REDCOATS
AND REBELS

REDCOATS AND REBELS

The War for America
1770-1781

Christopher Hibbert

Pen & Sword
MILITARY

First published in Great Britain in 1990 by Grafton Books
Reprinted in 1992 by HarperCollins Publishers
Re-published in this format in 2008 by
PEN & SWORD MILITARY
an imprint of
Pen & Sword Books Ltd
47 Church Street
Barnsley
South Yorkshire
S70 2AS

ISBN 978 1 84415 699 3

Printed and bound in Great Britain
By CPI UK

Pen & Sword Books Ltd incorporates the imprints of
Pen & Sword Aviation, Pen & Sword Maritime, Pen & Sword Military,
Wharncliffe Local History, Pen & Sword Select,
Pen & Sword Military Classics and Leo Cooper.

For a complete list of Pen & Sword titles please contact
PEN & SWORD BOOKS LIMITED
47 Church Street, Barnsley, South Yorkshire, S70 2AS, England
E-mail: enquiries@pen-and-sword.co.uk
Website: www.pen-and-sword.co.uk

CONTENTS

Table of Principal Events   vii
Author's Note and Acknowledgements   xi
Prologue   xvii

Part One

 1 Sons of Liberty   3
 2 First Blood   17
 3 Bunker Hill   42
 4 Washington Takes Command   64
 5 'An Ugly Job'   76
 6 The War in Canada   88
 7 Disasters in Virginia   101

Part Two

 8 The Declaration of Independence   113
 9 The Battle for New York   119
10 Generals at Loggerheads   133
11 Winter on the Delaware   143
12 The Fall of Philadelphia   153
13 The Army of the North   162
14 Surrender at Saratoga   182
15 The English Debate   201
16 Intrigues at Valley Forge   212
17 Fighting at Monmouth Court House   220
18 Enemies of the French   227

Part Three

19	Marching through Georgia	239
20	Quarrels in New York	248
21	Butchers and Patriots	256
22	Slaughter on King's Mountain	270
23	The Traitor and the Spy	290
24	With Cornwallis in the Carolinas	298
25	The Road to Yorktown	314
	Epilogue	333
	The Fate of Characters Whose End Is Not Recorded in the Text	339
	Bibliography	347
	Illustration Credits	359
	Index	361

TABLE OF
PRINCIPAL EVENTS

1765
Stamp Act

1766
Declaratory Act

1767
Townshend's American
Import Duties Act

1770
5 Mar: Boston Massacre

1773
16 Dec: Boston Tea Party

1774
5 Sept: Meeting of First Continental
Congress

1775
19 April: Skirmishes at Lexington and
Concord (Massachusetts)
10 May: Allen and Arnold capture
Ticonderoga (New York)
25 May: Howe, Clinton and
Burgoyne arrive in Boston
17 June: Battle of Bunker Hill
(Massachusetts)
3 July: George Washington takes
command of rebel army
investing Boston
26 Sept: General Gage recalled and
Howe takes over command

31 Dec: Arnold and Montgomery
lead assault on Quebec

1776
20 Jan: General Clinton sails for
South
17 Mar: Boston evacuated by British
6 May: British garrison in Quebec
relieved
28 June: Commodore Parker attacks
Sullivan's Island,
Charleston (South Carolina)
4 July: Declaration of Independence
22 Aug: British land on Long Island
(New York)
15 Sept: British enter New York
11 Oct: Naval battle on Lake
Champlain
28 Oct: Battle of White Plains
(New York)
26 Dec: Washington attacks Trenton
(New Jersey)

1777
3 Jan: Battle of Princeton
(New Jersey)
6 July: Burgoyne captures
Ticonderoga (New York)
16 Aug: Battle of Bennington
(New York)
11 Sept: Battle of Brandywine
(Pennsylvania)
19 Sept: Battle of Bemis Heights
(New York)

25 Sept:	British enter Philadelphia	**1780**
4 Oct:	Battle of Germantown (Pennsylvania)	12 May: British take Charleston (South Carolina)
17 Oct:	Burgoyne surrenders at Saratoga (New York)	10 July: Ternay and Rochambeau land on Rhode Island

25 Sept: British enter Philadelphia

4 Oct: Battle of Germantown (Pennsylvania)

17 Oct: Burgoyne surrenders at Saratoga (New York)

1778

4 Feb: Sir Henry Clinton succeeds Howe as Commander-in-Chief

6 Feb: Franco-American treaty of alliance signed

13 April: Earl of Carlisle appointed chief of commission to negotiate peace with America

13 April: Comte d'Estaing sails from Toulon

18 June: Clinton withdraws from Philadelphia

28 June: Battle of Monmouth Court House (New Jersey)

11 Aug: French fleet dispersed off Rhode Island

29 Dec: Archibald Campbell takes Savannah (Georgia)

1779

16 June: Spain declares war

16 July: Anthony Wayne captures Stony Point (New York)

14 Aug: Admiral Collier disperses American fleet at Penobscot Bay (Maine)

18 Aug: Henry Lee captures Paulus Hook (New Jersey)

7 Oct: British evacuate Rhode Island

9 Oct: Failure of Franco-American assault on Savannah

26 Dec: Clinton and Arbuthnot embark for South Carolina

1780

12 May: British take Charleston (South Carolina)

10 July: Ternay and Rochambeau land on Rhode Island

16 Aug: Battle of Camden (South Carolina)

14 Sept: Rodney arrives in New York

2 Oct: Major André hanged at Tappan (New York)

7 Oct: Battle of King's Mountain (South Carolina)

29 Oct: Cornwallis reaches Winnsboro (South Carolina)

1781

17 Jan: Battle of Hannah's Cowpens (South Carolina)

15 Mar: Battle of Guilford Court House (North Carolina)

25 April: Battle of Hobkirk's Hill (South Carolina)

17 June: Nathanael Greene abandons siege of Ninety-six (South Carolina)

6 July: Cornwallis defeats Wayne at James River

5 Aug: De Grasse sails for America

5 Sept: Naval battle of the Capes

8 Sept: Battle of Eutaw Springs (South Carolina)

28 Sept: Washington and Rochambeau leave Williamsburg (Virginia)

19 Oct: Cornwallis surrenders at Yorktown (Virginia)

1783

3 Sept: Treaty of Paris signed

MAPS

1 The American colonies in 1775   xvi

2 The Siege of Boston   38

3 The Northern Campaigns, 1775–6   96

4 Charleston and environs   106

5 New York and environs   120

6 Howe's Philadelphia campaign, 1777 147

7 The Northern Campaigns, 1777   168

8 The Southern Campaigns   236

9 The Siege of Yorktown   320

AUTHOR'S NOTE
AND ACKNOWLEDGEMENTS

This is a narrative history of the American War of Independence told largely from the British and loyalist points of view and incorporating as much interesting new material as I have been able to find. It is intended for the general reader rather than the student, although I hope the student to whom the field is new may find it a useful introduction to the works of those scholars listed in the bibliography to whom I am myself indebted. No references to sources are given in the text; but, for any readers who might be interested in consulting them, annotated copies of the book, giving references to all manuscript material, have been deposited, in London, at the libraries of the National Army Museum, Royal Hospital Road, Chelsea, and the Institute of United States Studies, Tavistock Square; and, in the United States, at the William L. Clements Library, the University of Michigan, Ann Arbor, and the Mugar Memorial Library, the University of Boston.

For their help when I was working in England I am most grateful to the staffs of the British Library, the Bodleian Library, Oxford, the London Library, the National Army Museum, the County Record Offices of England and Wales, the Scottish Record Office and the Royal Commission on Historical Manuscripts. I am in particular indebted to J. F. J. Collett-White, Senior Records Officer, Bedfordshire Record Office; C. Payne, Assistant Archivist, Berkshire Record Office; John S. Williams, Bristol City Archivist; H. A. Hanley, Buckinghamshire County Archivist; Dr P. C. Saunders, Deputy County Archivist, Cambridge; Mrs S. I. Dench, Cumbria Record Office; J. M. Draisey, Devon Record Office; Mrs Chandhuri, East Sussex Record Office; J. T. Smith, Essex Record Office; K. Haslem, Searchroom Supervisor, Gloucestershire Record Office; Miss J. Coburn, Head Archivist, Greater London Record Office; Peter Walne, Hertfordshire Record Office; R. Hale, Humberside Record Office;

Miss Kathleen Topping, Kent Archives Office; Miss Sharp, Lanca-
shire Record Office; Stephen M. Dixon, Assistant Keeper of Ar-
chives, and Mrs Valerie Joyce, Archives Assistant, Leicestershire
Record Office; S. J. Woods, Cataloguer in Military History, Newarke
Houses Museum, Leicester; Dr G. A. Knight, Principal Archivist,
Lincolnshire Record Office; Miss Jean M. Kennedy, Norfolk County
Archivist; Miss Rachel Watson, Northamptonshire County Archi-
vist, and Ms Sue Grove, Deputy County Archivist; Mrs Annette M.
Burton, Northumberland County Archivist; Richard Childs, Princi-
pal Archivist, Central Library, Sheffield; Miss S. Berry, Senior Archi-
vist, Somerset Record Office; D. A. Stoker, Assistant Archivist,
Staffordshire Record Office; Miss Jane E. Isaac, Assistant Archivist,
Suffolk Record Office; Miss Monica Ory, Deputy County Archivist,
Warwickshire Record Office; Mrs Patricia Gill, County Archivist,
West Sussex Record Office; and J. A. Burg, West Yorkshire Archive
Service, Leeds. My thanks are due also to Ian Hill of the Historical
Search Room of the Scottish Record Office, Edinburgh.

For their help in the United States I am also most grateful to Samuel
R. Gammon of the American Historical Association; Professor A.
Roger Ekirch of the Virginia Polytechnic Institute and State Univer-
sity, Blacksburg; Ms Melanie Yolles, Manuscripts Specialist, New
York Public Library; Ms Roberta Zonghi, Curator of Rare Books,
Boston Public Library; Mrs Arlene P. Shy, Head, Reader-Research
Services, and Roy Kiplinger, Manuscript Curator, William L. Clem-
ents Library, Ann Arbor; David Wigdor of the Manuscript Division,
Library of Congress, Washington; Dr Mary L. Robertson, Curator
of Manuscripts, Huntington Library, San Marino; Mrs Ella Greene,
Genealogical Assistant, Schenectady County Historical Society; Ms
Nanci A. Young, Archivist, Yale University Library; Ms Rosalind
Libbey, Reference Librarian, New Jersey Historical Society, Newark;
Ms Louise T. Jones, Historical Society of Pennsylvania, Philadelphia;
Ms Lisa Macbride, Library Assistant, Connecticut Historical Society,
Hartford; Ms Kaleta Riner, New England Historic and Genealogical
Society, Boston; Ms Joanne Hohler, Reference Archivist, State His-
torical Society of Wisconsin, Madison; Ms Rhonda Evenson, Minne-
sota Historical Society; Richard C. Roberts, Connecticut State
Library, Hartford; Dr Howard B. Gotlieb, Director, Mugar Mem-
orial Library, Boston University; Richard K. Barry of San Francisco;
and Bruce E. Burgoyne of Dover, Delaware.

For their help in a variety of ways I want also to thank John G. Simmons, Emeritus Fellow of All Souls College, Oxford; Michael Hurst, Fellow of St John's College, Oxford; Miss Alison Cowden, Librarian of the Institute of United States Studies, University of London; Richard Johnson of Grafton Books; Eric P. Swenson of W. W. Norton; Bruce Hunter of David Higham Associates; Claire Smith of Harold Ober Associates; Normand Redden; Esther Jagger; Hamish Francis; Mrs Alison Riley; Mrs Margaret Lewendon; and, as always, my wife for having compiled the index. I am also most grateful to Miss Katherine Everett for her help in choosing the illustrations.

Grateful acknowledgement is made to the owners of manuscript material listed in the bibliography and in particular to the State Historical Society of Wisconsin for permission to quote from the Lyman Copeland Draper Collection; to the William L. Clements Library for material from the Lexington and Concord Collection; to the Huntington Library for the journal of Richard Pope; to the Schenectady County Historical Society for the diaries of Captain John Davis; to Boston Public Library for the Joseph Merriam Papers; to the New Jersey Historical Society for the William Barton Collection; to the Minnesota Historical Society for the journal of Solomon Dwinnell; to the Historical Society of Pennsylvania for the journals of William Jennison and Thomas Sullivan; to the New York Public Library, Rare Books and Manuscripts Division, Astor, Lenox and Tilden Foundations for the Horatio Gates Papers; to the Scottish Record Office for the Seafield Muniments; to the Staffordshire Record Office for letters to the Viscountess Grimston; to the Lancashire Record Office for the Barcroft Letters; to the Northamptonshire Record Office for the Fitzwilliam (Burke) Papers; to the Northumberland Record Office for the Percy Papers; to the West Yorkshire Archive Service for the Rockingham Letters in the Ramsden Archive; to the Lincolnshire Record Office for the Fane Papers; to the Warwickshire Record Office for the Feilding Papers; to the Humberside Record Office for the Grimston Papers; and to the Gloucestershire Record Office for documents relating to the hanging of Major André and the capture of Fort Washington. The papers of Sir Francis Carr Clerke, held by the Bedford County Record Office, are quoted with the kind permission of the Lady Lucas of Crudwell and Dingwall. For his help with the papers of his forbear, the fourth Earl of

Sandwich, First Lord of the Admiralty during the American War, I am most grateful to John Montagu.

Finally I want to say how much I am indebted to Professor Esmond Wright, Emeritus Professor of American History in the University of London, for giving me so much useful advice and for having been kind enough to read the typescript.

Christopher Hibbert

For Bob and Peg Tessier
with love

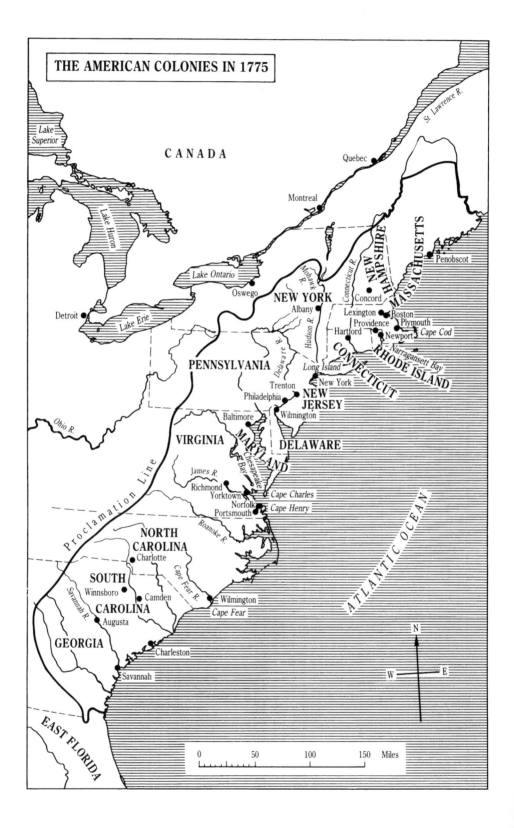

THE AMERICAN COLONIES IN 1775

Lake Superior

CANADA

St. Lawrence R.

Quebec

Lake Huron

Montreal

Lake Ontario

Oswego

Detroit

Lake Erie

Mohawk R.

Concord

NEW HAMPSHIRE

MASSACHUSETTS

Penobscot

Connecticut R.

NEW YORK

Albany

Lexington

Boston

Plymouth

Cape Cod

Providence

Hartford

Newport

Hudson R.

Narragansett Bay

CONNECTICUT

RHODE ISLAND

PENNSYLVANIA

Delaware R.

Long Island

Ohio R.

Trenton

New York

Philadelphia

NEW JERSEY

Wilmington

Baltimore

VIRGINIA

MARYLAND

DELAWARE

James R.

Chesapeake Bay

Richmond

Yorktown

Cape Charles

Norfolk

Cape Henry

Portsmouth

Proclamation Line

Roanoke R.

NORTH CAROLINA

Charlotte

Cape Fear R.

SOUTH

Winnsboro

Camden

Wilmington

CAROLINA

Cape Fear

Savannah R.

Augusta

GEORGIA

Charleston

Savannah

ATLANTIC OCEAN

N

W   E

EAST FLORIDA

0   50   100   150   Miles

PROLOGUE

'I breakfasted with Temple,' James Boswell recorded in his journal on 10 April 1763, 'and then went to [church] and heard a very good sermon on "Set thy house in order for thou shalt shortly die."' Later on that day Temple's kinsman, George Grenville, was called upon by King George III to become His Majesty's chief minister and to set the troubled affairs of the nation in order.

It seemed to many an unfortunate choice. After a conventional education at Eton and Christ Church, Oxford, George Grenville had abandoned the law for politics and had since conscientiously filled the various offices of Lord of the Treasury, Treasurer of the Navy, Secretary of State for the Northern Department and First Lord of the Admiralty. No one doubted his ability, his industry or his integrity. But everyone agreed that he was a most insufferable bore. Formal, exact and obstinate, he was also cold, suspicious, touchy and tactless. Men found it difficult to believe that he had nine children or even that he had a home life at all. According to Edmund Burke, soon to be elected Member of Parliament for Wendover, Grenville's one pleasure in life was to be found in the conduct of public affairs: he seemed to 'have no delight except in such things as in some way related to the business that was to be conducted within the House of Commons'. Horace Walpole added that his favourite occupation was talking, and 'brevity was not his failing'.

The King found him unendurable, complaining of his 'tiresome manner', his 'selfish disposition'. 'When he has wearied me for two hours,' His Majesty once remarked, 'he looks at his watch to see if he may not tire me for an hour more.' 'That gentleman's opinions,' he remarked upon another occasion, 'are seldom formed from any motives than such as may be expected to originate in the mind of a clerk in a counting-house.' The King eventually decided that he would rather have the Devil as a visitor at Buckingham Palace than be forced to listen to George Grenville. Yet, tedious and irritating as Grenville undoubtedly was, the King, a notoriously frugal man himself, warmly supported him when he turned his attention to the financial affairs of the country and decided that strict economy in their conduct was essential.

The ruinously expensive Seven Years' War with France had just ended with the Treaty of Paris which, signed but a few months before Grenville became chief minister, had established Britain as the world's leading colonial power and had left her with vastly increased territories to administer in North America. The most splendid victories in this war had been won when Britain's destinies were in the hands of the great William Pitt, who was married to Grenville's sister; but it was said of Grenville that he would have preferred a national saving of two inches of candle to all the marvellous victories of his famous brother-in-law, who treated him with much contempt. Now the time had come to pay not only for these victories which, in Grenville's opinion, the American colonists had done very little to achieve, but also for the cost of defending and administering the territories which they had secured. In helping to meet these expenses, Grenville considered that it was only proper that at least part of the high cost of maintaining a force of ten thousand men in America, as a safeguard against French revenge and Indian depredations, should be met by the American colonists themselves. After all, it was their homelands which were to be protected, and their taxes were so relatively slight that it was calculated that an American paid no more than sixpence a year against the average English taxpayer's twenty-five shillings. In 1764 Grenville accordingly announced that a direct tax would be imposed upon the colonies within a year if no other suggestions as to how the required sums might be raised were forthcoming. He also announced that there must be reforms in the ways in which customs duties were collected and evaded in America. Smuggling must be stopped and an end put to the present disgraceful mismanagement, whereby it cost £8000 to collect £2000 worth of customs duties in American ports.

It had long been accepted in England that the main purposes of the country's overseas possessions were to serve the business interests of British merchants and manufacturers and to provide the mother country with raw materials. Long lists of what were known as 'enumerated' commodities had been drawn up and all items on these lists, such as sugar, rice, cotton, tobacco and furs, could be exported from the colonies only to British ports. Additionally, for over a century, almost all commodities from countries on the continent of Europe could not be re-exported to the colonies except from Britain. The colonists, it was felt, had little cause to complain about this British monopoly of trade, since not only did their own goods thus enjoy a ready sale in protected markets, but exceptions were made from time to time in the lists of 'enumerated' goods: in 1730, for instance, the rice growers of Carolina had been permitted by law to export their crop direct to southern Europe. Besides, it was well known that the widespread prevalence of smuggling served to take the hard edge off all the measures by which the British Parliament and the British Navy endeavoured to control transatlantic trade.

To Grenville's fussily legalistic mind the slapdash way in which the Trade and Navigation Acts had been administered in the past was abhorrent. His answer was a new Revenue Act or, as it came to be known, Sugar Act, which imposed a duty of threepence per gallon on imported molasses. This was a reduction of the duty formerly imposed on foreign molasses by an Act of 1733; but, whereas that Act had been largely evaded, Grenville intended that the new Act should be vigorously enforced both at sea and in the colonial courts of law.

In a further attempt to relieve the British taxpayer of the burdens which weighed so much more heavily upon his shoulders than upon those of the colonists, Grenville also brought forward a direct tax in the form of the Stamp Act of 1765. As with the Sugar Act of the previous year, this was considered a perfectly unobjectionable measure by Parliament and the country at large. Stamp duties had long been imposed in England; there was no reason at all, so it was contended, why Parliament, in the proper exercise of its duties as the supreme constitutional authority in the empire, should not impose such duties in America also. So, without much notice of it being taken in England, the Stamp Act became law.

It decreed that from the beginning of November 1765 all manner of legal and other documents were declared to be null and void in America unless bearing stamps of varying denominations which had to be purchased from official distributors. Passports had to bear stamps, as did liquor licences, playing cards, ships' papers, insurance policies, almanacs, newspapers and pamphlets. The stamps had to be paid for in sterling; and cases involving breaches of the law were to be tried in the courts in which offences against maritime law were considered and in which judges, appointed by the government, decided the issue without reference to juries. The proceeds realized from the financial penalties imposed upon those found guilty in these courts were to be divided equally among the informer, the provincial governor and the local official responsible for selling the stamps. The money raised from the sale of stamps was to be used expressly for the pay of troops and the salaries of officials in the American colonies.

There was nothing in the Act which could be said to be contrary to the Bill of Rights of 1689, the constitutional outcome of the Glorious Revolution which had ensured the Protestant succession to the English throne and had established the principles of parliamentary supremacy. So unexceptionable, indeed, did this perfectly legal piece of legislation appear that it was not even mentioned in the lengthy correspondence that passed between the King and George Grenville. English public opinion and English newspapers, when they took notice of it at all, were quite satisfied as to its fairness and propriety. Yet in America the Act was seen in a quite different light. When news of the colonists' violent reaction to it reached England, it was recognized, as Edmund Burke put it, that the question which Grenville and his government should have asked themselves was not so much what a lawyer said *could* be done but what humanity, reason and justice told them *ought* to be done. By then, though, it was too late.

PART ONE

1

SONS OF LIBERTY

'One single Act of Parliament has
set people a-thinking in six months
more than they had ever done in
their whole lives before.'

James Otis

The first reports came from Boston, a town of some sixteen thousand inhabitants many of whom worked in its distilleries, fisheries, rope-walks and shipyards. It had once been the most prosperous port on the American coast, but was now a less flourishing and less orderly place in which a third of the adult population had no regular employment and the carriages of rich merchants were likely to be insulted and even pelted by crowds in the poorer parts of the town down by the wharves. Early in the morning of a hot August day in 1765 a large crowd of Bostonians could have been seen advancing on Hanover Square. Here from an elm, soon to be known as the Liberty Tree, hung an effigy of Andrew Oliver, a wealthy merchant who had accepted the office of Distributor of Stamps for Massachusetts Bay. On one arm of the effigy was pinned a paper inscribed with the words:

> What greater joy did New England see
> Than a stampman hanging on a tree.

Throughout the day all passers-by were stopped and required to go through the mock ceremony of buying a stamp as a means of showing them how irksome and burdensome the new imposition would be. The effigy was then carried up to Tower Hill and placed upon a huge bonfire. Encouraged by a masterful cobbler, Ebenezer MacIntosh, dressed in the colourful clothes he habitually wore on 5 November when effigies of the Pope and the Devil were burned on bonfires in Boston, the crowds then converged upon a building which was under construction on Oliver's wharf and which was believed to be his intended stamp office. They pulled the building down; marched to his house; hurled stones at his windows which were filled with glass imported from England; smashed his garden fences; plucked fruit from his trees; and forced their way through his front door in search of the man himself. They might well have carried out their declared intention of throwing him out of his smashed windows together with his broken furniture, wainscoting, glass and silver, had not his brother-in-law, Thomas Hutchinson, the rich and unpopular Chief Justice and Lieutenant Governor of Massachusetts, arrived on the scene with the sheriff. The mob shouted insults and threw broken bricks at these men, both known to be trusted servants of the British Crown and to be committed Tories, as those with loyalist sympathies were known.

The next day, a delegation presented itself at Oliver's house to warn him that if he did not resign his office as stamp distributor forthwith 'his house would be destroyed and his life in continual danger'. Oliver felt compelled to heed the warning and not long afterwards a broadside announced: 'The True-born Sons of Liberty are desired to meet under LIBERTY TREE at XII o'clock, This Day, to hear the public Resignation, under Oath, of ANDREW OLIVER, Esq., Distributor of Stamps for the Province of the Massachusetts-Bay. A Resignation? YES.'

Thomas Hutchinson was also called upon to resign, but he stood firm. He disclosed in private that he disapproved of the Stamp Act; yet his loyalty to the King and government in London prevented him from making his views generally known in Boston, where he was deeply envied for his wealth and widely disliked for holding and continuing to hold his office of Lieutenant Governor, in addition to the various other offices he had managed to amass as a member of one of the oldest families in Massachusetts. His splendid house, like Oliver's, was attacked by a mob shouting 'Liberty and Property!', a cry which, as the Governor, Francis Bernard, caustically observed, was 'the usual notice of their intention to plunder and pull down a house'. Unlike Oliver's, Thomas Hutchinson's house did not escape with broken windows and furniture. Some years before, when it had caught fire accidentally, the crowds who gathered to watch the conflagration had shouted, 'Let it burn!' Now the mob completely wrecked it, threw smashed furniture and family portraits into the street, destroyed numerous documents and manuscripts, including a history of Massachusetts which Hutchinson had written, and broke into a strongbox to steal all the money it contained. Hutchinson himself was considered lucky to have escaped with his life.

Elsewhere, as unrest spread throughout the American colonies, other Loyalists were not so fortunate.

At that time the population of America comprised about two and a half million people living in provinces stretching down the Atlantic seaboard from Nova Scotia in the north to East Florida in the south. The whites were mostly of British descent, the six hundred thousand or so blacks nearly all from Africa or the descendants of slaves imported from Africa. Formerly the colonies were held by royal charter, like Pennsylvania which had originally been given by King Charles II to William Penn, the Quaker and social philosopher, in payment of a debt of £16,000 owed to Penn's father, Admiral Sir William Penn; or like Maryland, which, named after the Queen of King Charles I, was founded by Lord Baltimore who had been granted a charter for the land as a refuge for Roman Catholics anxious to escape from the restrictions placed upon them in England. By 1763, however, only these two colonies remained proprietary; only two others, Rhode Island and Connecticut, were chartered colonies with elected governors; all the rest were Crown colonies with governors appointed in London, occasionally members of leading and wealthy American families like Thomas Hutchinson of Boston, in other cases poor English gentlemen, often of dubious reputation, for whom an appointment far away from London was desired by their families, the government or the court.

Before the Seven Years' War with France, successive British governments had taken but a spasmodic interest in their growing empire. And in these years of neglect the American colonial assemblies had attempted to assume powers which were, in the eyes of the administration in London, properly exercised by governors appointed by the Crown. The new interest which the British government was taking in America seemed to many colonists to be a threat to their liberties and a challenge to local assemblies, which they regarded as American counterparts to the British Parliament. Having fought in the past against the encroachments of royal prerogative, the assemblies now saw themselves faced by a new enemy in the House of Commons bent upon passing Acts attacking both their freedom and their pockets.

A case in point had been the establishment of the Proclamation Line in 1763. In the summer of that year the Indian chief, Pontiac, fearing that his ancestral lands would soon be overrun by white settlers, organized a concerted attack by his own and other tribes on British-occupied forts between Lake Superior and the Lower Mississippi, Pontiac himself laying siege to Detroit. Pontiac's Conspiracy, as the English called it, resulted in the capture of nearly all the forts, the annihilation of their garrisons and the plundering of the settlements they had been established to protect. After these reverses the British government were convinced that, since the colonists evidently could not or would not protect themselves, measures must be taken to deal with the problem for them. The Proclamation issued that October created a dividing line between Americans and Indians along the watershed of the Appalachian Mountains; the intention was to keep the two races separate, reserving the far western lands for the Indians, and encouraging white settlement both of the eastern territories and of the new provinces established by the Proclamation as a result of Britain's victory in the Seven Years' War – the colony of Quebec in the north and, in the south, the two provinces of East and West Florida. Regarded in England not only as an act of justice for the Indians but also as a means of encouraging the timber and fur trades in the north, as well as the sub-tropical resources of the empire in the south, the Proclamation was seen by American objectors as yet another interference by London in their lives, a frustrating curb on the activities of land speculators and adventurous frontiersmen, and an excuse to keep in America a large force of British troops which, while there ostensibly to keep the peace along the frontier, might one day be employed against the colonists themselves.

Such fears were not yet widespread in America, where the great majority were far too busy with the toil of their private lives to concern themselves with matters of which they knew little, with the constitutional status of town assemblies or with the legal problems of taxation. Ninety-five out of every hundred colonists lived in the countryside, many of their communities – in which most were tenants rather than freeholders – separated from the next by a long day's journey. That half of the population who were women, whether or not they took an interest in public affairs, had little or no influence over them. As in England, they were subordinate first to their fathers, then to their husbands. When a woman married, her property became that of her husband. If she were not pregnant at the time of her marriage – as about half New England brides were – she was almost certain to become pregnant soon afterwards and then, as likely as not, to bear children with regularity.

The blacks in America had even fewer rights. They were mostly slaves, and whereas a domestic servant in a rich and kindly family in New York would lead a very different kind of life from that of workers in the tobacco fields of Virginia or the rice farms of Carolina, all slaves were legally deprived of the rights to learn how to read and write as well as to the possession of their own bodies and those of their children. On occasions they were sent off as presents from one owner to another, as were two slaves belonging to the Governor of New Hampshire who shipped them to England in the 1770s as a gift to the Marchioness of Rockingham, writing to her:

> By the Tama Sloop of War I have this day embarked Two Negro men slaves (named Romulus & Remus) who are good [performers] on the French-Horn, and Remus a remarkable good taste to Music. In the hopes that they might be some Amusement in the Country, I have taken the liberty to ask your Ladyship's condescension to honor me with their acceptance. They have been with me from their childhood, and are faithful, honest and free from vice.

While blacks and, to a lesser extent, women could be little more than onlookers in the impending struggle, most male white settlers, even of the better-educated classes – though traditionally jealous of the freedom which they had learned to prize – took no deep interest in the arguments about the sovereignty in America of the House of Commons until the realities of the Stamp Act were brought home to them. They had generally subscribed to the familiar cry of 'no taxation without representation', but the propositions, full of classical allusions, contained in the speeches and pamphlets of such propagandists as the young Virginian lawyer, Patrick Henry, whose words, 'Give me freedom or give me death!' were to echo round the world, and the rich Daniel Dulany from Maryland, author of *Considerations on the Propriety of Imposing Taxes in the British Colonies . . . by Act of Parliament*, were of little concern to them. The Stamp Act, however, was of real concern: this was something which would affect nearly everyone in America, not just the rich landowners and merchants of the towns and burgesses anxious not to lose the privileges and authority of their assemblies.

Those most vociferous in their opposition to the Stamp Act were naturally those whose incomes would be most affected by it; and these men happened to be among the most influential in American society, newspaper owners and printers, lawyers, tavern keepers, planters and merchants. Yet people of all classes were affected by it in some degree, consumers as well as producers, poor as well as rich. And once the House of Burgesses in Williamsburg, Virginia had passed a series of resolutions against the Act, other assemblies, from Rhode Island, Massachusetts and New York to Pennsylvania and South Carolina, followed suit; all in their various ways insisted upon their right to tax themselves by consent of their own representatives, protesting that the actions of the British government seemed intent upon reducing Americans to slavery, and reflecting the view of William Pitt's friend, the lawyer Lord Camden, soon to become Lord Chancellor, who said that it was impossible for one 'petty island' in Europe to presume to hold in dependence a 'mighty continent, increasing daily in numbers and strength'.

Admittedly that continent could scarcely yet be described as a nation. Its colonies were frequently in dispute with one another, usually over conflicting claims to territory or quarrels about trade; and the ways of life of their inhabitants were vastly different. A genteel visitor from Rhode Island might well feel himself in a different country in Charleston, South Carolina where, while their black slaves were left to work themselves to death in the fever-ridden rice fields, planters came to the coast with their families to escape the unhealthy summer heat and to buy replacements for the slaves who would have been buried by the time their owners went home again.

Yet, different as the histories, traditions and customs of the American colonies were, some of their leading inhabitants were beginning to unite in response to the British threat. As it became more or less common ground that Americans should resist helping to pay for the consequences of a war that had been fought by Britain for her own imperial aggrandizement – and that her new government's policy was being framed for the benefit of British merchants – no fewer than nine colonies sent representatives to a Stamp Act Congress in New York in October 1765; and others would have done so had not their governors refused to sanction the appointment of representatives. As might have been foretold, the Congress, in a long Declaration of Rights and Grievances, contended that the 'only representatives of the people of these colonies are persons chosen by themselves, and no taxes ever have been, or can be, constitutionally imposed upon them but by their respective legislatures'.

By this time all over the continent were springing up secret organizations known as Sons of Liberty in allusion to a phrase used in a speech in Parliament by Isaac Barré, the massive and swarthy Member for Chipping Wycombe, son of a French refugee living in Dublin, and sympathizer with the American cause. In colonies with a long tradition of unrest and street violence, these 'Sons of Liberty', or, as their victims called them, 'Sons of Violence', organized attacks on stamp distributors and royal officials, tarring and feathering them beneath trees of liberty and forcing them to resign. It became unsafe in certain places 'for a man even to speak a word for the King Except He Knows What Company he is in', Ambrose Barcroft of Philadelphia wrote to a cousin in Lancashire. 'At Trenton in West Jersey they tar'd and feather'd a Man just for Drinking the King's health.'

In New York on 1 November 1765, when the Stamp Act was about to take effect and flags were flown at half mast in mourning for the death of American liberty, a large crowd gathered to watch the burning of an effigy of the Lieutenant Governor, Cadwallader Colden, as unpopular a figure as Thomas Hutchinson of Boston. They burned the effigy with Colden's carriages, which they had dragged out of his coach-house, marched to the house of an equally disliked British army officer and burned his house to the ground.

Learning of this and similar riots in other American towns by the so-called 'Sons of Liberty', who were said to be merchants and dissident intellectuals as well as artisans, the British government were obliged to conclude that, while it was simple enough to pass a Stamp

Act through the House of Commons, it was impossible to enforce it in America so long as officials were prevented from collecting the dues.

Opposition to the Stamp Act was not confined to the colonies. William Pitt, who said that he rejoiced in America's resistance, was opposed to it, as were Lord Camden and Edmund Burke. So were several lesser-known Members of Parliament in addition to Isaac Barré. Even those who approved of it in principle suggested it was impracticable: British merchants were losing business because one of the most effective American responses to it had been to impose an embargo on trade with Britain. Besides, the only way to enforce obedience was to send out more British troops. But where were these to be found? And how were they to be paid? These were questions to which the administration in London were now being forced to find answers.

Grenville declared that he had no doubt as to what should be done: the law must be enforced at all costs. Grenville, however, was no longer in office. The King had managed to rid himself of his tiresome Minister whose place had been taken by the Marquess of Rockingham, a thin, thirty-five-year-old man of great wealth and influential family connections, though 'weak, childish and ignorant', in Horace Walpole's opinion, 'by no means fit for the head of Administration'. He advised repeal of the Act. The King, who shared the common view that Parliament had as unquestionable a right to tax American colonies as it had to tax British citizens, yet who appreciated the difficulties of enforcement, suggested that perhaps the Act might be modified. Rockingham replied that the ministry intended to stand by repeal as an issue of confidence. If they lost the vote they would resign. At the contemplation of the prospect of having to take back Grenville, the King made no further objections to repeal; and so, in February 1766, after a powerful speech by Pitt, a motion by Grenville to enforce the Stamp Act was lost by 274 votes to 134. Yet, while this particular Act was repealed, it was almost universally agreed that the Americans must not be allowed to suppose that Parliament had abandoned its right to tax the colonies in future. Accordingly, a Declaratory Act was passed confirming Parliament's power 'to make laws and statutes . . . to bind the colonies and people of America . . . in all cases whatsoever'.

The next year the government made a further attempt to tax the colonies. The Chancellor of the Exchequer was now the Hon. Charles Townshend. A clever young man, witty and energetic, possessed of a marvellous talent for mimicry and repartee, with a loud voice, an even louder laugh, and a taste for high living which earned him the nickname 'Champagne Charlie', Townshend would have been, as Tobias Smollett, the novelist, said, 'a really great man if he had had any consistency or stability of character'. Full of self-confidence, he announced that he had devised a plan to reduce taxation in England and tax the colonists in a way that they would not find objectionable. His plan was to impose new customs duties in America; and, since these would be 'external' taxes collected at the ports and not the 'internal' taxes imposed at places of business, the colonists – who had, after all, accepted the Trade and Navigation Acts – would not complain that they were an unconstitutional imposition. The port duties were to be levied on glass, red and white lead, painters' colours, paper and tea. Those accused of evading the duties were to be tried in the kind of courts without juries which were used for offences against the Navigation Acts. This provision alone, despite Townshend's blithe confidence, was certain to raise protests; but the main objections to his legislation were its creation of a Board of Customs Commissioners under direct British control, the sanction of searches by customs officials in homes as well as in stores and offices, and, most objectionable of all, the establishment of an American civil list from which money could be drawn for the payment of governors, judges and other royal officials whose salaries had previously been in the hands of colonial assemblies.

Once more the colonists loudly voiced their protests, and once again boycotts on imports from England were organized. Letters and pamphlets poured from the presses. James Otis, the unpredictable Boston lawyer and pamphleteer who was credited with coining the slogan 'Taxation without representation is tyranny', and John Dickinson from Pennsylvania, another pamphleteer who had been trained as a lawyer in England, both added to this flood of printed complaint and exhortation. There were riots in which customs officers were abused and attacked, tarred and feathered. In New York there were clashes between demonstrators and soldiers who, by a recent Quartering Act, were entitled to occupy rooms in taverns and empty houses if barracks were inadequate or unavailable. In Boston there were similar outbreaks, in one of which a boy was killed by a customs informer who fired on a crowd demonstrating outside his house, providing an excuse for an expensive and highly emotional funeral. Samuel Adams, a failed businessman who had graduated from Harvard in 1740 and was a passionate, eloquent, occasionally disingenuous and always shrewd champion of the colonists' rights and liberties, composed an angry denunciation of the Townshend Acts for the Massachusetts House of Representatives. Outside the big Beacon Hill house of Adams's friend John Hancock, an affluent, also Harvard-educated young Bostonian merchant, the son of a man who had made a fortune from smuggling, a bonfire was lit to burn the boat of a collector of customs who had seized Hancock's sloop *Liberty* for some infringement of the new legislation. And then, in March 1770, there occurred what became known as the 'Boston Massacre'.

The trouble began on Friday, 2 March when a group of British soldiers, redcoats of the 29th Regiment, went to a ropewalk to try to obtain some spare-time work so as to augment their meagre pay. Their regiment had been in Boston for several months and the men – most of whose fellow-soldiers had not long before been condemned by General James Wolfe, the conqueror of Quebec, as 'rascals and *canaille* . . . terrible dogs to look at' – were much disliked by Bostonians in general for their taking on part-time jobs for less than the going rate of pay, their rough and rude behaviour when off duty in the streets, their noisy band practice and drilling during religious meetings and church services, their drunkenness and chasing after women, and their various other misdemeanours reported, exaggerated and sometimes invented by the *Boston Gazette*, the *Evening Post* and other local newspapers.

One of the workers at the ropewalk told Private Patrick Walker of the 29th that if he wanted work he 'could go and clean [his] shit house'. The soldier lost his temper, dashed forward and was knocked down. Soon eight or nine soldiers of his regiment appeared before the ropewalk with clubs and challenged the workers to come out and fight them. The workers, who outnumbered them, rushed out with the thick slats they used in their work and beat them off. The soldiers 'very speedily returned to the ropewalk', recorded an eyewitness, 'reinforced to the number of thirty or forty, and headed by a tall, negro drummer'.

'You black rascal,' someone called out. 'What have you to do with white people's quarrels?'

The drummer replied, 'I suppose I may look on.'

Once again there was a fight; and once more the soldiers were beaten off 'with considerable bruises'.

Three evenings later, as snow lay thick underfoot, there was another fight between the redcoats and gangs of young men of the town. This was stopped by the regiment's officers; but, after a fire bell had been rung, more people turned out into the streets, many of them armed with planks torn from a demolished butcher's stall and with clubs and the bats used in playing the game of tipcat. Other fire bells were now ringing; fire engines were being pushed along the streets; scores of apprentices were running through the snow, shouting threats at the British soldiers, the 'lousy rascals', the 'scoundrel lobster sons of bitches'. Outside the Custom House, where a British sentry stood guard in his box, one of the apprentices made an insulting remark to a passing British officer, then taunted the sentry, who hit him over the head with the butt of his musket.

A dense crowd gathered and pelted the sentry with snowballs, icicles and lumps of ice from the frozen gutters. The sentry fixed his bayonet and loaded his musket, striking the butt threateningly on the ground as the throng provoked him with cries of, 'Fire, damn you, fire! Fire and be damned! You coward, you dare not fire!'

Shouting, 'Where are the damned buggers? Where are your Liberty Boys?' a detachment of soldiers, their bayonets fixed, marched at double-time through the streets in the moonlight under the command of the duty officer of the day, a sensible, forty-year-old Irishman, Captain Thomas Preston. When they arrived before the Custom House, Captain Preston ordered his men to load their muskets. Having done so, they held their ground in front of the building while the Boston youths with sticks in their hands continued to shout provocative insults, tapping the soldiers' muskets with their sticks, daring them to fire. 'Damn you, you sons of bitches, fire!' one voice was heard calling above the rest. 'You can't kill us all!'

A merchant, Richard Palmer, a club in his hand, went up to Captain Preston and said, 'I hope you do not intend they shall fire upon the inhabitants.'

'By no means, by no means,' Preston replied. After all, he added, he was standing in front of his men: if he ordered them to open fire he would be killed first himself. But then, behind his soldiers, another voice, supposed to be that of an American Tory, shouted to them to fire. 'Fire!' this voice called out. 'Fire! By God! I'll stand by you whilst I have a drop of blood. Fire!'

At that moment one of the soldiers was knocked over by a lump of wood. When he got up he raised his musket and, urged on all sides to fire – except by Captain Preston who had now moved to the rear of his men – he pressed the trigger. Within seconds the other soldiers began firing too. A sailor from Salem later deposed:

> Immediately after the principal firing, I saw three of the people fall down in the street. Presently after the last gun was fired off the officer who commanded the rascals sprung before them, waving his sword or stick, said, 'Damn ye rascals, what did you fire for?' and struck up the gun of one of the soldiers who was loading again, whereupon they seemed confounded and fired no more. I then went where one of the people was lying, to see whether he was dead . . . There were four or five people about him, one of them saying that he was dead; whereupon one of the soldiers said, 'Damn his blood, he is dead. If he ever sprawl again I will be damned for him.'

Two other men had also been killed and seven wounded, two of them mortally. On the day of the funerals, shops in Boston were closed and church bells tolled all over the town and in the surrounding countryside. Thousands of people, not all of them mourners, lined the streets as the hearses drove by. One clergyman of loyalist sympathies remarked, 'They call me a brainless Tory. But tell me, which is better – to be ruled by one tyrant three thousand miles away, or by three thousand tyrants not one mile away?'

Captain Preston and his men were tried for murder. They were defended in court by Josiah Quincy and Samuel Adams's second cousin, John Adams, lawyers who both bravely incurred the anger of the more militant rebels by declaring that freedom would not be won in defiance of the dictates of humanity and the rule of law.

John Adams had been born in Braintree, Massachusetts in 1735, the son of a farmer who had once been a shoemaker. Like Samuel Adams and John Hancock, he had been to Harvard and, having been admitted to the Boston bar after a time spent as a schoolmaster, he had married the clever and amusing daughter of a minister from a nearby town. A forceful opponent of the Stamp Act and author of skilfully reasoned arguments against it in the *Boston Gazette*, he was at the same time an opponent of violent demonstrations. Frequently rude, quarrelsome and argumentative, he could also be gentle and courteous, though he was impatient with those who disagreed with his outspoken views. Never averse to the limelight, he and Quincy defended the British soldiers with singular determination, extracting admissions from one witness that he had carried a sword with which he was prepared to cut off the soldiers' heads, from another that he had had his hand on Preston's shoulder when the loud shout to fire was followed by the first shot, from two black slaves who swore that the order did not come from Preston, and from other witnesses who testified as to the provocation the soldiers had received. Quincy would have liked to emphasize this provocation; but he was dissuaded from doing so. Samuel Adams was in court, clearly determined that the soldiers must be punished and obviously annoyed that much was made by the judge, Thomas Hutchinson's brother-in-law, Peter Oliver, of a man who had been seen amongst the crowd, a man in a red cloak such as the characteristically stained and shabby one Samuel Adams was himself known to wear on cold nights. John Adams, too, did not want to allow it to appear that the soldiers had been incited by a calculating mob. He was prepared to agree that the victims *were* part of a mob, 'a motley rabble of saucy boys'. But he would not permit the defence to suggest that they had been manipulated by political puppeteers.

After two and a half hours' deliberation, the jury, in which Tory sympathizers were prominent, returned to give their verdict. Captain Preston had already been acquitted in a separate trial. Now, all but two of the soldiers were acquitted too. The two who did not escape were convicted not of murder but of manslaughter, branded with the letter M on their thumbs, then permitted to rejoin their regiment.

The 'Boston Massacre', nevertheless, passed into American folklore as a characteristically brutal attempt by the military to put down peaceful protest by ill-used citizens. Articles were published in the *Boston Gazette* and elsewhere condemning the practice of quartering troops in populous and well-regulated towns; ministers preached sermons on appropriate texts such as the 'Slaughter of the Innocents'; and engravings appeared of Captain Preston, standing behind his men, waving his sword and encouraging them to fire – one of them by a Boston master silversmith, Paul Revere, who, without permission, copied it from a picture of the scene by Henry Pelham, half-brother of the artist John Singleton Copley.

For years, until 4 July became a day of national celebration instead, 5 March was annually commemorated in Boston as a day worthy of the most solemn remembrance. Elsewhere there was a feeling that the Bostonians might have gone too far in their provocation of the British. 'Property will soon be very precarious,' observed the *New York Gazette*. 'It's high time a stop was put to mobbing.' Nevertheless the 29th Regiment was withdrawn from the city and the Townshend Acts did not long survive the 'Boston Massacre': once again the British government gave way.

2

FIRST BLOOD

*'The die is cast, and more mischief
will follow.'*

William Knox

By now King George III's prime minister was Lord North, though
North himself refused to acknowledge that any such office was
recognized by the British constitution, considering himself a kind of
agent for the King. The only son of the first Earl of Guilford, North
was born in Albemarle Street, London in 1732. His grandfather was
the Earl of Halifax, his godfather the Prince of Wales, and his
upbringing as privileged as such connections usually implied. He was
educated at Eton and Trinity College, Oxford, spent three years on
the Grand Tour, and at the age of twenty-two entered the House of
Commons as Member for the family borough of Banbury which he
represented until succeeding his father as Earl of Guilford. Never an
orator, though skilled and often amusing in debate, he soon became
one of the best-liked and most respected men in Parliament. Easy-
going, consistently good-natured, if, on occasion, obstinate, he was
well described by Edward Gibbon as 'one of the best companions in
the Kingdom' and by Edmund Burke as 'a man of admirable parts,
of general knowledge, of a versatile understanding, fitted for every
sort of business, of infinite wit and pleasantry, of a delightful temper,
and with a mind most perfectly disinterested'. He was an astute
manager of the House of Commons and a shrewd leader of a coalition
whose members were drawn together by a common desire for office.

Burke felt compelled to add, however, that Lord North 'wanted something of the vigilance and spirit of command that the time required'. North himself readily agreed with this view. He told the King more than once that he was not suited to leading a government in time of war. 'Upon military matters,' he said, 'I speak ignorantly, and therefore without effect.' In appearance he was not well favoured. His movements were decidedly clumsy, and his gait peculiarly awkward. 'He had,' said Walpole, 'two large prominent eyes that rolled about to no purpose (for he was utterly short-sighted). A wide mouth, thick lips, and inflated visage gave him the air of a blind trumpeter.'

To the King, to whom he bore so close a resemblance that it was rumoured they must be intimately related, he was to prove a most faithful servant. For his part the King got on with him better than he had done with any of his former prime ministers, trusted his judgement and clung to him so insistently that the very thought that he might lose him as head of his government brought on the most alarming agitation.

Although it was decided that the Townshend duties must be withdrawn, that on tea was retained 'as a mark of the supremacy of Parliament'. 'There must always be one tax to keep up the right,' the King insisted. 'And as such I approve of the Tea Duty.' So, although a period of prosperity and quiet in the colonies encouraged the government to hope the American problem was over, the central issues remained unresolved. Foreign tea continued to be smuggled into Atlantic ports; customs officers and other officials found the law as difficult to enforce as ever; and there were still violent disturbances whenever a conscientious official or naval officer insisted upon carrying out his instructions to the letter.

One such incident occurred in June 1772 when the commander of the Royal Navy schooner *Gaspee*, which sailed about Narragansett Bay, Rhode Island officiously looking for ships to stop and search, ran his ship aground near Providence. The people of the town, delighted to have the detested officer at their mercy, climbed aboard the *Gaspee*, set fire to it and put the wounded commander and his crew to sea in small boats. An inquiry was appointed to investigate the incident; but no one was found willing to turn king's evidence other than a runaway slave whose testimony would, in any case, have been discounted.

So this provocation had to be overlooked. An incident that occurred the following year in Boston, however, was to have far more fateful consequences. It concerned imported tea which patriotic Americans now ostentatiously declined to drink, terming it 'the beverage of traitors', though they consumed enormous quantities brought in by smugglers, mostly from the Netherlands, and lesser quantities of a drink made from the flowers of the sassafras tree. Lord North's government saw tea as the answer to the problems of the East India Company, which had been brought close to bankruptcy by increased administrative costs and declining profits from its trade, and which had between 15 and 20 million pounds of tea leaves mouldering away in the storehouses of Madras and other ports in the Bay of Bengal. If the East India Company were to be excused the British customs duty which would otherwise have fallen on it and were to be permitted to send the tea direct to the colonies, the price of imported tea would drop by half from about £1 a pound to a mere 10s. It would be even cheaper than smuggled tea, so American tea drinkers would be induced to drink it; and, at the same time, the finances of the East India Company would be put on a sounder basis.

Over three hundred chests of tea were accordingly and immediately despatched to Boston where it was intended they should be sold through the Company's own agents. However pleased the ordinary American tea drinker might have been by these arrangements, the smugglers who brought in foreign tea, as well as the merchants who were making fortunes from its distribution, naturally regarded Lord North's ingenious measure in a very different light. So did Samuel Adams, who had recently founded the Committee of Correspondence of Boston to maintain contact with similar dissident bodies in other towns, and who seems already by this time to have decided that complete independence from Britain was the goal towards which all patriotic Americans should be striving. An extraordinarily skilful manipulator and opportunist, Adams, unlike some other radical politicians and polemicists, had never relaxed his attacks on British · policy in America when the government in London made concessions to colonial feeling. He had been largely instrumental in securing the withdrawal of British troops from Boston, and in the importation of the British East India Company's tea into Boston he recognized a provocation ideally suited to his form of propaganda and protest.

The British ship *Dartmouth*, with a cargo of this tea, entered Boston harbour in November 1773. Previously, ships carrying tea to America had been turned away and sent back to England; tea agents in New York, Philadelphia and Charleston had been forced to resign their offices, as the stamp distributors had been a few years before. The *Dartmouth*, however, was permitted to tie up in Boston harbour; and Thomas Hutchinson, now Governor of Massachusetts, to whose two merchant sons part of her cargo of tea had been consigned, insisted that the chests must be unloaded, pending the issue of the necessary clearance forms. He ordered the port guns to open fire should the master of the *Dartmouth*, whose cargo had been entered at the Custom House, be persuaded to sail her away before the tea duty had been paid.

Demands that the ship must sail forthwith had been made in Boston's Old South Meeting House, where an assembly known as 'The Body' held frequent debates. A meeting held on the afternoon of Thursday, 16 December 1773 attracted so many thousands of people that most had to wait in the rain outside. It was announced that the Governor, after days of negotiation, remained obdurate in his refusal to let the still unloaded ship and two others, the *Eleanor* and the *Beaver*, which had since entered the harbour, sail away. The announcement caused uproar in the crowd; and, when order had been restored, Samuel Adams declared in a loud voice, 'This meeting can do nothing more to save the country.'

Soon afterwards a number of men disguised as Mohawks, with faces darkened by soot and representing themselves as symbols of oppressed America, appeared at the door of the assembly hall, gave a war whoop and then, followed by hundreds of onlookers, made their way down to the wharf. John Hancock called after them, 'Let every man do what is right in his own eyes.'

Shouting, 'The Mohawks are come!' and 'Boston harbour a teapot tonight!' they marched down to Griffin's Wharf, clambered aboard the ships in the moonlight, broke open the tea chests with their tomahawks, hurled their contents into the water and threw the splintered containers after them. There were 342 chests in all, containing 35,000 pounds of tea; and, before the last one had been emptied, the piles of leaves on top of the water had risen so high that quantities of them were falling over the sides of the ships on to the decks and had to be shovelled back again into the harbour. The temptation proved too much for one of the men, who was seen stuffing leaves into the lining of his coat. But he was chased off the ship; and, so that none of the others could be accused of theft, they were all made to shake out their shoes before jumping back on to the wharf. The decks were swept clean and the first mates of all three ships were asked to confirm that nothing other than tea chests had been touched. A small padlock belonging to the master of one of the ships had been accidentally damaged, and a replacement for it was afterwards procured and sent to him. As the Mohawks marched away, in Indian file, to the tune of a fife, Admiral John Montagu, Commander-in-Chief on the North American Station, threw up a window in the house of an American loyalist friend with whom he had been dining and called out to them, 'Well, boys, you've had a fine, pleasant evening for your Indian caper, haven't you? But mind, you have got to pay the fiddler yet.'

'Never mind, Squire,' one of them shouted back, 'just come down here, if you please, and we'll settle the bill in two minutes.'

Following Boston's lead, the citizens of other towns either destroyed such tea as had been landed, kept it locked up in warehouses where it rotted, or made public declarations never to drink the beverage again. In New York demonstrators clambered aboard the ship *Nancy*, threw its cargo of tea overboard, then burned the chests in which it had been packed. At Edenton, a seaside town on Albemarle Sound in North Carolina, a gathering of ladies signed a well-publicized declaration of their intent never again to drink tea, nor to wear English cloth. In Boston – where some people went so far as to give up eating fish caught in the harbour 'because they had drunk of the East India Tea' – a provocative customs official, John Malcolm, who had already been tarred and feathered in Maine, was dragged out of his house near North Square, tarred and feathered again and paraded through the streets in a cart which was halted from time to time so that he could be beaten.

When reports of these disturbances reached England – together with a parcel from John Malcolm containing a bit of his tarred and feathered skin sent in the successful hope of obtaining a pension – there was general agreement that the colonists had now overstepped the limits of tolerable misbehaviour and that there could be no further concessions to their revolutionary leaders. Benjamin Franklin, the tenth of seventeen children of a Boston candlemaker and himself a printer,

publisher, author, inventor and diplomat, who was then living in
London as agent for Pennsylvania and various other colonies, reported that 'the violent destruction of the tea seemed to have united
all parties'. 'I am more and more convinced that we have both the
right and power on our side,' declared Edward Gibbon, Member of
Parliament for Liskeard, who had just begun work on his *Decline
and Fall of the Roman Empire*, 'and that though the effort may be
accompanied with some melancholy circumstances, we are now
arrived at the decisive moment of persevering or of losing for ever
both our trade and Empire.' Gibbon's fellow-member of The Club,
Samuel Johnson, was even more forthright. His pamphlet, *Taxation
no Tyranny, An Answer to the Resolution and Address of the American
Congress*, stated the government's case in the most uncompromising
terms. Johnson maintained that 'he who accepts protection, stipulates
obedience', and that, since 'we have always protected the Americans,
we may, therefore, subject them to government'. Throughout the
British dominions, which were 'governed by English laws, entitled
to English dignities, regulated by English counsels, and protected by
English arms', the English Parliament reigned supreme. Its Members
had a perfect right to impose taxes on the American colonies as
payments 'exacted by authority from part of the community for the
benefit of the whole'. Since the American rebels refused to agree to
these incontrovertible and unexceptionable propositions, they must
be forced to accept them with, however, 'the least injury possible to
their persons and possessions'. If they remained obdurate, Johnson
continued in passages which outraged the feelings of the rebels and
their friends, 'let us give the Indians arms, and teach them discipline,
and encourage them now and again to plunder a plantation'. And not
only should Indians be armed but black slaves also. Johnson's black
servant, Francis Barber, whom he dearly loved, was the son of a
slave and had himself been brought up as a slave in the West Indies;
and Johnson regarded slave owners with exceptional animosity.
Arming people to whom slave owners denied the freedom which
they so loudly demanded for themselves was an act 'which surely the
lovers of liberty cannot but commend'.

Johnson's pamphlet aroused the most passionate protests. A
counterblast of a publication asked how an English heart could
'conceive such ideas, even in jest, what horror! – But the virulent
spirit of an inveterate Tory can calmly contemplate the idea of savages

turned loose upon the friends of freedom – he can imagine himself the huntsman of the Indian pack – hallooing forward his bloodhounds to carnage.' Other writers attacked Johnson as 'a sycophantic slave', 'a mercenary reptile', 'the bookworm, the tool of traitors'. Benjamin Franklin, alluding to the state pension which the government had bestowed upon him after the publication of his *Dictionary*, decried him as a mere 'court pensioner'.

There were many, however, who agreed with Johnson. 'Had I been George III, and thought as he did about America,' observed Robert Orme, the contemporary historian, 'I would have given Johnson three hundred a year for his *Taxation no Tyranny* alone.' As James Boswell said, the pamphlet was, indeed, 'congenial with the sentiments of numbers at that time'. One of those who approved of it was John Wesley, the first religious leader of importance to join the protest against slavery and a man who, so Johnson said, could talk well on any subject. Indeed, Wesley incorporated some of Johnson's arguments into his own *Calm Address to our American Colonies* which he published in 1775 and which elicited a letter from Johnson expressing satisfaction at having 'gained such a mind as yours'.

Johnson was highly pleased not only by the commendations bestowed upon his pamphlet by like-minded people such as John Wesley, but also by the uproar it provoked amongst the rebels and their supporters. 'I think I have not been attacked enough for it,' he announced at a dinner party soon after the pamphlet had appeared. 'Attack is the re-action. I never think I have hit hard, unless it rebounds.'

Thereafter, whenever opportunity offered, he condemned American *soi-disant* patriots in the most vituperative terms. They were 'a race of convicts, and ought to be thankful for anything we allow them short of hanging'. He was willing to love all mankind, he averred on a later occasion, '*except an American*'. He numbered several Americans among his friends and confessed that he 'set a high value upon their friendship'; but, he said, indulging in that hyperbole to which in calmer moments he confessed himself prone, they were in general 'rascals, robbers and pirates'. He would willingly burn and destroy them. A less intemperate member of the company bravely remarked that here was an instance 'that we are always most violent against those whom we have injured'. This predictably made Johnson more furious than ever, and he roared out another tremendous volley that James Boswell thought might well have been heard across the Atlantic.

Over other dinner tables views similar to Johnson's were constantly expressed. Within a matter of weeks in 1775 over 140 addresses were sent to the King condemning the Americans' rebellion. Even William Pitt, now Earl of Chatham and living in retirement, could not deny that the actions of those who had taken part in the various 'tea parties' in America were 'certainly criminal'. With a few notable exceptions, both his former supporters and opponents agreed that these recent provocations could not be ignored: the time of appeasement was over; the rebellion must be suppressed. One Member of Parliament, Charles Van, went so far as to declare in the House that Boston ought to be knocked about the ears of its inhabitants and destroyed like Carthage. 'I am of opinion,' he said, 'you will never meet with that proper obedience to the laws of this country until you have destroyed that nest of locusts.'

The King, who had previously been inclined to be less severe towards the Americans than some of his Ministers, now agreed with Lord North that a firm stand was essential. At the beginning of February he spoke to Lieutenant-General the Hon. Thomas Gage, a brave but not notably talented officer who had seen much service in America and was now returning as Commander-in-Chief of the land forces there. Gage told the King that, so long as the British behaved like lambs, the colonists would play the part of lions, but that if the government were resolute the Americans would 'undoubtedly prove very meek'. This opinion was confirmed by Thomas Hutchinson who, having resigned as Governor of Massachusetts, had come to London to give advice on American affairs and who assured the King that firm legislation would result in 'speedy submission'. Army officers serving in America shared this view. One was convinced that the colonists' talk of taking up arms to resist the force of England was 'mere bullying' and would 'go no further than words'. Another was of the opinion that, while the colonists boasted of their determined resistance, they would do little when the time for action came: 'To hear them talk you might imagine they would attack us and demolish us every night; yet, whenever we appear, they are frightened out of their wits.'

Thus encouraged, Lord North's Ministers brought in a series of

Acts, mostly directed at the rebels of Massachusetts, in the expectation that other colonies would come to heel once they realized what might be their lot if they continued recalcitrant. Boston was to be closed as a port until the cost of the tea destroyed had been met and compensation had been paid to the revenue officials. By the Administration of Justice Act, the Governor of Massachusetts was permitted to transfer trials to England if he considered local prejudices might interfere with justice. By the Government of Massachusetts Act, members of the upper house of the legislature were to be nominated by the Crown instead of being elected by the House of Representatives. By a Quartering Act, British troops were to be brought back into Boston. The appointment of Governor of Massachusetts, vacant since the resignation of the American Hutchinson, was to be filled by General Gage, the British Commander-in-Chief. 'The die is cast,' wrote the King, 'the colonies must either submit or triumph. I do not wish to come to severe measures, but we must not retreat. By coolness and an unremitted pursuit of the measures that have been adopted I trust that they will come to submit.' Even now, they were to be given every encouragement to give way peaceably. Gage was instructed by Lord Dartmouth, Secretary of State for the American Colonies, to 'use every endeavour to quiet the minds of the people', and 'by mild and gentle persuasion to induce submission'. The troops must, of course, be ready to meet any opposition, but the King hoped that 'such necessity [would] not occur'.

The King's hope was not to be realized. Other ports declined to take advantage of Boston's predicament; and one after the other, responding to Samuel Adams's plea that Boston should be considered 'as suffering in the common cause', colonies expressed their sympathy for Massachusetts. In Philadelphia, Boston's principal rival as a port on the Atlantic seaboard, Christopher Marshall recorded in his diary for 1 June 1774:

This being the day when the cruel act for blocking up the harbour of Boston took effect, many of the inhabitants of this city, to express their sympathy and show their concern for their suffering brethren in the common cause of liberty, had their shops shut up, their houses kept close from hurry and business; also the ring of bells at Christ Church were muffled, and rung a solemn peel at intervals, from morning till night: the colours of the vessels in the harbour were hoisted half-mast high; the several houses of divine worship were crowded . . . Sorrow, mixed with indignation, seemed to be in the countenances of the inhabitants, and indeed the whole city wore an aspect of deep distress, being a melancholy occasion.

Elsewhere sympathy for Boston was quite as publicly expressed as it was in Philadelphia. In several ports ships were loaded with supplies for Boston's poor and unemployed; more Committees of Correspondence were set up for the purpose of keeping the colonies in touch with each other; in New York, in Rhode Island and in Virginia, as well as in Massachusetts, calls were made for a meeting of the colonies' various representatives in a general congress.

In Williamsburg, Virginia, a young lawyer, Thomas Jefferson, came into prominence. The son of a surveyor who had left him comfortably off, Jefferson, already something of a classical scholar, had entered the College of William and Mary in Williamsburg in 1760 and, although rather lonely and introspective, he had soon earned the friendship and esteem of various men distinguished in Williamsburg society, including Francis Farquier, the Lieutenant Governor of Virginia. He was still in his twenties when he became a member of the lower house of the colony's legislature; and he was no more than thirty-one when he published his learned, persuasive and eloquent *Summary View of the Rights of British America* in which he argued that the Houses of Parliament in London had no right to pass legislation binding upon the people of America. Although more at ease with a pen in his hand than when addressing his fellow-representatives on the legislature, he proposed a day of fasting and prayer on behalf of Boston, inducing the Governor to dissolve the House of Burgesses, whose members continued their debate in a tavern. It was subsequently resolved that trade with Britain would again be stopped, and that a general congress must be convened without delay.

This congress, to be known as the First Continental Congress, was to meet in Philadelphia on 5 September 1774. As the delegates travelled from north and south to Pennsylvania that summer, there was much apprehensive talk about the Quebec Act which Parliament had passed in order to provide for the better administration of Canada. This Act not only extended the boundaries of Canada down to Illinois and Detroit, thus barring westward expansion from the seaboard colonies, but also left French civil law in force and gave recognition to Roman Catholicism, thus both alarming and deeply offending the Protestants of New England. Here, it seemed, was yet another threat to the liberties and religion of Americans.

The delegates, nearly half of them lawyers, who met in Carpenters' Hall, Philadelphia in the late summer of 1774 were not, however, yet committed to independence. Indeed, the more moderate, like Joseph Galloway of Pennsylvania, were for a policy of compromise; but Galloway's proposals offering reconciliation were rejected. While not yet generally advocating a complete break with the mother country, the radicals were determined not to back down. They insisted that Parliament's recent Acts must all be denounced, that commerce with Britain – except for some trade allowing southern states to sell their crops – must cease, and that to achieve this end patriotic Americans must practise the strictest frugality and economy. They must put a stop to 'every species of extravagance and dissipation, especially all horse-racing and all kinds of gaming, cockfighting, exhibition of shows, plays, and other expensive diversions and entertainments'. The radicals had their way; and when a delegate from Massachusetts rode into Philadelphia with a number of resolutions passed in Suffolk County, including a resolve that the Americans must be prepared for a defensive war, the Congress endorsed them, promising to stand by Massachusetts and to help defend the liberties for which their fathers 'had fought and bled'. Before returning home, the delegates agreed to meet again in May if their demands had not been met.

General Gage, who had now returned to America and had failed to bribe Samuel Adams with the offer of an extremely large pension, was deeply alarmed by the growing unrest. 'Affairs here are worse than even at the Time of the Stamp Act,' he reported. 'I don't mean in Boston but throughout the country . . . If you think ten thousand men enough send twenty; if a million [pounds] is thought enough, give two; you will save both blood and Treasure in the end.' While waiting for the few reinforcements which, despite his pleas and warnings, were all that the government were prepared to allow him at this stage, General Gage sent out officers in civilian clothes to make maps of the surrounding countryside and to draw plans of places likely to be centres of resistance. At the same time, determined to place all military supplies in the area well out of reach of the rebels, he despatched troops to remove the powder from a magazine at Charlestown and armaments from a fort at Portsmouth, New Hampshire and from Salem, Massachusetts. He was making arrangements for a raid upon a reported store of rebel guns and ammunition at Concord, north of Boston, when the sloop *Nautilus* sailed into harbour with a despatch from the Secretary of State for the Colonies authorizing him to take strong action, on the grounds that it would surely be better if the conflict ('if necessary') were brought on now rather than later, when the rebels had had more time to organize armed resistance.

The rebels, though, were already better organized than the government in London supposed. Special militiamen, known as minutemen because they undertook to take up arms at a moment's notice, had been called into existence, and arrangements for spreading a call to arms from town to town and settlement to settlement had been perfected. Workshops were being equipped for the making of gunpowder; and messengers held themselves ready to ride by day and night to carry warnings and despatches wherever they were needed. One such was Paul Revere, the Boston master silversmith, who had already carried the Suffolk County Resolves to Philadelphia and a warning of the British commander's order to remove military supplies from the fort at Portsmouth.

Revere, who was to become one of the folk heroes of the coming revolution, was the son of a French Huguenot immigrant, Apollos Rivoire, who had changed his name to Revere because, so he said, 'the bumpkins pronounce it easier'. As well as making the elegant teapots – one of which he is seen holding in his left hand in the celebrated portrait of him by John Singleton Copley – Paul Revere made and fitted false teeth, sold spectacles, constructed surgical instruments and engraved copper plates, such as 'The Bloody Massacre Perpetrated in King Street, Boston on March 5th 1770'. The father of several children, a man with experience of soldiering in the Seven Years' War, and a highly regarded figure amongst the craftsmen of Boston, he had been one of those dressed in Indian clothes who had taken part in the Boston Tea Party and was now the chief messenger for the town's Committee of Safety. It was he who was chosen to carry the warning to Concord that the military stores there were in danger of expropriation and to ride to Lexington to tell the rebel leaders, John Hancock and Samuel Adams, that the British intended to arrest them.

It had been realized for several days in Boston that some sort of military expedition was afoot. Although the British had taken precautions to keep it secret, the rebels had been given general warning of it by, amongst others, a Boston lady who employed the wife of a British soldier as her maid. The troops detailed for the operation, a force of picked companies detached from their regiments, were commanded by an officer remarkable for his obesity, Lieutenant-Colonel Francis Smith of the 10th Regiment, whose second-in-command was John Pitcairn, an active, ambitious and hard-drinking major in the Marines. They were to march quietly out of Boston on the night of 18 April 1775 without being told of their destination or even knowing of the exercise until woken by their sergeants. Leaving the barracks by a back door so that the sentries would be unaware of their departure, they were to make for boats waiting on a secluded part of the waterfront to take them across the bay to a landing place near a farm south of the road to Cambridge. The boats were to be rowed with muffled oars, and the men were to wade ashore.

Despite the care taken, it proved impossible to keep the preparations secret from the spies who kept a constant watch upon the movements of the British troops; and, as soon as the march from the barracks to the waterfront began, two messengers were sent to Lexington to warn Adams and Hancock that the soldiers were on their way. One messenger, a young shoemaker named William Dawes, rode by land across Boston Neck; the other, Paul Revere, was rowed across to Charlestown in a boat whose oars were muffled by the torn-up petticoat of the boatman's girlfriend. From Charlestown, Revere 'set off on a very good horse' belonging to John Hancock for Charlestown Neck.

Since it was thought likely that any horseman riding out of Boston in either direction that night would be intercepted, it had already been agreed that warning of the British approach would be given to the surrounding settlements by lanterns placed briefly in the North Church steeple. One lantern was to be lit if the soldiers left by land across Boston Neck, two if they went out by water.

It was a bright night as Revere galloped across Charlestown Neck and the road was clear; but soon after eleven o'clock he saw two horsemen in front of him under a tree. He recorded:

> When I got near them, I discovered they were British officers. One tried to get ahead of me, and the other to take me . . . I turned my horse very quick and galloped . . . for the Medford Road . . . I got clear . . . and went through Medford, over the bridge, and up to Menotomy. In Medford I awakened the captain of the minute men; and after that I alarmed almost every house, till I got to Lexington. I found Messrs. Hancock and Adams at the Rev. Mr Clark's [and] told them my errand, and enquired for Mr [William] Dawes, [the other messenger]. They said he had not been there [but] after I had been there about half an hour he came. We refreshed ourselves, and set off for Concord to secure the stores etc. We were overtaken by a young Dr [Samuel] Prescott whom we found to be a high Son of Liberty . . . I mentioned that we had better alarm all the inhabitants till we got to Concord. The young Doctor much approv'd of it and said he would stop with us, for the people between [Lexington] and Concord knew him and would give the more credit to what we said.
>
> [When] we had got nearly halfway, Mr Dawes and the Doctor stopped to alarm the people of a house. I was about one hundred rods [550 yards] ahead when I saw two men, in nearly the same situation as those officers were near Charlestown. I called for the Doctor and Mr Dawes to come up; in an instant I was surrounded . . . The Doctor, being foremost, he came up and we tried to get passed them; but they being armed with pistols and swords, they forced us into the pasture. The Doctor jumped his horse over a low stone wall and got to Concord.
>
> I observed a wood at a small distance and made for that. When I got there, out started six officers on horseback and ordered me to dismount. One of them, who appeared to have the command, examined me, where I came from and what my name was? I told him. He asked me if I was an express. I answered in the affirmative. He demanded what time I left Boston. I told him, and added that there would be five hundred Americans there in a short time, for I had alarmed the country all the way up.

Revere was then questioned by another officer, Major Edward Mitchell, who held a pistol to his head and threatened to blow his brains out if he did not tell the truth. Revere answered as before, whereupon he was told to remount his horse and to accompany the officers back to Lexington. As they approached it, a volley of shots rang out from the direction of the meeting-house which had been occupied by the militia. 'This appeared to alarm [the British officers] very much'; but after a while they rode on towards the meeting-house, leaving Revere free to escape to the parson's house where he found Adams and Hancock. They all left together for Woburn, about three miles away.

The men of the Lexington Provincial Company were commanded by Captain John Parker, a middle-aged farmer, who had drawn them up on Lexington Green in front of the meeting-house, surrounded by a large crowd of spectators standing on the edge of the Green. They waited there in the gathering light as an alarm gun was fired from time to time and an occasional peal of church bells could be heard in the distance. After an hour or so they voted to break up, some of them going home, others walking across to Buckman's Tavern which overlooked the Green. But almost seventy of them were still standing on the Green in their country clothes of leather jerkins and broad-brimmed hats when the British detachment on its way to Concord came upon them. There are conflicting reports as to what then occurred. According to one John Robbins, who was standing in the front rank of Captain Parker's company and who later testified under oath before a notary public, 'there suddenly appeared a Number of King's troops, about a thousand as [he] thought, at a distance of about Sixty or Seventy yards . . . They were huzzaing & on a quick pace Towards us with Three officers in there front on horse back & on full gallop Towards us the foremost of which cryed through down your arms you villans you Rebels.' Another American eyewitness, also testifying under oath, declared

That being in a Pasture near the Meetinghouse at said Lexington . . . about half an hour before sunrise I saw a Number of Regular Troops pass speedily by . . . and after they had passed by said Meetinghouse I saw three officers on horse back advance to the front of said Regulars when one of them being within six rods [about a hundred feet] of said Militia cryed out Disperse you rebels emediately [another witness gave the words as 'lay down your

arms, you damned rebels or you are all dead men . . . Disperse ye
villains, ye rebels! Disperse! Lay down your arms!'] on which he
brandished his sword over his head three times. Meanwhile the
second officer who was about two rods behind him fired a Pistol
Pointed at said Militia and the Regulars keeps huzzaing till he had
finished brandishing his sword and when he had thus finished his
dashing his sword he Pointed it Down Towards said Militia.

Both Major Pitcairn, who was in command of the leading British
detachment, and Captain Parker had ordered their men not to fire;
and there had been no retaliation when a man in the crowd at the
edge of the Green tried to shoot one of Pitcairn's subalterns with a
musket whose powder flashed in the pan. But suddenly a shot rang
out, perhaps from Buckman's Tavern or from behind a stone wall
beside it. Most American witnesses agree that orders to fire were
then given to the British troops, though English reports suggest that
Pitcairn's men responded to the fire spontaneously. 'The foremost of
the three officers ordered their men saying fire by God fire,' deposed
one of the American witnesses. 'I observed an officer at the head of
said troops flourishing his sword,' said another, Simon Winship of
Lexington, 'and he with a Loud Voice gave the word fire fire.' 'I
testify and declare,' deposed a third, 'that I heard the words of
command given to the troops to fire, fire damn you fire.'

Certainly the British troops, having opened fire, kept discharging
their muskets as the Americans dispersed and ran for cover, killing
eight and wounding ten, including Captain Parker who was shot in
the leg. The British then charged wildly forward after the retreating
Americans, shouting so loudly, a British subaltern said, that 'they
could hear no orders'. Several of them dashed towards Buckman's
Tavern and began battering on the door.

'There was not a gun fired by any of Captain Parker's men within
my knowledge,' recorded a member of his company. 'I was so
situated that I must have known it, had anything of the kind taken
place before the total dispersion of our company, [though another
provincial] told me, many years since, that after Parker's company
had dispersed . . . he gave [the British] "the guts of his gun"'.
Perhaps this man was responsible for slightly wounding an English
soldier, the only casualty suffered by the British during the affray.

When Colonel Smith came upon the scene he was clearly horrified by what had happened. He found a drummer to beat a tattoo to lay down arms; then, having castigated Pitcairn's men for opening fire without orders, he sent them off to Concord into which they marched to the music of pipe and drum at eight o'clock that morning.

Here there was another and more serious skirmish. All had gone quietly at first. The British officers had sat at their ease in chairs outside the clapboard houses, Major Pitcairn stirring a glass of brandy and water with his finger, while their soldiers had searched the town for the stores of arms and ammunition which were known to be concealed there. But then, down by the North Bridge, one of the two bridges across the Concord River, a single shot rang out, as it had done in Lexington, and the British soldiers responded without orders. Major Buttrick, commander of the Concord militia, was not, however, prepared to disperse his men as Captain Parker had been. 'Fire, fellow soldiers!' he called out. 'For God's sake, fire!'

They did so, and by the first volley four British officers were wounded and three soldiers killed. By now hundreds of militia-men had collected in Concord, where it was rumoured that they were scalping the wounded soldiers and where a simple-minded youth had certainly killed a British prisoner by a blow to the head from a tomahawk. Colonel Smith, himself to be wounded in the retreat, decided that the time had come to march back to Boston.

It was not a well-conducted withdrawal. Indeed, so disorderly did it become that men, tired out by their long day's march, running and stumbling towards Lexington, clinging to riderless horses, had to be stopped by officers drawn up in a line across the road and threatened with death unless they pulled themselves together, resumed their proper places in the ranks, and prepared to defend themselves.

Even so, the British, many of whom had now expended all the thirty-six rounds of ammunition with which they had been issued, suffered far more on their march back to Boston than they had while engaged with the minutemen at North Bridge in Concord. They would have suffered even more severely had not a large detachment with cannon been sent to cover their retreat under the command of the thirty-four-year-old Colonel Lord Percy, later Duke of Nor-thumberland, whose men marched thirty miles in ten hours to escort them home.

From farm walls, hedgerows and wayside boulders, from the windows of houses and the roofs of barns, hundreds of rebels, including women, kept up a steady fire on the retreating troops, shooting many in the back. A British officer wrote:

> We were fired on from all sides, but mostly from the rear, where people had hid themselves in houses till we had passed and then fired. The country was an amazing strong one, full of hills, woods, stone walls, &c, which the rebels did not fail to take advantage of, for they were all lined with people who kept up an incessant fire upon us, as we did too upon them but not with the same advantage, for they were so concealed there was hardly any seeing them. In this way we marched between nine and ten miles, their numbers increasing from all parts, while ours were reducing by deaths, wounds and fatigue, and we were totally surrounded with such an incessant fire as it's impossible to conceive; our ammunition was likewise near expended.

Another officer, Lieutenant Frederick MacKenzie of the Royal Welch Fusiliers, recorded how the rebels disappeared out of sight as soon as they had fired

> until they had loaded again . . . In the road in our rear they were most numerous, and came on pretty close, frequently calling out, 'King Hancock for ever.' . . . Some houses were forced open in which no person could be discovered, but when the column had passed numbers sallied forth from some place in which they had lain concealed . . . Many houses were plundered by the soldiers, notwithstanding the efforts of the officers to prevent it. I have no doubt that this inflamed the Rebels, and made many of them follow us further than they otherwise would have done. By all accounts some soldiers, who stayed too long in the houses, were killed in the very act of plundering by those who lay concealed in them.

According to other accounts, several innocent people were killed in the houses as well as armed rebels; and in one house a woman who had recently given birth was, she wrote, alarmed by three soldiers who burst into her bedroom.

One of the said soldiers immediately opened my [bed] curtains with his bayonet fixed and pointing . . . to my breast. I immediately cried out, 'For the Lord's sake, don't kill me!'

He replied, 'Damn you.'

One that stood near said, 'We will not hurt the woman if she will go out of the house, but we will surely burn it.'

I immediately arose, threw a blanket over me, went out, and crawled into a corn-house near the door with my infant in my arms, where I remained until they were gone. They immediately set the house on fire.

An officer in the Royal Navy found excuses for the conduct of the British troops:

The Enthusiastic Zeal with which these [rebels] have behaved must convince every reasonable man what a difficult and unpleasant task General Gage has before him. Even Weamin had firelocks. One was seen to fire a Blunderbuss between her Father and Husband from their Windows . . . In another House which was long defended by 8 resolute fellows, the Grenadiers at last got possession when After having run their Bayonets into 7, the 8th continued to abuse them with all the [fury] of [a] true Cromwellian, and but a moment before he quitted this World apply'd such epethets as I must leave unmentioned.

Writing home to England, Lord Percy confirmed the toughness of spirit displayed by the Americans, many of whom had advanced to fire within ten yards of him and other officers, 'though they were mortally certain of being put to death themselves in an instant'. While expressing shock at 'the cruelty and barbarity' of rebels who 'scalped and cut off the ears of some of ye wounded men who fell into their hands', Percy was forced to conclude that they were far from being 'an irregular mob . . . They have men amongst them who know very well what they are about, having been employed as rangers among the Indians.'

This opinion of the rebels was shared by John Wentworth, Governor of New Hampshire, whose wife told her kinswoman, the Marchioness of Rockingham:

The King's troops have too mean an opinion of the Americans –
they think them Fools and Cowards, but indeed, my Lady, they
are neither. Undisciplined and to be conquer'd they no doubt are,
but they are far from the despicable set thought for – their numbers
makes them formidable and they take all possible pains to improve
themselves in military skill.

The 'Sons of Violence' were likewise fired by 'an enthusiastic
passion', Frances Wentworth continued.

They declare their abhorrence of all under Lord North whose very
name they detest beyond words . . . Its shocking, my Lady, to pass
the streets and hear what imprecations are thrown out against the
King's Ministry.

Not a night since [the troubles began] have all my family been
in bed but one or more sits up. We watch lest we are in our sleep
surprised and taken . . . and fall a sacrifice to the Sons of Violence.
Thus is the once peaceful habitations of this Country turned to
desolation and misery . . . The Governor is so distressed at the
times – it preys upon him. He has lost a great deal of flesh and all
his Spirits. I tell him but he dont own it . . . There is no protection
for the Crown Officers except one 20 Gun ship which is at a distance
from the Town [Portsmouth] – and in case of a general insurrection
which is constantly feared – its doubtful if we shou'd be able to get
on board.

Less than a fortnight after this letter was written, the attack which
Frances Wentworth feared was made upon her house.

Colonel Fenton had dined with us that day, and was sitting with
The Governor when the rabble . . . came arm'd and insisted on Col
Fenton's appearance. The Governor refused when their insolence
became abominable. They stove at the House with Clubs, brought
a large Cannon and placed it before the Door and swore to fire
through the House. They were so cruel as to affirm no one person,
man, woman or child, shou'd escape with life. And when we found
resistance was vain Col Fenton surrendered himself and was made
to walk 15 miles from Portsmouth to Exeter on foot (tho' very
unwell) which he did not accomplish till daybreak . . . [We our-

selves] quit the house with great haste. It was sun-down and damp
air. We got into the Boat with our poor Child – who had never
been exposed and always used to the utmost delicacy – and hurried
away. We had not time to get a hat or Blanket for him but thought
ourselves fortunate to get him off alive . . . They were so cruel as
to say – If they could get the Governor's fat child they would split
him down the Back and broil him.

From all over New Hampshire and Massachusetts rebels were now
marching to surround Boston, into which the exhausted British
contingents had withdrawn from Concord. Having lost well over
250 men, they had spent the night of 19 April on Bunker Hill, the
most westerly of the three eminences on the Charlestown peninsula
which juts out into the estuary north of Boston.

The small town of Charlestown itself, which lay at the foot of
these three hills, was separated from Boston by a channel less than
half a mile wide. But, since its three hundred or so houses were
dominated by the guns of British ships, the colonists had evacuated it,
while the British did not have enough troops to occupy it themselves.
Charlestown and the peninsula on which it stood had thus become a
no-man's-land between the opposing forces.

As the days passed, General Gage became increasingly concerned
by the position into which he had now been forced. On the hills
around him, the rebels, scores of whose fires could be seen burning
at night, were gathering in ever-increasing strength, making encampments, digging entrenchments and collecting supplies by cart and
carriage. Before the end of April, it was calculated that there were at
least ten thousand men looking down upon Boston and the ships in
the harbour. An appeal for even more was made by Dr Joseph
Warren, President of the Massachusetts Provincial Congress, who
had helped to draft the Suffolk County Resolves which had been
carried to Philadelphia by Paul Revere, and who now spread lurid
stories of 'women in childbed' being 'driven by the soldiery naked
into the streets', of 'old men peaceably in their homes' being 'shot
dead', of 'such scenes exhibited as would disgrace the annals of the
most civilized nations':

The barbarous Murders of our innocent Brethren . . . has made it
absolutely necessary that we immediately raise an Army to defend

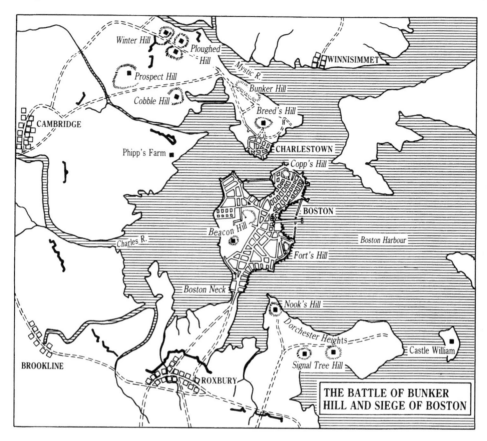

THE BATTLE OF BUNKER
HILL AND SIEGE OF BOSTON

our Wives and our Children from the butchering Hands of an
inhuman Soldiery, who, incensed at the Obstacles they met with
in their bloody Progress, and enraged at being repulsed from
the Field of Slaughter, will without the least doubt take the first
Opportunity in their Power to ravage this devoted country with
Fire and Sword: We conjure you, therefore, by all that is dear, by
all that is sacred, that you give all Assistance possible in forming an
Army . . . We beg and entreat you . . . that you will hasten and
encourage by all possible Means, the Inlistment of Men and send
them forward to Head-Quarters at Cambridge, with that Expedition which the vast Importance and instant Urgency of the
Affair demands.

Men responded to such appeals in their hundreds. Within a matter
of weeks the number of men in the revolutionary camps around

Boston had increased to some fifteen thousand, most of them still wearing the homespun clothes in which they had left their farms. They were placed under the command of Artemas Ward, a major-general of the Massachusetts militia, a cautious stout man suffering from a painful kidney stone, who looked more like the farmer he was than the military strategist he could not pretend to be. Ward gave his most trusted senior officer, John Thomas, the responsibility of occupying Roxbury opposite Boston Neck with nearly half his available forces. Most of the rest were kept in reserve at Cambridge under commanders whose independent spirit gave Ward grounds to fear that concerted attacks might be difficult to mount. Independent though they were, however, all these commanders had past experience of warfare. One of them, Israel Putnam, known affectionately as 'Old Put', a short, burly, energetic farmer and a lieutenant-colonel in the Connecticut militia, had seen service in the recent wars against the French. Another, William Prescott, also a farmer in civilian life and grandfather of the future historian of *The Conquest of Mexico*, had likewise seen service in those years and, before he was twenty, had been offered a commission in the British Army which he had declined because of the bad treatment which many colonial officers received. The third senior officer, Colonel Richard Gridley of Massachusetts, had accepted a British commission and had fought as an artillery officer under Wolfe at Quebec, but had declared his support for the rebels once the issues had become clear.

The rivalries between the rebel commanders and their respective contingents were highlighted when a wealthy merchant from New Haven, Connecticut, who had been appointed a captain in his state militia, rode into the American headquarters at Cambridge. This was Benedict Arnold, then thirty-four years old, the son of a drunken cooper whose grandfather had been a most distinguished citizen of Rhode Island but whose family had since come down in the world. Benedict had been a wild boy and a quarrelsome young man. He had run away to join the British Army in the Seven Years' War and, after keeping a shop which sold medicines, books and other items imported from England, had made a large amount of money out of shipowning, smuggling and selling Canadian horses to the plantation owners of the West Indies. He had become one of the foremost men in the society of New Haven, where he lived in a large house in Water Street and, as captain of the Governor's Foot Guards, could often be seen, in his splendid red and white uniform, parading with his men on the green.

A small, dark-skinned, rough-tongued man with a long nose, heavy jaw, sharp mind and highly self-confident manner, Arnold suggested that the heavy cannon which the rebel force surrounding Boston so badly needed might be supplied by a raid on the British fort of Ticonderoga. It was agreed that the attempt was well worth making. Ticonderoga, formerly known as Fort Carillon, had been established by the French as a fortress of strategic importance between Lake Champlain and Lake George on the main route between Canada and the upper Hudson valley. It was 150 miles inland from Boston as the crow flies; but it was believed to be lightly defended, and known to be in poor structural condition and to contain the cannon which would prove so invaluable to the colonists' operations on the coast.

Arnold was given permission to recruit men for this raid; but, while he was doing so, he learned that another rebel, Ethan Allen, a massive frontiersman, a former lead miner and farmer who had also been born in Connecticut, was organizing for the same purpose volunteers from a band of farmers known as the Green Mountain Boys, after those ranges of the Appalachian Mountains which extend through the middle of what is now Vermont. The Green Mountain Boys had been formed to resist a sheriff's party sent from New York to evict residents who had received grants of land from New Hampshire on the grounds that New Hampshire had no right to dispose of any land west of the Green Mountains. The Boys were a notoriously tough set of men, reluctant to take orders from anyone other than Ethan Allen; and when Arnold rode off to confront Allen and to demand that he himself lead the expedition in the name of the Massachusetts Committee of Safety, the Boys soon made it obvious that they would never obey him. So, after angry discussions, it was agreed that the two leaders should co-operate in a joint enterprise.

The raiders, storming into the fort about half past three in the morning, caught the defenders by surprise and both the commanding officer and the second-in-command asleep in bed. The second-in-command described Benedict Arnold as requesting surrender in a 'genteel manner' but Ethan Allen as being highly agitated, brandishing a sword as he demanded the keys of the fort 'and all the effects of George the third (those were his words)'. 'Come out of there!' he cried. 'Come out, you damned old rat!' What was his authority? the English officer asked him, standing up on his bed, his breeches in his hand. 'In the name of the Great Jehovah and the Continental Congress,' Allen later claimed to have shouted, striding off to find the commander of the fort.

'Damn you, what does this mean?' the commanding officer angrily asked when Allen found him; but, on being told that his men had already been disarmed, he obediently gave up his sword.

By this time the Green Mountain Boys were rampaging round the fort, where they had found several casks of rum. Arnold endeavoured to restore order, but some of the Boys spat at him and one threatened him with a musket when he returned a valuable possession to a British soldier from whom it had been looted. At length the men were brought under control; and about midday on 10 May the captured British soldiers were taken down to the landing-stage on the shores of Lake George, then rowed over the still waters to be marched down through Vermont to Hartford in Connecticut. The artillery which they left behind them included over a hundred iron cannon, the best of which, with several mortars, were soon to be brought south for the use of the rebels by a young and enterprising colonel of artillery, Henry Knox, a former bookseller.

3

BUNKER HILL

*'I wish we could sell them another
hill at the same price.'*

Nathanael Greene

A fortnight after the surrender of the fort at Ticonderoga, towards
the end of May 1775, His Majesty's ship *Cerberus* sailed into Boston
harbour carrying no fewer than three generals sent to America by
the British government, who had come to the conclusion that Thomas
Gage was not capable of dealing with the deepening crisis. Whether
or not these three new generals were much better qualified to handle
it was a question which had been much debated in London. 'I don't
know what the Americans will think of them,' Lord North was
quoted as saying. 'But I know that they make me tremble.'

The senior of the three was the forty-five-year-old the Hon.
William Howe, the tall, dark, younger son of the second Viscount
Howe, a notably brave officer who had served under Wolfe at
Quebec. A Whig Member of Parliament for Nottingham, with an
inarticulateness rivalled only by that of his brother, the admiral,
Richard, Lord Howe, William Howe had opposed the government's
colonial policy and had once declared he would never accept a
command in America. Like his brother, however, he had been
anxious for profitable employment and had persuaded himself that,
if the rebels proved intractable, measures must be taken to stop
America cutting herself loose from Britain and, as Lord Howe put it
in a letter to Benjamin Franklin, to prevent American trade 'passing

into foreign channels'. The Howes had not found employment difficult to obtain. Their mother was widely believed to be an illegitimate child of King George I, and their family were certainly well regarded at court. Their attitude towards America was indulgently considered as a kind of aberration by King George III, who protested in only the mildest way when Lord Howe was reported to have condemned His Majesty's 'invincible obstinacy' towards the colonists. Perhaps, so it was offered in mitigation of the Howes' attitude, their sympathetic feelings for the Americans owed something to the fact that the people of Massachusetts had thought so highly of their elder brother, who had been killed in 1758 at Ticonderoga, that the General Court of Massachusetts Bay had voted £250 for a monument to be erected to his memory.

On leaving Eton, William Howe had been bought a commission in the Duke of Cumberland's Light Dragoons. In the Seven Years' War, he had commanded a battalion which General Wolfe, not a lenient critic, described as 'the best trained in all America'. Known to be a strict disciplinarian, he was respected as a tactician and was well liked by both his officers and his men. He also clearly enjoyed the company of women; and, while he was believed to be fond of the attractive wife he had left behind in England, he was not expected to be faithful to her. He had been a major-general for three years, but his capacity to lead an army had not yet been put to the test; and, since his active service had been limited to America, certain officers who had fought in Germany, and who tended to despise those who knew only of colonial warfare, maintained that his training and experience scarcely suited him for high command.

Next to Howe in seniority, although at forty-five the youngest of the three generals who arrived in the *Cerberus*, was Major-General Henry Clinton. Like Howe, he came from an aristocratic family: a grandson of the sixth Earl of Lincoln and cousin of the second Duke of Newcastle, he could scarcely have been better placed to call upon relations for advancement in his career. His father, Admiral the Hon. George Clinton, although suffering from what he termed a 'family bashfulness' that prevented him from 'pushing [his] fortune', had been quite shameless in this respect. An officer of severely limited talents, he would certainly not have reached his high rank in the

Navy nor been appointed Governor of New York without the badgering to which he constantly subjected his relations.

Henry, his only surviving son, who arrived in America with his parents at the age of thirteen, attended a school at Hampstead, Long Island for a time, before obtaining a commission in the New York militia. After service on Manhattan Island he sailed for Louisbourg, the fortress on the coast of Cape Breton Island, Nova Scotia which the colonists of New England, with the help of a small British fleet, had recently captured from the French. Soon afterwards, having returned to New York, he said goodbye to his family and sailed back to London where, in 1751, with the help of the Duke of Newcastle, he was commissioned into the 2nd Foot Guards.

Any satisfaction that his father may have felt at this appointment was soon dissipated by Henry's bills which, so the elderly Admiral protested, he could not afford to pay. His salary as Governor of New York was supposed to come from some of the rents of the province; but these were always months in arrears, while the provincial assembly were deaf to all pleas for financial help. He hated New York and longed to go home. But the government seemed 'resolved to keep [him there] on purpose to try if the climate' would kill him or not; and when, having disposed of his furniture and having had his luggage sent aboard ship, he was told that he could not sail home until a successor had been found, his wife, whose mental state was already giving cause for concern, was flung into 'violent fits', while his daughter, who had but recently recovered from malaria, 'was not much better'. At length, after over ten years in his detested office, he returned to England where he resumed the importuning of Lord Lincoln and the Duke of Newcastle for a seat in the House of Commons, a naval command, a pension, and 'some genteel post' for his son whose bills as a guards officer were mounting up intolerably.

His requests on his son's behalf did at least bear fruit; and in 1756, when he was twenty-six, Captain Henry Clinton was appointed an aide-de-camp to Sir John Ligonier, the old Huguenot general who had served with great distinction under Marlborough and was shortly to be appointed Commander-in-Chief of the British Army. This appointment did not, however, do much to improve the state of Captain Clinton's finances, for at the age of seventy-seven Ligonier was as lively and sportive as he had ever been. He maintained that no woman past the age of fourteen was worth the trouble of pursuing and kept four mistresses whose combined ages were less than sixty. He expected his aides-de-camp to enter into the spirit of his frolics; and since he did not care to go down alone to his country house in Surrey, Cobham Place, one or other of his military family were always required to go with him. This was not a duty to Captain Clinton's taste.

Although so frequently in debt, he was not by nature a gregarious young man. He had friends but he made them with difficulty; and lost more than one by a shyness, diffidence and sense of insecurity which made him appear both touchy and suspicious. For a time his marriage in 1767 transformed him. His bride, seventeen years younger than himself, was a cousin of Edward Gibbon's friend, John Baker Holroyd, later first Earl of Sheffield, but she was otherwise not particularly well connected and certainly not rich. He married her in a haste which suggests that she may perhaps have been pregnant when the ceremony took place at St George's, Hanover Square. She had four other children and, after giving birth to the last of these, died at the age of twenty-six after little more than five years of marriage. Clinton was desolate. He withdrew from the society of his acquaintances; he neglected his duties; he left his only close friend, Colonel William Phillips, a fat, friendly and amiable artillery officer and one of Ligonier's other aides-de-camp, to let his country house at Weybridge and to rent a more modest one for him in London; he declined to take up the seat in Parliament to which he had been elected through the influence of the Duke of Newcastle; he ignored his mounting debts. For months he refused to be comforted; and it was not until the spring of 1774 when he left England to inspect the Russian army which the Empress Catherine had assembled to fight the Turks that the clouds of misery which enveloped him began to lift. He remained a lonely, aloof and introspective man, quick to take offence and difficult to befriend; but he began to take an interest once more in his career.

This had not so far been remarkable, despite such efforts as were made to promote it by his family and by the King's brother, the Duke of Gloucester, to whom, at their suggestion, he was appointed Groom of the Bedchamber. He had received his lieutenant-colonelcy in the 1st Foot Guards in 1758, and, after serving as aide-de-camp to the Prince of Brunswick in Germany – where he was wounded and then, in his own words, 'hacked by an ignorant German surgeon' – he had been promoted full colonel. He had subsequently gone out to Gibraltar as second-in-command of the garrison there and had displayed not only a determination to familiarize himself with every detail of the fortress's defences and the conditions of the troops stationed there, but also a capacity to offend his superiors by tactlessly voicing his views as to the inadequacy of their arrangements.

By 1772 his worth, however grudgingly, had been recognized: he was promoted major-general; and three years later, leaving his four children in the care of his dead wife's family, he climbed aboard the *Cerberus* for the voyage across the Atlantic with General Howe, from whom at first he kept his distance and to whom he seldom spoke, being, as he confessed, 'a shy bitch' as well as dreadfully seasick.

The third British general to arrive in Boston that day, John Burgoyne, also had aristocratic connections. Fifty-two years old, he was widely believed to be an illegitimate son of Lord Bingley, a clever, unscrupulous and immensely rich man of humble Yorkshire stock who had once been Chancellor of the Exchequer. Certainly Burgoyne was born in a house belonging to Lord Bingley, who left Burgoyne's mother well provided for in his will, in which he also forgave her husband, Major John Burgoyne, a debt he owed him. Major Burgoyne was the son of a baronet and, in the words of a young member of his family, 'one of those fine gentlemen about town who contrive to run through their means and finish their days in a debtors' prison'. Having spent his rich wife's fortune, Major Burgoyne did, indeed, land up in a debtors' prison; but by then enough money had been found to send his son to Westminster School and then to buy him a commission in the Horse Guards.

After spending several years in the Horse Guards without promotion, Burgoyne exchanged into the 1st Royal Dragoons in which he served in Flanders and later in Lancashire, where he met and fell in love with Lady Charlotte Stanley, daughter of the 11th Earl of Derby. Since the Earl declined to contemplate the marriage of his daughter to a poor young officer of dubious provenance, Lady Charlotte and Burgoyne ran away together, were married at a chapel in Curzon Street and went to live in France on the money that Burgoyne received from the sale of his commission.

When the Seven Years' War broke out in 1756, the Burgoynes returned to England where Lady Charlotte became reconciled to her father, who made her a handsome allowance, while her husband returned to the Army, buying a captaincy in the 11th Dragoons with whom he took part in raids on the French coast. His rise in the Army, thanks to his father-in-law's influence, was now far faster than it had been when he was an unknown officer in the Horse Guards. He soon became a lieutenant-colonel and received permission to raise a cavalry regiment to be known as the 16th Regiment of Light Dragoons. To encourage men to enlist in this new regiment, he prepared a notice to be posted in all the towns and villages around Northampton where its headquarters were to be:

> You will be mounted on the finest horses in the world, with the finest clothing and the finest accoutrements; your pay and privileges are equal to two guineas a week; you are admitted by the fair, which together with the chance of getting switched to a buxom widow or of brushing with a rich heiress renders the situation truly enviable and desirable for young men out of employment or uncomfortable – Nick in instantly and enlist.

Having provided himself with a satisfactory and splendidly uniformed regiment, Burgoyne then addressed himself to the acquisition of political influence. He obtained a seat in Parliament, first as Member for Midhurst, then for Preston, Lancashire, which he represented until his death.

After distinguished service in Portugal as brigadier commanding the cavalry, Burgoyne returned to England where he concentrated upon ensuring that his regiment became so obviously well drilled and efficient that it was not one of those disbanded at the end of the war. In this he was so successful that, when the King and Queen reviewed Burgoyne's Light Horse on Wimbledon Common, His Majesty gave instructions that the regiment should henceforth be known as the Queen's Light Dragoons. A successful and distinguished cavalry officer, Burgoyne was also by now well known as a man about town, a frequenter of smart clubs, green rooms and race meetings, and as a guest in the most fashionable houses. And, although the prose of his official communications was so laboured, pompous and verbose as to be scarcely intelligible, he was becoming known as a writer for the theatre – David Garrick put on his *Maid of the Oaks* at Drury Lane.

Indeed, when his appointment to a command in America was

announced, it was suggested by some that Burgoyne – 'a vain, very ambitious man' in the opinion of Horace Walpole, who called him Julius Caesar Burgonius – was too much the dilettante to make a good soldier. He himself, so he told Lord North, would prefer to go on his own to New York rather than 'make up a triumvirate of reputation' in Boston. As Governor of New York, 'a military man, clothed in that character only, going in his station at the head of three or four regiments', he might succeed where others had failed in reopening negotiations with the rebel leaders. He had already spoken in the House of his hope that the Americans could be persuaded to return to their old loyalties by peaceful means rather than by the sword; and he would like to be given an opportunity to initiate negotiations. Lord North listened politely but was evidently not convinced, and eventually decided against Burgoyne's proposal as well as a similar one made by William Howe.

To Lord Barrington, the Secretary-at-War, Burgoyne now confessed that he was reluctant to go to America at all because of the ill health of his wife; and certainly, despite many reported infidelities, he was deeply attached to her. But when it was explained to him that the King had particularly asked for his services and that, unless he were to be given a separate command or other circumstances forbade it, he would have leave to return home the following winter, Burgoyne agreed to go.

Immediately upon landing, all three generals were disturbed to find what Clinton described as 'nothing but dismay among the troops', who were besieged in Boston by what appeared to be an ill-equipped and largely amateur force of colonists – or 'peasants', as Burgoyne is said to have described them. Admittedly the rebels were 'amazingly well situated', in Howe's words, since the countryside around Boston was ideal for the kind of warfare that suited their experience and resources, being 'Covered with woods and small stone wall Inclosures, Exceedingly uneven and much Cutt with Ravins'. The Americans were also well supplied with horses, whereas the British had very few and not nearly enough wagons or landing craft. Yet, with his force recently increased to 5700 men, there seemed no excuse for General Gage's inactivity or for his failure to carry out any proper reconnaissance.

After making their own examinations of the terrain, the newly

arrived generals concluded that an attack on Cambridge across Boston
Neck and the Charles River must be mounted as soon as possible
while diversionary raids were made on the high ground overlooking
Boston, to the north on Charlestown peninsula and to the south-east
on Dorchester Heights. Before this plan could be put into force, rebel
spies in Boston learned of it; and on the starlit night of 16 June some
thousand or so American militiamen, carrying picks and shovels,
advanced towards the Charlestown promontory, walking up the
gentle slopes of Bunker Hill then down and across the plateau to the
next shallow eminence, known as Breed's Hill. While two companies
were sent down into the empty streets of Charlestown to keep watch
across the water to the British lines, the rest began vigorously to dig
a long, shoulder-high earthwork above the town. By dawn the
fortification was complete; and British sailors aboard the *Lively*, lying
at anchor beneath it, were astonished at the sight of the upturned soil
which had so suddenly transformed the landscape above the roofs of
the small town. The captain of the *Lively* gave orders for a broadside
against the fort. But most of the balls, having struck harmlessly
against the earthen wall, rolled slowly back down the slope; while
many of the guns of other ships could not be sufficiently elevated to
reach the works at all. General Gage, watching the cannonade, noticed
a figure, standing behind and sometimes on top of the parapet, who
seemed to be in charge of the rebels' operations and to be recklessly
urging his men to stand firm under their alarming first experience of
cannon fire. He handed the glass to an American Loyalist on his staff,
Abijah Willard, asking him if he knew who the man was. Willard
took the glass and immediately recognized his rich and distinguished
brother-in-law, William Prescott.

'Will he fight?' Gage asked.

'I can't answer for his men,' Willard replied, 'but Prescott will
fight you to the gates of hell.'

Many of Prescott's men were not so resolute. When one of them,
a young farm-hand, was killed by a cannon ball which tore off his
head and – instead of being buried quietly and quickly, as Prescott
wished – was given a solemn funeral, several of his distressed companions wandered home demoralized. And when others were sent
back with entrenching tools, they, too, disappeared for good. Nor
did all those who remained work as hard as they might. Israel Putnam
came upon a corporal who stood idly by, contemplating the men of

his squad as they dug up a large stone. 'My lad,' Putnam said to him, 'throw that stone up on the middle of the breastwork.'

The corporal, touching his hat with his hand, said to the general, 'Sir, I am a corporal.'

'Oh,' replied Putnam, dismounting from his horse and throwing up the stone himself, 'I ask your pardon, sir.'

Like General Gage, General Burgoyne was also looking across to the rebel works and later reported: 'On the 17th, at dawn of day, we found the enemy had pushed intrenchments with great diligence during the night, on the Heights of Charlestown, and we evidently saw that every hour gave them fresh strength; it therefore became necessary to alter our plan and attack on that side.'

Gage and Howe considered landing on the Charlestown promontory from the estuary of the Mystic River, but the shallow waters here were rendered hazardous by mud flats and, since they had no flat-bottomed boats at their disposal and would have to rely on the fleet's longboats for landing craft, it was concluded that the main assault would have to be made, under the protection of shipping, on the outward side of the promontory beneath the eminence known as Morton's Hill, and that reinforcements would subsequently have to be landed nearby under Breed's Hill. To protect their left flank from snipers in the houses in Charlestown, the fleet was to open fire with red-hot shot to set the place ablaze.

Clinton was of a different opinion: concerned that the rebels should not be allowed to escape across the isthmus to the north of Breed's Hill, he proposed that, while Howe landed on the southern shore of Charlestown Neck opposite Boston, he himself should launch a simultaneous assault behind the American main defences and so cut off their retreat. But his advice was disregarded. 'Mr Gage,' he complained with characteristic peevishness, 'thought himself so well informed that he would not take any opinion of others, particularly of a man bred up in the German school, which that of America affects to despise . . . These people seem to have no idea of any other than a direct [attack].'

General Gage's frontal assault accordingly took place in the early afternoon of 17 June 1775, the soldiers marching down to the landing craft in their winter uniforms of thick scarlet cloth, carrying rolled blankets on their backs and three days' supply of boiled beef and bread in their heavy packs. 'Gentlemen,' Howe had addressed them,

'I am very happy in having the honour of commanding so fine a band of men. I do not in the least doubt that you will behave like Englishmen and as becometh good soldiers . . . I shall not desire one of you to go a step farther than where I go myself at your head.'

Watched by Clinton and Burgoyne, who had been required to help direct the artillery on Copps' Hill, and by immense crowds of spectators on the surrounding hills and rooftops of Boston, the first wave of British troops were rowed across the water from Long Wharf, while the cannon on Copps' Hill and the guns of the fleet maintained a covering fire of deafening intensity. The landing was initially unopposed; the twenty-eight barges scraped ashore and, as they were pushed off again by the sailors who rowed back fast for the next wave, the soldiers jumped on to the beach and ran forward up the slope of the hill to establish their bridgehead. The rebels had evidently been caught by surprise at the prompt response to the appearance of their entrenchments.

The earthworks on the slopes of Breed's Hill were, however, not the only defences which had been built on the promontory and were now being manned. Behind them on Bunker Hill another thousand militiamen were preparing positions; while yet more men were being called over to the Charlestown peninsula from wherever they could be spared. Israel Putnam, riding back to Cambridge for reinforcements, encountered several hundred armed men from Connecticut; and Artemas Ward despatched a messenger to the New Hampshire regiment commanded by John Stark, whose troops were as renowned for their strange clothes as for their marksmanship. A contemporary recorded:

> To a man they wore small-clothes, coming down and fastening just below the knee, and long stockings with cowhide shoes ornamented by large buckles . . . The coats and waistcoats were loose and of huge dimensions, with colors as various as the barks of oak, sumach and other trees of our hills and swamps could make them, and their shirts were all made of flax and, like every other part of the dress, were homespun. On their heads was worn a large round-top and broad-brimmed hat. Their arms were as various as their costume. Here an old soldier carried a heavy Queen's Arm, with which he had done service at the conquest of Canada twenty years previous while by his side walked a stripling boy, with a Spanish fusee . . .

which his grandfather may have taken at the Havana, while not a few had old French pieces that dated back to the reduction of Louisbourg. Instead of the cartridge box, a large powder horn was slung under the arm, and occasionally a bayonet might be seen bristling in the ranks. Some of the swords of the officers had been made by our Province blacksmiths, perhaps from some farming utensil; they looked serviceable, but heavy and uncouth.

The arrival of Stark's men brought heart to Prescott's tired Massachusetts militiamen on Breed's Hill, several of whose companions had already had enough of warfare and had decided to follow the example of those who had deserted earlier that day and to go home to their farms and families. Prescott's men were also encouraged when the tall and handsome figure of Dr Joseph Warren, President of the Massachusetts Provincial Congress, appeared amongst them carrying a musket, ready, it appeared, to fulfil an earlier promise to die if necessary 'up to [his] knees in blood'. When Prescott offered to give up his command to him, Warren said he had come not to give orders but to fight.

Slowly the British, in three red lines of heavily laden soldiers, advanced towards the rebels up the slope through the long grass, past clay pits, kilns and apple trees. They stumbled on the jagged rocks and had to clamber over the low stone walls and fences, the left wing under heavy fire from snipers in Charlestown until red-hot shot was sent crashing into the houses, setting the whole place alight within minutes, and making the wooden church steeples, so John Burgoyne said, look 'like great pyramids of fire above the rest'.

The main body of the Americans held their fire, while shot and shells from the British batteries and fleet thudded and roared in the earth around them, sending up showers of dust in the grass. John Stark had given strict orders to his men not to open fire too soon. They were short enough of ammunition as it was, Stark reminded them, having no more than fifteen musket balls per man. They were on the left of the American line where the ground fell down to the Mystic River, concealed behind a rail fence draped with bunches of grass and by a rough wall of stones which they had themselves rapidly thrown up between the end of the fence and the river. The men behind the wall were told not to open fire until the British had passed a stake which Stark had driven into the earth by the water's edge; and the men behind the grass-strewn fence were given similar orders not to fire a single shot until they could see the gaiters of the enemy troops as they came up the slope.

To their right the militia had also been told to hold their fire: they were to wait until they could see the whites of the British soldiers' eyes, then to aim for 'the gorgets and fancy vests of the officers'. The best shots had several firearms each, ready to be passed to them by loaders. Many of their muskets, so a British surgeon later testified, were 'charged with old nails and angular pieces of iron' so as to occasion 'infinite Pain'; and many of their balls, so another surgeon asserted, were encrusted with a white matter 'which is supposed to have been some poisonous mixture, for an uncommon rancorous suppuration followed in almost every case'.

The effect when the Americans did fire, and fired in devastating unison, was astonishing. Scores of British soldiers fell at once; at a second volley, as more men were killed, whole ranks faltered and retreated, although officers and sergeants did all they could to halt them, prodding the men with halberds, bayonets and the tips of swords. General Howe, leading the main assault in person as he had promised to do and supported by Brigadier Robert Pigot with the 43rd and 52nd Foot, found himself on three occasions quite alone, all the staff around him lying dead or wounded.

John Burgoyne was still closely watching the action from a commanding battery directly opposite Charlestown. It was, he wrote in a private letter, 'one of the greatest scenes of war that can be conceived':

> If we look to the height, Howe's corps, ascending the hills in the face of intrenchments, and in a very disadvantageous ground, was much engaged; to the left the enemy pouring in fresh troops by thousands, over the land; and in the arm of the sea our ships and floating batteries cannonading before them; straight before us a large and noble town in one great blaze . . . Behind us, the church steeples and heights of our own camp . . . and the hills round the country covered with Spectators all in anxious suspense . . . The roar of Cannon, Mortars, and Musquetry; the crash of churches, Ships on the Stocks & whole Streets falling in ruin to fill the ear. The storming of the Redoubt to fill the eye. And a reflection that a

> Defeat was perhaps the loss of the British Empire in America to fill
> the Mind, made the whole a picture & a complication of Horror &
> Importance beyond any it ever came to my lot to Witness.

Brave as the Americans were in defence, the British were equally
determined in attack. Twice repulsed with appalling losses on both
occasions, Howe regrouped his men and, supported by Henry Clinton, who led a supporting force from Copps' Hill across to the
promontory, he made a third attempt upon the American position.
This time he broke through. The Americans had run out of ammunition and powder, and at the sight of the British advancing steadily
with fixed bayonets, shouting and screaming, 'stepping over the
bodies of their comrades as if they were logs', throwing off their
packs and, in some cases, discarding even their red coats, the militiamen broke.

Untrained in tactics though they were, they retreated in good
order; but when they reached Bunker Hill and came upon their
fellow-colonists, who had shrunk from fighting in the forward line,
nearly all of them joined in a headlong flight. Standing firm in the
rearguard, still 'in his best cloaths', as a British officer described him,
wearing a pale blue coat over a lace-trimmed, satin waistcoat, Dr
Warren was shot in the head and fell into a trench. A British soldier
plunged a bayonet into his body, then stripped him of his clothes.
'Nothing could be more shocking than the carnage,' a British officer
wrote. 'We tumbled over the dead to get at the living who were
crowding out of the redoubt.'

Over four hundred Americans were killed or wounded that day.
But the British losses had been far more severe. No fewer than
sixty-three officers had been wounded and twenty-seven had been
killed, including Major Pitcairn who had been shot 'by a Villain from
behind a Tree whom he took for a Deserter and it is said had ordered
his life to be spared'. He had been carried off the field by his son, so
Frances Wentworth was told, 'which being observed by the soldiers
and hearing the young gentleman say "my father", they replied "*our*
father", so much they loved him'.

Of the British soldiers engaged, 226 had been killed and 828
wounded; nearly 40 per cent of their total strength. Indeed, William
Prescott thought that the British might well have been driven off
altogether if Putnam had properly organized the men who were

milling about on the slopes of Bunker Hill. 'Why did you not support me, General, with your men?' Prescott asked him.

'I could not *drive* the dogs up.'

'If you could not drive them up, you might have *led* them up.'

Since Howe held the battlefield he claimed the victory; but it was not a victory to celebrate: the day's fighting had witnessed much 'disgraceful disorder' in the British ranks, and the army had suffered too many casualties and was too exhausted and by now too disorganized to pursue the Americans far. 'All was confusion,' General Clinton commented. 'Officers told me that they could not command their men and I never saw so great a want of order.' After the battle the bodies of officers were carried off the field for burial in Boston, but ordinary soldiers were interred where they had been killed; and all night long the groans of wounded men could be heard on the slopes of the hill. It was not until the next day that the last of them were removed to the hospitals in Boston, which were by then so crowded that many of them had to lie out in their courtyards.

The Americans had fought with a spirit which came as a shock to British officers, who still supported the common view expressed by General James Murray, a former Governor of Quebec, that the native American was 'a very effeminate thing, very unfit for and very impatient of war'. Now they were compelled to concur with Lord Percy and Frances Wentworth and with General Gage who maintained that the colonists were not 'the despicable rabble too many had supposed them to be', that they had shown 'a conduct and spirit against us they never showed against the French and everybody has judged them from their former appearance and behaviour'.

They might have been defeated at Bunker Hill, but the British were still surrounded in Boston. And who could tell, as one English officer asked, how long they would be able to hold it before the rebels built forts which would make the harbour unsafe for shipping?

Writing home to complain that General Gage was 'unequal to his present station', John Burgoyne made it clear that he thought the army should not have been in Boston, anyway, a view with which Gage heartily agreed. 'I wish this cursed place was burned,' he told the Secretary-at-War. 'The only use is its harbour . . . but in all other respects it is the worse place either to act offensively from, or defensively.' New York, Burgoyne contended, was the place from which offensive operations should begin. From here the British, taking full advantage of their command of the sea and making intelligent use of the Hudson River, could move either north or south, north up the Hudson to Lakes George and Champlain and to Canada, south to Delaware and Chesapeake Bays, to Virginia and the Carolinas.

It had been recognized by the British high command during the Seven Years' War that the American continent's geography severely limited the lines of attack. Because of impenetrable forests, wide and fast-flowing rivers, and long mountain ranges, there were only three main routes upon which armies could successfully manoeuvre and fight. One of these lines ran north-west from Virginia across the valleys in the Pennsylvania mountains; a second ran west from Albany along the River Mohawk to Lake Ontario; the best ran due north from New York towards the St Lawrence River and Quebec.

New York was one of several towns along the Atlantic seaboard east of the Appalachian Mountains to which the French had endeavoured to keep the British confined. North of New York were Newport, at the southern end of Rhode Island, Plymouth, the first permanent settlement by Europeans in New England, and Boston; to the south was Philadelphia at the confluence of the Delaware and Schuylkill Rivers, by the 1770s a city of some 30,000 people, the most important commercial centre in the British Empire after London and Liverpool. South of Philadelphia were Baltimore, a busy port at the head of the Patapsco River estuary above Chesapeake Bay; Norfolk at the mouth of the Chesapeake; Wilmington, the principal seaport of North Carolina, on the Cape Fear River, thirty miles above its mouth; and Charleston in South Carolina from whose harbour at the mouth of the Ashley and Cooper Rivers sailed ships loaded with cotton and rice. But by far the most strategically important of these towns was New York, the key to operations both to north and south.

Moreover, in New York the British could support the many Loyalists there were believed to be in Albany and the Mohawk valley, and at the same time give encouragement to the people of the Hampshire Grants who were still in dispute with the Continental Congress over boundary claims and administration. The Green Mountain Boys and their leader, Ethan Allen, had become heroes to the patriots of New York since the capture of Ticonderoga; but, so long as the disputes over land grants remained unresolved, the area, Burgoyne contended, was ripe for British recruitment.

There were also the Indians to consider. If the British were in control of the Hudson River and of Lakes George and Champlain, they would form a barrier between the rebels and both the Iroquois League of Six Nations – the Mohawk, the Oneida, the Onondaga, the Cayuga, the Seneca and the Tuscarora – and the Indians of the Western Confederation. These Indians, some 160,000 of them in all, might then be used in the British service – perhaps, so Burgoyne suggested, in carrying arms to the black slaves of the south; they could certainly be prevented from joining the rebels.

But for the moment Burgoyne could do no more than advise and suggest. Without a proper command, he felt himself *de trop* in America, 'a mere military cipher', as he put it himself. Gage passed on to him the task, required by the government, of issuing a proclamation offering a pardon to any rebel who deserted and went home. But, having regard to Burgoyne's literary style, this work could scarcely have been left in more unsuitable hands, and the resulting proclamation was as ludicrously grandiose in its wording as it was unavailing in its purpose. Pleading that 'private affairs of consequence' required his presence in England, Burgoyne set sail for England on 5 December 1775.

Left behind in Boston, General Clinton continued to express his own outrage at what he considered the bungling of the recent battle and at the way in which his own efforts to secure a worthwhile victory had been either thwarted or misunderstood. Not only had the rejection of his plan resulted in the escape of so many rebels, but he considered himself slighted in the Commander-in-Chief's despatch which seemed to him to imply that he had followed the reinforcements up the hill rather than led them. Worse than this, when reports of his action reached England, his cousin the Duke of Newcastle, in congratulating him on his gallantry, incautiously expressed the hope that in future he would be content with doing what was '*right*; for volunteering is not *necessary*'. Taking this to be a criticism of his acting without the express instructions of his commander as well as an accusation that he had behaved no better than an 'idle, wanton volunteer', Clinton fired off a furious blast to the Duke, which elicited a humble apology and an assurance that the head of his family loved him as a man, was proud of him as a relative, honoured and respected him as a soldier, and was 'a good deal flurried by this unlucky event'.

Concerned as he was for his own reputation, Clinton was deeply worried, too, about the condition of the army as a whole and the evident inability of either the Commander-in-Chief or the government to form any coherent plan to suppress a rebellion which was now spreading over 'the whole country'. The troops had behaved bravely enough in the recent engagement; but Clinton was far from being alone in complaining of their indiscipline, their 'wild behaviour' when advancing under fire. All was 'confusion, anarchy, and wretchedness' now, Clinton lamented; and he saw little prospect of any improvement in the army's affairs so long as Gage remained in charge of them. If matters were left to him, he contended in one of those long memoranda whose composition occupied so much of his time, he would demand large forces to be sent to both Canada and New York, and then maintain communication between the two armies by way of the Lakes and the Hudson River and thus encourage resistance to the rebels amongst both American Loyalists and Canadian Indians. Alternatively, if no such large land forces could be mustered, he would place garrisons in Florida and Canada and leave the rebellion to exhaust itself, while constantly harrying the Atlantic coastline, burning American ships and destroying harbours. As it was, the rebels were day by day entrenching themselves ever more securely in the country around Boston which was, in any event, a terrain peculiarly ill suited to the deployment of regular troops, though ideal for the rebel marksmen.

While Clinton set down his ideas in that scarcely legible script which was the despair of his family and correspondents in England, the Adjutant-General, Edward Harvey, wrote from London to complain of the 'damned' impossibility of carrying on a land war at this distance and to seek advice from the field commanders as to what should now be done. 'For God's sake elec[trify] a little,' Harvey begged them, 'and let us know what you and your comrades think as to what the forces can do, and what you want that can possibly be furnished from our skeleton of an army.'

For the time being life in Boston that summer for the officers of the army was not unpleasant, though hard enough for the wounded rebels held prisoner in the Stone Gaol. The fish landed in the harbour from the rivers and the sea was excellent; lobsters and turtles abounded, as well as haddock and cod. Fruit and vegetables were plentiful; and, so an officer recorded, the Navy brought in occasional supplies of provisions, cows and sheep 'from Fishers and other islands adjacent'. Most regimental messes had no difficulty in supplying their tables with wine; and, according to one British officer, the Boston women were very handsome and very susceptible. 'Our camp,' he added, 'has been as well supplied in that way since we have been on Boston Common, as if our tents were pitched on Blackheath.'

Clinton lived in comfort in the house of John Hancock, who had left it in the care of a servant to whom the General gave the key of a room in which was locked all the furniture not for the moment required. In this house Clinton entertained his fellow-officers and their wives, played the violin for them after dinner and endeavoured to compose a long-standing quarrel between General Gage and Vice-Admiral Samuel Graves, the naval commander in America, whose respective wives were scarcely on speaking terms.

Presiding over the management of the house was Mary Baddeley, daughter of an Irish gentleman and married to a soldier, a carpenter by trade, who had been demoted from sergeant to private because, so it was said, his colonel had had designs on his wife and she had spurned his advances. Hearing of her attractions and the misalliance which had distressed her family, Clinton found work as a carpenter for her husband, employed her as his housekeeper and 'could have been', so he confessed, tempted to a closer 'connection with her', but was at first dissuaded from proposing it by her 'uniformly discreet conduct' and by her already being pregnant by her husband, even though Private Baddeley himself 'seemed rather to wish a certain degree of intimacy' might be arranged between the General and his wife. After a time, however, Mrs Baddeley admitted Clinton 'to certain liberties', as he put it, and although he 'never could prevail upon her to grant the last', eventually 'resentment did what opportunity and importunity and a warm attachment could not effect. She detected her h[usband] in an intrigue with a common strumpet.' 'She came to me directly,' Clinton added. 'She told [her husband] she would, and she surrendered.' As a reward for her complaisant husband, by now a sergeant-major, Clinton managed to obtain him a commission in a provincial corps, despite General Howe's objections.

Baddeley ultimately became a captain in Colonel Beverley Robinson's Loyal American Regiment, in which he served without notable distinction, dying of fever in Charlestown in 1782, while Mrs Baddeley remained the General's mistress for the rest of his life. She bore him children to whom he was devoted and whom he remembered in his will, together with his legitimate children and his daughter by a woman whom he had known before his short-lived marriage.

Clinton's comfortable life in the Hancock house came to an end when General Gage sailed home and William Howe became Commander-in-Chief. At first Clinton and Howe got on well together. Howe assured Clinton that he hoped to have the constant benefit of his advice throughout the period of his new command; and Clinton, for his part, promised to do just as Howe would wish and to carry out his instructions to the letter. But this amity between the two incompatible men could not last for long; and Clinton's insistence on offering gratuitous advice – for which he was eager to be given full credit when it was accepted and as ready to grumble when it was not – soon led to a breakdown in their friendly relationship and to Clinton's preference for the camp on Charlestown Neck to garrison life in Boston.

'I like this sort of life best,' Clinton wrote from his new headquarters. Here he was able to indulge his taste for giving military instruction and retailing military anecdotes of his campaigns in Germany to the young officers of his staff, prominent among whom was the young Captain Lord Rawdon, a conscientious and ambitious pupil who had had two bullets through his cap at Bunker Hill and was gratifyingly happy 'at receiving instructions from one whom [he regarded] as a thorough master of his profession'.

If Clinton was as content as he could ever be, his men were far from being so. The summer of 1775 had given way to a cold and wet winter in which provisions were in short supply, even though 'great numbers of People [had] obtained Passes to quit the Town and the greatest part of the inhabitants [had] gone', being allowed to take with them, said Richard Pope of the 47th Regiment, 'nothing except their bedding and household furniture'. Lieutenant William Feilding reported:

> Our Troops have been attacked with severe fluxes & many have
> died for want of fresh provisions which have been so very scarce

that when any have been procured for the Hospitals they allowed only 4 ounces per Man Officers included. I have eat fresh meat but 3 times these six weeks. Fish & Salt pork are our constant food.

'No sort of provisions goes into Boston,' Frances Wentworth told Lady Rockingham.

They exist on salt meat at a great price . . . Its said The Admiral by his little vessels obtains provisions for his Table which is kept nearly as regular as before the Battle but no other Person has even the comforts of common Food which is very dreadfull as there used to be a plentiful Market. It is painfull to me to see our table [in Portsmouth] with sufficient on it, when I know how distress'd my friends are for common necessarys, and its as much as one's life is worth to send a joint of meat to anyone. I have two Sisters married in Boston . . . but I dare not assist them tho I know they now suffer, having nothing but salt meat for their Babies and children.

When ships did arrive with fresh provisions the prices were beyond the reach of most men's pockets. As Captain John Bowater wrote home on 19 January 1776:

Several Vessels have Arrived with porter, potatoes and sour crout for the Army which is of infinite Service as many of the soldiers are much Afflicted with the Scurvy. The sheep which these Vessels took on Board at London all died to very few as scarce a Ship brought in above 8 or 10 out of a Hundred and fifty each . . . Several Vessells of late have Arrived from Halifax, and Annapolis with quarters of Beef, Mutton etc – which has been sold at the most Exhorbitant prices . . . which with the Exchange of Money is enough to Ruin the Subalterns of this Army. We are happy to find the people of England have open'd a Subscription for sending fresh Provisions to the Soldiers. Were the Soldiers Allow'd their rations without paying for [them], it wou'd be of Infinite service in getting them Warm Clothing and other Nessissarys which at present the Captains are Oblig'd to provide to the Ruin of their pocketts and the distress of the poor Soldiers from the heavy Stoppages they unavoidably are Obliged to be put under.

Not only scurvy and dysentery were rife but also other forms of disease, and funerals were almost as common as punishments. A characteristic General Order for 3 January decreed:

> Thomas MacMahan, private soldier in His Majesty's Forty-third Regiment of Foot, and Isabella MacMahan, his wife . . . tried by . . . court martial for receiving sundry stolen goods, knowing them to be such, are found guilty of the crime laid to their charge, and therefore . . . the said Thomas MacMahan [is] to receive a thousand lashes on his bare back with a cat-of-nine-tails . . . and the said Isabella MacMahan, to receive a hundred lashes on her bare back, at the cart's tail, in different portions and the most conspicuous parts of the town, and to be imprisoned three months.

Fresh food became increasingly difficult to come by; and even Lord Rawdon considered himself lucky to get 'a red herring, some onions and some porter' for his supper. The men slept in leaky tents while slowly building huts by day in constant fear that the rebels surrounding them, far more comfortably quartered in barracks and the entrenchments which they were so quick and expert in constructing, would at any moment open fire on their exposed position.

This position, so Colonel William Phillips told Clinton, who knew it himself only too well, was 'useless', 'impotent' and 'disgraceful', being 'surrounded by enemies'. 'You may be lions,' Phillips added disobligingly, 'but you are lions confined in a den; and the provincial rebels are your keepers.'

On 20 January 1776, Clinton was able to escape. Orders had arrived from England at last. To the dismay of Howe, who was most unwilling to divide his already too small army, it had been decided to send a force from Boston to North Carolina to meet troops and a naval squadron which were being despatched from England to the Cape Fear River. This combined expedition, it was hoped, would encourage the Loyalists of Carolina to fight for the re-establishment of constitutional government. Gratified as he was to be given his first independent command, Clinton, always happier in proposing plans than in carrying them out, immediately began to complain of the difficulties of his assignment and the lack of the support he should have been given by Howe, under whom it was a 'mortification' to have to serve. He was to be allowed no more than 1500 troops at the most, and what could he achieve with so few? 'I could not help telling our chief,' he grumbled in a letter to Burgoyne, that, 'had I been in his station, he should have had all he asked . . . If I do return [to Howe's command] I hope not to stay long.' Like Burgoyne, he was 'tired of being a subordinate'; but, unlike Burgoyne, his confidence faltered at the prospect of acting on his own.

As he sailed south, Clinton was assured by the former Governor of North Carolina and the present Governor of Virginia, both of whom had been driven from their homes to seek shelter aboard ships at sea, that he would be sure to find thousands of Loyalists eager to join him as soon as he reached Cape Fear. In this, as in other expectations, he was soon to be profoundly disappointed.

4

WASHINGTON TAKES COMMAND

*'Everyone is made to know his
place and keep in it.'*

William Emerson

A fortnight after the fighting on Bunker Hill, the man recently appointed by Congress as Commander-in-Chief of their Continental Army arrived in Boston. This was George Washington.

He was a tall, thin, muscular man, 'straight as an Indian', as a friend described him, with bluish grey eyes beneath prominent brows and a wide, thin mouth, firmly set over decaying teeth. His uniform was remarkably well cut; his highly fashionable civilian clothes were bought in London. Upon encountering him for the first time, meeting the gaze of those searching eyes and being gripped by an extremely large, firm, rough-skinned hand, strangers often found his presence formidable, even forbidding. Yet friends spoke of his generosity as a host, the ease – no less pleasant for being hard-earned – with which he entertained guests on his Virginian estate, the pleasure he took in barbecues and picnics, in dancing, playing billiards and cards, in gambling and in going to the theatre, to musical evenings and to cockfights. In the opinion of John Adams's wife, Abigail, he possessed 'dignity with ease'. He was an enthusiastic and skilful horseman; he enjoyed hunting, shooting and fishing, and considered farming the 'most delectable of pursuits'.

He shared, indeed, most of the tastes of his English forbears who had lived for generations on an estate in Northamptonshire given to them by King Henry VIII. His great-grandfather had sailed for America in 1657, having fallen on hard times after the English Civil

War, and had settled in Virginia where his grandson Augustine, George's father, who had been sent home to school in England, had much enlarged the family's estates on his return, eventually acquiring ten thousand acres and fifty slaves as well as ten children by two wives.

George, who was eleven when his father died in 1743, was not sent to school in England as his two eldest half-brothers had been, so learned less of the classics than they had done but a great deal more of practical matters, and he soon decided that he would like to become a surveyor. His eldest half-brother, who had taken care of him since their father's death, was married to the daughter of Colonel William Fairfax, who acted as agent in America for his cousin, Thomas Fairfax, sixth Lord Fairfax of Cameron, owner of some five million acres in Virginia; and it was through the influence of Lord Fairfax, who went to live in America in 1746 and who thereafter befriended him, that at the age of eighteen George Washington became official surveyor of Culpeper county, which was named after the family of Fairfax's mother. As a resourceful and adventurous as well as conscientious surveyor, Washington developed a keen interest in the settlement of lands in the American west and, having become a speculator in various western enterprises, was naturally annoyed when the British government introduced the Proclamation Line defining the limits beyond which white settlement was not to be tolerated.

By this time his half-brother had died and Washington had inherited 2500 acres and several slaves. Intent upon fame and reward, he had also embarked on a military career and had fought bravely against the French and their Indian allies as an officer on the staff of General Edward Braddock, the British commander who had died from wounds received near Fort Duquesne, the present site of Pittsburgh. After Braddock's death, Washington, though not yet twenty-four, had been appointed to the command of all the troops of Virginia; and by the time of his marriage in January 1759, having resigned his commission as brigadier-general, he had been elected to the Virginian House of Burgesses.

His wife was a wealthy widow, slightly older than himself, the mother of two children of whom he grew extremely fond. To his own estate of Mount Vernon she brought a further fifteen thousand acres and a large number of slaves, whom their new master treated with that firm but just hand to which his own were already accustomed. The marriage was by no means a passionate attachment, but it seems to have been happy enough, and Washington settled down to his life as a rich young landowner with quiet satisfaction, becoming less selfish than he had been in his younger days, less touchy, less ambitious.

He had had occasional brushes with the British authorities in the past. Once he had resigned his commission in protest at the ruling from London that provincial officers, whatever their rank, were to consider themselves subordinate to those who held the King's commission and who were far better paid than their colonial counterparts. Washington had subsequently been deeply disappointed not to be granted a regular commission. Yet throughout the earlier disagreements between the British government and the colonists he had, as his benefactor, Lord Fairfax, would have wished, maintained a loyal attitude to the country from which his ancestors had come, and had spoken rarely in the House of Burgesses. As the quarrel intensified, however, while Fairfax remained a forthright Loyalist, Washington began to reconsider his position until he was openly declaring that it might be necessary to resist by force of arms those whom he termed 'our lordly masters' if the liberties of the colonists were in danger of being lost. He did not yet seek independence from Britain; but he made it clear that he was prepared to fight for the rights and privileges which were 'essential to the happiness of every free state'.

As one of Virginia's delegates to the First Continental Congress he took his seat in uniform; and by the time the second Congress met in Philadelphia, although he had shown himself to be a far from effective speaker in those few debates in which he took part, his sincerity, sound common sense and energy, his determination and experience as a soldier, rendered him an obvious contender for the post of military commander at Boston. But his appointment was not unanimous. Many delegates felt that a Massachusetts man should be given the command, and several supported the claims of the increasingly ostentatious John Hancock, who was certainly most anxious to obtain it. Washington himself considered General Andrew Lewis the most suitable man for the post. Others advocated the appointment of Colonel William Byrd. But John Adams was a strong supporter of Washington, who let it be known that he would accept no salary; and there was wide agreement with Adams's view that the appointment of a Virginian would encourage patriotic feelings in the south. So, to Hancock's obvious disappointment and, so Adams thought, 'mortification and resentment', Washington was appointed Commander-in-Chief of the Continental Army. 'You may believe me, my dear Patsy,' he told his wife,

> when I assure you in the most solemn manner that, so far from seeking this appointment, I have used every endeavour in my power to avoid it, not only from my unwillingness to part with you and the family, but from a consciousness of its being a trust too great for my capacity . . . But as it has been a kind of destiny that has thrown me upon this service, I shall hope that my undertaking it is designed to answer some good purpose.

As soon as he arrived in camp outside Boston, Washington realized the appalling difficulties of his command. Discipline was lax and officers were treated with little respect; drunkenness and malingering were common, provisions meagre, ammunition so low that for a time no man had more than three rounds, powder equally difficult to obtain, despite the supplies that came across the Atlantic in Dutch ships and the best efforts of the American Navy, which was created by an Act of the Second Continental Congress in October 1775. The camps were filthy and perfunctorily guarded by sentries who frequently strolled away from their posts before they were relieved or even went over for a chat with the enemy. Moreover, since the troops had been enlisted only until 1 January 1776 or, in some cases, even earlier, Washington was faced with the imminent dispersal of an army only too anxious to go home as soon as possible. Many men, indeed, did wander off to their farms, or to those of their officers, from time to time and for days on end; and several were never seen in camp again. Officers were driven to advertising for their discovery:

> Deserted from Colonel Brewer's regiment and Captain Harvey's company, one Simeon Smith, of Greenfield, a joiner by trade, a thin spare fellow about five feet, four inches high, had on a blue coat and black vest, a metal button on his hat, black long hair, black eyes, his voice in the hermaphrodite fashion, the masculine rather

predominant. Likewise, one Mathias Smith, a small, smart fellow, gray-headed, has a younger look in his face, is apt to say, 'I swear! I swear!' and between his words will spit smart; had on an old red great coat; he is a right gamester, although he wears a sober look. Likewise one John Daby, a long, hump-shouldered fellow, drawls his words, and for 'comfortable' says 'comfabel', had on a green coat, thick leather breeches, slim legs, lost some of his fore teeth . . . Whoever will take up said deserters and secure them or bring them into camp, shall have two dollars reward for each, and all necessary charges paid.

Officers from different provinces frequently declined to co-operate with each other, even when they were in the same regiment; and, on occasions, they advised their men not to re-enlist when their time was up but to go home and to get back to work at the earliest opportunity. 'Such a dearth of public spirit' Washington had never seen before and hoped never to see again. Mercenary attitudes so pervaded the army that he would not, so he confessed, be surprised at any disaster. 'Could I have foreseen what I have experienced and am likely to experience,' he added,

> no consideration on earth would have induced me to accept the command . . . I have already broke one colonel and five captains for cowardice and for drawing more pay and provisions than they had men in their companies. There are two more colonels now under arrest and to be tried for the same offences. In short they are by no means such troops as you are led to believe of them from the accounts which are published . . . I daresay the men would fight very well (if properly officered) although they are an exceedingly dirty and nasty people.

Washington agreed with Prescott that the battle which had recently been fought outside Boston might have been won had the forward troops been more fully supported by officers, who shrank from the conflict. He had eight more officers court-martialled; and one flogged in front of his company. He sought permission from the Continental Congress to hang deserters; and issued a succession of orders intended to bring cleanliness and order to the camps and to subdue all manner of breaches of discipline, from drunkenness to lewdness. 'The general does not mean to discourage the practice of bathing while the weather is warm enough to continue it,' one of these orders ran. 'But he expressly forbids it at or near the bridge in Cambridge, where it has been observed and complained of that many men, lost to all sense of decency and common modesty, are running about, naked, upon the bridge whilst passengers, and even ladies of the first fashion in the neighbourhood, are passing over it, as if they meant to glory in their shame.'

Every day Washington rode about the camps, usually in the company of Major-General Horatio Gates, his Adjutant-General. An Englishman, the son of a duke's housekeeper from Essex and of a man described at different times as a greengrocer, a customs officer and a parson, Gates had emigrated to a farm in Virginia after serving in America in the British Army, from which he had retired as a major without much hope of further advancement, being neither rich nor well-connected. A kindly, if devious and decidedly ambitious man, at thirty-seven he was five years younger than Washington, though he looked considerably older. Grey-haired and round-shouldered, with spectacles constantly slipping down his long nose, he seemed more like an elderly schoolmaster than an officer in early middle age, and was known as 'Granny' Gates.

Washington was also often accompanied on his rounds by Major-General Charles Lee, who was, like Gates, an Englishman by birth and who, also like Gates, had served as a junior officer with Washington during the Seven Years' War. He was the son of a wealthy British officer in the 1st Foot Guards and was a former officer himself both in the Polish Army and in the British Army. A quarrelsome, arrogant, avaricious and caustic man, Charles Lee was tall, thin and uncommonly ugly with an immense nose, a penchant for smart, though rarely clean, uniforms and a high opinion of his talents and of the recondite knowledge which he aired with tireless garrulity. Because of this seemingly ceaseless flow of talk he was known as 'Boiling Water' by the Mohawks, from one of whose chiefs he had taken a daughter for a wife, though he declined to consider himself properly married and did not pretend to be a faithful husband.

Having decided to emigrate to America, Lee had obtained a grant from the Crown of twenty thousand acres in Florida, and had subsequently purchased an estate in the Shenandoah valley, Virginia,

not far from that of Horatio Gates. As an experienced professional
soldier, he outspokenly derided the amateurs and civilians amongst
his fellow senior officers, dismissing Artemas Ward as a 'fat church-
warden' and treating Washington, who was only a few months
younger than himself, as though he were an immature backwoods-
man who had been placed above him for political reasons. Lee was
undoubtedly a 'queer creature', Samuel Adams conceded, and you
had to love the dogs that invariably accompanied him if you were to
gain his own regard and 'to forgive a thousand [oddities] for the sake
of the soldier and the scholar'.

The camps through which Washington rode outside Boston presented
a most strange appearance. Occupied by rather more than sixteen
thousand men, they were, so a chaplain, the Rev. William Emerson,
recorded, 'as different in their form' as their occupants were in their
dress. Some were made of boards and some of sailcloth, others of
'stone and turf, brick or brush. Some thrown up in a hurry, others
curiously wrought with doors and windows, done with wreathes
and withes in the manner of a carpet; some [were] proper tents and
marquees, looking like the regular camp of the enemy. In these [were]
the Rhode Islanders, who [were] furnished with tent-equipage, and
everything in the most exact English style.' The countryside around
the camps was 'cut up into forts and entrenchments, and all the lands,
fields, orchards laid common, with horses and cattle feeding on the
choicest mowing land and whole fields of corn eaten down to
the ground and large parks of well regulated [trees] cut down for
firewood'.

Outside observers confirmed Washington's pessimistic opinion of
the army occupying these camps. One visitor recorded:

> The army in general is not very badly accoutered, but most wretch-
> edly clothed, and as dirty a set of mortals as ever disgraced the name
> of a soldier. They have no women in the camp to do washing for
> the men, and they in general not being used to doing things of this
> sort, and thinking it rather a disparagement to them, choose rather
> to let their linen, etc., rot upon their backs than to be at the trouble
> of cleaning 'em themselves. And to this nasty way of life, and to
> the change of their diet from milk, vegetables, etc., to living almost
> entirely upon flesh, must be attributed those putrid, malignant and

infectious disorders which broke out among them soon after their taking the field . . .

Notwithstanding the indefatigable endeavours of Mr Washington and the other generals, and particularly of Adjutant General Gates, to arrange and discipline the army, yet any tolerable degree of order and subordination is what they are totally unacquainted with in the rebel camp. And the doctrines of independence and levellism have been so effectively sown throughout the country, and so universally imbibed by all ranks of men, that I apprehend it will be with the greatest difficulty that the inferior officers and soldiers will be ever brought to any tolerable degree of subjection to the commands of their superiors . . . Many of their leading men are not insensible of this, and I have often heard them lament that the existence of that very spirit which induced the common people to take up arms and resist the authority of Great Britain, should induce them to resist the authority of their own officers, and by that means effectively prevent their ever making good soldiers.

As the weeks passed, Washington managed gradually to disband the ill-disciplined army he had taken over and to raise another in its place. Orders were read out to the men every morning after prayers; and thousands of men were set to work on the fortifications each day as dawn began to break. 'The strictest government is taking place,' William Emerson reported, 'and great distinction is made between officers and soldiers. Everyone is made to know his place and keep in it, or be tied up and receive forty or fifty lashes according to his crime.'

Reinforcements of three thousand men from Pennsylvania and Maryland in the north and from Virginia in the south arrived at the beginning of July, and by February 1776, despite many desertions, Washington had well over seventeen thousand men under his command. It was an army now worthy of the 'United Colonies' whose formation he felt justified in celebrating by raising a new flag, already in use in the American Navy, with thirteen stripes, six red and seven white, representing the thirteen American colonies, with the crosses of St Andrew and St George of the British Union Jack in the upper left-hand corner. Washington had also much enlarged his stocks of ammunition; and since 24 January, when Colonel Henry Knox arrived from Ticonderoga with sleighs and carts and pack animals laden with forty-three cannon and sixteen mortars captured there, the Commander-in-Chief, though still beset by a lack of powder, had the artillery he needed to begin a proper siege of the British in Boston.

While Washington was doing all he could to improve discipline in the American camps, the British forces – Parliament's army or the ministerial army as its enemies often called it – had been enduring months of idleness and frustration in Boston. The tedium was occasionally broken by a sudden call to arms – as, for instance, one evening when a party of rebels raided an outpost just before the intended opening of a performance in the Faneuil Hall, 'a famous place where the sons of sedition used to meet', now 'fitted up very Elegantly for a Theatre'. Lieutenant William Feilding reported:

> A new farce call'd *The Blockade of Boston* (written by Genl Burgoyne) was to have been introduc'd, but unfortunately as the Curtain drew up to begin the Entertainment, an Orderly Sergeant came on the Stage, and said the Alarm Guns were fired, which Immediately put everybody to the Rout, particularly the officers who made the best of their way to their Respective Corps and Alarm Posts, leaveing the Ladies in the House in a most Terible Dilema.

General Howe, Gage's successor as Commander-in-Chief, had been authorized to evacuate the town if his situation did not improve. But he did not have enough ships to do so in one move, and dared not take the risk of dividing his army and moving in two; and in the meantime his twelve thousand troops, bored and gloomy, with not enough to eat and nothing constructive to do, continued to suffer and fall ill in the cold winter weather. Discipline became more and more lax and punishments savage. Time after time the men were called out to witness the floggings of men or women, at one of which a drummer, sickened by his task, threw his cat-o'-nine-tails to the ground and refused to carry on with his bloody punishment. 'Robberies and housebreakings have got to such a height in this town,' Howe reported, 'that some examples had to be made.' Executions were carried out as well as floggings; and the men were warned that in future an executioner would accompany the Provost Marshal on his rounds and would 'hang upon the spot the first man he should detect in the act without waiting for further proof by trial'.

Thomas Sullivan, an Irish sergeant in the 49th Regiment, recorded many of these privations and depredations in his journal:

> Upon our first coming into Boston Provisions were very cheap . . . very good beef 2d. a pound . . . a gallon of West India Rum 2s., Brandy half a doller or 2s. 3d. per gallon . . . Spruce Beer commonly a halfpenny a Quart. But now 'all very expensive' . . . and the water very brackish which was very destructive to the troops, giving them (it was supposed) the Flux, and good many of the Inhabitants as well . . . And after the first engagement what happened on a Common at a place called Concord, the troops grew more cruel against the Inhabitants, so that they began in most parts of the town to pull down the fences . . . around the houses [which] are about two thirds built of wood; and one third of Brick, notwithstanding the repeated orders the Commander-in-Chief issued to the contrary. After the Battle at Bunker's Hill they were so inveterate against the Rebels on account of the dreadful spectacles that presented themselves after that action, they destroyed everything they could come at without Scruple. When the troops went into winter Quarters the General gave Orders that all the Old houses in every part of the town should be pulled down for firing for the Army, the river being (that time) almost frozen so that the Shipping could not get out of the Harbour to bring timber from other Parts . . . The one-fourth part of the town was either pulled down for firing in that manner or otherwise destroyed in making Batteries; so that the most-part of the houses that was damaged were Irrepairable.

General Howe contemplated an attack on the besieging rebels; but in the unlikely event of this being successful, it would have served no purpose, since he had no transport to allow him to take advantage of it by pursuing a defeated enemy. He decided that he had no choice, therefore, but to wait for the ships to take his men and equipment away.

He was still waiting for these ships when, on the night of 2 March, the Americans opened up a heavy bombardment of the town as a preliminary to their landing a force of some two thousand men on Dorchester Heights, the high ground immediately to the south-east of Boston Neck which Howe had neglected to occupy. By 4 March, the day before the anniversary of the 'Boston Massacre', they were in full possession of these heights on which they had sited some twenty or so cannon. The ground was still frozen too hard to dig entrenchments; but they had built defensive walls, strengthened by fascines which they had brought with them in three hundred heavily loaded carts, and by the trunks of trees which they had felled in nearby orchards. Beside these defences, which they had thrown up with the skill and rapidity they had shown on Breed's Hill eight months before, they had stacked scores of barrels, filled with earth and stones and chained together, which they intended to roll down the smooth, steep hill against the British should they attempt to ascend it.

Howe made plans to do so on the night of 5 March. But on the evening of that day the rain that had been falling intermittently throughout most of the afternoon grew heavier and more persistent, until it stormed down torrentially on Boston and Dorchester Heights. A heavy wind now blew across the harbour, rocking the ships at their moorings and hurling spray across their swaying decks. Howe was forced to call off his proposed attack; and, by the close of the next day, he had decided to wait no longer for the transport ships which had been expected for so many days and to leave Boston, taking with his men over a thousand American Loyalists – whose 'Hurry and Confusion' was 'dreadful' to behold – and ordering that all military stores and equipment, for which no room could be found in the holds of such ships as were available, should be destroyed. Boston was accordingly evacuated on Sunday, 17 March in an 'Astonishing silence', the operation being undisturbed by the Americans on Howe's assurance that the town would not be burned. Ten days later, after 'a great many children [had been] Suffocated' in the crowded holds, the ships sailed out to sea, packed with their human cargoes and with as many horses and stores as could be crammed aboard them.

The triumphant men of the Continental Army marched down into Boston as the British ships disappeared beyond the horizon on their sixteen days' voyage to Halifax, Nova Scotia. Here provisions and stores were almost as hard to come by as they had been in Boston; the price of meat was eventually to rise to the equivalent of £3 a pound and eggs were sold for as much as £9 for six. The soldiers who, of course, could not afford such prices became increasingly dispirited, and longed to get away from 'this dreadful hole'. 'Of all the Misserable places' Captain John Bowater had ever seen, Halifax, where the snow still lay thick on the frozen ground in April, was 'the Worst'. Yet Howe was forced to remain there throughout the spring of 1776, keeping his men occupied in making cartridges or in work on the docks and fortifications while himself preparing plans for an attack on New York which would, he hoped, make amends for his recent misfortunes.

5

'AN UGLY JOB'

'The ardour of this nation in this cause has not arisen to the pitch one could wish.'

Lord North

'America is an ugly job,' General Harvey, the Adjutant-General, told General Howe, 'a damned affair indeed.' The first reports of the fighting in America to be received in England had come from rebel sources which had suggested that British troops, having initiated hostilities, had 'shot down the unarmed, the aged and the infirm', had killed the wounded, had mangled their bodies 'in a most shocking manner', had, in short, been guilty of a 'cruelty not less brutal than the Americans' venerable ancestors had received from the vilest savages of the wilderness'. While the London *Gazette* officially informed its readers that no reliable information had yet been received from America, one of the rebels' agents in London circulated all newspaper offices with a note to the effect that the horrifying reports so far received were perfectly reliable and that the affidavits of eyewitnesses were available at the office of the Lord Mayor of London.

The Lord Mayor at this time was John Wilkes, the most 'wicked and agreeable fellow' that William Pitt had ever met, a charming, cross-eyed demagogue who had become Member of Parliament for Aylesbury at the age of twenty-nine, after marrying a local heiress whose fortune helped him to bribe the voters. Wilkes had subsequently been pronounced an outlaw for a seditious libel he had published against the King and for obscene libel in a parody of Pope's *Essay on Man*. On his return from exile, he had been elected Member of Parliament for Middlesex as an outspoken and highly popular opponent of the government; and, when his right to sit in the House of Commons was denied him, he had pursued his campaign against the ministry in the City of London, becoming Lord Mayor in 1774. He had subsequently become one of the most vociferous supporters of the American rebels, and of the London merchants who opposed the war as damaging to their trade and who were among the principal subscribers to the Constitutional Society which, at a meeting at the King's Arms tavern on Cornhill, inaugurated a fund for the 'relief of widows [and] orphans . . . of our beloved American fellow subjects . . . inhumanely murdered by the King's Troops'.

Such sentiments, common enough in the City, were far from widespread in the country at large, where letters were being received from men serving in America who painted very different pictures of the rebels from those portrayed by John Wilkes, Isaac Barré and the City merchants. 'I hope the Rebels will get heartily thrashed,' Lieutenant William Feilding wrote in a characteristic letter to his kinsman, Lord Denbigh. 'I would be content to loose a leg & an Arm to see them Totally defeated and their whole Country laid waist.' If Feilding had had his way, Boston, that 'nest of Rascals', would have been burned to the ground. As for those who spoke out on behalf of the rebels, wrote another of Denbigh's correspondents, Captain John Bowater, castigating men like the Duke of Richmond and the 'Scoundrel Barre', 'we flatter ourselves with the pleasing prospect of seeing their Heads ornament Temple Barr when we Return, for they certainly have led these wretches into their present unhappy situation'. In a subsequent letter Bowater wrote:

I every day curse Columbus and all the discoverers of their Diabolical Country . . . The Natives are such a Levelling, underbred, Artful Race of people that we Cannot Associate with them. Void of principal, their whole Conversation is turn'd on their Interest, and as to gratitude they have no such word in their dictionary & either cant or wont understand what it means. (For instance as to levelling) I met a man of very good property a few days ago who had a Complaint to make and I refer'd him to Lord Percy. I heard him enquire at his Lordships door for Mr Percy. Thinking him

Ignorant I stept up & told him again Lord Percy. He replied to me
he knew no Lord but the Lord Jehovah. Thus it is throughout
America and a sad set of Presbyterian Rascals they are . . . Their
dress is so formal and their words come up so Slow, that I frequently
long to Shove a Soup ladle down their throats . . . I think nothing
but a total Extirpation of the Inhabitants of this Country will ever
make it a desirable object of any Prince or State.

It was generally agreed by less intemperate commentators that a
war fought against an entire continent 3500 miles distant would not
be easily won; but that it would have to be fought was a proposition
more often reluctantly conceded than denied. 'The sword alone can
decide the dispute,' the *Morning Chronicle* declared. And the sword
would now have to be used 'to prevent the ruin of the British Empire
which [would] inevitably take place' were the King's troops to be
defeated. How such a defeat might be averted was a question of
constant debate.

General Harvey, the Adjutant-General, thought it would be quite
impossible to subdue the whole continent with the British Army as
it stood at present; to propose to do so was 'as wild an idea as
ever controverted common sense'. Those who agreed with Harvey
suggested that the problem ought to be solved by the Royal Navy,
that American ports should be taken over as naval bases and that a
determined war should be waged against American trade: such a
policy would soon bring the colonists to heel. As an English resident
in New York put it in a letter to Lady Grimston, 'We should depend
on our Navy for the destruction of the [rebels'] trade, and our troops,
instead of running a wild goose chase after the rascals in the country
should be employed in occupying the most essential ports on the
coasts to cooperate with the fleet in this intention.' Lord Barrington,
Secretary-at-War, endorsed this use of the Navy; so did John Burgoyne, but Burgoyne also insisted that a large army must be formed
in the colony of New York and another in Canada, and that Indians
should be enlisted as well as black slaves.

Others argued that the situation was not nearly as gloomy as this.
Far from all colonists were rebels; in some provinces, in fact, those
who were loyal, if not active Loyalists, outnumbered revolutionaries
– and everywhere sentiment swung with the fortunes of war. This
optimistic view was not ill founded. Perhaps a fifth, possibly a quarter

of the population remained loyalist in sentiment – as many as a hundred thousand Loyalists are believed to have emigrated before the troubles were over – and many other Americans would have declared their support of the British cause more openly had not they been intimidated by the more violent Sons of Liberty and the mobs called out in the name of patriotism. Several members of America's leading families had opposed the rebels from the beginning; others, who had supported the earlier protests, had drawn back at the thought of independence. Among the ranks of the Loyalists could be found such distinguished names as that of the honourable and widely respected Lawrence Washington, with whom George had spent much of his childhood after their father's death. Walter Dulany, a loyalist officer from Maryland, spoke for many Americans when he wrote to the British commander in New York: 'My duty as a subject; the happiness which America enjoyed under the British government; and the miseries to which she would be reduced by independence were the motives which induced me to join the British Army; nor are there any dangers or difficulties that I would not cheerfully undergo to effect a happy restoration.' Moreover, Loyalists were to be found in all classes of society. In a list of so-called Tories drawn up in Delaware were the names of innkeepers, pilots, smallholders, coopers, mariners, tradesmen and labourers as well as professional men and merchants.

Nor did the numbers of those actually prepared to bear arms against the British represent a very large proportion of the adult male population: indeed by 1780, the total number of men in the American Continental Army and the state militia combined was still under one-sixteenth of the national manpower. During the course of the war as many as forty loyalist regiments were formed or reorganized, among them the Royal Greens, the Roman Catholic Volunteers, the Black Pioneers and Butler's Rangers. Some of these loyalist regiments were eventually absorbed as regular regiments in the British Army; the Royal American Regiment, for example, became the 60th Rifles, later the King's Royal Rifle Corps. But if Loyalists were numerous, they were certainly not well organized, nor well led by William Franklin, son of Benjamin, the Governor of New Jersey and head of the Board of American Loyalists. It also had to be conceded that many who were loyalist in sentiment were soon deterred from supporting the redcoats by the threat of rebel reprisals.

The view that potential Loyalists outnumbered revolutionaries was supported by Major-General James Robertson, who had served in America for several years and was one day to be appointed Governor of New York. The rebels, in Robertson's view, were merely 'a few artful folks'. The mass of the population would side with the King if given proper encouragement and capable leaders to help them escape from 'Congress's tyranny'.

This complacent opinion was endorsed by several colonial governors. The Governor of North Carolina, for example, assured London that the rebels in his territories were only a small and tiresome minority; while the Governor of Virginia wrote with confidence of his being able to recover his province with a mere three hundred men. Encouraged by such claims as these, an officer stood up in the House of Commons to declare that he would require no more than five thousand regular troops to march 'right through America'. Even after the costly battle of Bunker Hill, it was still maintained by other officers who had served there that the people were too ill disciplined to make satisfactory soldiers, and that they were mostly indifferent to the issues which disturbed the agitators. A few good British regiments would soon restore order.

The government, while not sharing this blithe confidence, hoped that differences of opinion in the colonies and traditional jealousies between them would eventually soften the resistance of the trouble-makers. In the meantime, though, the country would have to steel itself for what Lord North called a war that had 'now grown to such a height that it must be treated as a foreign war', much as this distressed all those who shared the feelings of General William Phillips, who could not forget that when he struck an American he 'wounded a brother', and of the King who warned that notes of triumph after victories would not be proper, since such successes would 'be against subjects, not a foreign foe'. Yet, in order to overcome the enemy in the kind of war that now seemed inevitable, a large number of troops would have to be raised either by increasing the strength of existing regiments or by creating new ones.

Both the Army and the Navy had been allowed to decline in recent years. The establishment of the Navy had been reduced to sixteen thousand from twenty-one thousand seamen in 1774, while the condition of the ships in which they sailed was described by one senior officer as being 'quite as intolerable as they had ever been'.

They were scarcely more manoeuvrable in heavy seas than they had been at the time of the Spanish Armada; their crews, often ill and largely composed of the scourings of press gangs, were trained with difficulty – and with frequent recourse to the lash – to perform the complicated operations required for the positioning, loading, firing and sponging of guns and for the movement of sails known as tacking. Their officers, bound by the rules contained in the manual *Fighting Instructions*, were for the most part unlikely to inspire much confidence except by their undoubted bravery.

The Army was also in a far from encouraging state. Its strength on paper was 48,647 men, 39,294 of them infantry, 6,869 cavalry and 2,484 artillery. About sixteen thousand of these men were in England and Scotland, twelve thousand in Ireland, nine thousand in various garrisons in India, Africa, Minorca, Gibraltar and the West Indies, and some eight thousand in America. As with other British institutions, the regiments in which these men served were distinguished by class: there were the three smart household regiments of the 1st, 2nd and 3rd Foot Guards and the three regiments of Horse Guards. This élite corps, which had developed from the sovereign's personal guard, rarely served abroad, though a Brigade of Guards, consisting of men selected from the various companies of the household infantry, was eventually formed for service in America.

The ordinary regiments of the Army, the regiments of the line, were, of course, far more numerous. In 1775 there were twenty-five cavalry regiments and seventy-two infantry regiments, most of the cavalry regiments having 231 men divided into six troops each, and the infantry having 477, divided into ten companies each. One of these ten companies was a grenadier company, another a company of light infantry. When first introduced into the Army in 1667, grenades were extremely heavy, and tall, strong men were required to throw them effectively. The weapons had gone out of use but the name 'grenadier' had been retained, and grenadiers were still the picked men of the regiment, together with the men of the light infantry, the more recently created companies of skirmishers – agile, enterprising soldiers who were also good marksmen.

All companies were armed with the smooth-bore flintlock musket known as the Brown Bess, a counterpart of the Brown Bill, the halberd used by infantry before muskets came into use. The Brown Bess was a clumsy weapon. It had a barrel three feet eight inches

long and a priming pan into which the powder was sprinkled. Care
had to be taken that rain did not get into the pan to wash the powder
out, or dampen it so that it would not ignite. In windy weather the
powder might well be blown from the pan; and men shooting into
a high wind were often burned and temporarily blinded by the
back-blown flare from the touch-hole. Even in the best conditions
the musket was not an easy weapon to load quickly or to fire
accurately. It had an effective range of three hundred yards but
could not be relied upon over a hundred, and the most skilled and
experienced soldiers could not load and fire more than five times a
minute; most managed only two or three shots in that time. To load,
the soldier had to tear the end off the cartridge with his teeth, then,
having sprinkled powder into the priming pan, ram the ball and
cartridge down the muzzle of the barrel with an iron rod. When a
bayonet was fixed, it was difficult if not impossible to ram down the
charge; while the bayonet, which weighed over a pound and was
well over a foot in length, made accurate shooting more difficult than
ever.

An improved form of breech-loading rifle had been constructed
and its efficacy had been demonstrated to the Adjutant-General and
other senior officers at Woolwich. The inventor had fired six shots
a minute and, so a contemporary recorded,

> then poured a bottle of water into the pan and barrel of the piece
> when loaded, so as to wet every grain of powder; and in less than
> half a minute, he fired with her, as well as ever . . . Lastly, he hit
> the bull's eye lying on his back on the ground. Incredible as it may
> seem, considering the variation of the wind, and the wetness of the
> weather, he only missed the target three times during the whole
> course of the experiment.

Yet, although a certain number of his rifles were manufactured and
a small corps of riflemen was authorized for service in America, the
musket remained standard equipment in the British Army for many
years to come, being still in use in some regiments when the Crimean
War broke out in 1854, despite the superiority of the rifle which the
fighting in America had demonstrated. Also still in use were halberds,
a combination of spear and battle-axe seven feet long, which were
carried by sergeants, and spontoons, a shorter version of the halberd,

which were preferred by some officers to swords, and fusils, the light flintlock muskets which gave their names to the various regiments of infantry known as fusiliers. In addition to these personal weapons, each foot regiment was generally allotted two pieces of field artillery known as battalion guns.

Commissions were still bought and sold, frequently for very large sums much in excess of those recognized as standard by the Secretary-at-War; the prices were considerably higher for commissions in the Guards than in regiments of the line, and usually higher for commissions in the cavalry than in the infantry. A lieutenant-colonelcy in the 1st Foot Guards, for instance, might fetch the equivalent of £300,000 in today's money; a captaincy in certain regiments of the line £100,000. Those with small means and without recourse to the patronage of a great family had, therefore, to be content with slow advancement, and in some regiments there were grey-haired lieutenants of great experience serving under the young sons of rich and noble families whose money and influence had secured them not only high rank in the Army but the seats in Parliament which helped to further their careers.

As well as its fighting soldiers, each regiment of foot had its fifers and drummers and in each cavalry regiment there were a number of trumpeters. All regiments also had a surgeon, who was not required to hold a medical degree and not allowed a uniform, and a surgeon's mate, commonly an ordinary soldier, who in most cases had had no medical training at all and who relied upon the wives and other women of the regiment to help him in such nursing of the sick and wounded as was considered practicable. All regiments were also meant to have a chaplain; but many colonels, while pocketing a chaplain's pay, considered that the services he might offer were not required.

The pay that the soldiers received was negligible. Recruiting sergeants spoke of eight pence a day for private soldiers in the infantry, but by the time all the numerous deductions had been made from this sum there was very little left for the paymaster to hand over. The meagre pay was divided into two parts, known as 'subsistence' and 'gross off-reckoning'. 'Subsistence' was meant to pay for the soldiers' food, but in fact was used additionally for other purposes such as the repair of shoes and stockings and firearms; a proportion of it also went to the regimental surgeon and paymaster. The Paymaster

General of the Forces took a share of the 'gross off-reckoning'; so did the regimental agent; so did the governors of Chelsea Hospital, an asylum for veterans since 1689. The 'net-reckoning' that remained after these deductions had been made was applied to the cost of the soldiers' uniforms.

Since pay was such a pittance, recruiting was a very difficult process. Much was made of the smartness of a soldier's uniform, the thick red coat with its buttoned-back lapels, the stock and handsome gaiters, the dashing hats. But the recruit found that his clothes were tight-fitting and uncomfortable, that the greased, powdered and clubbed pigtails required by regulation caused endless trouble as well as discomfort, and that his attire was as likely to bring insults upon him as compliments: the soldier had never been a popular figure in England and was suspected as a possible instrument of tyranny, unlike sailors who were seen rather as guardians of liberty. Samuel Johnson was expressing a common sentiment when he suggested that life guardsmen and felons were equally undesirable in respectable company.

Certainly felons and soldiers were often disciplined with the same brutality. In most good regiments officers treated their men with humanity, even with kindness; but punishments for misbehaviour could be ferocious. Miscreants were confined in dark, cramped cells for hours on end, beaten with sticks or belts, made to run the gauntlet or to sit on a wooden hump-backed horse with heavy weights tied to their feet. Sentences of flogging for quite minor offences were not uncommon; and men guilty of more serious misdemeanours were liable to be sentenced to eight hundred or a thousand lashes on the back with a cat-o'-nine-tails. Sentences of two thousand lashes were not unknown, although it was rare for more than two hundred and fifty to be inflicted on one day. A week was usually allowed to elapse between floggings, a bucket of salt water being thrown over the wounds to prevent infection at the end of each session of punishment. It is not surprising that Americans called British soldiers 'bloody-backs' as well as 'lobsters' and redcoats.

Since the beginning of the war in America, the government had endeavoured to win more recruits by shortening the terms of enlist-ment, by offering bounties to volunteers and pardons to malefactors. It had also been decided to lower the standards of physical fitness which had, indeed, never been high. Recruits for the infantry had been required to be no shorter than five feet six and a half inches and to be certified by a surgeon as having 'no rupture nor ever troubled by Fits . . . and no way disabled by Lameness'. But as the war progressed these standards became even less rigorous: recruits of five foot three were acceptable, and all convicted smugglers, 'all disorderly Persons who could not, upon Examination, prove themselves to exercise and industriously follow some lawful Trade or Employment', and 'incorrigible rogues . . . convicted of running away from and leaving their Families chargeable upon the Parish' were liable to impressment. At the same time bounties were increased and promises of exemption from future parish service were given to volunteers. Indeed, the government resorted to every expedient considered tolerable in a free society.

In his anxiety to bring in more recruits than the existing measures could supply, the King had suggested 'sending beating orders to Ireland'; but this had been objected to in Cabinet. He had also proposed that 'nobility and gentry of property [should] be persuaded separately in their parishes to give half a guinea in addition to the levy money for the encouragement of each of their parishioners enlisting in the Army'. But, as North said, conscious of the growing opposition to the war amongst merchants and those put out of work by the decline in the American trade, 'the ardour of the nation in this cause' had 'not arisen to the pitch one could wish'; and recruitment into existing regiments was disappointingly slow. The alternative of raising new regiments was not favoured by the King, who shrank from being pestered with requests for the granting of commissions and promotions to unsuitable candidates and who knew only too well that, when the new regiments were disbanded at the end of the war, all officers who had served in them would add to the general expense by demanding half pay. The King decided, therefore, that he would have to look to Germany for the men he could not find in England. In August 1775 five regiments of Hanoverians became mercenaries for the British, four of them being sent to Minorca and Gibraltar to release British troops from the garrisons there. The King's uncle, the Landgrave of Hesse Cassel, was persuaded to lend some of his soldiers; other regiments came from the ruling families of Mecklenburg Strelitz and Brunswick Wolfenbüttel, though an approach to Russia was quickly rebuffed by Catherine the Great who did not have 'the civility to answer in her own hand' but, as the King said, threw out 'some expressions that may be civil to a Russian ear but certainly not to more civilized ones'.

The Opposition were soon strongly protesting against this use of mercenaries and the proposed enlistment of Indians against the Americans; and, when the government proposed to prohibit all trade and communication with America so long as the rebellion continued, the attacks became more biting than ever. In the House of Commons, Charles James Fox accused the present Ministers of 'want of policy, of folly and madness'. They were utterly unfit to govern America. Lord North was condemned as a 'blundering pilot who had brought the nation into its present difficulties. Lord Chatham, the King of Prussia, nay, Alexander the Great, never gained more in one campaign than the noble Lord has lost – he has lost a whole continent.' Virulent assaults were also made upon Lord Sandwich, the ugly, dissipated, though undeniably charming man of fashion and inveterate gambler who was First Lord of the Admiralty and who employed the immense patronage at his disposal for personal and political motives. Attacked with comparable vehemence was Lord George Germain who, as Secretary of State for the American Department, an office instituted seven years before, was largely responsible for the conduct of the war in America and for defending it in the House.

Germain, the youngest and favourite son of the Duke of Dorset and, until inheriting a large estate and fortune from Lady Elizabeth Germain on condition that he changed his name, known as Lord George Sackville, had been a lieutenant-general. But his failure to obey an order of his superior, Prince Ferdinand of Brunswick, during the Battle of Minden had led to his dismissal from the service. He had demanded a court-martial with dogged persistence; and, although he defended himself with remarkable energy and skill before the court, he had been 'adjudged to be unfit to serve his majesty in any military capacity whatever'. Since then, however, despite the vindictiveness of his opponents and the diligently spread rumours of his homosexuality, he had gradually rebuilt his reputation and, having coolly and bravely fought a duel with a fellow Member of Parliament who expressed surprise that he should be so concerned about his country's honour when he cared so little for his own, Lord George Germain was said by Horace Walpole to have become a hero 'whatever Lord George Sackville may have been'.

A strong supporter of firm action against the colonists, Germain was appointed American Secretary, in succession to the more moderate Lord Dartmouth, on 10 December 1775 at the age of fifty-nine; and in that office, so his Under-Secretary Richard Cumberland said, he displayed 'all the requisites of a great minister, unless popularity and good luck are to be numbered amongst them'. He was 'a tall man', according to the Marquess of Lansdowne, 'with a long face, rather strong features, clear blue eyes . . . and a mixture of quickness and a sort of melancholy in his look which runs through all the Sackville family'. His manner was haughty, distant and coldly polite, yet in private, so another contemporary, Nathaniel Wraxall, said,

> no man unbent himself more. In the midst of his family [he had five children] and in the company of a few select friends, he soon forgot the toils annexed to public life, the asperities of debate, and the vexations of office. Even after the latest night in the House he always sat down to a delicately served table . . . drank a pint of claret, unbent his mind and passed in review the incidents of the preceding evening . . . He rarely dined from home, except for Cabinet dinners.

In his office he was brisk and forthright and soon became master of the business transacted there. While in the House of Commons, though liable to lose his temper when goaded, he was skilled in debate and nearly always spoke well, concisely and to the point without those literary and classical allusions which were so dear to his contemporaries but for which he had no taste, rarely opening any of the books in his extensive library.

In his first speech as a Minister he declared that he had always held the view that Parliament had the right to tax the colonies and what he had so consistently believed he now stood in office to maintain, making the pledge that, were the Americans to persist in their obstinacy, the government would certainly provide the forces necessary to establish and maintain 'the power of this country in America'. He promised, in the pursuit of his objectives, to be 'decisive, direct and firm'. He had not been long in office when news reached England from Canada that greatly encouraged his supporters, dismayed the Opposition, and had a profound effect upon public opinion in Britain as a whole.

6

THE WAR IN CANADA

*'One or two dogs were killed
which the soldiers ate with good
appetite, even the feet and skins.'*

Major R. J. Meigs

In command of such British troops as there were in Canada at this
time was an experienced fifty-year-old Irish officer, Major-General
Guy Carleton, the Governor of Quebec, a highly conscientious and
humane man though one intolerant of any criticism and, like General
Clinton, ever ready to take offence. Much respected by the French
in Canada because of his endorsement of the Quebec Act, which had
allowed Roman Catholics the free exercise of their religion and
re-established the authority of French law in Canada, Carleton was
regarded with suspicion and widespread dislike by British settlers.
He had also been much disliked by the King's grandfather, King
George II, not least because of some excessively impolite remarks
concerning Hanoverian troops which he was said to have made; and,
as a young colonel, he had consequently had great difficulty in
obtaining His Majesty's permission to take up an appointment on
the staff of his odd, conceited and heroic friend, James Wolfe, whose
army had taken Quebec in 1759. The King's objections being finally
overcome, Carleton had fought under Wolfe at Quebec where he had
been badly wounded. Wounded again more than once in subsequent
campaigns, he had made a name for himself as one of the bravest and
most talented officers in the Army, and had been appointed acting
Governor of Quebec at the age of forty-three in 1767.

He had since then had occasion frequently to complain of the weakness of the garrisons in Canada, vitally placed though they were *vis-à-vis* the American colonies, and the reluctance of successive administrations in London to reinforce them. When he heard that two thousand American troops were on the march, bent upon conquering Canada and thus pre-empting a strike against the rebels from the north, Carleton, with no more than eight hundred regular troops under his command, feared that he would be unable to resist them.

The American forces, approaching in two columns across country considered virtually impassable, were led by Benedict Arnold, who had been commissioned by General Washington to take Quebec, and by Richard Montgomery, an Irishman and former officer in the British Army, who was ordered to take Montreal and then join Arnold for the attack on Quebec. Montgomery, a courageous and attractive man with an American wife from New York, had set out from Ticonderoga at the end of August 1775 with 2400 men. By 10 September he had arrived at St John's, a fort on the River Richelieu north of Lake Champlain. Here he was held for a time by the garrison which Carleton had reinforced with five hundred men and by a hundred Canadian volunteers.

With his stocks of ammunition rapidly diminishing, Montgomery decided to turn aside for the moment and to attack the nearby post of Chambly, whose garrison, having quickly and discreditably surrendered, handed over to him stores and ammunition sufficient to enable him to return to St John's, which fell on 3 November. Carleton, repulsed when he had marched to the relief of St John's with a pitiably small force, was now forced to withdraw from Montreal which Montgomery's forces entered on 12 November, eagerly seizing upon the red, warm, winter uniforms of the British troops piled up there in store and so wantonly plundering the houses of the town that a British officer believed that General Carleton would soon have as many Canadian volunteers anxious to fight the American rebels as he could possibly desire.

Carleton himself was almost captured, and was obliged to escape from the town in a whaleboat disguised as one of its fishermen. He arrived in Quebec a week later; and immediately set about preparing its fortifications, and encouraging the few and mostly ill-trained and poorly disciplined men under his command to defend them with spirit. By the time Montgomery's men arrived before Quebec at the beginning of December, Carleton had succeeded in making their task far more difficult than it would have been a month before.

The eleven hundred Americans under Benedict Arnold had faced an appallingly severe task when they had set off in September to advance up the Kennebec and Chaudière rivers through the deserted forests of Maine. For three weeks they had been on the march, struggling through mile after mile of wilderness and swamp, their coarse cloth hunting-shirts torn to shreds, their provisions running so low that they had been obliged to eat boiled candles and moccasin and even their dogs, and eating them, so one of their officers recorded, 'with good appetite [including] the feet and skins'. Even so, some men died of starvation, others of exhaustion and exposure, their feet wrapped in flour bags and animal skins after their boots had worn out. Several became too ill to keep up with the march and had to be sent back; some three hundred, including a colonel, deserted. One of the survivors of the march reported:

> It rained heavily and turned to a snowstorm, and the snow fell [knee] deep. Our company was obliged to kill a dog and eat it for breakfast, and in the course of that day I killed an owl, and two of my messmates and myself fared in the repast . . . The day following, we waded a river thirty rods wide. We came soon to a house where we drew a pound of beef and three potatoes each . . . Went from the house into the woods and found an Indian camp and lodged for the night. Next day started, and I was taken sick of a kind of camp distemper. Could not walk far in a day. Went on five miles and came to another house where we got one pound of beef, three potatoes, and a pint of oatmeal each. We then went on, when I became so feeble that myself and two more hired a Frenchman to carry us at our expense for thirteen miles . . . We then went on, all very much enfeebled by reason of sickness and hardship, for four or five days until we reached Quebec.

Another survivor, a corporal in a company of riflemen from Pennsylvania, recorded similar experiences:

> 13 July 1775.   Marched from Carlisle . . .
> 26th.   Got to the Log gaol where we tarred and feathered one

of the ministerial tools who refused to Comply with the Resolves of our Continental Congress.

31st. Rested at New Windsor to get our Linnen washed, and ourselves recruited, being weary marching in Exceeding hot weather.

3rd August. Marched thro' Litchfield . . . Here they tarred and feathered another Ministerial tool and, after his making acknowledgements, he was drummed out of Town . . .

18th September. Embarked in Newberry Port . . . most of our people very seasick . . .

23rd. Got up to Fort Western where we embarked on 22 Batteaux . . . sometimes rowing against the Rapid stream and sometimes setting with Poles in the Shallow places . . .

24th October. Provisions growing scarce, and our people sickly and much dispirited . . . A company of musketmen returned, being discouraged by the many Difficultys they meet with . . . Several of our boats were overset, and much baggage lost.

27th. . . . Crossing many ponds and carrying places, thro' swamps and muddy grounds and over mountains and rocks such as we believe were never passed by man before . . . Our shoulders so bruised by carrying the boats that we could suffer nothing to touch them . . .

28th. We shared out our last flour . . .

31st. Travelling through pathless woods and steep mountains and wading rapid rivers, sometimes up to our waists and then going forward in our wet cold cloths . . .

2 November. . . . Many fell behind, Quite faint for want of provisions . . . We passed some musketmen devouring two dogs which they had roasted, skin, guts and all, and were making a hearty meal of it, not having eat anything for 2 or 3 days. I saw one of them offer a Dollar for a bitt of Cake not 2 ounces. After lying all night on the cold ground in our wet Cloths we are so weak and fieble in the morning as scarcely to be able to stand. However we sett out staggering in the Evening, and met some Cattle sent to our relief by Col. Arnold . . . It was the most joyful sight we ever saw . . .

8 November. Arrived at Point Levi . . . Remained till the 15th when most of the people that were alive came up. They informed us that several had died on the Road of Hunger and Cold.

When Arnold himself arrived before Quebec he had scarcely more than six hundred men left. After leading an attempted sortie against the town, he realized that it was now far too strongly defended for him to attack with such a depleted and ill-equipped force; so he withdrew to Pointe aux Trembles to await the arrival of Montgomery.

As soon as Montgomery arrived with about three hundred men – the rest having been left at garrisons in the forts he had taken – he and Arnold advanced upon Quebec together, occupying houses and convents in the suburbs of the town, thankful for any shelter from the wind. It was bitterly cold now and the ground was frozen hard. The men did their best to dig siege lines beneath the walls of the town; but the frozen earth seemed as hard as iron, and they had to content themselves with building walls of snow to give an impression of strength to the enemy.

General Carleton was not misled. He had intercepted messages carried by Indian runners between the American commanders and knew pretty well how matters stood. The forces at his disposal had recently been increased by almost four hundred recruits brought into Quebec by forced march from Sorel by Colonel Allan Maclean, who was raising a regiment there. Even so, Carleton had only about twelve hundred men at his disposal and of these less than seventy were British, the rest of doubtful reliability.

Montgomery and Arnold had just as little ground for confidence. They had no siege artillery, nor any hope of obtaining any. A bombardment by field guns had done no discernible damage. Many of their men, who had enlisted only until the end of the year, were anxious to get home to New England. If an assault were to be made, it would have to be attempted as soon as possible. The two commanders decided to wait only until the next snowstorm concealed their movements from the town.

The snow clouds gathered in a high wind on the last day of the year. Orders were therefore given for the attacks to begin at two o'clock in the morning of 31 December, Montgomery on one flank, Arnold on the other, while two feint attacks were made on the centre of the lower town between them.

The snow fell heavily through the wind, concealing the Americans' movements from Quebec; but the two false attacks were made too soon, and the enemy garrison, alerted to their posts by drums beating and bells clanging in every church, opened up a heavy fire with musket and grapeshot on both Montgomery's and Arnold's columns. Running forward with his men, their shoulders crouched against the snow, doing their best to keep their powder dry, Montgomery was shot through the face and both legs and died in the arms of a young lieutenant. Arnold was wounded and had to be carried away across the ice on a scaling ladder.

Despite his wounds and their repulse and the ever-increasing cold, Arnold refused to withdraw. Although many of the men who remained with him were suffering from smallpox, and although stores were running low, he was still in camp before Quebec on 1 April when the bucolic, hard-drinking General David Wooster arrived from Montreal with heavy guns to take over the command of the besieging forces. Arnold, deeply resenting his replacement as a personal slight, asked to be assigned to other duties.

Wooster did not remain in command long. Having thrown everything into confusion, he was soon himself replaced by General John Thomas, who shortly afterwards died of smallpox. The command was then given to Major-General John Sullivan, a vain and pugnacious New Hampshire lawyer. By now the thick ice was at last melting in the St Lawrence River and relief for Quebec was on its way from Britain.

Lord George Germain had long recognized the advisability of 'coming down upon the American rebels from the north' and of pouring 'an army from Quebec on the back of the colonies'. He had listened favourably to Carleton's request for ten thousand men and to Howe's request for a further fifteen thousand for the defence of New York and for operations beyond it. The Secretary for the American Department had also accepted that a large number of those flat-bottomed river-boats known as bateaux would be required, as well as several gunboats for amphibious operations on the St Lawrence River and on Lake Champlain. Yet, although Germain ordered four hundred bateaux, the officer who was instructed to supply them argued that it would be far better to have them made in the forests of Canada as and when they were needed, even though this would mean their being constructed of greenwood rather than of seasoned wood, and though there might not be either time or men skilled enough to make them in Canada, anyway. Consequently, only a few of the bateaux ordered by Germain were supplied; and, while the order for gunboats was fulfilled, these were constructed without masts and sails and supplied without anchors, as the requisition to the Admiralty had not been sufficiently specific to satisfy the bureaucratic requirements of its officials.

The raising of the army for Canada was fortunately not attended by such difficulties. About three thousand men were to come from Germany and rather more than five thousand from the British Army, including six regiments from Ireland under Brigadier-General Simon Fraser and a regiment to be transferred from Boston. All regiments were to be allowed to take sixty women and forty-two servants each. They were also to take sixteen horses each and 68 tons of baggage, though only four wagons for personal baggage. The headquarters staff were more generously provided for in this respect: Burgoyne, who was to take the reinforcements out as Carleton's second-in-command, and his two aides-de-camp were to have no less than forty tons of baggage between them.

As on the eve of his departure the year before, Burgoyne was reluctant to leave his wife who was now critically ill. He asked that the date of his departure for Canada might be postponed. But he was told that the fleet could not be delayed any longer; and so, assuring the King in his grandiloquent way that private misfortune would not interfere with the trust reposed in him, and that every faculty of which he was master would be exerted to his last breath to forward His Majesty's service, he left for Portsmouth. Here he found that the fleet was not ready to sail after all, because some of the crews of the transports which were leased from contractors were on strike for higher wages. He was also told that the German regiments had lost their boots on the Continent and that the packing cases of footwear sent over to take their place had been found to contain five thousand pairs of dancing pumps.

It was, therefore, not until 4 April that the fleet set sail. But Burgoyne bore the delay with equanimity. He had been promoted lieutenant-general, and had been assured by Germain that the captain of the *Blonde*, in which he was to make the voyage, was very rich, so that he 'need not fear putting him to expense'.

Two months before, the fifty-gun *Isis* had set out for Quebec with orders to get through at all hazard. No pains must be spared, Lord

Sandwich had told Captain Douglas, to get his ship to Quebec where the British garrison was close to starvation: the fate of Canada was in his hands. Captain Douglas was determined to succeed. The *Isis*, followed closely by a frigate and a sloop, sailed fast across the Atlantic, passing vast icebergs towering above her mast-head and arriving in the second week of April in the Gulf of St Lawrence, where a huge icefield closed her passage. Undeterred, Douglas, believing it 'an enterprize worthy of an English ship of the Line in our King and Country's sacred Cause', made up his mind to batter his way through by force of sail. He rammed the *Isis* against the ice at what appeared to be its narrowest point and, as chips of the bow and the hull were splintered off his ship, the ice cracked and parted and the *Isis* squeezed through. For nearly two hundred miles she sailed on, her sails hard with ice, her decks covered with snow, 'describing her path all the way', as Captain Douglas said, 'with bits of sheathing off the ship's bottom', occasionally held fast by the ice on which the troops she was carrying were paraded up and down for exercise, watched by Esquimaux with beards so thick that one officer found it 'difficult to distinguish any features of the face', other than 'little eyes looking wild, and large, very foul teeth'.

When eventually the *Isis* broke out into clearer water she was almost immediately joined by the two other ships which had been following her, then by another and by five transports from one of which three despairing soldiers had thrown themselves overboard. At dawn on 6 May a gun salute from the basin awoke Quebec to the exciting realization that relief had come. 'People half dressed ran down to the Grand Battery', as the frigate *Surprise* bombarded the American entrenchments, while from the other ships the long-awaited reinforcements were disembarked.

All hopes that the Americans had of taking Quebec were now frustrated: orders were given to withdraw and, as the rebels began the long march south, British troops burst forth from the town to hasten them on their way, capturing several pieces of their artillery and much of their baggage, finding their tents still standing and their breakfasts laid out on tables, so precipitate had been their departure.

John Burgoyne and the main body of Sir Guy Carleton's reinforcements were still at sea. But as soon as he landed, on 29 May,

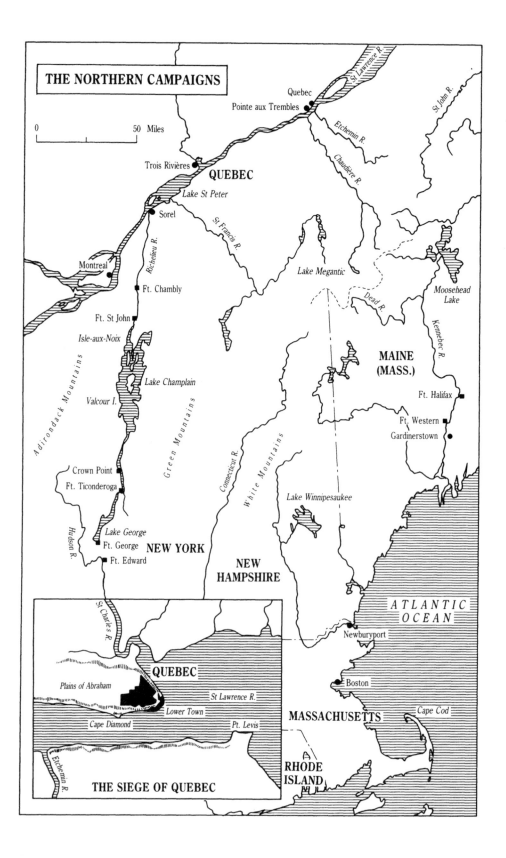

THE NORTHERN CAMPAIGNS

0   50 Miles

Quebec
Pointe aux Trembles
St. Lawrence R.
St. John R.
Etchemin R.
Chaudière R.
Trois Rivières
QUEBEC
Lake St Peter
Sorel
Richelieu R.
St Francis R.
Montreal
Lake Megantic
Moosehead Lake
Dead R.
Ft. Chambly
Ft. St John
Isle-aux-Noix
MAINE (MASS.)
Kennebec R.
Adirondack Mountains
Lake Champlain
Valcour I.
Green Mountains
Ft. Halifax
Ft. Western
Gardinerstown
Crown Point
Ft. Ticonderoga
Connecticut R.
White Mountains
Lake Winnipesaukee
Hudson R.
Lake George
Ft. George
NEW YORK
Ft. Edward
NEW HAMPSHIRE
ATLANTIC OCEAN
Newburyport
St Charles R.
QUEBEC
Plains of Abraham
St Lawrence R.
Lower Town
Cape Diamond
Pt. Levis
Boston
Cape Cod
Etchemin R.
THE SIEGE OF QUEBEC
MASSACHUSETTS
RHODE ISLAND

Burgoyne chased after Carleton in a cabriolet, coming up with him at Champlain, some 75 miles south-west of Quebec.

Immediately upon disembarking, the troops that Burgoyne had brought with him also moved south, marching quickly up the St Lawrence towards Trois Rivières, the British regiments on the right bank, the Germans on the left under the command of Major General Adolf Friedrich von Riedesel, who was accompanied by his wife, their two little daughters and the family's two maids.

At Trois Rivières William Thompson, General Sullivan's tough and boastful second-in-command, attempted to drive the British back. His attack, however, was ill conceived. Within minutes sixty of his men were killed and nearly three hundred were marched away as prisoners through the woods, their faces burning from the bites of swarms of black flies. The rest of Sullivan's forces escaped to Sorel, where they burned the buildings and spiked the guns, then moved on to Chambly, many of them suffering from smallpox or malaria, deserted by nearly all their officers.

When Burgoyne reached Chambly, where he was to establish his headquarters, he found that this fort, too, had been almost burned to the ground by Sullivan whose small army, disintegrating though it was, managed to evacuate two thousand patients from the military hospital on the Ile aux Noix, to drag the sick, as well as their stores, in bateaux over the rapids of St John's, and to reach the safety of Crown Point. Here at the southern end of Lake Champlain, the Americans, under the energetic direction of Benedict Arnold, threw themselves into the task of building a fleet of sloops and galleys, gondolas and schooners with which to oppose a crossing of the long stretch of water by the British, who were also busy assembling a fleet at the other end of the lake, 120 miles to the north.

From his headquarters at Chambly, Burgoyne rode to Montreal to talk to the chiefs of two thousand Indians who were assembled there for a pow-wow. He proposed to lead fifteen hundred of these Indians, together with three British battalions and some Canadian volunteers, up the St Lawrence to Oswego on Lake Ontario, and from there to come down the Mohawk valley to the Hudson, thus threatening the rebels' rear and, so he hoped, putting a stop to their boat-building on the shores of Lake Champlain. At first Carleton seemed interested in the plan, but eventually decided against it, telling Burgoyne to send all but a few of the Indians home. Burgoyne,

already annoyed with Carleton for not pursuing the rebels with
vigour after their repulse at Trois Rivières, decided that the command
of the British troops in Canada was not in good hands. His poor
opinion of Carleton was confirmed when the Commander-in-Chief
vetoed another proposal for an attempt to get behind the Americans
before their fleet was ready. Carleton had decided to wait, he said,
for the completion of his own fleet. So the army remained largely
inactive while sailors and chain-gangs of Canadian convicts brought
materials down from the north and carpenters and shipwrights
worked all day long on their flat-bottomed boats, on schooners,
sloops and bomb-ketches, on an immense raft, which they named
the *Thunderer*, on two schooners, the *Marie* and the *Carleton*, and on
a warship, the *Inflexible*, which had been dismantled and dragged
piece by piece from the St Lawrence to the Richelieu River.

The Americans were nearing the end of their task. One after the
other their boats were prepared for battle – their *Liberty*, the *Providence*
and the *Success*, the *Spitfire*, the *Congress* and the *Revenge*, the *Enterprise*
and the *New York*, the *Boston*, the *Philadelphia*, the *New Haven* and
the *Jersey*, the *Washington*, the *Lee* and the *Royal Savage*, an old sloop
formerly bearing the name of King George III, which was the flagship
of Captain Jacobus Wynkoop, Arnold's predecessor as commodore
of the fleet.

On the morning of 11 October 1776, the wind being favourable,
all the ships of the British fleet set sail, followed by some five hundred
small boats packed with soldiers sitting on the thwarts with their
muskets between their knees. Arnold reported:

> At half-past twelve, the engagement became general, and very
> warm. Some of the enemy's ships, and all their gondolas beat and
> rowed up within musket-shot of us. They continued a very hot
> fire, with round and grape shot until five o'clock . . . The *New
> York* lost all officers, except the captain. The *Philadelphia* was hulled
> in so many places that she sank . . . The *Congress* received seven
> shot between wind and water and was hulled a dozen times . . .
> The *Washington* was [also] hulled a number of times. Both [these]
> vessels are now very leaky . . . The whole killed and wounded
> amounted to about sixty. The enemy landed a large number of
> Indians on each shore, who keep an incessant fire . . . We suffered

much for want of seamen and gunners . . . It was thought prudent
to return to Crown Point.

Further damage was inflicted on the American ships as they beat
their way back towards Crown Point, which Arnold reached with
less than two hundred men and four ships. Accepting that it would
be futile to defend the place, he set fire to it and withdrew to
Ticonderoga, where the camp was thrown into uproar by reports
of the imminent arrival of the British soldiers. A captain from
Pennsylvania recorded:

> A general alarm was fired and every one hurryed to his post. All
> was bustle; the whole camp presented a terrific blaze of fire arms
> . . . Collom after collom presented their fronts along the lines, with
> fixed bayonets . . . The sounds of the drums to arms, the reports
> of the alarm cannon, and the crye of the sergeants to the men in
> hurrying them from their tents of 'Turn out! Turn out!' would
> make even a coward brave . . . I will throw a vail over some names,
> who but the evening before bosted over a glass of grog what feats
> they intended to do on the approach of the enemy, now shrunk
> with sickning apathy within the cover of their tents and markees,
> never appeared to head their men, leaving their tasks to their
> subalterns to perform. On finding at last the enemy had made a
> halt . . . they came out as boald soldiers as ever, complaining only
> of a little headake . . .

There were, however, more brave men than cowards, and when
this officer looked into the faces of his own men 'not a ray of fear'
was 'depicted in the face of any of them'. He was confident that,
had the British attacked, 'they would not have dishonoured either
themselves or their country'.

But Carleton had decided not to push his success too far. Getting
his army across Lake Champlain in the face of American resistance
had been a lengthy process: he had now lost too much time to fulfil
his plan of joining Howe for an assault on New York. Had he begun
his expedition four weeks earlier, so the German General Baron von
Riedesel believed, 'everything would have ended this year'. As it
was, it was now too late for further operations. Winter was coming
on again: the first snow of what threatened to be a severe season had

fallen. Carleton dared not stretch his lines of communication any further. Indeed, he was forced to conclude that they would already be too extended to keep open during the long, cold months to come. He decided, therefore, to withdraw into Canada.

Burgoyne left him to deal with his problems alone. He had just heard that his wife had died in London not long after his departure. Complaining that his mind was 'sunk in distress', that his constitution was 'unfitted to severity of cold', and that 'all his plans [had] been disappointed', he sailed home, without leave, for England.

7

DISASTERS IN
VIRGINIA

---

*'I never was uneasy on not having
a retreat, because I never imagined
the enemy could force me to that
necessity.'*

William Moultrie

The British government's long-cherished hope that there were thousands of steadfast Loyalists eager to fight for the rights of the Crown
was still bolstered by regular reports from governors of the southern
colonies. One of the most sanguine was John Murray, fourth Earl of
Dunmore, the impetuous and self-important Governor of Virginia
who gave it as his 'considered opinion' that the present disturbances
would soon be over, that they had been brought about by just a few
young men, no doubt well-intentioned 'but spoil'd by a strange,
imperfect desultory kind of Education which has crept into fashion
all over America'. What was needed, Dunmore insisted, was a firm
hand. He himself had twice prorogued the House of Assembly
in Williamsburg when it passed resolutions which he considered
unacceptable; and in April 1775 had seized several cases of gunpowder
stored in the town's magazine and had them carried aboard the
Magdalen man-of-war in the James River. The angry demonstrations
which this action provoked had been quietened only when he consented to pay for the powder confiscated. Dunmore had given further
provocation to the people of Williamsburg when, having hastily left
his house for the safety of the frigate *Fowey*, after a riot in the town
on 5 June, he required the burgesses to attend upon him there before
giving his assent to various bills passed by their Assembly. When the

Assembly responded by declaring that the Governor had abdicated
and by transferring his power to a committee of public safety,
Dunmore retaliated by collecting and manning a flotilla in the river,
by carrying out a series of attacks on settlements and plantations
along the river banks, by boarding fishing vessels, impounding crops
of tobacco, taking prisoners including two young women whom he
was said to have employed as 'bedmakers', endeavouring to win the
support of the Ohio Indians, and proclaiming freedom for all black
slaves who were prepared to run away from their masters and enlist
in a regiment of 'Loyal Ethiopians'.

A number of these black recruits formed part of a raiding party
which Dunmore despatched at the beginning of December 1775 to
attack a force of about nine hundred colonists commanded by Colonel
William Woodford. They took up positions at Long Bridge, some
twenty miles south of Norfolk at the far end of a long causeway over
a swamp. In addition to the black troops and American Loyalists,
there were several British sailors and about sixty regular soldiers, all
under the command of Captain Charles Fordyce. They were far
outnumbered by the American militia, expert marksmen, mostly
backwoodsmen experienced in Indian fighting, who were securely
entrenched behind a loop-holed stockade seven feet high and well
supplied with ammunition.

The outcome of the ensuing battle at the bridge was predictable.
It was, in the opinion of one young British officer who had to
take part in it, 'an absurd, ridiculous and unnecessary attack, an
extravagant Folly'. The stubborn and opinionated Governor was
strongly urged not to attempt it; yet he could not be dissuaded from
going ahead with the 'mad enterprise'.

The British troops, obliged to march up the causeway in single
file, were soon exposed to the Americans' accurate fire, as one of
them recorded:

Captain Fordyce fell within four Yards of their Breastwork . . .
covered with 11 wounds . . . Lieutenants Napier, Leslie & Bates
[also] fell, the last is still living a Prisoner with the Enemy. The
Rebels behaved with the greatest Humanity, ceasing to fire when
we were retreating with the wounded . . .

They paid the greatest respect to poor Fordyce's Body, burying
it with all the Honours of War. They call him the brave Fordyce &

say his Death would have been that of a Hero, had he met it in a
better Cause. They were astonished at Men marching up with such
Courage, or rather Madness to certain Death. They had only one
Man wounded slightly in the Hand . . . His Lordship has much to
answer for – besides sacraficing a handfull of brave Men, he has
ruined every Friend of Government in this Colony, & done the
Cause much Disservice . . .

   We are now retired on board Ship, cut off from all Communications from the Shore.

In North Carolina attacks on the rebels were equally misguided
and equally unfortunate. Here, too, was a Governor, Josiah Martin,
who assured London that the Loyalists needed but little encouragement to rise up in defence of the Crown: an expeditionary force
landed on the coast would sweep ashore and, in conjunction with its
American allies, soon reduce the colony, and, indeed, the whole
south, to perfect obedience. There were at least some grounds for
this optimistic belief: around Cross Creek, now Fayetteville, along
the upper reaches of the Cape Fear River, there was a large colony
of emigrants from the Scottish Highlands predisposed to support the
King who, by the Act of Union of 1707, was their monarch as much
as England's. One of these Highlanders was Flora MacDonald, the
Jacobite heroine who had helped the Pretender, Prince Charles Edward, to escape to Skye following his defeat at Culloden. After
imprisonment in the Tower of London for this offence, she had
married Allan MacDonald with whom she had emigrated. When the
war broke out in America, MacDonald, as a trusted Loyalist, was
appointed brigadier-general by the Governor, while she – who had
assured King George's father that she would have helped him in
distress just as she had befriended the Pretender – rode about the
countryside from neighbour to neighbour, urging them all to fight
for the British Crown against the ungrateful rebels.
   Many of the Highlanders whom Flora MacDonald approached did
join the Royal Emigrant Regiment, which two Scottish officers in
the King's service were sent into North Carolina to raise. But the
response to calls for volunteers was not as ready as the Governor had
hoped, while far more men than he had expected enlisted in the
North Carolina Continentals. These Continentals were not an imposing sight on parade as they marched raggedly up and down in

their shirtsleeves to the uncertain time of an ill-beaten drum, yet they were all as good marksmen as the men at Long Bridge had proved themselves to be. At Widow Moore's Creek they inflicted a defeat upon the Loyalists which ensured that, when the British squadron which the Governor had asked for arrived off Cape Fear, there was little hope that the officer in command of it would receive much assistance from the local inhabitants.

This officer was Commodore Sir Peter Parker who had joined the Royal Navy as a boy and who had been promoted captain and given command of a frigate when he was in his early twenties. The son of an admiral and the father of a boy who was to become one, Parker had never known, nor ever wanted, any life other than that of the sea. Until now he had had little opportunity for the display of his talents, having been on half pay for ten years and then captain of a guardship at Portsmouth before being given his present command.

When Parker's flagship, the *Bristol*, reached Cape Fear in May 1776, General Clinton, commander of the British land forces in the area, had already been there long enough to realize that talk of great numbers of Loyalists flocking to the British flag was absurdly optimistic, and that the government's belief that battalions of Americans formed under British protection would be able to take care of themselves when left to their own devices was ridiculous. 'Tis clear to me,' Clinton wrote,

> that there does not exist in any one [province] in America a number
> of friends of Government sufficient to defend themselves when the
> troops are withdrawn. The idea is false and if the measure is adopted
> . . . all the friends of Government will be sacrificed *en détail*. This
> is the case in Georgia, will be in South Carolina, is already in North
> Carolina and in Virginia, will probably be in Boston, and must in
> my opinion be everywhere.

While waiting for Parker to arrive, Clinton had become increasingly depressed. Satisfactory provisions for his troops were in severely short supply. The men's diet of biscuits, dried meat and flour could occasionally be supplemented by oysters and a local cabbage which tasted like artichoke hearts when boiled and was admittedly quite wholesome; but there was no fresh meat, no salt, and an almost sickening surfeit of molasses which Clinton had

managed to secure from the master of a French schooner who had
been intercepted off the coast on his way to Newfoundland. Having
an abiding interest in natural history, the General was able to while
away the long hours of waiting by studying the fauna and plants
with which the neighbourhood abounded. The wild honeysuckle
was 'beyond description'; aloes, prickly pears and tuberoses grew in
profusion, and birds flew across the sky 'in the greatest variety'.
Clinton spent hours on end watching hawks seize fish from the sea
and, as they flew away with them, eagles from the forests rising high
above them, then swooping down. 'The hawk, to save himself, quits
his prey; and the eagle seizes it before it reaches the sea.'

But correspondents were not allowed to suppose he was living in
a kind of Eden. 'What is not bog, salt marsh [or] quicksand,' he told
one of them, 'is cedar grove, and as full of all sorts of offensive beasts,
birds, and serpents as any part of the known globe. Among other
extraordinary things we have the whipping snake, which meets you
in the road and lashes you most unmercifully. We are told that two
or three of them will kill a horse.'

'Of all the countries for climate I ever visited,' he continued in
another letter, 'nothing can equal this. As the season advances, it
must be intolerable. In the space of two hours every change that can
happen – such thunder and such rain is, I thank God, not to be met
with [anywhere else]. The *agrément* of mosquitoes is not wanting,
and the sand fly of a particular sort and size is here in perfection. We
have nothing to eat [and] execrable water.'

The arrival of Peter Parker and the troops sent out from England
under the command of Major-General the Earl of Cornwallis brought
Clinton no comfort: the new arrivals were in a sorry state after three
months' buffeting at sea; the condition of his own men was not much
better; the instructions which the Commodore handed to him gave
him little guidance. Had he been authorized to decide for himself
what to do, he would have called off the invasion of South Carolina
altogether after learning of the Loyalists' defeat at Widow Moore's
Creek.

Parker, however, was keen to take action; and, since there were
reports that work on the defences of Charleston were still in hand
and that the existing fort commanding the entrance to the harbour
was not a strong one, Clinton reluctantly agreed that the attack
should be made. The commanders, meeting in a Council of War,

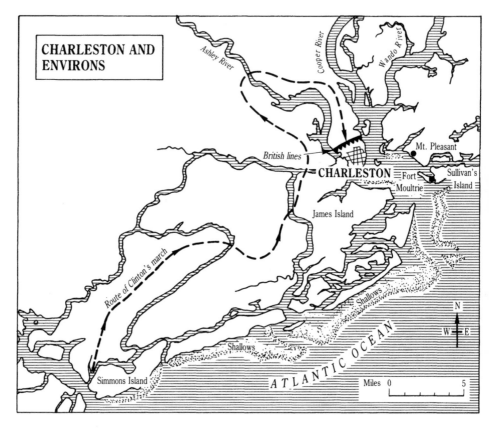

CHARLESTON AND
ENVIRONS

decided to abide by this determination even after further letters
arrived from Lord George Germain, who now doubted that an
assault on Charleston was wise and suggested that Clinton should
rejoin Howe unless it were considered that success was virtually
certain.

Assured that the waters between Long Island, the offshore island
(now the Isle of Palms) where his troops were to disembark, and
Sullivan's Island, which guarded the south approaches to Charleston's
wide harbour, were so shallow that they could easily be forded at
low water, Clinton considered it safe to proceed with the attack. It
was decided, therefore, that the fort on Sullivan's Island should be
approached from the rear, across the shoals from Long Island, by
most of the two thousand men under Clinton's command, reinforced
by Loyalists, while Parker's frigates bombarded the fort from the
deeper waters in front.

The American commander on Sullivan's Island was William Moultrie, a member of the Provincial Congress and a colonel in the South
Carolina Regiment, who had been trained as a soldier in fighting
the Cherokee Indians. The fort, to be named Fort Moultrie as a
compliment to his zeal in defending it, was made of sand and logs
cut from the small, tough, stringy palm which grew thickly on the
island. It did not appear to be too sturdy a structure, yet Moultrie
professed himself unconcerned when the bridge of hogsheads ordered
by his superior, Charles Lee, as a means of retreat to the mainland
sank beneath the waves. 'I never was uneasy on not having a retreat,'
he wrote, 'because I never imagined the enemy could force me to
that necessity.' If the enemy's guns flattened his fort – which Charles
Lee described as a 'slaughter pen' – he and his men would lie down
behind the ruins and 'prevent their men from landing'.

As it happened, there was to be no question of an assault by British
infantry. The waters through which Clinton had been led to believe
his men could wade at low tide were far from shoals on the day
chosen for the attack, 28 June. Banked up by high wind, the tide did
not run out as expected and the water remained between seven and
eight feet deep, while in front of the fort the water was so shallow
that Parker's ships could not get close enough to fire on it effectively.
Many of the shells which reached the fort landed in a morass in the
middle of it and were consequently, in Moultrie's words, 'swallowed
up instantly. And those that fell in the sand in and about the fort
were immediately buried, so that very few of them bursted amongst
us.' 'At one time,' Moultrie continued,

> the Commodore's ship [the *Bristol*] swung around with her stern to
> the fort, which drew the fire of all our guns that could bear upon
> her: we supposed he had the springs of her cables cut away. The
> words that passed along the platform by officers and men were
> 'Mind the Commodore!'
>
> Most of all the attention was paid [to the two fifty-gun ships, the
> *Bristol* and the *Experiment*] especially the Commodore's, who, I dare
> say, was not at all obliged to us for our particular attention to him.
> The killed and wounded on board those two fifty-gun ships confirm
> what I say. During the action, General Lee paid us a visit through
> a heavy line of fire, and pointed two or three guns himself; then he

said to me, 'Colonel, I see you are doing very well here, you have
no occasion for me. I will go up to town again.'

When three or four broadsides hit the fort at the same time they
caused so loud a roar and violent a tremor that Moultrie feared his
defences would crumble. But when the smoke cleared they were seen
to be more or less intact; and the men, sweating in the intense heat
of a stiflingly hot summer's day and taking the occasional gulp of
grog from the fire-buckets that were passed along the platforms,
remained steadfastly at their posts. 'General Lee exposed himself to
great danger,' Sergeant Lamb recorded. 'As the balls whistled about
he observed one of his aide-de-camps shrink every now and then,
and by the motion of his body seemed to evade the shot. "Death,
sir!" cried Lee. "Why do you dodge like that? Do you know that
the King of Prussia lost above an hundred aide-de-camps in one
campaign?" "So I understand, sir," replied the officer, "but I did not
think you could spare so many."'

After a time the fort's flag was shot away, and people watching
the action from the town thought that the island had been surrendered. But a sergeant named Jasper jumped through one of the
embrasures, brought the flag back through heavy fire, tied it securely
to a sponge-staff and planted it upon the ramparts once more.

For hours the bombardment continued, the guns of the Americans
falling into silence for a time when Moultrie was informed that
British troops were landing on the island and he decided that he must
conserve his dwindling stock of powder for his muskets. But the
report was proved false, so the guns opened up once more and
continued firing until night, when Moultrie could hear quite distinctly
the shot striking the hulls of the British ships.

The damage inflicted upon the British fleet was devastating. The
vessels returned to their former anchorages in what one observer
described as a 'very shattered Condition'. Parker's flagship, the *Bristol*,
had lost her mizzen and main mast; and her captain, who had had
one arm shot off in the engagement and had been severely wounded
in the hand of the other, had since died. The captain of the *Experiment*
had also lost an arm; and it was feared that he, too, would not live.
All five frigates had been damaged, and one, the *Actaeon*, having run
aground, was set on fire and abandoned. Nevertheless, a party of
Americans boarded her while she was still on fire, pointed her guns

at the other ships, fired them, then brought off the ship's bell and flag before scrambling overboard again, minutes before she blew up and was consumed by flames down to the water's edge.

In all nearly two hundred men on the British side had been killed and wounded, while the Americans for their part had lost no more than twelve men killed and twenty-four wounded. It was a defeat which, as one British officer gloomily commented, would 'scarcely be believed in England'. The palmetto logs, packed in with earth, had offered a far better protection against shot than had seemed likely; and the only serious damage had been done by shells which, as chance would have it, came through the embrasures.

The Americans had good cause for celebration. While the British troops endured the heat of Long Island, eating their salt pork and stale biscuits, swallowing their grog and contending with snakes and mosquitoes, Colonel Moultrie's men received the hearty congratulations of the people of Charleston. Sergeant Jasper was presented with a sword by John Rutledge, the American lawyer who had been elected Governor in Dunmore's place; and another prominent citizen of Charleston sent 'his compliments to Col. Moultrie and the officers and soldiers on Sullivan's Island', begging 'their acceptance of a hogshead of old Antigua rum, which being scarce in town at this time, will be acceptable'.

Dismayed by the British repulse, Henry Clinton was determined not to be blamed for it. He immediately despatched his secretary, a former Boston customs officer, Richard Reeve, to London where the general feeling seemed to be that, instead of making the fatal attempt upon Charleston, the army should have been taken to the Chesapeake as Lord George Germain's orders permitted. As much was suggested in an account of the action which appeared in the *Gazette* and which, in its implied criticism of the commanders, drove Clinton to fury. He was sure that he recognized the hand of the Secretary for the American Department behind the report. It was clear that 'that rancorous Minister' had merely been waiting for an opportunity 'to vent his spleen'. If anyone were to blame, it was Sir Peter Parker; and Clinton refused to rest until this had been established, at least to his own satisfaction, and until Parker, after an acrimonious correspondence, wrote a letter of guarded apology for having advised so disastrous an attack.

PART TWO

8

THE DECLARATION OF INDEPENDENCE

'How is it that we hear the loudest
yelps for liberty among the drivers
of Negroes?'

Samuel Johnson

On the last day of November 1774, Tom Paine, then aged thirty-eight, 'an ingenious, worthy young man', arrived in America from England. The description of him is that of Benjamin Franklin who had met him in London where their mutual interest in scientific subjects had brought them together. Paine was an ambitious man with a red face, eager, dark eyes and an extremely large nose; up till now his career had been marked by a succession of failures. Born in Norfolk, the son of a Quaker who had endeavoured to augment the modest living he made as a manufacturer of corsets by keeping a small farm, Thomas had been found employment in his father's business when he was fourteen. Finding this a humdrum occupation, he had gone to sea, at first in a privateer, then aboard the *Terrible*, commanded by Captain Death. Brought back by his father, he had returned to the corset workshop, and had afterwards set up on his own account in a business in Kent that failed. He then became an excise official until dismissed for neglect of duty. After a spell as a schoolmaster, he was readmitted as an exciseman; but having drawn up a statement of his fellow-officials' grievances and demands for higher pay, he was again dismissed, suspected of dealing in smuggled tobacco and certainly in debt. The tract which he had written for the excisemen had, however, displayed a talent for political argument which he had already revealed in debates in political clubs in England

and which was to bring him fame in America. He arrived in America alone: his first wife had died and he was separated from his second.

In Philadelphia, where he first settled, Paine soon became acquainted with a number of people through the letters of introduction with which Benjamin Franklin had kindly supplied him. One of these was a bookseller who was just about to publish a magazine, the *Pennsylvania Magazine or American Museum*, to whose first number Paine contributed and whose editor he later became with a salary of £50 a year. His own articles in the magazine, reflecting his strongly radical views, considered such subjects as the injustices of slavery and of the inferior position of women in society. It was only to be expected that he would soon turn to the question of the relationship between the British Crown and the colonies. But what could not have been foreseen was the extraordinarily widespread influence his opinions were to have when they found expression in his pamphlet *Common Sense*, published anonymously on 10 January 1776 and, before its real authorship became known, ascribed to Franklin and several others, including John Adams – though Adams, while believing that Paine was a 'better hand in pulling down than building', admitted that he 'could not have written anything in so manly and striking a style'.

Up till then the idea of independence from Britain, while often enough considered in private, had rarely been brought into public debate. It was now spoken of everywhere. About 150,000 copies of *Common Sense* were sold, far more than even the most successful of the productions of previous pamphleteers and greatly to the profit of the Continental Congress to whom its copyright was assigned. The reason for its success was indicated by its title: it was straightforward, easy to comprehend, written in clear yet striking prose which all men, the Philadelphian mechanic as well as the Boston lawyer, could readily understand. It also seemed to be written from the heart, with a warmth of feeling so often lacking in publications of its kind. An assault on monarchy in general, it was also a spirited attack upon British monarchy in particular, upon the 'royal brute', King George III, and upon the absurdity of American allegiance to a British King. 'America is only a secondary object in the system of British politics,' Paine wrote. 'England consults the good of this country no further than it answers for her own purpose . . . Reconciliation is now a fallacious dream.' What America needed was a republic and a republic independent and self-governing. The cause of Americans was, indeed, 'in large measure the cause of all mankind'.

Such forcefully expressed views, while naturally alarming the more conservative, appealed to those delegates to the Second Continental Congress in Philadelphia who realized that, if independence were to be achieved, foreign alliances would be required and that these alliances could never be formed until the American colonies had their own permanent and separate government. At last, it was felt, the time had come to make formal declaration of America's independence as a state in her own right, to take the step which, for so many reasons, had for so long been delayed. Franklin supported this view; so did John and Samuel Adams; so did Patrick Henry and Richard Henry Lee, the tall and eloquent Virginian delegate to the Congress who proposed that 'these United Colonies are, and of right ought to be, free and independent States, that they are absolved from all allegiance to the British Crown, and that all political connection between them and the State of Great Britain is, and ought to be, dissolved.'

All these leading delegates agreed that their fellow-member of Congress, the rich Virginian planter Thomas Jefferson, with what John Adams termed his 'happy talent of composition', was ideally qualified to make the momentous announcement to the world, in words that would stir the hearts of Americans and encourage them to support the revolution, without losing the sympathy of such autocratic monarchs as the King of France whose help in the struggle was deemed essential to victory. Jefferson had already published his *Summary of the Rights of British America* in which he had argued that the British Parliament's claim to authority over the colonies was utterly invalid, that there was no reason why '160,000 electors in the island of Great Britain should give law to four millions in the states of America, every individual of whom is equal to every individual of them'. It was hoped that he would now present the case for independence in an equally vivid and convincing manner. Entrusted with the task of composing the declaration, Jefferson withdrew to his first-floor lodgings in Market Street, Philadelphia, well aware of his responsibility to 'place before mankind', as he put it himself, 'the common sense of the subject in terms so plain and firm as to command their assent, and to justify ourselves in the independent stand we are to take'.

He worked alone for days on end to produce the first draft of the fateful document which, after laborious amendments and corrections, he presented to his colleagues in committee on 28 June. It began with a general statement of purpose and went on to list a formidable number of grievances against the King, including the charge that he had encouraged slavery in America in defiance of the wishes of the American people, an accusation that some thought rather hard to substantiate since Jefferson himself, like many other members of Congress, owned slaves and had no intention of relinquishing them.

Although John Adams, as Jefferson's spokesman, urged its retention, this particular charge was deleted from the final text when the Declaration came to be considered by Congress. So were several other passages, while the wording of yet others was altered. Jefferson was distressed that his work was amended in this way. But at least its second paragraph remained, declaring to the world in brave and moving words which, while not capable of bearing too close an examination as to their exact meaning, were to become for ever renowned as an avowal of man's right to freedom:

> We hold these truths to be self-evident: that all men are created equal; that they are endowed by their Creator with certain inalienable rights; that among these are life, liberty, and the pursuit of happiness; that to secure these rights, governments are instituted among men, deriving their just powers from the consent of the governed; that whenever any form of government becomes destructive of those ends, it is the right of the people to alter or to abolish it, and to institute new government, laying its foundations on such principles, and organizing its powers in such form, as to them shall seem most likely to effect their safety and happiness.

There were critics of these assumptions who maintained that Jefferson's claims went far beyond those of John Locke and the other philosophers, several of them Scottish, whose works had so often been cited in previous debates. Could it really be argued, they asked, that governments were instituted to secure man's right to the pursuit of happiness? Was it as axiomatic as Jefferson proposed that all men were created equal?

Despite these doubts and objections, on the evening of 4 July 1776 the text was formally approved. The Declaration was signed, and the American colonies became independent communities.

In London news of the Declaration of Independence was greeted in some quarters with an enthusiastic approval voiced by certain opposition newspapers such as the *Public Advertiser*, which declared that 'the despised Americans' were 'manifestly not those cowards and poltroons which our over-hasty, ill-judging, wrong-headed Administration styled them'. Other publications, however, were less complimentary. The *Gentleman's Magazine*, for example, considered:

> The declaration is without doubt of the most extraordinary nature both with regard to sentiment and language, and . . . reflects no honour upon either the erudition or honesty [of its authors]. We hold, they say, these truths to be self-evident: That all men are created equal. In what are they created equal? Is it in size, strength, understanding, figure, moral or civil accomplishments, or situation of life? Every plough-man knows that they are not created equal in any of these. All men, it is true, are equally created, but what is this to the purpose? It certainly is no reason why the Americans should turn rebels.

The *Morning Post* also ridiculed Jefferson's high-flown cadences, while another newspaper described a 'patriotic' clergyman reading out the Declaration to an attentive audience on a hot summer's day in South Carolina, while a slave held a parasol over his head with one hand and fanned him with the other. Many Englishmen, indeed, agreed with Samuel Johnson who continued to wonder how it was 'that we hear the loudest yelps for liberty among the drivers of Negroes?' Even the caricaturists – though for the most part still anti-government and therefore pro-American – were beginning to advance such opinions as that expressed in *The Patricide: A Sketch of Modern Patriotism*. Engraved for the *Westminster Gazette* at this time, it showed America in the form of an Indian woman, with dagger in one hand and tomahawk in the other, attacking Britannia under the complacently approving gaze of John Wilkes, Lord Chatham, Charles James Fox and other members of the Opposition who, 'with an effrontery beyond example in any other age or nation . . . assume the name of Patriots'. For Johnson, of course, this kind of patriotism was 'the last refuge of a scoundrel'.

9

THE BATTLE
FOR NEW YORK

*'There is something exceedingly
mysterious in the conduct of the
enemy.'*

George Washington

A week after the Declaration of Independence was signed in Philadelphia, General Henry Clinton left the coast of South Carolina and,
with the troops who had failed to take Charleston, sailed north to
New York. Here, at Staten Island in New York harbour south of
Manhattan, he joined forces with General Howe who had brought
his nine thousand men down from Halifax, Nova Scotia a few weeks
before.

Howe, in conjunction with his brother, Admiral Viscount Howe,
who had been appointed naval Commander-in-Chief in North America, had been charged to treat with the rebel Americans and to take
measures for the restoration of peace with the colonies. But this was
before the Declaration of Independence; and when the Admiral
arrived in America, Washington declined to see him, while Congress
refused to withdraw the Declaration, which the brothers had orders
not to accept. Since the Americans would not consider using this
'door to retreat', as Lord George Germain described it, further force
must be used 'to crush [their] rebellious resistance'.

Lord Howe's arrival in American waters aboard the *Eagle* was soon
followed by that of the reinforcements and the camp equipment for
which his brother had been waiting. By the middle of August General
Howe had some thirty thousand troops, a quarter of them Germans,

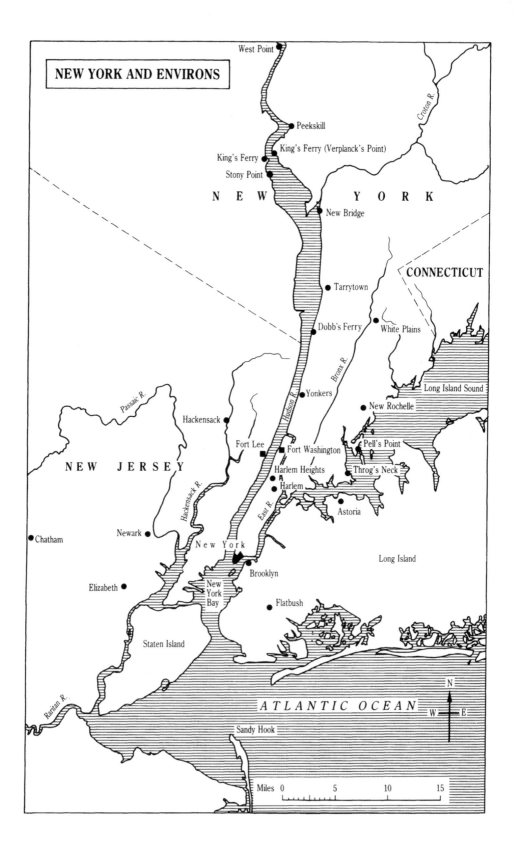

NEW YORK AND ENVIRONS

West Point

Peekskill

King's Ferry (Verplanck's Point)

King's Ferry

Stony Point

N E W   **Y O R K**

New Bridge

CONNECTICUT

Croton R.

Tarrytown

Dobb's Ferry

White Plains

Long Island Sound

Passaic R.

Hudson R.

Bronx R.

Yonkers

New Rochelle

Hackensack

Pell's Point

Fort Lee

Fort Washington

N E W   J E R S E Y

Harlem Heights

Throg's Neck

Harlem

Hackensack R.

East R.

Astoria

Chatham

Newark

New York

Long Island

Brooklyn

Elizabeth

New York Bay

Flatbush

Staten Island

Raritan R.

A T L A N T I C   O C E A N

N

W — E

Sandy Hook

Miles 0   5   10   15

under his command, including the regiments that General Clinton and Lord Cornwallis had brought up from Cape Fear. They were in much better heart than the British army had been in Halifax, and far better disciplined, Howe was sure, than the greatly outnumbered forces at Washington's disposal. With naval support of ten ships of the line and twenty frigates, and in command of the largest British army which had ever been landed on an alien shore, Howe was ready at last to make his long-planned assault on New York, to take command of the Hudson River, the most convenient overland route to Canada, and thus to drive a wedge between the rebels who could then be defeated separately, first above New York and then below it.

Throughout the summer Washington had been preparing his defences, which now stretched across Long Island, and had occupied forts commanding the Hudson River as well as entrenchments on Brooklyn Heights. Although many of his men were anxious to get home, spirits in camp had been high ever since news of the Declaration of Independence had reached New York on 9 July, to be greeted with cheers whose reverberating echoes were carried across the waters of the Narrows. That day a large crowd of militiamen and civilians had broken through the gate in the railings that surrounded the statue of King George III in Bowling Green, had knocked off the head, which was put on display in a tavern, and, to the beating of drums and the playing of pipes, to cheers and singing, had marched off with the lead body which was melted down for bullets.

A few weeks later, on the morning of 22 August 1776, after a stormy night during which the wind howled across the encampments, numerous small boats carried wave after wave of British and German soldiers across the Narrows to Gravesend on Long Island, the British sitting down in the boats with their muskets, bayonets fixed, between their knees, the Germans standing stiffly to attention, Hessian grenadiers in blue, Jägers in green with red facings. All seemed eager for the fight, and their officers were glad to get them on the move. The Germans had behaved well enough on Staten Island, despite their reputation for being avid plunderers, 'without any discrimination', so Governor Wentworth said, 'of rebel or loyalist'. They had sung hymns as loud as the Yankees, Lord Rawdon thought, though it had to be 'owned they have not the godly twang through the nose which distinguishes the faithful'; and, affecting to despise the colonists, whom they looked forward to 'lambasting mightily', they had not generally bothered their women. The British troops, on the other hand, had become as 'riotous as satyrs' after eating the fresh meat of which they had been so long deprived. 'A girl cannot step into the bushes to pluck a rose,' Rawdon had said, 'without running the most imminent risk of being ravished, and they are so little accustomed to these vigorous methods that they don't bear them with the proper resignation, and of consequence we have the most entertaining court-martials every day.' In the south the women behaved 'much better in these cases', Rawdon added, if he could judge from the instance of one who had been raped by seven of his men. She had gone to him to complain of her treatment: not of this sexual abuse, she assured him, but because one of the men had 'taken an old prayer book for which she had a particular affection'.

The first wave of troops were landed on Long Island without opposition; and, as the American advance parties retired, burning behind them all buildings which might afford the enemy shelter, four British battalions moved forward to the small village of Flatbush where from a nearby wood they came under a troublesome fire which, by the night of 25 August, had cost them about forty casualties.

The next evening the advance was resumed, General Clinton, followed by Major-General Lord Percy, moving towards the Americans' left, and then turning east over the high ground and behind their rear towards Bedford. At the same time the German General, Philip von Heister, advanced against the rebels' main body in the centre, where Major-General John Sullivan was in command; while James Grant, with nine battalions and ten guns, attacked the Americans' right along the Narrows' coast, supported by Lord Cornwallis. This plan of attack had been largely proposed by Clinton who, anxious to repair the damage done to his reputation by the débâcle at Charleston, had gone on a lengthy reconnaissance, over ground he remembered from his boyhood, with Lord Rawdon and Sir William Erskine, a young staff officer, who had taken the plan enthusiastically to headquarters. Evidently annoyed by Clinton's interference, Howe at first rejected the scheme: it was framed in typical 'German jargon' and altogether savoured 'too much of the German school'. According to Erskine, Howe went so far as to say that, since 'the rebels [knew] nothing of turning a flank, such a movement would have *no* effect'. On reflection, however, the Commander-in-Chief recognized the virtue of Clinton's plan and decided to adopt it.

The operation was completely successful. The British, out-manoeuvring the Americans, obtained their objectives with the loss of fewer than four hundred men and twenty-one officers killed and wounded. They took almost two thousand prisoners, including the general officer commanding the right flank, William Alexander, a man from New Jersey who, in defiance of a ruling of the House of Lords, claimed the title of Earl of Stirling. American casualties amounted to a further three thousand or so officers and men, several of whom were drowned as they retreated through a swamp. One young American said:

> It is impossible for me to describe the confusion and horror of the scene: the artillery flying with the chains over the horses' backs, our men running in almost every direction, and run which way they would, they were almost sure to meet the British or Hessians. And the enemy huzzahing when they took prisoners made it truly a day of distress to the Americans. I escaped . . . and entered a swamp or marsh through which a great many of our men were retreating. Some of them were mired and crying to the fellows for God's sake to help them out; but every man was intent on his own safety and no assistance was rendered. At the side of the marsh there was a pond which I took to be a millpond. Numbers, as they came to this pond, jumped in, and some were drowned . . . Out of the eight men in our company who were on guard the day before . . . I only escaped. The others were either killed or taken prisoners.

The British were encouraged not only by their victory over the American troops but by their reception by the civilians of Long Island. 'The Inhabitants received us with the Utmost Joy,' Captain John Bowater told Lord Denbigh, 'having been long oppress'd for their Attachment to Goverment. They sell their things to the Soldiers at the most Reasonable Terms ... . They like our Gold and Silver better than the Congress paper money.' The welcome accorded to their troops on Long Island deeply gratified the British command. It was, after all, more important to win the confidence of the American people than to defeat their rebel soldiers. As General James Robertson was to put it, 'I never had an idea of subduing the Americans; I meant to assist the good Americans to subdue the bad.'

Howe was, however, as reluctant to follow up his victory as he had been to begin the attack until he had received all the men and equipment he could reasonably expect. 'There is,' Washington said, 'something exceedingly mysterious in the conduct of the enemy.' Israel Putnam thought so too. 'General Howe,' he commented, 'is either our friend or no general.' While the rebels remained entrenched on Brooklyn Heights, the British General was evidently unwilling to risk either the heavy loss of life which his army had suffered in taking Bunker Hill or the possibility of a defeat which would have such widespread political consequences. Also, he hoped that Washington's retreat would be cut off by British ships sailing up the East River between Brooklyn and Manhattan; and this the Royal Navy might well have accomplished had not a violent storm, which flooded both camps, prevented the ships from sailing. As it was, anxious to get away from Brooklyn while he still could, Washington gave orders for the whole of his force there to be evacuated and brought back immediately into New York across the stretch of water now spanned by Brooklyn Bridge.

His men were exhausted and soaked by the constant rain; their powder was wet, their firearms clogged with mud; their only food was pickled pork. Facing them were over twenty thousand well-trained troops, almost twice the number of men at his own command.

As they marched down to the scores of small craft assembled along the waterfront, the noise they made as they stumbled through the dark aroused a woman who had so annoyed her neighbours by making no secret of her preference for English tea that her house had been fired at. When she saw what was going on, she sent a black servant to warn the British; but, as he tried to get through to Howe's headquarters, the man was intercepted by a German officer who, unable to understand a word the man said, had him arrested as a spy.

Fortune favoured Washington in other ways, too; part of the American rearguard withdrew prematurely; but he sent them back and they arrived in their sodden trenches before their absence had been noted. And then, as dawn approached and all would otherwise have been revealed, a thick fog descended, hiding his men's movements from view. By seven o'clock on the morning of 30 August all his men and most of his stores were safely on the other shore of the East River.

Once again it was felt that, as soon as the withdrawal had become known in the British camp, Howe should have acted to disrupt it. It was rumoured that, even now, he was hoping that the colonists might be persuaded to come to terms. Indeed, his brother, the Admiral, did have a meeting with John Adams and other members of Congress at this time at a house on Staten Island, where Lord Howe entertained them to a splendid meal of cold meats and excellent claret; but nothing came of the meeting other than an exchange of guarded pleasantries. In any event, the only response the British made to the withdrawal was a scattered firing by their picquets on the rearguard. 'The having to deal with a generous, merciful *forbearing* enemy who would take no unfair *advantages*,' Sir George Collier, commander of the frigate *Rainbow*, wrote sardonically,

> must have been highly satisfactory to General Washington . . . For *many succeeding* days did our brave veterans . . . stand on the banks of the East River, like Moses on Mount Pisgat, looking at their promised land, little more than half a mile distant. The Rebels' standard waved insolently in the air, from many different quarters of New York. The British troops could scarcely contain their indignation at the sight and at their own *inactivity*. The officers were *displeased and amazed*, not being able to account for the strange delay.

Their commander, however, had decided that New York could be won without further loss of life, since Washington's position there was now virtually untenable. And Howe was far from being alone in believing this. 'Everything seems to be over with them,' wrote Lord Percy. 'I flatter myself that this campaign will put an end to the war.' British ships could now be seen both in the East River and, on the other side of New York, in the Hudson River, sailing as far up the Hudson as Bloomingdale and in the East River to Turtle Bay. Moreover, while the British and German troops were eager to press on, having given the rebels what one of their officers described as a 'damned crush', the Americans were thoroughly dispirited. Many, persuading themselves that the war was as good as over, had set off for home; others remained only to plunder. Washington and the Rhode Island ironmaster, Major-General Nathanael Greene, made up their minds, therefore, that New York must be abandoned, and Greene insisted that it should first be burned to the ground: two-thirds of it, so it was estimated, belonged to Tories, anyway. Some officers on Washington's staff, however, advised delay.

On 15 September Howe took the initiative by sending a strong force under General Clinton across the East River to land at Kipp's Bay on Manhattan Island, an inlet now the site of 34th Street, about three miles above New York, while the fleet bombarded the Americans' entrenchments.

'As we approached [Kipp's Bay] we saw the breastworks filled with men and two or three large columns marching down in great parade to support them,' recalled Lord Rawdon.

> The Hessians, who were not used to this water business and who conceived that it must be exceedingly uncomfortable to be shot at whilst they were quite defenceless and jammed so close together, began to sing hymns immediately. Our men expressed their feelings as strongly, though in a different manner, by damning themselves and the enemy indiscriminately with wonderful fervency.
>
> The ships had not as yet fired a shot but upon a signal from us, they began the most tremendous peal I ever heard. The breastworks were blown to pieces in a few minutes, and those who were to have defended them were happy to escape as quick as possible through the ravines. The columns broke instantly, and betook themselves to the nearest woods for shelter. We pressed to shore, landed, and formed without losing a single man. As we were without artillery, upon an island where the enemy might attack us with five times our number, and as many cannon as he thought proper, it was necessary to attain some post where we might maintain ourselves till we were reinforced, which we knew could not be done quickly. We accordingly attacked and forced a party of the rebels from the Inchenberg, a very commanding height, taking from them a new brass howitzer, some waggons of ammunition, and the tents of three or four battalions who were encamped on it.

About three hundred Americans and sixty-seven of their guns were captured; and, although Washington succeeded in withdrawing most of the rest of his forces to Harlem Heights – where they took up a strong position protected from the British fleet by two forts on opposite banks of the Hudson River, Fort Lee and Fort Washington, and by batteries commanding Harlem Creek – the British entered New York in triumph. Cheering Tories came out in the streets to welcome them, lifting officers shoulder-high, waving British flags and pointing out the houses of leading rebels which were marked with the letter R.

Soon after the British occupation of New York, in the early hours of 21 September, a fierce fire broke out in a timber grog shop near Whitehall Strip. No warnings could be given, as church bells had been carted off to melt down for ammunition; and no fire-engines could be found. So, within hours, the flames spread throughout the town. Nearly five hundred buildings were destroyed, and before the flames were at last extinguished, a large part of New York had been reduced to ashes. Supposed to be the work of incendiaries who, so Captain William Congreve said, 'even set fire to houses when they saw our Sailors and Soldiers pursuing them and were killed in the very act', the fire was certainly as much a misfortune for Howe, who had intended using the houses of New York as winter quarters for his men, as it was advantageous to the American commanders who, in General Greene's words, had good cause to thank 'Providence, or some good honest fellow', for doing more for them than they were disposed to do for themselves. Ambrose Serle, General Howe's secretary, had no doubt who was responsible for the fire:

> Some rebels who lurked about the town, set it on fire, and some of them were caught with matches and fire-balls about them. One man, detected in the act, was knocked down by a grenadier and thrown into the flames for his reward. Another who was found cutting off the handles of the water buckets to prevent their use, was first hung up by the neck till he was dead and afterwards by the heels upon a sign post by the sailors. Many others were seized on account of combustibles found upon them, and secured and, but for the officers, most of them would have been killed by the enraged populace and soldiery. The New England people are maintained to be at the bottom of this plot, which they have long since threatened to put into execution.

The fire was at least partially responsible for Howe's failure yet again to follow up his victory against a disheartened enemy whose forces, so spies reported, were on the verge of breaking up and whose conduct in the recent fighting had much disappointed their leaders. 'Good God!' Washington was reported to have cried as he flung his hat to the ground in despair at the unwillingness of his men to stand their ground, 'Good God! Have I got such troops as those!' For once he had lost control of himself, and had lashed out with his cane at the officers and men of a Connecticut brigade who had fled past him in their anxiety to escape the advancing redcoats.

For over three weeks the two armies faced each other on Manhattan Island, occasionally shouting good-natured insults across the lines and even exchanging presents. Indeed, according to the American General, William Heath, they were

> so civil to each other, on their posts, that one day, at a part of the creek where it was practicable, a British sentinel asked an American, who was nearly opposite to him, if he could give him a chew of tobacco: the latter, having in his pocket a piece of a thick twisted roll, sent it across the creek to the British sentinel who, after taking off his bite, sent the remainder back again.

It was not until 12 October that Howe, after careful preparations, resumed his ponderous attack by embarking most of his men in boats, sending them north-eastwards in a thick fog through the perilous channel known as Hell Gate and landing them on Throg's Neck, the peninsula jutting out into Long Island Sound. Howe's intention had been to advance along Throg's Neck over a causeway across swampy ground to strike at the Americans' entrenchments from their flank and rear. But Washington, having had the causeway demolished, had taken up a strong position at its far end; and so Howe embarked his men again and landed them further up the East River at Pell's Point. From here he advanced to New Rochelle.

Nine days had now passed since the British had resumed their advance; and Washington had been given time to alter his dispositions to meet the threat which the British now posed. He had brought his men round to face the enemy; and, leaving garrisons in Fort Washington, which stood above the Hudson River looking across to New Jersey, and in Fort Lee on the opposite bank of the river, he established a series of entrenchments along the high ground stretching from Kingsbridge in the south to White Plains in the north, his front protected by the deep Bronx River every ford of which he defended.

As the British advanced north towards the clapboard houses and Presbyterian church of White Plains, with the river on their left, Washington drew in as many men as he could afford to defend his threatened camp. The ensuing battle on 28 October was a fierce one. The Germans were the first to receive the fire of Washington's advance party and, as one of the American officers wrote, they were 'scattered like leaves in a whirlwind, and retreated so far' that his own men were able to run forward, pick up the arms and equipment of the Germans who had been killed, and to carry off a quantity of their rum which they drank before the enemy resumed their attack.

> They advanced in solid columns . . . The scene was grand and solemn; all the adjacent hills smoked as though on fire, and bellowed and trembled with a perpetual cannonade and fire of field pieces, howitzers and mortars. The air groaned with streams of cannon and musket-shot. The hills smoked and echoed terribly with the bursting of shells; the fences and walls were knocked down and torn to pieces, and men's legs, arms and bodies, mangled with cannon and grapeshot all around us.

A soldier from Connecticut was appalled by the sight of this mutilation, which he could never forget. One ball 'first took off the head of Smith, a stout heavy man, and dashed it open, then took Taylor across the bowels. It then struck Sergeant Garrett of our company on the hip [and] took off the point of the hip bone . . . he died the same day . . . Oh! What a sight it was to see within a distance of six rods those men with their legs and arms and guns and packs all in a heap.'

The British advance, steady but slow, came to a halt the next day, while Howe, cautious as ever and waiting to be joined by a German division which had just disembarked, prepared batteries to fire upon the Americans' main position at White Plains. At last, on 31 October, all was ready for the final assault. But then a heavy rainstorm led him to cancel his orders and the next day Washington, who well knew that he 'should on all occasions avoid a general action', retired while he still safely could, withdrawing five miles across the Croton River to a strong position at North Castle.

Content to leave him there for the moment, Howe turned his attention towards Fort Washington whose garrison, under command of Colonel Robert Magaw, was now isolated. Magaw, however, was convinced that he could hold out for at least a month. The position was certainly an extremely strong one. To the rear was the river over which Magaw intended to escape, if he must, to New Jersey. The steep slopes in front were densely wooded; and where the approaches were not protected by natural defences, by rocks and deep ravines, they were barred by entrenchments and batteries. General Greene supported Magaw in his belief that Fort Washington was virtually impregnable; and although Washington himself, not sharing their confidence, felt that both this stronghold and Fort Lee should be abandoned, he allowed himself to be persuaded to hold on to them.

On 15 November, General Howe, who had fallen back from White Plains to Dobb's Ferry on the Hudson River, sent one of his staff to Fort Washington with a drummer and another soldier carrying a white flag. The American commander was formally invited to surrender and given the traditional warning that, if he failed to do so, his entire garrison would be killed when the fort was taken. Having received the reply that Colonel Magaw, 'activated by the most glorious cause that mankind ever fought in', would defend the place 'to the last extremity', the British began their assault as the guns of the *Pearl* in the Hudson River and the batteries on the eastern bank of Harlem Creek cannonaded the American defences.

The British attacked on four well-directed fronts, Germans, Highlanders, Light Infantry and nine battalions of the line all advancing with determination under a heavy fire, scrambling over rocks, dragging cannon up steep, rough roads, clinging where necessary to the bushes which sprouted from the crevices, the officers urging their men forward with shouts and waving swords, and slowly driving the American outposts back. Lord Percy's column, originally intended as a diversion, prepared to lead the main assault against the fort where a little dog darted about behind the breastworks, tearing the fuses out of shells with its teeth until one exploded in its face.

At one o'clock the Americans, surrounded now by cannon and by troops with fixed bayonets, sent out a white flag of surrender. Some of the Germans seemed intent on fulfilling Howe's threat to put the entire garrison to the sword; but they were ordered to calm down and to take the men captive instead. Over 2800 prisoners were marched away, and immense stores of ammunition as well as guns were carted off. Howe had lost 440 men killed and wounded; two-thirds of them Germans and half of the rest from the 42nd Highlanders. But he was now in possession of the whole of Manhattan Island, and was well placed to seize Fort Lee on the New Jersey shore.

Lord Cornwallis and a flying column of 4500 men were sent across the river without delay. So sudden, indeed, was this attack on Fort Lee that the Americans had scarcely time to get away before the British were upon them. When Cornwallis's men burst into the fort only twelve men remained, all of them incapably drunk. The garrison's tents still stood unfolded; outside them pots were boiling on camp fires; tables were laid for the officers' dinner, loaded guns abandoned.

The British set off in pursuit of an enemy that constantly eluded them, 'neither fighting nor totally running away', as one British officer put it, 'always keeping a day's march out of reach'. On 6 December, Cornwallis and Howe joined forces and continued their advance together as Washington's army seemed ever closer to disintegration.

By the time he reached Princeton, closely followed by Howe's advance guard, Washington had scarcely three thousand men with him; and when, soon afterwards, he crossed the Delaware at Trenton many of these had deserted. Having removed all boats on the river, he was able to frustrate Howe's further advance and to escape into Pennsylvania. But his position there seemed desperate enough: New York and Manhattan Island were lost; General Clinton had been landed at Newport by Sir Peter Parker and had, without resistance, occupied Rhode Island as a base for harassing American shipping. The British appeared well placed to end the war as soon as the winter was over.

Certainly in England there was a general feeling that the uprising in the colonies was as good as suppressed. Compliments were showered upon the Howe brothers in newspapers, in official despatches and in private letters. Lord Howe was warmly congratulated by Lord Sandwich, General Howe by Lord George Germain. Hans Stanley, Governor of the Isle of Wight, expressed the general opinion when he wrote to a friend in America to say, 'You will hear from others, and may easily imagine the general Joy which your successes have occasioned, the great Honour and Popularity the two Howe Brothers have acquired.'

10

GENERALS AT LOGGERHEADS

'We never had agreed upon any single question.'

Sir William Howe

The optimistic mood in the British camp after the rebels had been driven from New York seemed to General Clinton wholly unjustified. General Howe in particular, so Clinton thought, had little cause for self-congratulation. Admittedly he had pushed Washington back from New York, the city which dominated communications in the American colonies; but he had not succeeded in bringing him to a decisive battle.

In the later stages of the campaign, Clinton had besieged the Commander-in-Chief with letters of advice and criticism until Howe was utterly exasperated. When Clinton took it upon himself to modify slightly some minor order which Howe had given him and, characteristically, pointed out at some length his reasons for doing so, the Commander-in-Chief brusquely instructed his subordinate to stop arguing and do as he was told. 'I cannot bear to serve under him,' Clinton expostulated to Cornwallis. He would rather have just three independent companies than be second-in-command in such a man's army. 'If I cannot serve with them I like,' he complained on another occasion, 'I had rather not serve at all.'

He made up his mind to apply for leave and go home. He had been quite long enough away from his children and from his dead wife's sisters, of whom he was so fond. He longed to escape from Howe;

he was also deeply anxious to make it clear to all in authority at home
that the blame for the Charleston fiasco did not lie with him. As soon
as permission was received, Clinton accordingly left for England,
leaving Lord Percy in command on Rhode Island.

Percy was not there long. Clinton had been careful not to offend
the Rhode Islanders: he had ordered his officers to keep an exceptionally firm hold over their men; and so successful had they been in
doing so that only one case of rape was reported, and little was stolen
other than fencing for use as firewood in the intense cold. The local
people, many of them Quakers, responded by promising to return
to their allegiance to the King – against whom, in any event, their
religious convictions prevented them from taking up arms. Before
leaving, Clinton had impressed upon Lord Percy the importance of
doing nothing to disturb this peace, in fact 'to do everything but act'.
Howe had advised an attack on Providence; but, in Clinton's opinion,
this was out of the question in the present weather conditions. The
naval commander, Peter Parker, 'according to custom', did not agree
with Clinton: on the contrary, he thought 'something should be
tried', and, to the General's fury let it be known in London that he
had advocated an action that might well have seemed feasible there
but was certainly not to be contemplated by officers on the spot.

After Clinton's departure, Lord Percy, another officer of the 'German' persuasion, was criticized by Howe for the way the Rhode
Island operation had been conducted. Since the enemy had had 'no
force whatever at Providence' when possession had been taken of
Rhode Island, Howe contended, it 'would have been a most important
stroke' to have occupied the town. Howe went on to criticize the
subsequent administration of the Rhode Island garrison, the size of
the staff and the methods of command, and to insist that support
must be given to Commodore Parker in any naval operation he
considered appropriate. Lord Percy was as unwilling to submit to
such blunt reproach as Clinton had been. He refused to lay himself
open to 'indignity', maintaining that he would rather 'quit the service
than remain here any longer'. He wrote to Howe to tell him so: 'As
I find, Sir, that the accounts of commissaries, midshipmen, and others
are so much more depended on than any information I have the
honour to transmit . . . permit me to return home to England.'

While protesting he was 'most sensibly hurt' by Lord Percy's letter,
Howe granted the request. Percy returned to England where, having

fallen foul of King George III who complained of that 'peevish temper for which he has ever been accused', he became a troublesome member of the Opposition to Lord North.

Between bouts of heavy drinking and evenings spent in the company of Elizabeth Loring, the pretty and complaisant wife of an American Loyalist, Joshua Loring, whom he had appointed to the profitable office of Commissary of Prisoners of War, Howe considered his plans for the coming year's campaign. He had first proposed an advance upon Albany in two strong columns from New York and Rhode Island, while a third column came down from Canada. But now he turned his attention to Philadelphia, the largest city in America, an attractive place of pale red brick which the Continental Congress had adopted as their headquarters. Since so many people in New Jersey and Pennsylvania had been coming in of late in response to a British proclamation promising pardons for past offences to those who submitted to royal authority, Howe expressed his confidence that the fall of Philadelphia would decide the issue once and for all. He outlined his new plan in a letter to Lord George Germain a few days before Christmas. This plan, he wrote in a subsequent letter, would require reinforcements of between fifteen and twenty thousand men.

Germain confessed that he had been 'really alarmed' by a previous request for reinforcements on this scale; he had decided then that Howe would have to be content with a further 7800 men which, so Germain calculated, would bring his total strength up to 35,000. He now replied to Howe that even that figure was out of the question; he could expect reinforcements of no more than 2900. But as to Howe's plan for a move against Philadelphia, Germain assured him that the King entirely approved of it, 'being of the opinion that the reasons which had induced him to recommend the change in his operations were solid and decisive'.

Howe's ability to carry out these operations successfully would largely depend upon the support he could expect from the army in Canada and the skill with which it was led. Overcoming his personal dislike of the man, he himself proposed that General Clinton should be given command of this army, and his proposal was at first approved by both Germain and the King.

*   *   *

The Government's handling of the Canadian command had already outraged General Carleton, still Governor of Quebec, a particular *bête noire* of Germain's whose dislike of him was fervently returned. Carleton had been created a Knight of the Bath after his success in driving the Americans from Quebec; and he had since been assured by Germain that the King placed complete confidence in his zeal and loyal attachment to his service. But he had also been told that his account of his recent operations and present strength was regrettably brief. To this he huffily replied that he had been rather occupied of late driving the Americans out of Canada, 'a task which was happily executed long before [he] could profit by any Instructions [his] Lordship might think it necessary to favour [him] with'. Since then Carleton had been informed that his services were no longer required in military command, only in his civil capacity as Governor of Quebec: it was proposed to place the army in other hands for the forthcoming campaign. To his further annoyance and dismay, Carleton had not only not been invited to join the Howes' peace commission, as he felt he should have been, but he had also been given the most detailed instructions by Germain as to how to administer the complicated internal affairs of his province. Adding fuel to his resentment, the American Secretary had subsequently informed him that Lieutenant-Colonel Gabriel Christie, the officer who had failed to provide Carleton's bateaux for the previous campaign, was being sent out as his Quartermaster-General, an appointment which he had already given to his brother, Thomas Carleton. When Christie, a known opponent of the Quebec Act, arrived in Canada, which he knew well, Carleton informed him that his services were not required and demanded that he be recalled. Christie retaliated by sending his friend Germain a long letter detailing Carleton's utter incompetence.

Carleton had good reason to feel that his position and authority in Canada were also being undermined by his second-in-command, John Burgoyne, who, as soon as he had arrived in England, had set about promoting his own interests at the expense of his rivals. Carleton did not doubt that Burgoyne was assuring the government that their forces ought to have pushed on to Ticonderoga after successfully defending Quebec, and should not have been withdrawn to Canada. Carleton also felt sure that Burgoyne was condemning him for abandoning Crown Point after his subordinate's departure for London. And in this Carleton was quite right. 'I must honour

Carleton's abilities and judgement,' Burgoyne had written home shortly before his departure for London. 'I have lived with him on the best terms and bear him friendship. I am therefore doubly hurt that he has taken a step in which I can be not otherwise serviceable to him than by silence.'

Burgoyne did not, however, remain silent when, the day after his arrival in England, he had an interview with Lord George Germain. Nor did he hide his reservations about Carleton's behaviour to the King, who received him a fortnight later and who was clearly not impressed by the rather vague memorandum of Carleton's proposals for future operations which Burgoyne had brought with him and submitted to the government. 'Perhaps,' the King commented, 'Carleton may be too cold and not so active as might be wished.' This was a view shared by Germain, who described the recent Canadian campaign as being 'conducted without sense or vigour' and who was not unhappy to find a man whom he so disliked being subjected to royal criticism.

It was generally agreed, in fact, that Carleton must not be left in command in Canada, that his withdrawal from Crown Point had, in Germain's words, allowed a 'very considerable number of the insurgents' to march from Ticonderoga to join the 'rebel forces in New York and Jersey, thus threatening the winter quarters that were taken up by the army under the command of Sir William Howe'. It was also agreed that Carleton's furious and vituperative response to all criticisms of his conduct made his removal virtually inevitable. Yet by the end of February 1777 it had still not been decided who was to succeed him.

General Clinton remained the favourite candidate. He had sent his aide-de-camp, Captain Duncan Drummond, to England before he himself sailed, to find out how matters stood and how he was likely to be received. Drummond had been to see Germain, who seemed cordial enough until mention was made of the manner in which the Charleston affair had been reported in England. Germain said that it appeared from his 'laconic way of writing' that General Clinton was 'hurt at what had happened'. Drummond replied that Clinton was, indeed, upset, 'very much so, at only an extract of his letter', explaining the reasons for the setback at Charleston, being published. 'The conversation upon this was immediately dropped.'

The Charleston affair and Clinton's attitude towards it were also mentioned when Drummond was received by the King. 'How does Clinton do?' the King asked in his hurried manner. 'Is his mind easy? Why does he plague himself so much, when it was impossible for him to do more? I am thoroughly well satisfied with every part of his conduct. I have as high an opinion of him as any officer in my service.'

When Clinton received Drummond's report of these conversations, he was not altogether convinced that he was regarded as favourably as the court and government would have him believe. In his mistrustful way he thought it significant that his aide-de-camp had been given £500 on announcing the news of the capture of Rhode Island but, although the 'oldest captain in the world', had not been promoted as officers bearing such news so often were.

Clinton considered himself better suited to the Canadian command than any other general, certainly more so than Burgoyne who, while older than himself, was junior in rank and had seen so much less service in America. Yet the government was coming to the view that Burgoyne – who was better liked in the Army than either the reserved and formal Carleton or the touchy, fretful Clinton – was the man for the Canadian campaign. To expect Clinton to work amicably with Carleton was absurd, whereas Burgoyne's charm might help to alleviate the jealousy his appointment was certain to arouse. In fact, when Burgoyne's appointment was finally announced, Carleton was so enraged that he demanded his own immediate recall as a victim of gross injustice.

Burgoyne owed his appointment at least partly to a lengthy memorandum about future operations in America which he had submitted to the government as an appendix to Carleton's far less impressive and far shorter document. He had proposed three alternative schemes and had suggested that the government choose the one that seemed most practicable. The forces required for the implementation of the plans were quite modest: eight thousand regulars, a suitable complement of artillery, a corps of watermen, two thousand Canadians and about one thousand Indians. The government and the King were convinced by Burgoyne's arguments. With some modifications they accepted the second of his three proposals; and, in March 1777, they informed him that he would have the responsibility of carrying it into effect.

In its essentials the plan of campaign, designed to isolate New

Right: British troops of the 29th Regiment open fire on a threatening mob in 'the Boston Massacre' of 5 March 1770. Captain Preston is shown in the left foreground attempting to prevent them

Above: Crowds cheer as rebels, disguised as Mohawks, hurl chests of imported tea into Boston harbour by Griffin's Wharf on 16 December 1773

Left: Frederick, Lord North, King George III's Prime Minister throughout the war from 1770 until his resignation in 1782, after the surrender at Yorktown

Left: John Burgoyne, general, playwright and man about town, whose forces surrendered to the American rebels at Saratoga in October 177

Above: Major-General Sir Henry Clinton, the shy, tactless and touchy officer who was appointed Commander-in-Chief in America in 1778

Left: Lord George Germain, as Secretary of State for the American Department in Lord North's administration, was responsible for the conduct of the war from November 1775 until he was replaced in 1782, shortly before the Government's resignation and the abolition of his office

Left: Charles Lee, the eccentric, English-born officer who was appointed by Congress to high command in the rebel army in June 1775. According to Samuel Adams, you had to love his dogs if you were to gain his own regard. This caricature by Barham Rushbrooke was 'allowed by all who knew General Lee to be the only successful delineation either of his countenance or person'

Right: 'Bunker's Hill or America's Head Dress'. The extravagant hair styles of the time are burlesqued as well as the conduct of the British soldiers, who are shown firing at each other beneath flags decorated with a goose, an ape and women holding darts of lightning

Below: 'Six-Pence a Day'. In this anti-recruiting satire, the lot of the British soldier and his starving family is contrasted with that of the sedan chairman and the coachman. Even the chimney-sweeper's climbing-boy earns twice as much as the redcoat who is under fire from the cannon of American rebels

Left: On 9 July 1776 the statue of King George III in Bowling Green, New York – which had been erected there by the city's General Assembly after the repeal of the Stamp Act – was pulled down and destroyed. Those responsible were white militiamen and civilians, no black slaves as shown in this engraving by François Xavier Habermann

Right: Soon after the British occupation of New York, a fire, believed to be the work of incendiaries, broke out in a timber grog shop. Almost five hundred buildings were destroyed

Right: General Burgoyne's camp on the Hudson River, three miles above Stillwater, in September 1777. The drawing, from Thomas Anburey's *Travels through the Interior Parts of America*, shows Brigadier-General Simon Fraser's funeral procession winding its way round the hill on the right

Above: 'The Conference between the Brothers How to get Rich': a caricature of October 1777, the month of Saratoga, attacking the Howes for what was alleged to be their inaction and greed. 'The nation from impatience of news, grew much dissatisfied,' wrote Horace Walpole, 'and the Howes were infinitely abused and accused of thinking of nothing but their vast profits.' The cabbages in the background are a reference to the profits which the Howes were supposed to be making from the perquisites of their respective commands. 'To cabbage' meant to pilfer, as tailors did the pieces of cloth ('the cabbages') which they cut off when making clothes

Left: A self-portrait of Major John André, Clinton's versatile adjutant-general, drawn shortly before his execution by hanging as a spy on 2 October 1780. 'The sympathy of the American officers was universally expressed.'

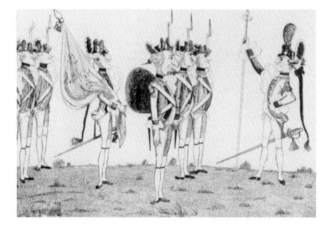

Below left: 'The Count de Rochambeau, French General of the Land Forces in America, Reviewing the French Troops': a caricature published in London in November 1780, one of a number issued at this time burlesquing the French army and its intervention in America. Rochambeau, who was narrowly to escape the guillotine in the French Revolution, had landed at Rhode Island in July 1780 with some six thousand men

Foot: On 15 March 1781 Lord Cornwallis defeated the rebels at Guilford, North Carolina. Tarleton's dragoons, which were in fact held back in reserve, are here shown advancing from a copse. Cornwallis's field guns, one of which is in action on the left, brought down as many British guardsmen as rebel soldiers

Above: 'The Savages let loose or the Cruel Fate of the Loyalists.' It was widely felt in England that Loyalists were not being sufficiently protected by the peace negotiators. The losses incurred by Loyalists in the war were eventually referred by Congress to the various states, which declined to settle them. Many Loyalists escaped to Canada and Nova Scotia where they were compensated by the British Government

Above: A caricature of May 1782 showing Britannia and America embracing as France and Spain try to pull them apart. Fox tells Admiral Keppel to give the interlopers 'a Spank', while Holland stands by awaiting the outcome and smoking complacently. The European powers were anxious to profit by the rebels' victory either at Britain's or America's expense

Left: A British drummer and fifer

Below: German mercenaries of the Prince Carl Regiment

Below: American infantry sketched by Baron von Closen, aide-de-camp to the French commander, the Comte de Rochambeau. From the left, a black light infantryman of the 1st Rhode Island Regiment, a musketeer of the 2nd Canadian Regiment, a rifleman, and a gunner of the Continental Artillery

England from the other colonies, was simple enough: Burgoyne, assisted by William Phillips in command of his artillery, was to lead his army down from Canada, through Ticonderoga and Lake George, to Albany where he would 'effect a junction with General Howe, or after cooperating so far as to get possession of Albany and open the communication to New York, to remain upon the Hudson River, and enable that General to act with his whole force to the southward'. At the same time Lieutenant-Colonel Barry St Leger was to make a diversion with a much smaller force of about seventeen hundred men, half of them Indians, down the Mohawk River. St Leger, too, was then to advance to Albany to support Howe. Howe himself was to cross the Delaware into Pennsylvania, to strike at the heart of revolutionary resistance, Philadelphia, then to move towards Albany.

When these plans were approved in principle and Burgoyne was given a letter of detailed instructions to hand over to Carleton, Germain added, 'I shall write to Sir William Howe from hence by the first packet.' This undertaking seems never to have been fulfilled. It appears that, after weeks of hard work in his office, Germain was anxious to get away to his country house in Sussex for the Easter holiday. As he was signing letters before his departure, his first deputy-secretary, William Knox, reminded him that no letter had been written to Howe to 'acquaint him with the plan and what was expected of him in consequence of it'. 'His Lordship,' so Knox said, 'started'; and when D'Oyley, his second deputy-secretary, said that he would write a few lines in a moment for his signature, Germain exclaimed, 'So, my poor horses must stand in the street all the time and I shan't be to my time anywhere.' D'Oyley then suggested that Lord George should leave; he himself would write to Howe and 'tell him everything that he would want to know'.

'With this, his lordship was satisfied, as it enabled him to keep his time, for he could never bear delay or disappointment.' But D'Oyley also was apparently in a hurry to get away for the holiday, since all he sent to Howe, it seems, was a covering note enclosing a copy of the instructions which were being taken by Burgoyne to Canada. Howe could therefore claim, and afterwards did claim, that he had never been instructed to advance towards Albany, while Burgoyne never knew for certain how or when his colleague was expected to co-operate with him.

★ ★ ★

Since Burgoyne was to be given the Canadian command, the King and the government realized only too well that Clinton would have to be compensated for his disappointment, particularly so since his ready sense of grievance might induce him to make trouble by publishing his own version of the events at Charleston and thus create further friction between the Army and the Navy. Why not, the King proposed, offer him a knighthood? There was at present no vacancy in the Order of the Bath, but this need not deter them in offering him a red ribbon. In return for this, General Clinton would surely agree not to publish any damaging revelations about Charleston and would consent to return as second-in-command to Howe.

Harvey, the Adjutant-General, was delegated to make the approach. Clinton, as might have been expected, regarded the offer with suspicion: it was clearly intended as recompense for an injury; in any case, he could not afford the fees payable for knighthood. Was he expected to meet them out of his own pocket? Clinton's suspicions were deepened when, later on that day, he went to see Lord George Germain who claimed that it was himself and not the King who had proposed the knighthood. The King, in fact, so Germain said, had not been too keen on the idea, suggesting that General Howe might object to a subordinate being honoured in this way. But Germain had put his mind at rest and the King had eventually agreed. It was hoped, however, that Clinton would now be willing to return to America as second-in-command and that no more would be said about Charleston. Yet, while agreeing reluctantly to go back, Clinton was unwilling to commit himself about the Charleston despatch. He must himself, he said, be the best judge of that affair. Germain 'argued', so Clinton commented, 'and I bowed'.

The conversation then passed to a general discussion about American strategy. Finally Germain assured Clinton that if 'any accident happened to Sir William Howe', he would have confidence that 'everything was safe' with Clinton, adding as a parting shot that he was confident, too, that Clinton would 'be cordial with the Navy'.

Upon his return to his 'very mortifying' command in America, Clinton was dismayed to find that the general plan of campaign conceived in London seemed to have no unifying theme: Burgoyne in his operations from the north appeared to have no very clear idea of what he was to do in co-operation with Howe once he had reached

Albany. Howe was apparently so taken up with his own invasion of Pennsylvania that he gave the impression of considering the ultimate co-operation with Burgoyne of little importance. Clinton himself was to be left behind on Manhattan Island with a dangerously small garrison of seven thousand men, nearly all of them Loyalists and Germans, and no very definite idea as to what to do with them. Letter after letter arrived from London; but none of them contained clear instructions which would have drawn the Generals' separate enterprises into a coherent whole.

In one of these letters, Germain, always optimistic on this point and ready to misinterpret despatches which contradicted his own opinions, expressed his belief that once the British army appeared in Pennsylvania, Loyalists would flock to their colours. Washington would be unable to oppose so strong a combined force and, provided that Howe's campaign was over in time for him to co-operate with Burgoyne's army, the 1777 campaigns would satisfactorily end the war. Neither Clinton nor Howe could share this blithe confidence. Disappointed in the number of reinforcements he had been promised, and well aware of the difficulty of bringing the Americans to battle – since they moved so much more quickly than his own heavily laden troops – Howe was forced to confess that his hopes of 'terminating the war this year [had] vanished'. Clinton, for his part, considered the whole proposed strategy 'misguided' and he did not hesitate in making his opinion known. It was absurd, he contended, to disperse the British forces in the way proposed. If Howe's army got into difficulties in Pennsylvania, if his men were to become debilitated by sickness in the heat of summer there, Washington would be able to strike at either Burgoyne or at Clinton's garrison in New York, which was scarcely strong enough to defend itself let alone take the American forts to the north of it, as Howe cheerfully proposed. Far better, Clinton suggested, for Howe to march north from New York, to effect a junction with Burgoyne and thus cut Washington's line of communications with New England. This really might well bring Washington to a general action. As it was, the rebels were being given an opportunity to 'murder' Clinton in New York.

The two men talked and argued, by turns acrimonious and conciliatory, at one moment endeavouring to come to an agreement, at another resigning themselves to irreconcilable differences. 'We never had agreed upon any single question,' Howe eventually contended.

Clinton responded by complaining that Howe had never thought well of him as an officer and that the army as a whole suspected this. No doubt he *was* rather awkward in manner, Clinton conceded; he *did* find it difficult to mix with people; he *was* of a reserved, shy nature. Yet he *did* feel compelled to offer his objections to a plan of campaign which might prove disastrous. One of Howe's own staff, Sir William 'Woolly' Erskine, agreed with Clinton that a march north towards Burgoyne would be far preferable to an invasion of Pennsylvania. But Lord Cornwallis derided them both. 'Faugh! Faugh!' he said flippantly, '"Woolly" only wants a junction with Burgoyne so that he may crack a bottle with his friend Phillips.'

Howe would not give way. Strongly supported by Lord Cornwallis – whose recent conduct, so Clinton said, 'displayed the most consummate ignorance' he had ever heard of 'in any officer above a corporal' – Howe insisted that he was not to be deflected from his purpose. 'I have sent my plan home,' he kept repeating, 'and it has been approved.'

11

WINTER ON THE DELAWARE

'Many of our soldiers had not a shoe to their feet and their clothes were ragged as those of a beggar.'

John Greenwood

There were times that winter when Washington despaired of bringing his army into the field against the British. A visitor to his headquarters one day in December 1776 found him 'much depressed'. He 'lamented the ragged and desolving state of his army in affecting terms'.

A week later he spoke to the men on parade, begging them not to go home as so many of them intended to do as soon as their period of enlistment was over, assuring them that their services were greatly needed, that they could do more now for their country than they would ever be able to do in the future. In 'the most affectionate manner', he 'entreated us to stay', wrote one of those whom he addressed:

> The drums beat for volunteers, but not a man turned out. The General wheeled his horse about, rode in front of the regiment, and addressing us again said, 'My brave fellows, you have done all I asked you to do, and more than could be reasonably expected; but your country is at stake, your wives, your houses, and all you hold dear. You have worn yourselves out with fatigues and hardships, but we know not how to spare you. If you will consent to stay only one month longer, you will render that service to the cause of liberty, and to your country, which you probably never can do

under any other circumstances. The present is emphatically the crisis which is to decide our destiny.' The drums beat a second time. The soldiers felt the force of the appeal. One said to another, 'I will remain if you will.' Others remarked, 'We cannot go home under such circumstances.' A few stepped forth, and their example was immediately followed by nearly all who were fit for duty in the regiment, amounting to about two hundred volunteers. An officer enquired of the General if these men should be enrolled. He replied, 'No! Men who will volunteer in such a case as this, need no enrolment to keep them to their duty.'

The soldiers whom Washington was able to induce to stay with his army, however, were still pitiably few; and many who might well have joined him were enticed away by the higher pay and bounties offered by the state militia. The foreign allies who, it was hoped, would join the army after the Declaration of Independence, had not yet arrived. Several units, notably the militiamen from Connecticut, had behaved so badly in the recent fighting that they could not be trusted to stand firm, while many officers were wholly unworthy of their commissions. Some officers, indeed, who were elected by their men and were expected to share their pay with them, were treated with as 'little respect as broomsticks'. Others, 'not fit to be shoeblacks', joined their soldiers on plundering expeditions; one acted as company barber; yet another was convicted of selling the company's blankets. Their captors were astonished by the sort of men among the prisoners of war who turned out to be American officers: 'Of those we took one major was a blacksmith, another a hatter. Of their captains there was a butcher . . . a tanner, a shoe-maker, a tavern-keeper, etc. Yet they all pretended to be gentlemen.' Many appeared to make no effort to ensure their men were even reasonably well clothed: some militiamen looked like beggars with torn coats and holes in their boots.

'At this time our troops were in a destitute and deplorable con-dition,' an American sergeant confirmed. 'The horses attached to our cannon were without shoes, and when passing over the ice they would slide in every direction and could advance only with the assistance of the soldiers. Our men too were without shoes or other comfortable clothing.' Even when a picked company was marched about to give encouragement to the civilian population, they did not look very impressive or well disciplined. They did not have 'quite the Air of Soldiers', wrote John Adams of a regiment which was marched through the streets of Philadelphia. 'They dont step exactly in Time. They dont hold up their Heads quite erect, nor turn out their toes so exactly as they ought. They dont all of them cock their Hats – and such as do, dont all wear them the same way.'

A French officer who served as Washington's engineer-in-chief was even less impressed by the drill of the American troops and considered that many of them were remarkably listless. 'They move without spring or energy,' he wrote, 'without vigour and without passion for the cause in which they are engaged. There is a hundred times more enthusiasm for [the] revolution in any one coffee house at Paris than in all the Thirteen Provinces united.'

There was, Washington told Congress, an urgent need for 'gentlemen and men of character' to come forward as officers, as well as for reliable men to be enlisted as soldiers for longer than the short terms previously considered appropriate. Congress eventually concurred, agreeing to raise an army of sixty thousand men enlisted for three years or for the duration of the war, and granting Washington powers to raise a further fifteen thousand men if he considered they were necessary. This new army could not, of course, be created quickly; and in the meantime, after the dispersal of so many of the regiments which had fought at New York, he had scarcely more than three thousand men under his command; and one of his leading generals, Charles Lee – who had clearly indicated his reluctance to serve under a Commander-in-Chief, a 'certain great man' whom he described as 'damnably deficient' – had disappeared somewhere in New Jersey, evidently hoping that Congress, given time, would recognize that he himself was far better qualified to lead their army than the Virginian amateur they had misguidedly appointed.

One day in December, Lee decided to take the evening off and to visit a place called Basking Ridge where an Irishwoman kept a tavern in which women could be enjoyed as well as liquor. After breakfast the next morning, Lee, dressed in exceptionally old and dirty clothes and wearing bedroom slippers, sat down to write a letter to Horatio Gates expressing his by now familiar opinions about the Commander-in-Chief who was unhinging 'the goodly fabrick' which other, more gifted, generals might create.

As Lee wrote, one of his aides, upon looking out of the window, was horrified to see a party of British cavalry in the uniforms of the Hon. William Harcourt's 16th Light Dragoons galloping down the lane less than a hundred yards away. The aide-de-camp, 'startled by this unexpected spectacle', exlaimed:

> 'Here, Sir, are the British cavalry!'
> 'Where?' replied the General who had signed his letter in the instant.
> 'Around the house' . . .
> General Lee appeared alarmed yet collected, and his second observation marked his self-possession: 'Where is the guard? – damn the guard, why don't they fire?' and after a momentary pause, turned to me and said, 'Do see what has become of the guard.'
> The woman of the house at this moment entered the room and proposed to him to conceal himself in a bed, which he rejected with evident disgust. I caught up with my pistols which lay on the table, thrust the letter he had been writing into my pocket, and passed into a room at the opposite end of the house, where I had seen the guard in the morning. Here I discovered their arms, but the men were absent. I stepped out of the door and perceived the dragoons chasing them in different directions.

Cornet Barnastre Tarleton, whom Colonel Harcourt had put in charge of the party, dispersed the guard and then, so he recounted, 'went on at full speed, when perceiving two sentrys at the door and a loaded wagon, I pushed at them, making all the noise I could . . . I fired twice through the door.' Lee's aide-de-camp, with a pistol in each hand, had taken up a position in the tavern where he could not be approached by more than one person at a time, while the Irish landlady endeavoured to squeeze the General into an upstairs hiding-place into which his long body would not fit. Suddenly they heard Tarleton's shout: 'If the General does not surrender in five minutes, I will set fire to the house.' There was a short pause. The threat was repeated. Then another voice declared, 'Here is the General. He has surrendered.'

'The trumpet then sounded assembly,' the aide-de-camp reported, 'and the unfortunate Lee, mounted on my horse, which stood ready at the door, was hurried off in triumph, bareheaded, in his slippers and coat, his collar open and his shirt very much soiled from several days use.'

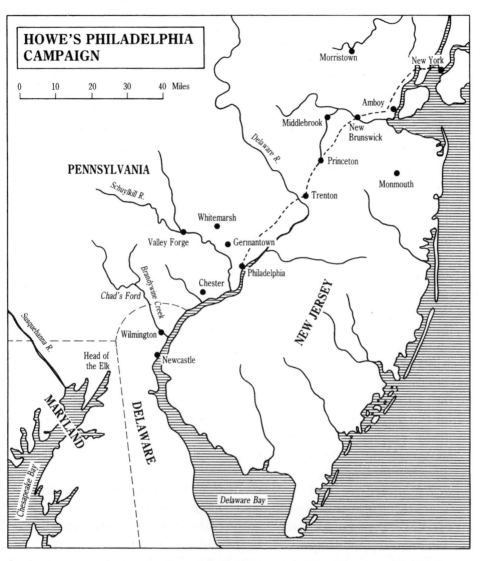

HOWE'S PHILADELPHIA
CAMPAIGN

0   10   20   30   40 Miles

PENNSYLVANIA

Schuylkill R.

Delaware R.

Morristown

New York

Amboy

Middlebrook

New
Brunswick

Princeton

Monmouth

Trenton

Whitemarsh

Valley Forge

Germantown

Philadelphia

Chester

NEW JERSEY

Brandywine Creek

Chad's Ford

Susquehanna R.

Wilmington

Head of
the Elk

Newcastle

MARYLAND

DELAWARE

Chesapeake Bay

Delaware Bay

The loss of General Lee caused the utmost dismay in the American
camp. Six senior German officers who had been captured in New
York were offered in exchange; but Howe declined to accept the
bargain. Strange as his appearance and behaviour were, and disloyal
as he was to Washington, he had been a skilful officer and the
Commander-in-Chief knew how sorely his most senior subordinate
would be missed. He had few enough officers of his gifts and
experience; and, four months after Lee's capture, he still had fewer

than four thousand men under his command. 'If Howe does not take advantage of our weak state,' he wrote, 'he is very unfit for his trust.'

Washington was still showing himself far from unfit for *his* trust, despite Lee's strictures. Only too well aware of how sorely a victory was needed to put new heart into the flagging revolutionary cause after the loss of New York – and hoping at least temporarily to divert the British threat to Philadelphia, for whose safety he confessed that he trembled – he decided to make an assault upon Howe's frontier posts with as many men as he could muster, including volunteers from Philadelphia, a regiment of German immigrants, units from Charles Lee's command and some five hundred men who had joined him under Horatio Gates – about six thousand men in all. On Christmas night 1776, through a storm of sleet, his men were ferried across the Delaware, then 'full of ice', and marched towards Trenton, some of them leaving trails of blood in the snow from their bare or bandaged feet, their sergeants prodding them from time to time during halts for fear lest they fell into a sleep from which they never woke. The next morning, his nose turned comically red by the cold wind, Washington was outside Trenton ready for the attack. He had chosen that day because the Hessians occupying the place were, as one of his officers said, known to 'make a great deal of Christmas in Germany'. They would, no doubt, drink quantities of beer and have a dance on Christmas night and the next day would be sleepy. 'Washington,' he added, 'will set the tune for them about day-break.'

The conceited and insolent German commander at Trenton, Colonel Johann Gottlieb Rall, had declined to believe that he was in danger from these 'country clowns' of Americans, and had not even troubled to throw up redoubts for the defence of his post. When urged to do so, he had cheerfully replied, 'Let them come! We want no trenches; we'll have at them with bayonets!' Taken completely by surprise, Colonel Rall, who had as usual been drinking heavily the night before, was in his nightshirt when given news of the attack. Dressing quickly, he rushed downstairs and was soon mortally wounded in the street-fighting which had broken out on all sides. By nightfall Washington had gained his sorely needed victory and a thousand of Rall's men had been captured, together with nearly all his stores – including, to the Americans' delight, numerous fine

German swords and, more immediately welcome, forty hogsheads of rum.

Lord Cornwallis, who had been packing up to go home to England on leave, had been ordered not to sail and to rush back towards Princeton. Leaving one brigade there under the command of Colonel Charles Mawhood, he marched with the remainder, seven thousand strong, along a muddy road through woods in which his men were repeatedly fired upon by snipers. He was determined, he said, to fall upon Washington at Trenton and to 'bag the old fox'.

Cornwallis had just celebrated his thirty-eighth birthday. A 'rather corpulent' man, as he described himself, his expression was sad in repose, his manner agreeable though politely reserved. Occasionally he made a humorously sardonic remark; but his fellow-officers were inclined to regard him as rather stuffy. He did not drink much and, unlike Howe, Burgoyne and Clinton, preferred to sleep alone when he could not sleep with his wife, to whom he was devoted. She was the very modestly provided for daughter of a Colonel James Jones, an affectionate, rather plain young woman whom he had married for love. He was devoted also to his two children, and to the country pursuits he had been able to enjoy on the estate in Suffolk which he had inherited from his father, the first Earl Cornwallis. Indeed, had not a sense of duty persuaded him to offer his services to the King in a conflict he had initially opposed, he would have chosen to remain at home, living the life of a contented, conscientious country gentleman. Having chosen to join the Army, however, he had done his best to master his profession, to reform the obvious abuses in the regiments he commanded, giving all the matters that came within his province the attention of an earnest and orderly if not penetrating mind. An honest, kindly, concerned and sympathetic officer, he was far better liked in the Army than such men as Clinton or Carleton could ever hope to be.

Having caught the Americans with their backs to the Delaware at Trenton, Cornwallis was confident that he could bring them to battle and defeat them. The river was frozen, so that boats could not cross it; but the ice was not thick enough to bear the weight of marching men. Some of his staff advised an immediate attack. But he demurred: it had taken all day to cover the ten miles of slushy road from

Princeton to Trenton; the men were tired; night was falling; exploratory attacks against the rebels by the advance guard had been repulsed. Cornwallis decided to wait until morning. 'The damned rebels,' he told an officer on his staff, 'are cornered at last.'

Washington skilfully eluded him, however. Unable to escape across the frozen river, he crept away on a recently built road towards Princeton at two o'clock in the morning, leaving his camp fires burning, muffling his artillery wheels in cloth, and instructing his rearguard to make as much noise as they could in digging the ground the rest of the army had left. He had less than five thousand troops with him. But after their victory over Colonel Rall's Germans, they were in more confident mood than they had been for months past. As the sun rose on the cold morning of 3 January 1777, Washington felt sure he could defeat the brigade which Cornwallis had left at Princeton before the main British army could come to their help from Trenton.

Washington was right. At the first clash of arms at Princeton, the American General Hugh Mercer was fatally wounded and his men ran back before a charge of British troops who plunged their bayonets through men trying to surrender. But when Washington galloped to the front on his white horse, he put an immediate stop to the retreat and rallied the men, apparently oblivious to the danger of his position which seemed to one of his officers, Colonel John Fitzgerald, so perilous that, as the British guns opened fire again, the Colonel pulled his hat over his eyes so that he would not be a witness to the General's death. When he raised his eyes again, however, Colonel Fitzgerald saw Washington still sitting in his saddle. He could not restrain his tears. 'Thank God,' he said, 'Your Excellency is safe!'

'Bring up your troops, my dear Colonel,' Washington replied. 'The day is our own.'

The British lost well over three hundred men in the brief and bloody battle at Princeton, as well as most of their guns and several men taken as prisoners.

[These prisoners] were a haughty, crabbed set of men, as they fully exhibited on their march to the country [an American sergeant recorded]. In this battle, my pack, which was made fast by leather strings, was shot from my back, and with it went what little clothing

I had. It was, however, soon replaced by one which belonged to a British officer, and was well furnished. It was not mine for long, for it was stolen shortly afterwards.

Immediately after the battle an officer observing blood on my clothes said, 'Sergeant you are wounded?' I replied 'No.' [But] on Examination I found the end of my forefinger gone, and bleeding profusely. When and how it happened I never knew; I found also bullet holes in the skirts of my coat, but, excepting the slight wound of my finger, I was not injured.

In this battle and that of Trenton, there were no ardent spirits in the army, and the excitement of rum had nothing to do in obtaining the victories. As I had tried powder and rum on Long Island to promote courage, and engaged here without it, I can say that I was none the less corageous here than there.

The Army retreated to Pluckemin mountains. The weather was extremely cold, and we suffered greatly from its severity . . . The inhabitants manifested very different feelings towards us from those exhibited a few weeks before, and were now ready to take up arms against the British.

Washington's dashing and successful action had succeeded in its purpose: it had encouraged a fresh revolutionary spirit amongst a people becoming disillusioned by a war in which they had had to endure the pillaging not only of foreign troops but also of bands of Americans who affected to believe that the farms and homesteads they plundered belonged to Loyalists or traitors, 'designing Tories and informers of all descriptions'. Encouraged by exaggerated and often fanciful reports of houses being invaded by British and Hessian troops, of innocent families being robbed of food and even linen and furniture, of cattle being driven off, of wives and daughters being raped, volunteers now began to come forward to join the militia and submit to a training which, irksome as it was to their independent spirits, was accepted as inevitable.

Throughout the spring of 1777 Washington worked hard to maintain this new spirit of hope and confidence, while gathering provisions and enlisting men for the major conflict with the enemy which – though he was anxious to avoid it until confident of success – might not now be long delayed. Occasional raids and skirmishes, some initiated by his own commanders, others by the enemy, resulted in casualties on both sides. But Washington was now better able to spare the men than was General Howe, even though he had lost many that winter through smallpox. Recruits were joining him all the time, often with their wives or other women, and sometimes with children, until he was obliged to issue an order to 'officers commanding brigades and corps to use every reasonable method in their power to get rid of all such as are not absolutely necessary'. There were far from enough uniforms to go round, some companies being distinguished only by the green sprigs they wore in their hats; and when the men appeared on parade it had to be admitted that their drill still left much to be desired: in some units the men marched along totally disregarding the music; in others it was difficult to get them to accept any sort of drill at all. All the same, at the beginning of August, Washington had a far more creditable army than it had seemed possible to raise a few months before; and by the beginning of September, after protracted manoeuvrings by both armies, he was in command of a force of about sixteen thousand men drawn up at Brandywine Creek across the road to Philadelphia.

12

THE FALL OF
PHILADELPHIA

*'They decamped with the utmost
precipitation, and in the greatest
confusion.'*

Robert Morton

The British troops had not enjoyed their summer in New York. The weather was sultry; the military hospitals were crowded; the inhabitants who remained were becoming increasingly unfriendly, complaining of chronic food shortages. Foraging parties sent out into the surrounding countryside were in constant danger of attack from marauding irregulars, who fell upon them with the same alarming ferocity displayed by the Tory band of James Delancey into whose hands fell a rebel foraging party, one of whom reported:

> The horse came upon the party full speed and were in the midst of the cattle and horses before the party could move through the drove, calling out, 'Surrender, you damned rebels, surrender!' Several of the party were struck down, when [I] presented [my] musket to surrender. Instead of receiving it, [I] was struck down to the ground, [my] skull fractured, and cut through the bone for four inches or more and, while lying on the ground, was rode over and struck four strokes in the head and several in the body with a cutlass. [Only one of the] party escaped . . .
>
> After [I] had been stripped of [my] neckcloth and silver shoe buckles and [my] pockets searched by the British, they discovered that [I] was not dead, for [I] had lain perfectly still before plundered.

The captain then asked [me] to what troops [I] belonged and how many there were of the party, which [I] told him. Captain said one had escaped and asked [me] if [I] could ride with them to the British lines. [I] answered [I] could not tell, as [I] did not know how bad [my] wounds were. [I] was then put onto a horse and told that [I] must try to ride. [I] rode on with them perhaps half or three-quarters of a mile, when [I] grew faint with the loss of blood and clung down by the horse's mane in the road and told them that [I] could go no farther with them.

Someone asked, 'Shall we kill him?' The captain said, 'No, let him alone. He will die soon himself.'

During these foraging expeditions women and civilians suffered as well as men in arms, both from the British and from rebels attacking Loyalists and supposed Loyalists. According to the Pennsylvania Council of Safety, 'Sixteen young women who fled to the woods . . . were seized and carried off'; a man, who had been forced to witness the rape of his wife and ten-year-old daughter, reported that 'another girl of thirteen years of age, was taken from her father's house, carried to a barn, there ravished' and afterwards raped by five other men. 'Furniture of every kind [was] destroyed or burnt, windows and doors broken to pieces; in short, the houses left uninhab-itable and the people left without provisions, for every horse, cow, ox, hogs and poultry carried off.' One 'blind old gentleman' was 'plundered of everything and on his door wrote, "Capt. Wills of the Royal Irish did this."'

On their return to New York, British foraging parties entered a city apparently in decay. 'Noisome vapours arise from the mud left in the docks and ships at low water,' a Loyalist serving with the British army complained.

Unwholesome smells are occasioned by such a number of people being crowded together in so small a compass almost like herrings in a barrel, most of them very dirty, and not a small number sick of some disease, the Itch, Pox, Fever, or Flux, so that altogether there is a complication of stinks to drive a person . . . into a consumption in the space of twenty-four hours. If any author who had an inclination to write a treatise upon stinks and ill smells, he never could meet with more subject matter than in New York.

[Also, to] anyone who had inclination to expose the vicious unfeeling parts of human nature, I recommend New York as a proper place to collect his characters. Most of the former inhabitants that once possessed this once happy spot are utterly ruined and from opulence reduced to the greatest indigence.

The price of provisions was so high that General Clinton spent as much as £25 a week, the equivalent of £1500 today, on his butcher's bill alone, until the arrival in New York of Mrs Baddeley, efficient as a housekeeper as she was accommodating as a mistress, brought some economy into a household which included as many as thirty servants who had been unwillingly acquired by the General to look after the regular influx of the numerous guests he was expected to entertain. 'Such,' he explained sardonically to his sister-in-law, 'is the pleasant accompaniment to this pinchbeck command, and absolutely unavoidable.'

The Loyalists, whose officers were so often to be seen at his table, had been dismayed to learn that, when the army moved on, most of them would be left behind as a garrison, together with seventeen infantry battalions and a small force of cavalry under Sir Henry Clinton. The rest of Howe's army, comprising about fourteen thousand men, were embarked aboard the 260 ships anchored in the harbour. It had been expected that they would make their way towards Philadelphia by way of the Delaware or across the Hudson River and through New Jersey, a route which would not take them too far away from Burgoyne, who might need Howe's support should Washington advance against the army of the north. But, on the advice of naval officers and to the amazement of several officers of his own staff, Howe had decided upon a more roundabout sea route by way of Chesapeake Bay. He himself, after spending a last night on shore with Mrs Loring, climbed aboard his brother's ship, the *Nonsuch*, at the beginning of the last week of July and set sail south by Sandy Hook towards the Virginia Capes. Storms and contrary winds delayed the expedition; several ships were struck by lightning; and it was not until 25 August that the troops, after forty-seven extremely uncomfortable days at sea, began to disembark near Head of Elk, Maryland, many of them with faces almost green from seasickness. One of them, Sergeant Thomas Sullivan of the 49th, recorded in his diary:

After forming the Line of march we arrived at a small town called Head of Elk, by reason of its being built at the head of that River. The Inhabitants fled before we reached the Town, leaving great quantities of stores in it and on board several sloops that was in the River, being informed or rather persuaded by the Rebels that our Army would kill and destroy them and their Families. Mister Washington as I was credibly informed dined there the Day before our arrival under a strong Guard.

Most of the horses the troops had brought with them had died on the voyage and those that survived looked as painfully thin as Sir William Howe's. The soldiers were reported to be 'in gloomy mood' as they marched slowly up the river towards Kennet Square, five miles from Washington's entrenchments above Brandywine Creek, occasionally plundering empty houses on the way, despite the floggings which were inflicted on the miscreants.

Washington himself was in command of the troops in the middle of his lines by Chad's Ford, a shallow crossing through Brandywine Creek commanded by well-sited batteries. He was supported here by Nathanael Greene and Anthony Wayne. Various regiments, well supplied with French firearms and cannon, were to their left behind high cliffs overlooking the Creek, which here became a torrent. To Washington's right was General Sullivan, a veteran of the Canadian campaign and of the fighting on Manhattan Island. It was a strong position which the British, whom the Americans slightly outnumbered, were not so likely to take by frontal assaults as by an outflanking movement against Sullivan's men in the wooded, hilly country to their left. 'The damned rebels', as Lord Cornwallis felt obliged to admit, did 'form well'.

Soon after dawn on 11 September the British advance began. As one column under the German General Wilhelm von Knyphausen came forward towards the centre of the American line at Chad's Ford, constantly fired upon by Washington's sharpshooters, another larger column of 12,500 men under Lord Cornwallis marched off towards the American right. It was some time, however, before Howe's intentions became clear. It seemed at first that, despite the difficulties facing him, Knyphausen, whose heavy guns were thundering against the American centre, intended to make a frontal assault across Chad's Ford; and, in order to forestall this assault,

Washington himself attacked, sending two thousand of his men over the Creek against the British and German troops deployed along the far bank. A British officer in Knyphausen's force described how the numbers of their opponents seemed to increase as he advanced towards Chad's Ford and 'in the course of two hours [his] lads underwent the fire of 2,000 men'. During a pause in the column's forward movement he caught sight of 'a rebel officer, remarkable by a hussar dress . . . followed by another dressed in dark green or blue, mounted on a bay horse, with a remarkably large cocked hat':

> I ordered three good shots to steal near . . . and fire at them, but the idea disgusted me. I recalled the order. The hussar in returning made a circuit, but the other passed again within a hundred yards of us, upon which I advanced from the woods towards him. On my calling he stopped, but after looking at me proceeded. I again drew his attention and made signs to him to stop, but he slowly continued his way . . . It was not pleasant to fire at the back of an unoffending individual who was acquitting himself very cooly of his duty, so I let him alone . . . I was telling this story to some wounded officers . . . when one of our surgeons, who had been dressing the wounded rebel officers, told us they had been informing him that General Washington was all that morning with a French officer in a hussar dress, he himself dressed and mounted in every point as above described. I am not sorry I did not know at the time who it was.

It was not until early afternoon that Washington was told that the assault on Chad's Ford appeared to be a feint, that his right was being outflanked and that Cornwallis, having crossed over both fords of the upper Brandywine, was advancing on Dilworth, thus threatening the American rear. Washington reacted quickly: he immediately withdrew the troops he had sent forward against Knyphausen and sent orders to Sullivan to take up a new position, at right angles to his former one, on high ground two miles to the north of Dilworth above a small chapel known as Birmingham Meeting House. Deciding to go over there in person, he approached an elderly man who lived in the area to take him there by the quickest way he knew. This man, Joseph Brown, was extremely reluctant to undertake the duty and tried to excuse himself; but he immediately agreed to go when one of Washington's aides-de-camp, jumping from his horse, threatened to run him through with his sword. When they reached the road half a mile from Dilworth, Brown said 'the bullets were flying so thick' he felt 'uncomfortable; and as Washington no longer required, nor paid any attention to his guide', he embraced the first opportunity to make his escape.

Sullivan had no sooner completed his dispositions than Cornwallis's men, having already marched eighteen miles that day, attacked him. 'There was,' an English officer recalled, 'a most infernal fire of cannons and musquetry, smoke and incessant shouting: "Incline to the right! Incline to the left! Halt! Charge!" The balls ploughing up the ground: the trees cracking over one's head; the branches riven by the artillery; the leaves falling as in autumn.'

At length Cornwallis drove the Americans back to Dilworth where Sullivan rallied his men, while the British commander – four of whose battalions had become entangled and lost their way in the thick woodland between Birmingham Meeting House and Dilworth – endeavoured to regroup the rest of his column so that the impetus of his attack could be maintained. He managed to force Sullivan out of Dilworth; but Washington had by now brought his reserve under General Greene round behind the village and was thus able to cover Sullivan's retreat to Chester. Fighting continued until dark when the Americans, 'much shaken', as one of them put it, 'though not dismayed', withdrew without further molestation.

By this time Knyphausen had taken advantage of the withdrawal of American troops from the centre to pour his men across Chad's Ford and to advance to Cornwallis's assistance. On gaining the other bank and advancing rapidly towards Dilworth, Knyphausen's men came upon men of the four battalions who had been lost in the woods and took them along with them towards their junction with Cornwallis. It was after nightfall, however, when the two British columns met, and by then they were both too exhausted to pursue the Americans any further. In all they had lost 557 killed and wounded to American losses of over a thousand casualties and 400 men taken prisoner.

The next day the British moved slowly forward on a wide front towards the Schuylkill, a tributary of the Delaware. Washington retreated over the river, leaving troops to delay the enemy at the fords and sending detachments of Pennsylvania Continentals under

Anthony Wayne against their left flank and rear to delay their advance. To rid himself of this tiresome harassment, Howe gave orders to Major-General Charles Grey to drive Wayne off. Grey did so with great skill and ruthless determination. Ordering the men of the three battalions he had been assigned for the operation to remove the flints from their muskets so there should be no temptation to open fire and thus betray their advance, 'No Flint' Grey, as he was afterwards known, fell upon Wayne in a sudden surprise attack by night near an inn known as the Paoli Tavern. 'The enemy was completely surprised,' wrote one of Grey's officers, describing how the whole British force, guided by the camp fires, rushed upon the Pennsylvanians, giving 'such a cheer as made the woods echo':

> The enemy . . . some with arms, others without, [ran] in all directions with the greatest confusion. The light infantry bayoneted every man they came up with. The camp was immediately set on fire, and this, with the cries of the wounded, formed altogether one of the most dreadful scenes I ever beheld. Every man that fired was instantly put to death. Captain Wolfe was killed, and I received a shot in my right hand, soon after we entered the camp. I saw the fellow present at me, and was running up to him when he fired. He was immediately killed. The enemy were pursued for two miles. I kept up till I grew faint from [loss of] blood and was obliged to sit down. Wayne's brigade was to have marched at one in the morning to attack our battalion while crossing the Schuylkill river, and we surprised them at twelve. Four hundred and sixty of the enemy were counted the next morning, lying dead, and not one shot was fired by us – all done with the bayonet. We had only twenty killed and wounded.

The day after what became known as the Paoli Massacre, Howe advanced to the Schuylkill, his men plundering the farms along their route; and on 22 September, after successfully misleading Washington into supposing he intended to force a passage further upriver, he crossed over at Flatland Ford. Three days later his army entered Philadelphia behind a parade of heavy guns with bands playing triumphant airs.

Having occupied the town from which the Congress, in what one observer described as 'the utmost precipitation and greatest confusion', had fled to York, a hundred miles to the east, Howe's immediate task was to open the Delaware to British shipping, to remove the booms and other obstacles which had been sunk into its bed and which stretched across the river from bank to bank, and to capture the forts whose guns had been sited to cover them. Until these operations were carried out, however, his supplies had to come overland from the Chesapeake River, whose waters debouched into the Atlantic in Maryland; and, to escort them safely across the intervening miles, he was obliged to detach three thousand men for this duty.

Taking advantage of Howe's temporarily reduced numbers, Washington – whose own forces had been recently reinforced and now numbered about eight thousand Continentals and three thousand militia – decided to make an attack upon the main British camp at Germantown, then a village whose widely separated houses straggled on either side of the road which led north out of Philadelphia towards Washington's camp at Skippack Creek. The attack began in the early hours of the morning of 4 October; but the dawn light was obscured by so thick a fog that visibility was reduced to a few yards. Even on a clear day Washington's intricate plan would have been difficult for inexperienced troops to execute. On a day such as this it might not have proved impossible had not so many of his troops, both officers and men, been drunk. As it was, the action, which lasted for nearly three hours with only occasional respite, was a confused affair with the Americans, wearing pieces of white paper in their hats for purposes of identification, more than once firing on their own men through the fog and smoke. 'Our orders were not to fire until we could see the buttons on their clothes,' an American private wrote, 'but they . . . would not give us an opportunity to be so curious, for they hid their clothes in fire and smoke before we had either time or leisure to examine their buttons.'

In growing fury and confusion the battle raged around Cliveden – a large stone house in the middle of the village belonging to one Benjamin Chew – first one side seeming to have the advantage, then the other. Shouting, 'Have at the bloodhounds! Revenge Wayne's affair!' a battalion of Americans fired a volley at a British regiment which returned the fire, cheered and charged.

> On our charging they gave way on all sides [Lieutenant Martin Hunter wrote] but again and again renewed the attack with fresh

troops and greater force. We charged them twice, till the battalion was so reduced by killed and wounded, that the bugle was sounded to retreat . . . This was the first time we had retreated before the Americans, and it was with great difficulty to get our men to obey our orders. By this time General Howe had come up, and seeing the battalion retreating, all broken, he got into a passion and exclaimed 'For shame, light infantry! I never saw you retreat before. Form! Form! It's only a scouting party.' However, he was soon convinced it was more than a scouting party, as the heads of the enemy's columns soon appeared. One, with three pieces of cannon in their front, immediately fired at the crowd that was standing with General Howe under a large chestnut tree. I think I never saw people enjoy a charge of grape before, but we really all felt pleased to see the enemy make such an appearance and to hear the grape rattle about the commander-in-chief's ears, after he had accused us of having run away from a scouting party. He rode off immediately full speed.

The losses on both sides were heavy, the British having 537 casualties, the Americans 652 with an additional 438 men taken prisoner. Yet neither commander could feel the lives had been well spent.

Washington had lost his chance of retaking Philadelphia; while Howe, withdrawing there for the winter, was so dispirited by the limited progress he had made and by a growing awareness that he was unequal to his task that he wrote to London to say that his orders were impossible to execute without reinforcements and that, if more troops were not forthcoming, he wished to resign his command. After having, with much difficulty and further loss of life, captured the Delaware forts and opened the river for his army's supplies, he had tried unsuccessfully to force another engagement upon Washington, who warily declined it, content to remain in a strongly entrenched position at Whitemarsh, fourteen miles from Philadelphia. From here Washington moved to Valley Forge where, towards the end of October, he was brought momentous news from the north.

13

THE ARMY
OF THE NORTH

---

*'I little foresaw that I was to be
left to pursue my way through such
a tract of country, and hosts of foes,
without any co-operation from
New York.'*

John Burgoyne

After forty days at sea aboard the frigate *Apollo*, John Burgoyne had
stepped ashore at Quebec on 6 May 1777 in his habitually immaculate
uniform. Sir Guy Carleton was naturally dismayed to be superseded
by an officer who had recently been his second-in-command and to
be forced to remain in Canada at the mercy of a Minister, Lord
George Germain, for whom his antipathy had much increased since
his arrival there. But, while waiting for a reply to his demand to be
recalled, he did what he could to support Burgoyne and help him in
his preparations; and for this Burgoyne expressed his gratitude.
Carleton's 'zeal to give effect to the measures in my hands,' he wrote,
'[is] equally manifest, exemplary and satisfactory . . . He could not
have done more than he did to comply with and expedite my
requisitions and desires.' Unfortunately, Carleton's instructions from
London allowed him little discretion in the despatch of troops to
reinforce Burgoyne or to garrison forts which would be captured on
the way to Albany. Lord George Germain had not only stipulated
which regiments were to form part of Burgoyne's force and which
were to remain in Canada but had even, so Carleton complained,
'pointed out where the latter were to be posted'. 'Whatever I may
think of his Lordship as an officer or a statesman,' Carleton explained

to Burgoyne, 'I must respect his office; and, as Secretary of State, signifying to me the King's pleasure, he must be obeyed . . . The conduct of the war having been taken entirely out of my hands, I have only to lament that, being limited by positive commands, I am not at liberty to assist you as fully as I wish or as, if it had been left to my discretion, I might have done.'

Burgoyne certainly needed all the help that he could get. He had expected to have at his disposal at least twelve thousand soldiers with a generous number of Canadian volunteers. In fact, when all his forces were assembled at Cumberland Point, on the shores of Lake Champlain, there were no more than three British and three German brigades, comprising about eight thousand men in all. In addition, a mere four hundred Indians, who were to prove a source of endless trouble, were enlisted; and, instead of the large numbers of eager volunteers which Burgoyne had anticipated, there were less than three hundred Canadians of no marked enthusiasm and a similar number of American Loyalists. There were, moreover, so few horses that, instead of the thirty days' supply of stores which the army had hoped to carry, only fourteen days' supply could be managed. Further strains on transport were imposed by an exceptionally heavy train of artillery and a numerous assortment of women, camp followers, cooks, servants and musicians.

With the means at his disposal the fulfilment of Burgoyne's plans would prove no easy task. But, cheered by the knowledge that, though his British regiments were few in number, their men were mostly experienced in war and their officers of remarkable quality – no fewer than thirty of them were to become generals – Burgoyne had lost none of his energy and self-confidence. If he had any deep reservations about the likely success of the forthcoming campaign, he was careful to conceal them from his staff. At the end of June his florid, not to say theatrical, General Orders were read out to his army:

> The Army embarks tomorrow to approach the Enemy. We are to contend for the King and the Constitution of Great Britain, to vindicate the Law and to relieve the Oppressed, a cause in which His Majesty's Troops and those of the Princes His Allies will feel equal Excitement.
>
> The Services required on this particular Expedition are critical

and conspicuous. During our progress occasions may occur in which neither difficulty, nor labour, nor Life are to be regarded. THIS ARMY MUST NOT RETREAT.

Few of those who listened to these words knew for sure where they were going or what they were expected to do when they got there. Even their commanding officers had only a general idea of what the overall strategy of the campaign was intended to achieve. Indeed, there was no very certain knowledge about this in London.

While severely limiting Sir Guy Carleton's freedom of action, Lord George Germain had allowed Sir William Howe considerable latitude in the interpretation of such orders as had been given him by the government; and Howe had taken full advantage of the scope accorded him. Germain was consequently driven upon more than one occasion that summer to suggest to his Commander-in-Chief in America that 'perhaps Sir Wm. Howe [would] acquaint [him] in what manner and when he [intended] to begin his operations' or to complain that he could not guess 'by Sir Wm. Howe's letters when he [would] begin his operations or where he [proposed] carrying them on'. Germain later protested that for a period of longer than two months he knew no more of the whereabouts of the General or of what he was doing than did the man in the street.

So far as Germain knew, Howe's intention was to move against Washington in Pennsylvania; and he had agreed to that action. But he had supposed that this operation would be over in time for Howe to co-operate with Burgoyne's army coming down from the north. Yet Howe still seemed not to attach the same importance to this co-operation as the King and his ministers. In one of his letters to London, before the long ensuing silence, he had outlined his plans for 1777 and had not so much as mentioned co-operation with the army from Canada; and, in a letter written three days later to Carleton in Quebec, he had warned him that any troops which might come down towards him from the north could expect 'little assistance from hence' because of 'the want of sufficient strength in this army'. Besides, Howe had added, 'I shall probably be in Pennsylvania when that corps is ready to advance into this province, [so] it will not be in my power to communicate with the officer commanding it as soon as I could wish. He must therefore pursue such measures as may from circumstances be judged most conducive to the advancement of his Majesty's service.'

It still seemed to General Clinton that Howe's operations in Pennsylvania were quite incompatible with Burgoyne's invasion from the north, to both of which Germain had given his approval; and he had regarded it as increasingly unlikely that Howe would have achieved victory in Pennsylvania in time to join forces with Burgoyne for a combined assault upon the rebels. Moreover, when Burgoyne reached Albany, he could hardly expect to exist there through the winter with a line of communications running north for mile after mile through a frozen wilderness.

Clinton had suggested to the Commander-in-Chief that it would be far better to move up the Hudson River to join Burgoyne in a concerted attack on Washington. But Howe could not be persuaded. He reiterated that his plan for operations in the south had been approved by the government, and that there was no point in discussing the matter further. A month or so after this conversation, Howe received a letter from Germain confirming that the King liked the idea of his southern expedition, but that he expected this to be completed in time for him to co-operate with Burgoyne. When Howe received this letter, however, he had already begun his operations and, because of advice received from naval officers, he had chosen to approach Philadelphia by way of Chesapeake Bay, rather than the Delaware River, and had thus not only prolonged his expedition by at least a fortnight but had also taken his army well over three hundred miles further away from Burgoyne's. Successful co-operation would now be extremely unlikely, particularly as Loyalists along the line of Howe's march were to prove far fewer than had been hoped. Indeed, excepting a few individuals, the inhabitants were 'strongly in emnity' against the British. 'By far the greater number deserted their dwellings, driving off at the same time their stock of cattle and horses.' 'It is with much concern,' Howe regretted, 'that in this particular [of co-operation with Burgoyne] I am to answer that I cannot flatter myself that I shall be able to act up to the King's expectations.'

In Montreal, Burgoyne had been astonished to see 'an account of his own intended operations so accurately predicted' that it might have been 'copied from the Secretary of State's letter'. But he was not dismayed. Despite the small size of his army, he was still confident that his men would prove more than a match for the rebels, who constituted no more than 'a preposterous parade of military arrangement'. He professed confidence in the Germans who, despite their rather mournful expressions, their homesickness, the tears that came into their eyes when they sang their hymns and psalms, and their ponderous rate of marching, were to be depended upon in battle. He expressed confidence, too, in the American Loyalists who had joined him, in their commander, Colonel John Peters, and in his American political adviser, the tall, eccentric, Scots-born Philip Skene, who, attended by black servants in splendid livery and powdered wigs, lived near Scots Bay in a house in which his mother's corpse reposed on a table so that she might still receive the annuity guaranteed her so long as she remained 'above ground'.

The weather that summer was bad enough to dampen the most ardent spirits. The rain poured down in torrents; bridges were washed away; roads became impassable; wagons broke down in the mud; uniforms and stores were soaked. Yet Burgoyne's apparent confidence remained unimpaired. When he reviewed the troops they cheered him as he smiled and raised his hat. When he spoke to the Indians they roared their approval of his words, though what he had to say to them was more of a warning than an encouragement: 'I positively forbid bloodshed when you are not opposed in arms. Aged men, women, children and prisoners must be held sacred from the knife or hatchet, even in the time of actual conflict. You shall receive compensation for the prisoners you take, but you shall be called to account for scalps.' These could be taken from the dead, but not from prisoners or the wounded.

'We receive you as our father,' replied one old chief on behalf of the rest, 'because when we hear you speak, we hear the voice of our great Father beyond the lake.' There were further cheers when the old man had finished his speech; and later a war dance was performed by the braves, their skins quite smooth, all hair being plucked out apart from the tufts that grew from the back of their heads which were also adorned with a feather for each man they had killed, their penises decorated with what an officer described as 'the head of some handsome bird'. William Digby of the 53rd commented:

> Their manner of dancing the war dance is curious and shocking,
> being naked and painted in a most frightful manner. When they

give the war whoop or yell, they appear more like infernals than of the human kind . . . They were much encouraged . . . as useful to the army in many particulars, but their cruel and barbarous custom of scalping must be shocking to any European, though practised on our enemies. They walk freely through our camp and come into our tents without the least ceremony, wanting brandy or rum, for which they would do anything, as their greatest pleasure is in getting beastly intoxicated.

As for their methods of scalping, Lieutenant Thomas Anburey, who seems to have witnessed the operation, was horrified by it. 'They sieze the head of the disabled or dead enemy,' he wrote,

and placing one of their feet on the neck, twist their left hand in the hair, by which means they extend the skin that covers the top of the head, and with the other hand draw the scalping knife . . . If the hair is short, and they have no purchase with their hand, they stoop, and with their teeth strip it off . . . They then tie their trophies in a small hoop with bark or deer's sinews to preserve it from putrefaction, painting part of the scalp and the hoop all round with red.

By 20 June 1777, when the army set off across the lake to the sound of music, the skies had cleared and the smooth water reflected the leaves of the tall trees growing by the banks. The Indians led the way in their canoes, followed by the Loyalists – some of whom were also wearing Indian dress and warpaint – and the Canadians in their white smocks. Then came the British troops who, once the enemy were encountered, were to be the spearhead of the advance; and in their wake came the boats of the main body. The headquarters staff were standing on board the *Maria*, Burgoyne prominent among them, the bateaux of the British regiments to his starboard side, those of the Germans to the port, boats laden with provisions, ammunition, cattle and all the army's servants, sutlers, tradesmen and hangers-on, sailing behind them with the women.

Having issued a proclamation, at once pious and threatening, and a final, high-flown General Order to the army, Burgoyne landed his troops on 30 June on the southern shores of the lake, a few miles from the fort of Ticonderoga. The next morning the fort could be

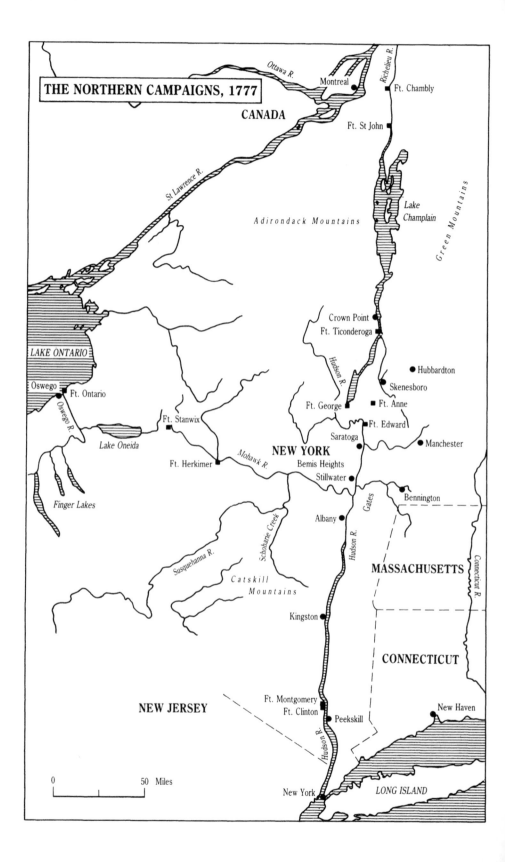

THE NORTHERN CAMPAIGNS, 1777

Ottawa R.

Montreal

Richelieu R.

Ft. Chambly

CANADA

Ft. St John

St. Lawrence R.

Adirondack Mountains

Lake Champlain

Green Mountains

LAKE ONTARIO

Crown Point
Ft. Ticonderoga

Hubbardton

Oswego
Ft. Ontario

Oswego R.

Ft. Stanwix

Hudson R.

Skenesboro

Ft. George

Ft. Anne

Lake Oneida

Ft. Edward

Manchester

Ft. Herkimer

Mohawk R.

NEW YORK

Saratoga

Finger Lakes

Bemis Heights

Stillwater

Gates

Bennington

Schoharie Creek

Albany

Hudson R.

Susquehanna R.

*Catskill
Mountains*

MASSACHUSETTS

Connecticut R.

Kingston

CONNECTICUT

NEW JERSEY

Ft. Montgomery
Ft. Clinton

Peekskill

New Haven

Hudson R.

0   50 Miles

New York

LONG ISLAND

clearly seen, its grey walls, stark and forbidding, surrounded by the green leaves and dark shadows of the forest. Before it, piled down to the water's edge, was a tangle of undergrowth and an abatis – a rampart of felled trees with their sharpened boughs pointing outwards. To either side of the fort were entrenchments, earthworks and gun emplacements. Guns could also be seen behind the battlements of the fort itself.

The place was defended by some three thousand Americans under General Arthur St Clair and General Anthony Wayne, who had occupied not only the main fort of Ticonderoga on the western shore of the lake but also, on the eastern shore, Mount Independence which was similarly protected by entrenchments and batteries and by a fort built on its summit. The two forts were connected by a bridge beneath which a boom of chains and tree trunks stretched from bank to bank, blocking the approach from Lake Champlain into Lake George and the South River. Yet, although known as 'the Gibraltar of the North', the defences at Ticonderoga were overlooked by the dominating height of Sugarloaf Hill which, in the words of a British engineer officer, 'had the entire command of the works at Ticonderoga'. If guns could be mounted here, the defences could be bombarded mercilessly. And the experienced artilleryman, General Phillips, had no doubt that guns *could* be hauled up the hill, whatever the rebels thought. 'Where a goat can go a man can go,' he said, 'and where a man can go, he can drag a gun.'

Burgoyne took his advice; and, while the British infantry encircled the position and threw up entrenchments around it, the artillery struggled to build a causeway up Sugarloaf Hill, through the maple and pine trees, out of sight of the Americans. With the help of oxen, the gunners laboriously dragged cannon after cannon up it, dismantling them on occasions and hauling up the parts by means of ropes lashed round the trunks of trees, and eventually they managed to erect a battery on the summit. By the evening of 4 July, the second anniversary of the Declaration of Independence, the guns were in position; and General St Clair was forced to conclude that his position at Ticonderoga had been suddenly rendered untenable. Orders were given the next day for the stores of the fort to be transported upriver to Skenesborough (now Whitehall) and for the garrison to withdraw by way of Castleton.

★　　★　　★

The British pursued the Americans closely. Burgoyne embarked part of his force in his bateaux to chase them up the South River in the wake of his gunboats, while Brigadier-General Simon Fraser, commander of the advance corps, with General von Riedesel in support, started at four o'clock in the morning with the light infantry and grenadiers for Castleton.

Having burst through the boom and sailed up the waterway beyond it – here so narrow that the cliffs on either side seemed almost to touch the ships' yardarms – Burgoyne came out into South Bay where the Americans, believing that it would take a day at least to dismantle the boom, could be seen preparing a meal on shore while their ships lay at anchor. At the sight of the British fleet suddenly debouching into the Bay they ran off into the trees, abandoning not only their camp kettles but also the sick and wounded, and leaving their ships to be destroyed or captured.

Meanwhile Fraser, pushing on hard through the forest towards Castleton, and returning the fire of the retreating American picquets, had discovered their rearguard near the small village of Hubbard-town. Although outnumbered almost two to one by marksmen far more at home in this well-wooded country than his own rigidly disciplined troops, Fraser at once attacked and kept the Americans hotly engaged until General von Riedesel came to his support. It was a bitter engagement. At one point, so Lieutenant Anburey recorded, a party of about sixty Americans came forward to a company of grenadiers as though surrendering, with their rifle barrels pointing to the ground. They approached to within ten yards of the British soldiers, then suddenly snatched up their rifles and fired a volley from the hip before dashing back behind the trunks of the trees. Several grenadiers were killed and more were wounded; but their enraged comrades dashed after the 'filthy scoundrels' who, throwing down their weapons and surrendering, were bayoneted to a man. When darkness fell on the night of 7 July the British had in all lost fewer than 140 men, whereas over two hundred Americans had been killed, including the commander of the rearguard, Colonel Francis; and two hundred more had been taken prisoner. Encouraged by news of this short engagement, Burgoyne sent a detachment south towards Fort Anne to cut off the retreat of the fugitives, then established his headquarters at Skenesborough, a village built by Philip Skene who had brought over settlers from Scotland to live with him there.

It was less than three weeks since the British had left Cumberland Point. They had already covered a hundred miles, had captured the enemy's most important fortress and had taken scores of prisoners as well as 128 guns at a loss of a very small fraction of their force. They had now only forty more miles to go before reaching Albany, where they could expect news of Howe's army in the south. But now Burgoyne's apparently relentless march began to falter. In their retreat from Skenesborough to Fort Anne and from Fort Anne to Fort Edward, the Americans had wielded their axes with astonishing vigour and had felled hundreds of trees across the road which the British would have to use for the transport of their ammunition and stores. 'We are obliged to wait for some time in our present position till the roads are cleared,' one of Burgoyne's officers wrote a week after they had first entered Skenesborough. 'Every ten or twelve yards great trees are laid across [our path].' As well as dragging away trees, the men had to work night and day in building wagons, and in constructing over forty bridges and causeways across the creeks and marshes beneath which the road disappeared with exasperating frequency.

It would have been better, some officers suggested, if Burgoyne had abandoned the land route to Albany altogether and had taken his army back by water to Ticonderoga, had crossed from there to Lake George, and had gone by boat down the lake to Fort George and then marched along the relatively short road to Fort Edward. But Burgoyne had decided against this route because, for one reason among many, he had been assured that by going overland he would be joined by numerous ardent Loyalists eager to fight for King George and England. Two or three hundred Loyalists, many without arms and most without training, did, indeed, offer their services; but others who might have come to the British camp were dissuaded from doing so by the intimidating activities of revolutionary committees and their agents who were instructed to decree that 'to give aid and comfort to the enemy would be punished as treason to the United States'. Of the thousands of men ready and determined to risk reprisals by rebels for supporting the Crown against the rebels there were, here as elsewhere in the colonies, no signs. 'The great bulk of the country is undoubtedly with Congress, in principle and in zeal,' Burgoyne told Germain,

and their measures are executed with a secrecy and dispatch that are
not to be equalled . . . Wherever the King's forces point, militia to
the amount of three or four thousand assemble in twenty-four
hours; they bring with them their subsistence, etc., and, the alarm
over, they return to their farms. The Hampshire Grants in particular
. . . now abound with the most active and the most rebellious race
of the continent.

Anti-British feeling in America was certainly much fostered by the
behaviour of the Indians whom Burgoyne had enlisted in his army.
Contemporary accounts are full of alleged Indian atrocities. The
sparse, laconic entries in the diary of Estes Howe, a surgeon on
General Gates's staff, for example, while otherwise almost entirely
devoted to medical matters, recount in some detail stories of Indian
depredations:

> 25 July 1777.   A number of Indians went to a house near Fort
> Edward and took two white women and a Negro man and woman
> and one of the white women they killed upon the hill and skalped
> her . . .
> 27 July.   Hear that the other woman is found dead this
> morning . . .
> 28 July.   A man killed . . . going after his hogs . . . The Indians
> fired through his Body and two of them held him and the other
> Skelped him . . . Our people ran to him and Brought him down
> to the River and Putt him in a Boat . . . I found him shot with two
> Baules and Skalpt. Thought it not worth while to dress him . . .
> Died in about two hours after . . .
> 29 July.   . . . We hear that the Indians have killed a family of
> seven and Skalped them . . .

Appalled by the conduct of the Indians in Ticonderoga, where they
had stayed behind to drink and plunder, and by the sight of scalps
hanging up to dry in the sun around their camps, Burgoyne had
repeated his warnings and orders to their chiefs, exhortations which
were later compared by Burke to the kind of admonition which
might be addressed by the keepers of the King's wild animals in the
Tower of London menagerie should there be a riot on Tower Hill:
'My gentle lions, my humane bears, my tender-hearted hyenas,

go forth! But . . . you are not to hurt any man, woman or child.'
Burke's scepticism was well justified. The Indians did not obey
Burgoyne's rules even in so far as they understood them. They
behaved 'like hogs', according to one German officer. 'When it comes
to plundering they are on hand every time; and most of them
have remained at Ticonderoga and Skenesborough . . . They filled
themselves with rum in true military style . . . and after every
campaign they get "full" and remain in that condition until they get
home, when they begin to brag of their deeds while away.'

News of one particularly horrifying depredation spread fast
throughout the colonies. The victim was a young, good-looking
woman, Jane McCrea, a Presbyterian minister's daughter, who was
engaged to a loyalist lieutenant in Burgoyne's army. With another
woman of loyalist sympathies, Mrs McNeill, a Scottish widow
who was a cousin of Brigadier-General Fraser, Jane McCrea was
apparently abducted by Indians from a house near Fort Edward.
The two women were carried into a wood where, according to an
American soldier who had also been captured by Indians and claimed
to have witnessed the scene, 'violent language passed between the
Indians, & they got into high quarrel, beating each other with their
muskets'.

> In the midst of the fray, one of the Chiefs in a rage shot Jenny
> McCrae in her breast, & she fell & expired immediately. Her hair
> was long and flowing, and the same chief took off the scalp, cutting
> so as to unbrace nearly the whole of that part of the head on which
> the hair grew. He then sprang up, tossed the scalp in the face of a
> young Indian standing by, brandished it in the air, and uttered a
> savage yell of exultation. When this was done the quarrel ceased,
> & the whole party moved off quickly.

As soon as he heard of this 'shocking' outrage, Horatio Gates wrote
a letter of vehement protest to Burgoyne: 'The miserable fate of Miss
McCrea was partly aggravated by her being dressed to receive her
promised husband; but met her murderers employed by you. Upwards of one hundred men, women and children have perished at
the hands of these ruffians, to whom it is asserted you have paid the
price of blood.'

In a characteristically grandiloquent reply, Burgoyne indignantly denied the charge that he had paid the Indians for scalps, though he admitted paying them for prisoners because this 'would prevent cruelty'. He protested that Miss McCrea's death 'wanted not the tragic display [Gates had] laboured to give it, to make it as sincerely abhorred and lamented' by himself as it could 'possibly be by the tenderest of her friends'. He explained that she had met her fate during a dispute between two Indians who had squabbled over her custody and that, having had the murderer brought before him, he had decided that a pardon 'would be more efficacious than an execution to prevent similar mischiefs'. Had he had the man executed, the Indians would have immediately deserted and created havoc in all the settlements they passed through on their way home. Protest as he would, however, the behaviour of the Indians did much to damage the reputation of the British, and the image of an Iroquois chief in their service carrying the scalp of a young American woman, the blood dripping through the carefully brushed fair hair, was a valuable gift to revolutionary propaganda.

Burgoyne's difficulties were now increased by his having had to deplete his force by several hundred men left behind as a garrison in Ticonderoga. He had hoped that this garrison duty would be undertaken by reinforcements sent there by Carleton who, however, protested that his orders from London forbade him doing so. The forces remaining to Burgoyne were further weakened by his chosen method of 'dividing his army into separate columns', a method which gave much encouragement to Washington. 'From your accounts [Burgoyne] appears to be pursuing that line of conduct which is of all others most favourable to us; I mean acting in Detachments,' Washington wrote to Philip Schuyler. 'This conduct will certainly give room to Enterprise on our part, and expose his parties to great hazards.'

So successful, indeed, were American attempts to slow him down that Burgoyne – hampered by the heavy train of artillery he insisted upon taking with him to batter down the strong timber forts which the Americans were so skilful in constructing – was able to cover the twenty miles between Skenesborough and Fort George at no faster a rate than one mile a day. In his front, as he lumbered forward past the charred ruins of farm buildings and fields of burning corn, set alight on the orders of rebel leaders so that the crops could not be harvested by the enemy, the whole population of the area, so it seemed, was moving south too, flying out of the way of the British and German soldiers and their Indian allies, the sight of whose painted faces suddenly appearing from the woods was greeted with screams of terror.

'Every one for himself was the constant cry,' wrote one of the American refugees, who described his mother trudging along with a baby on her arm and a club in her hand. Behind and in front of his family were carts filled with furniture, horses with two or even three riders on their backs, footsore men and women wearily walking they knew not where.

They passed through Fort Edward, which the American Army had deserted in favour of Stillwater, about thirty miles above Albany, and when, on 30 July, Burgoyne's advance parties arrived at Fort Edward the place appeared to be deserted and in smoking ruins. But, one after the other, figures appeared from hiding places where they had sought safety from the Indians. Protesting loyalty to the British cause, they asked pathetically for food, of which Burgoyne himself had by now the most meagre supply.

To maintain even the slow momentum of his advance, Burgoyne recognized that more baggage animals were essential. He determined, therefore, on Baron von Riedesel's advice, to make a raid upon a magazine established by the New England militia at Bennington where there were reported to be at least a hundred horses besides large supplies of food and ammunition. For the purpose of this raid Burgoyne detached about eight hundred men including eighty Indians and about two hundred Canadians and Americans under a dashing German officer, Lieutenant-Colonel Friedrich Baum, who, much to the amusement of those who presumed that secrecy of movement was to be desired, insisted upon taking with him a German band. Burgoyne would have sent more men, but he was assured that, although he had been disappointed in this respect in the past, the countryside around Bennington was full of Loyalists who would be sure to support Baum and would probably come to his help.

On their march through the forest, the trees dripping with rain after a heavy storm, the Indians running ahead, plundering and burning any homesteads they could find, Baum's soldiers struggled along in their immense boots, carrying loads which Lieutenant Anbu-rey described as being of an 'enormous bulk'. English soldiers were heavily laden enough with their arms and accoutrements, their sixty rounds of ammunition, their knapsacks and blankets, their haversacks of provisions, their canteens for water, their hatchets and their 'proportion of the equipage belonging to their tents'. But their burdens were 'almost light' when compared with those of the Germans, who, in addition to all this, were 'loaded with a cap with a very heavy brass front, a sword of an enormous size, a canteen that cannot hold less than a gallon, their coats very long skirted [and heavy leather gauntlets reaching almost to their elbows]. Picture to yourself a man in this situation, and how extremely well calculated he is for a rapid march.'

On his march to Bennington with such troops, Baum, who spoke no English, encountered a large party of professed Loyalists in countrymen's clothes. They offered to serve with him, and to swear the customary oath of allegiance. Skene, satisfied of their sincerity, assured Baum that he could confidently add them to his force. He accepted their oaths, signed them up, and gave them slips of white paper to wear in their hats so that the Indians would not molest them. 'How Colonel Baum became so completely duped as to place reliance on these men, I know not,' wrote one of his officers.

> But . . . he was somehow or other persuaded to believe [that they wished] to offer their services to the leader of the King's troops . . . I cannot pretend to describe the state of excitation and alarm into which our little band was now thrown. With the solitary exception of our leader, there was not a man among us who appeared otherwise than satisfied that those to whom he had listened were traitors . . . [But] he remained convinced of their fidelity.

He did not remain in ignorance for long. When his route was blocked by a force of militia considerably larger than his own, these new allies of his at first obediently took up positions around him and in his rear. But as soon as firing started in earnest they began shooting German officers in the back. Caught between two lines of fire, the Indians ran off into the forest, leaving Baum's troops dangerously exposed. A German officer, Lieutenant Glich, recorded:

> The vacancy which the retreat of the savages had occasioned was promptly filled up with one of our field pieces, whilst the other

poured destruction among the enemy in front. But the solitary tumbril, which contained the whole of our spare ammunition, became ignited and blew up with a violence which shook the ground under our feet, and caused a momentary cessation in firing, both on our side and on that of the enemy. The cessation was only for the moment. The American officers, guessing the extent of our calamity, cheered their men to fresh exertions. They rushed up the ascent with redoubled ardor, in spite of the heavy volley which we poured in to check them; and finding our guns silent, they [dashed towards us].

For a few seconds the scene that ensued defies all power of language to describe. The bayonet, the butt of the rifle, the sabre, the pike, were in full play; and men fell, as they rarely fall in modern war, under the direct blow of their enemies. But such a struggle could not, in the nature of things, be of long continuance. Outnumbered, broken, and somewhat disheartened by the late events, our people wavered, and fell back, or fought singly and unconnectedly, till they were either cut down at their posts, obstinately defending themselves, or compelled to surrender . . . Col. Baum shot through the body by a rifle ball, fell mortally wounded; and all order or discipline being lost, flight or submission was alone thought of.

A few survivors of the battle, having fought on until their ammunition was exhausted, escaped like the Indians into the forest, as another detachment of German soldiers under Lieutenant-Colonel von Breymann, sent to support Baum, came trudging slowly through the forest in the pouring rain, stopping at frequent intervals to dress their ranks. Never renowned for the speed of their progress in open country, Breymann's men were exceptionally slow in the thick, wet forests near Bennington. They took sixteen hours to march twenty-four miles; and when they arrived on the scene they 'noticed through the woods', in the words of Breymann's report, 'a considerable number of armed men (some of whom wore blouses and some jackets) hastening towards' them on their left flank. Breymann called the attention of Philip Skene to these men and 'received from him the reply that [they] were loyalists. But upon his riding towards them and calling to them, the matter was soon explained, for instead of returning an answer, they opened fire.' Breymann's men returned the fire until their ammunition was exhausted, then, like Baum's before them, they retreated, carrying off as many wounded as they could.

Altogether in these two actions Burgoyne lost four cannon, numerous muskets, tons of stores, nearly all his Indians and perhaps as many as nine hundred soldiers. One of the rebels wrote:

> We do not know how many we have killed. Our scouts daily find them dead in the woods. One of our scouts found, the beginning of this week, twenty-six of the enemy lying dead in the woods. They stank so they could not bury them . . . The wounded Hessians die three or four a day. They are all in Bennington Meeting House which smells so it is enough to kill anyone to be in it.

In his despatch to Lord George Germain, Burgoyne attributed his setback largely to the inhabitants of the settlements along the Hoosick River, who were 'the most active and most rebellious race of the continent'. But others blamed his own excessive confidence in the superiority of his own soldiers to those whom he had dismissed as 'preposterous' opponents.

While the American commander at Bennington, John Stark, who had raised 1500 New Hampshire militia within a week, was acclaimed by Congress, General 'Swagger' Burgoyne was criticized for spending too little time in careful planning and too much enjoying dinners in camp with his officers and their wives, drinking claret, listening to music and pleasuring himself with his new mistress, who was either the wife of a planter from Virginia who had been taken prisoner in Ticonderoga, as some maintained, or the wife of an English commissary, according to Baroness von Riedesel. When he had left Quebec, so it had been observed, no fewer than thirty carts had been required to transport his uniforms and other personal possessions; and now, Baroness von Riedesel complained, 'it was only too true that General Burgoyne liked to make himself easy, and that he spent half his nights in singing and drinking, and diverting himself with . . . his mistress who was as fond of champaign as himself'.

Distressing news for Burgoyne came not only from Bennington. Colonel St Leger's diversion through the valley of the Mohawk from Oswego had also fared badly. Having come up from Montreal, St Leger had landed at Fort Oswego on Lake Ontario in the middle of

July and had been joined there by a small party of Indians and a few Loyalists, considerably fewer than he had expected, predictions as to the number in the area brave enough to join him being as usual over-optimistic. With less than seventeen hundred men he had advanced through the forest to Fort Stanwix, not far from the source of the Mohawk River, and had invested the place. At that time there were less than six hundred Americans in the fort, which had been solidly constructed twenty years before by General Stanwix; but reports reached St Leger of eight hundred other rebels under command of a Dutchman, Nicholas Herkimer, marching to their relief. So he decided to ambush them as they approached the fort down the ravine that led to it at a place called Oriskany, which in the language of the Oneida Indians means Field of Nettles. But St Leger's plans went awry when the Indians, who had been told not to show themselves until the white men opened fire, were unable to restrain their impatience and attacked prematurely, enabling the American rearguard to escape. The remainder of the militiamen were surrounded, however, and were soon heavily engaged with the men who had been lying in wait for them. The fight lasted from nine o'clock in the morning until three in the afternoon, Herkimer himself being wounded soon after it began, though he continued to direct and encourage his men, sitting down on a log with his sword in his hand. In order to help him, a colonel in the New York Regiment, Peter Sansevoort, who was in command at Fort Stanwix, sent out his second-in-command, Marinus Willett, in a diversionary attack on St Leger's camp. This diversion was a complete success, so the *Continental Journal* reported,

> for after an engagement of an hour Lieut. Col. Willett had routed the enemy, took one Captain and four privates prisoners. The baggage taken was very considerable, such as money; bear skins, officers' baggage and camp equipage: one of the soldiers had for his share a scarlet coat, trimmed with gold lace to the full, and three laced hats . . . Col. Willett then marched with his booty into the Fort, where he arrived at four the same day, having not a single man killed or wounded.

St Leger's losses, on the other hand, were very heavy, particularly amongst the Indians, several of whose bravest warriors and chiefs had

been killed, causing deep resentment and anger. Indeed, according to
Willett, the garrison were warned that such was the rage of the
Indians that the consequences to the defenders of Fort Stanwix if it
fell into their hands would be 'terrible' and that, if it did not surrender,
the Indians 'were determined to go down the Mohawk River and fall
upon the inhabitants. The reply was "that such proceedings would
ever remain a stigma upon the name of Britain". For their part, the
garrison remained determined to defend the fort.'

St Leger, who had no intention of letting the Indians loose upon
the American riverside settlements, continued the siege, increasingly
doubtful of success with the forces at his command and with guns
far too light to make any impression upon the sturdy defences of the
star-shaped fort. He was obliged to make his way forward by digging
approaches, a lengthy and laborious process. He had, however, got
within a hundred and fifty yards of the outer defences of the fort when
rumours began to spread among the Indians of General Burgoyne's
imminent defeat and of a large war party of Americans on the march
against them, intent upon their destruction.

These stories had been artfully spread by agents of Benedict
Arnold, who had been sent from Albany to relieve Fort Stanwix
with some twelve hundred volunteers from Massachusetts. St Leger
did his best to dispel the rumours and to reassure the Indians; but to
no avail. Arnold had chosen his agents well. One of them was a
highly plausible Indian chief, the other a young American, apparently
insane, whose state of mind was calculated to awe the Indians into
belief in him as a messenger of supernatural powers. The more they
heard of the vengeful army marching against them, the less inclined
were the Indians to wait to receive them. One by one they slunk
away, then, after breaking out into drunken mutiny, the rest followed
their example. Left with so few regular troops, St Leger had no
alternative but to raise the siege, take to his boats and return to
Oswego.

Three weeks later General Burgoyne continued his march. Had the
decision been left to him, he would have remained where he was, he
told Germain, or perhaps have gone back to Fort Edward where he
would have been 'perfectly secure until some event happened to assist
[his] movement forward'. As it was, he was dangerously weak in
numbers, while the enemy's strength seemed to be constantly grow-

ing. Yet he felt bound by his orders, so he maintained, to 'force a junction with Sir William Howe', a junction for which, as it happened, Howe himself was still entirely unprepared. 'When I wrote more confidently,' Burgoyne added in his letter to Germain, 'I little foresaw that I was to be left to pursue my way through such a tract of country, and hosts of foes, without any co-operation from New York; nor did I think the garrison of Ticonderoga would fall to my share alone, a dangerous experiment would it be to leave that post in weakness, and too heavy a drain it is upon the life-blood of my force to give it due strength.'

14

SURRENDER AT SARATOGA

*'This Day General Burguine
Sined the Articels of Capitilation
. . . and the whole Armey Capi-
lated and the General officers came
out in the fore Noon & in the
afterNoon the rest of the Armey
came out and thay wair two hours
a marching out.'*

Solomon Dwinnell

As soon as he realized how matters stood with the British and that a junction between their armies was no longer a threat, Washington saw his opportunity. 'Now,' he said, 'let all New England rise and crush Burgoyne.' To enable the American forces north of Albany to achieve this victory he sent them as many additional troops as he could spare, including a brigade under Benjamin Lincoln, who had been released in an exchange of prisoners after his surrender at Charleston, and Daniel Morgan's by now celebrated riflemen with their distinctive coonskin caps and highly effective Pennsylvania flintlocks.

These men, on the advice of the Polish volunteer, Tadeusz Kościuszko, were directed to a strong defensive position a few miles from Stillwater, Bemis Heights, named after a man who kept a tavern beside the road which followed the course of the river below. Soon the American force gathered here beneath the oak and maple trees was to be far larger than the army which Burgoyne took across to the west bank of the Hudson River by a bridge of rafts on 13 September 1777.

Marching through a countryside still soaked by heavy rain, Burgoyne's officers were well aware of the daunting task that faced them. There were believed to be well over six thousand Americans at Bemis Heights, under the command of Horatio Gates, who had recently replaced Philip Schuyler as commander of the Northern Department. Gates was not as good a general as Schuyler, whom he intensely disliked and by whom he was as wholeheartedly disliked in return. But he was much more popular with New Englanders, who resented Schuyler's opposition to their claims during the quarrels over the New Hampshire Grants; and men who would have been reluctant to come forward to enlist under Schuyler, a proud, aloof disciplinarian of Dutch descent, had no such reservations about the friendly, cautious 'Granny' Gates. Admittedly, few of those who rallied to Gates had a high opinion of him as a general, but his men were relieved to discover that Benedict Arnold was also on Bemis Heights.

Burgoyne advanced against the rebel position in three columns. He decided to take personal command of the centre column, comprising four battalions and numbering just over one thousand men; the left-hand column was entrusted to Baron von Riedesel, with General Phillips and the artillery in support; Simon Fraser, supported by Breymann's reserve, was appointed to command the right-hand column which, having made a wide detour, was to attack the enemy's flank. Behind these columns trailed the familiar lines of women and cooks, hospital attendants and servants, smiths and carpenters, officers' wives in small carriages, wagons piled high with stores and ammunition, drovers with herds of cattle.

By dawn on 17 September, a cold morning on which the ground was white with frost, the advance guard were within four miles of the rebel lines. Here, near a place known as Sword's Farm, a field of potatoes proved too tempting a sight for a party of British soldiers who, disobeying orders which forbade foraging before the lifting of the morning fog, went to dig them up. While they were doing so, they were surprised by some of Daniel Morgan's riflemen who killed, wounded or captured about thirty of them as the others fled for their lives. Hitherto, Burgoyne's punishments had been comparatively mild, except for looters, some of whom had been sentenced to a thousand lashes; but the army was now informed that the 'Lieut.

General [would] no longer bear to lose his men for the pitiful consideration of potatoes or forage'. Soldiers' lives were 'the property of the King'; and, since 'neither friendly admonition, repeated injunctions nor corporal punishments' had had effect, the army must now understand that 'the first Soldier caught beyond the Centries of the Army [would] be instantly hanged'.

Annoyed as he was by displays of indiscipline in his army, and disgruntled as he might sound in his letters to Lord George Germain, Burgoyne maintained a cheerful confidence that infected his staff. One of his aides-de-camp, Sir Francis Carr Clerke, told a friend that the enemy's numbers were reported to be great but that the British were 'equal to anything'. The 'Americans pretend to be in spirits,' Clerke wrote, 'and threaten us a drubbing, but on the approach of the red Coats I rather believe it will be as usual; they will find out that they can take up better ground in their rear.'

> One proof of the spirit of our army, the Ladies do not mean to quit us. Lady Harriet Acland graces the advanced Corps of the Army, and Madame Riedesel the German brigades. We have frequent dinées and constantly musick; for my part . . . this campaigning is a favourite portion of Life: and none but stupid Mortals can dislike a lively Camp, good Weather, good Claret, good Musick and the enemy near. I may venture to say all this, for a little fusillade during dinner does not discompose the Nerves of even our Ladies . . . Therefore we set our faces forward, and mean to bite hard if anything dares to show itself. As to numbers of our foes, I believe them great, mais n'importe, what are not we equal to.

As soon as the British movement developed and he realized the nature of the threat to their position, Benedict Arnold urged Gates to attack the enemy on the march through the forest, where they would be unable to use their heavy artillery to best advantage or effectively to carry out their demoralizing bayonet charges. Gates, already annoyed with Arnold for giving so many of Schuyler's friends appointments on his staff, told him he preferred to wait. Arnold 'urged, begged and entreated' him to move; but, although scouts high up in the trees warned of the approach of the British infantry with their bayonets glinting, it was not until Fraser was in a position on Burgoyne's right and a signal-gun had been fired to let Riedesel know that the other two columns were ready to advance again that Arnold was given the orders he had so pressingly sought and allowed to counter-attack. He first tried to turn Burgoyne's right, but, being prevented from doing so by General Fraser's column, which up till then had been concealed from him by the forest, he turned upon the British centre column in a clearing known as Freeman's Farm. Here there was fierce fighting for several hours, first one side seeming to have the advantage, then the other.

'The conflict was dreadful,' recalled Sergeant Lamb of the 9th Regiment. 'For four hours a constant blaze of fire was kept up . . . Men, and particularly officers, dropped every moment on each side.' The three regiments most hotly engaged, the 20th, 21st and 62nd, made one bayonet charge after another; but as soon as a little ground was gained, Benedict Arnold threw more of his men into the fight to drive the British soldiers back. 'Nothing could exceed the bravery of Arnold on this day,' recorded one of his officers, Captain Wakefield of the New Hampshire Regiment. 'He seemed the very genius of war. Infuriated by the conflict, maddened by Gates's refusal to send reinforcements which he repeatedly called for, and knowing he was meeting the brunt of the battle, he seemed inspired with the fury of a demon.'

In the ranks facing him was Lieutenant William Digby who was appalled by the slaughter and the crackle and roar of the guns. 'Such an explosion of fire I never had any idea of before,' he wrote, 'and the heavy artillery joining concert like great peals of Thunder, assisted by the echoes of the woods, almost deafened us with the noise . . . This crash of cannon and musketry never ceased till darkness parted us.' Digby saw the British advance pickets engage a far larger number of riflemen from Virginia; and, because of 'the great superiority of fire' received from these expert marksmen, the British fell back, 'every officer being either killed or wounded except one'. Further along the line, although the British and Germans were fighting hard, standing their ground until driven back by the overwhelming power of the skilled American riflemen, many of their allies were less inclined to fight bravely against such odds. 'The Indians were running from wood to wood,' Lieutenant Anburey recorded. 'As to the Canadians, little was to be depended upon their adherence, being easily dispirited with an inclination to quit as soon as there was an appearance of danger. Nor was the fidelity of the [Loyalists] who had joined our army to be relied on, as they withdrew on perceiving the resistance of [their fellow-Americans] would be more formidable than expected.'

The British and Germans continued to fight throughout the afternoon and evening, losing so many men that, had Arnold been fully supported by Gates, they would almost certainly have been driven from the field. General Burgoyne 'was everywhere', William Digby said, 'and did everything that could be expected of a brave officer; & Brigadier-General Fraser gained great honour by exposing himself to every danger.' So did Baron von Riedesel who, by pressing hard on Arnold's flank, forced him to retire for a time; and so did General Phillips who, having used his guns to good effect, took personal command of the 9th Regiment. It was astonishing that none of these senior officers was killed, for rebel sharpshooters, clustered in the trees above their heads, picked off one target after another with unerring aim.

By nightfall, when the action ended, the British regiments engaged had lost almost a third of their strength. In the 62nd only about sixty men survived unscathed out of nearly four hundred who had eaten breakfast that morning. The artillery had lost all their officers and all but twelve of their forty-eight men. Burgoyne could claim a victory since he remained in possession of the field; yet as Digby said, it was a very dear victory since so many brave men had died and 'no very great advantage, honour excepted, was gained by the day'. 'During the night we remained in our ranks . . . unable to assist the wounded, not knowing the position of the enemy, and expecting the action to be renewed at day-break.' And throughout those hours of darkness, above the groans of the wounded, could be heard the cries of wolves as they fought each other over the corpses of the dead and snapped at dying men too weak to resist them.

When the dead could be buried they were tipped into common graves, as many as twenty in each hole, often with legs, arms and even heads appearing above the upturned earth, the officers being laid in holes separate from the men. In one hole three officers of the 20th Regiment were buried together; all of them were less than eighteen.

Since most of the wounded had had to be left in the open all night, so an officer in charge of a burial party wrote, 'from loss of blood and want of our timely assistance they inevitably expired'.

These poor creatures, perishing with cold and weltering in their blood, displayed such a scene, it must be a heart of adamant that could not be effected by it.

In the course of the late action, Lieutenant Harvey, of the 62nd, a youth of sixteen, and a nephew to the Adjutant-General of the same name, received several wounds, and was repeatedly ordered off the field by Colonel Anstruther, but his heroic ardor would not allow him to quit the battle while he could stand and see his brave lads fighting beside him. A ball striking one of his legs, his removal became absolutely necessary, and while they were conveying him away, another wounded him mortally. In this situation the Surgeon recommended him to take a powerful dose of opium, to avoid seven or eight hours of the most exquisite torture; this he immediately consented to, and when the Colonel entered the tent with Major Harnage, who were both wounded, they asked whether he had any affairs they could settle for him? His reply was that being a minor, every thing was already adjusted; but he had one request which he had just life enough to utter, 'Tell my uncle I die like a soldier!'

On the morning after the battle, while the British troops, constantly under sniping fire from American sharpshooters, cut down trees to strengthen their position, their General prepared plans for another attack the following day. He believed, with justice, that although numerous fresh troops had joined them since the fighting at Bemis Heights, the Americans were in almost as unhappy a condition as he was himself, that they had little food or ammunition left, that one last effort might drive them back if the British relied more on the bayonet than they had done in the recent engagement. 'Amidst these subjects of applause,' Burgoyne had felt it necessary to write in a General Order after the fighting at Freeman's Farm, 'the uncertain aim of the Troops in giving their fire and the mistake they are still under in preferring it to the Bayonet, is much to be lamented. The Lieutenant General is persuaded this Error will be corrected in the next Engagement.' Sergeant Thomas Sullivan of the 49th agreed with the General that the British troops should rely more on their bayonets, which 'were always a terror to the Rebels and put them to an immediate Rout'. 'If the King's troops kept at a distance,' he added, 'the Rebels stood firing with Mosquetry long enough . . . But they could never endure to stand for any time to the Bayonet.'

The British soldiers were, however, too exhausted to undertake a fresh engagement just yet either with musket or bayonet, so their officers informed Burgoyne, who therefore postponed the attack for twenty-four hours until 22 September. But when that day came, as foggy and wet as ever, the men were still not ready.

Further up the river at the head of Lake George, the Americans had already mounted a successful surprise attack on the British flotilla at anchor there and had captured all the ships as well as the three companies of the 53rd Regiment which had been posted there to guard them. When news of this misfortune reached Burgoyne's camp near Saratoga, he considered retreating to safety while he still could. But on that same day he also received a message from New York which persuaded him that, shrunken and battered though his army was, he should not retreat just yet: Sir Henry Clinton was preparing to make a diversion from New York in his favour.

Up till now Clinton had been of the opinion that the size of his force in New York did not permit any move in favour of Burgoyne. He had received a letter from Howe proposing some kind of diversion, provided Manhattan was not thereby exposed to attack; but he had concluded that Howe had only sent these instructions to place himself in the clear after receiving a letter from Lord George Germain, and that, in any event, the presence of strong rebel forces in the area put out of the question any operation which would reduce New York's defences. There had already been three well-conducted attacks on his outposts on 22 August. In one of these a young officer had been killed; his wife and child had escaped into the woods where the rebels had found them and, in the words of one of Clinton's staff, having stripped the mother, 'used her so ill that her child died of the fright the same night, and she continued delirious for some time and is now in miserable circumstances'.

While thus threatened by the rebels in New York, and without dependable news of either Howe or Burgoyne, Clinton had clung to his conviction that he could mount only minor diversions unless a direct and urgent request for help from Burgoyne provided him with the excuse for an attack upon the Hudson River forts which, if successful, might not only open up navigation of the waterway but also draw Sir William Howe away from his 'meaningless excursion' into Pennsylvania. Consequently on 11 September, on learning that

Burgoyne's advance appeared to have come to a halt forty miles from Albany, Clinton wrote him a letter which on the face of it was incomprehensible. The recipient was meant to read it with the help of a piece of paper with a hole in it cut in the shape of an hour glass. Burgoyne had lost the sheet but, remembering the rough shape of the hole, he cut another roughly like it, and eventually deciphered Clinton's message;

While you, my dear Burgoyne are reaping laurels
I am forced to sleep. You know my temper too well to doubt that I
do not cede them to you with goodwill, & are convinced that I take my share
in your success. You're not ignorant of my hopes of being able to
work at last upon poverty. If you think the young man more tractable,
I'll try him. Surely 2,000 men can assist Sir Wm importantly just now!
I'll send him there, for you effectually etc etc etc etc etc etc etc etc etc
etc etc etc etc etc etc etc etc I will make etc etc etc etc etc etc etc etc etc etc
etc etc etc etc etc etc etc a push at etc etc etc etc etc etc etc etc etc
etc etc etc etc etc etc etc [Fort] Montgomery etc etc etc etc etc etc etc etc
etc etc etc etc etc etc etc in about ten days etc etc etc etc etc etc etc etc
etc etc etc etc etc etc etc but ever jealous of etc etc etc etc etc etc etc etc
etc etc etc etc etc etc etc my flanks; if they make etc etc etc etc etc etc etc etc
etc etc etc etc etc etc a move in force on either etc etc etc etc etc etc etc
etc etc etc etc etc etc of them, I must return to etc etc etc etc etc etc etc
etc etc etc etc etc etc save this important post etc etc etc etc etc etc etc
etc etc etc etc etc etc I expect reinforcements etc etc etc etc etc etc etc
etc etc etc etc etc etc every day. Let me know etc etc etc etc etc etc etc
etc etc etc etc etc etc etc etc what you would etc etc etc etc etc etc etc etc etc
etc etc etc etc etc etc etc etc etc wish etc etc etc etc etc etc etc etc etc etc

This message took ten days to reach Burgoyne; the reply was a further eight days on its way back to New York; so that it was not until 29 September that Clinton learned precisely what Burgoyne's position was. The letter from Burgoyne, accepting Clinton's offer, was characteristically optimistic, though – as was to be expected of one which might be intercepted – carefully guarded. The messenger who brought it, however, reported verbally that Burgoyne's provisions were almost exhausted, and that his line of communications was stretched to the limit and in danger of being cut. Yet Burgoyne still believed that if a diversion were made in his favour he could push his way past Gates to Albany.

Reinforcements for Clinton had by now arrived, and he felt able to move at last. Before the end of the first week in October three thousand troops were embarked and ready for the planned attacks on the Hudson forts. Under cover of a naval squadron commanded by Commodore Como Hotham, the expedition moved north from New York beyond Fort Washington and Dobbs Ferry. Clinton first attacked Verplancks Point, which protected a place where stores were landed for General Israel Putnam's troops in Peekskill; and, having overwhelmed the small garrison here and captured their guns, he made attacks on two other forts three miles upriver. The first of these, Fort Montgomery, he captured with ease; in taking the second, Fort Clinton, called after his namesake, Governor George Clinton, he lost eighteen officers and 169 men killed and wounded. 'I never saw more gallantry and intrepidity shown,' one of his officers reported of the infantry, who had had to manage without artillery support because of the roughness of the tracks leading to the fort, which was out of range of Commodore Hotham's guns. 'It is impossible to give an idea of the strength of the country we had to march through to this attack. Well might they think it impregnable, for it certainly was so to any but British troops.' After a courageous defence in which they suffered severe casualties, the Americans were compelled to surrender with all their sixty-seven cannon and a large amount of ammunition and stores. Clinton marched off with three hundred prisoners and a ten-gun sloop. He would also have taken the ships of the American flotilla beyond the boom had these not been burned when contrary winds prevented their escape to the north.

'*Nous y voilà*,' Clinton wrote to Burgoyne from the captured Fort Montgomery on 8 October, 'and nothing now between us but Gates. I sincerely hope this *little* success of ours may facilitate your operations . . . I heartily wish you success.' This message, written on thin paper, was rolled up inside a small silver bullet and entrusted to a loyalist messenger, Daniel Taylor, who set off with it through the forest to General Burgoyne's camp. On the way he was intercepted. But, before he could be searched, he was seen to remove an object from his pocket and to swallow it. He was taken before Governor George Clinton who ordered him to be given 'a severe dose of emetic tartar'. 'This produced the happiest effect as respects the prescriber,' wrote the American surgeon, James Thacher, 'but it proved fatal to the patient. He discharged a small silver bullet which [he snatched and swallowed again but which on being discharged after another dose of emetic and] being unscrewed was found to enclose a letter from

Sir Henry Clinton to Burgoyne . . . The spy was tried, convicted and executed.'

The day before this letter was written, Burgoyne decided to make a desperate attempt to turn the Americans' left, despite the few men he could spare for such an enterprise. For nearly a fortnight his troops had been under repeated attack by raiding parties and under fire every night. Sentries were shot at their posts or attacked silently with tomahawks by Indians who were now in American employment. Provisions were becoming scarcer day by day, the flour having been ruined by rain. Over the whole area the stench of death filled the air as wolves, converging upon the battlefield in their thousands, dragged the rotting corpses from their shallow graves. 'They were similar to a pack of hounds,' an officer recorded, 'for one setting up a cry they all joined in and, when they approached a corpse, their noise was hideous until they had scratched it up.' Men, for the most part Germans, began to desert; and, to discourage others from following them, those Indians who remained with the British were told that scalping deserters was not a forbidden activity.

'It was the plan of the enemy,' Burgoyne reported, 'to harass the army by constant alarms, and their superiority of numbers enabled them to attempt this without fatigue to themselves . . . I do not believe that either officer or soldier ever slept [throughout this time] without his cloaths, or that any general officer, or commander of a regiment, passed a single night without being upon his legs occasionally at different hours and constantly an hour before daylight.'

On 27 September Burgoyne sent another message to Clinton reporting that he had only about five thousand troops left, whereas the enemy probably had about twelve thousand by now, with another four thousand ready to support them if necessary. He might still, he added, force his way through to Albany; but would Clinton be able to supply his troops there throughout the winter, once his own supply route to the north was cut? If not, he would have to retreat before ice blocked the river. He had only a fortnight left.

Within hours of writing this letter Burgoyne learned that Ticonderoga had been attacked by Benjamin Lincoln who, after taking many prisoners and burning or sinking several boats, had gone on to make an attempt upon Fort George where several other boats had been destroyed. Clearly Burgoyne's position was becoming more perilous with each passing day. He sent another, more urgent, message to Clinton, repeating his question as to whether his forces could be supplied if they managed to get through to Albany.

There being still no news from Clinton by 4 October, Burgoyne decided to call a Council of War, a measure to which he had not before felt the need to resort. Both Riedesel and Fraser suggested a retreat to Fort Edward; but Burgoyne was reluctant to withdraw just yet, and, since William Phillips did not commit himself either way, no firm decision was taken.

Three days later, however, Burgoyne made up his mind independently that his one chance of extricating himself and his men from their intolerable position without dishonour was to get behind the Americans and then away to Albany for the long-delayed junction with Howe. So, leaving eight hundred men to protect his camp, he set out shortly before noon on 7 October with fifteen hundred men and ten guns, Riedesel with his Germans in the centre, General Phillips in command on the left flank, he himself on the right, the few Indians and Loyalists who had not already deserted him making their way through the forest to create a diversion at the back of the American position.

No sooner had the British begun their operation than the Americans under Colonel Daniel Morgan, commanding what Burgoyne later described as 'the finest regiment in the world', fell heavily upon their left column; and when a company of grenadiers wheeled to protect it, the Americans extended their attack to the centre also, bringing four thousand men into action. Simon Fraser, who had been endeavouring to contain a simultaneous attack on the British right, withdrew the 24th Regiment and his light infantry to support the grenadiers as they faltered in the face of fierce fire from an overpoweringly greater force. Seeing Fraser riding across the British lines, Benedict Arnold said to Daniel Morgan, 'That officer upon a grey horse is of himself a host and must be disposed of.' Morgan passed the order on to one of his riflemen with the words, 'That gallant officer is General Fraser. I admire him, but it is necessary that he should die. "Do your duty."' Soon afterwards, so an American militiaman recorded, the bullets began to fly around Fraser. One shot cut the crupper of his horse; another grazed its ears. An aide-de-camp urged him to withdraw; but he rode on and immediately received a bullet through his stomach.

Also killed at this point was one of Burgoyne's aides-de-camp, taking a message for the artillery to retire.

Burgoyne had realized that to press the attack was suicidal. As well as Fraser, Sir Francis Carr Clerke had also been mortally wounded; General Breymann had been shot dead, reportedly by one of his own men whom he had been threatening angrily with his sword when they seemed reluctant to fight; Major John Dyke Acland, who had recently been badly burned when his tent caught fire after his dog had kicked over a candle, was shot through both his legs; Burgoyne himself had been shot through his waistcoat, collar and hat. He told Phillips and Riedesel to cover a general retreat into the entrenchments, drawing the main body back in remarkably good order despite the driving rain and the deep, sticky mud that covered the road, losing no prisoners and only six guns whose crews and horses had all been shot.

In eager pursuit of his initial success, Benedict Arnold lost no time in attacking the British right. He seemed almost hysterical with excitement now. Some of his men thought he was drunk as he roared out orders and whirled his sword. He struck one of his own officers, who threatened to shoot him, then, shouting still, he galloped off to another part of the line where his horse fell and, in rolling over, broke his leg. The troops here, light infantry under command of Alexander Lindsay, 6th Earl of Balcarres, who had succeeded Simon Fraser, stood their ground and drove the Americans off. But a subsequent attack upon Canadian volunteers who were on the light infantry's right broke through the British lines and, although strongly contested by German grenadiers and light infantry, the Americans were before nightfall so firmly established on his right flank that Burgoyne felt compelled to retire under cover of darkness and heavy rain to a new position on high ground above the river.

The next day this position also was threatened by an outflanking movement which forced Burgoyne to make a further retreat to Saratoga, leaving about five hundred men, who were too badly wounded or too ill to walk, to fall into the hands of the enemy. The survivors retreated through the still pouring rain and were so exhausted when they reached Saratoga on 8 October that they could not bring themselves to collect wood for fires. They lay down to sleep in their soaking clothes on the cold and marshy ground, several more of their comrades having slipped away in the darkness and deserted to the enemy camp.

They woke in the morning to another wet day and to the prospect of further retreat. Having marched before the fog had lifted, they stood for a time at bay on open ground ideally suited to the tactics in which they had been trained and to the use of the twenty-seven guns which, at Burgoyne's insistence, they had not abandoned. The fog still hid them from the Americans, who came on in close pursuit. But when the air cleared the Americans were seen not advancing but moving quickly back; for two deserters from the British army, stumbling into the American lines one after the other, had warned General Gates that he was falling into a trap. He had escaped just in time, denying Burgoyne the victory that might have saved him.

As it was, Burgoyne's troops were now beyond salvation. Almost completely surrounded by an army recently reinforced by John Stark's militiamen who had fought so well at Bennington, they sought shelter in their exposed encampment from the remorseless American bombardment and the ever-watchful snipers crouching in hollows or behind upturned carts, while hungry cattle roamed about amongst them in search of food or lay dead and putrefying on the bare slopes of the hill. 'Some of the rebels' balls fell very near our hospital tents,' Lieutenant Digby recorded, 'on which we were obliged to move [the wounded] out of the range of fire, which was a most shocking scene – some poor wretches dying in the attempt, being so very severely wounded.' Water was so scarce that men risked their lives in crawling down to fetch it from the river under the fire of rebel snipers, until a soldier's wife offered to take the buckets down herself, suggesting that the Americans would not fire on a woman. She walked down to the water's edge, filled her buckets and was allowed to return unharmed.

Baroness von Riedesel sought shelter with her children in a house which immediately became the object of a 'frightful cannonade', 'probably because the enemy believed, from seeing so many people flocking around it, that all the generals made it their headquarters. Alas! it harboured none but wounded soldiers, or women!'

> We were finally obliged to take refuge in a cellar. My children lay
> down on the earth with their heads upon my lap, and in this manner

we passed the entire night . . . A horrible stench, the cries of the children prevented me from closing my eyes. On the following morning the cannonade again began, but from a different side. I advised all to go out of the cellar for a little while, during which time I would have it cleaned, as otherwise we would all be sick. They followed my suggestion, and I at once set many hands to work, which was in the highest degree necessary; for the women and children, being afraid to venture forth, had soiled the whole cellar.

I had just given the cellars a good sweeping, and fumigated them by sprinkling vinegar on burning coals, and each had found his place prepared for him – when a fresh and terrible cannonade threw us all once more into alarm. Many persons, who had no right to come in, threw themselves against the door. My children were already under the cellar steps, and we would all have been crushed, if God had not given me strength to place myself before the door, and with extended arms prevent all from coming in; otherwise every one of us would have been severely injured.

Eleven cannon balls went through the house, and we could plainly hear them rolling over our heads. One poor soldier, whose leg they were about to amputate, having been laid upon a table for this purpose, had the other leg taken off by another cannon ball, in the very middle of the operation. His comrades all ran off, and when they again came back they found him in one corner of the room, where he had rolled in anguish, scarcely breathing. I was more dead than alive, though not so much on account of my own danger as for that which enveloped my husband, who, however, frequently sent to see how I was getting along, and to tell me he was still safe . . .

In this horrible situation we remained six days.

During this time the intrepid, bossy Baroness went in search of one of Burgoyne's aides-de-camp and, encountering Lord Petersham, instructed him to tell the General that several of his wounded officers had had no food for two days. Burgoyne came over and, with an elaborate politeness whose sardonic undertones were quite lost upon her, thanked her for 'teaching him his duty'.

He was by then in the midst of negotiations with the enemy. Escorted by Gates's young adjutant-general in a blue civilian frock-coat, Burgoyne's own adjutant-general, Major Kingston, had been taken blindfolded to the American headquarters.

The terms at first proposed by Horatio Gates were deemed unacceptable and Burgoyne submitted instead a proposal that he should be allowed to march his army out with the honours of war, that the men should pile their arms and go to Boston to be sent home from there by ship. In return Burgoyne undertook to ensure that they would not serve in America again so long as the present war lasted. He could hardly have expected that such a proposal would be entertained by the American commander, who could have dictated whatever terms he chose and who might well have protested that the undertaking not to serve in America again meant very little, since every soldier landed in England would release another for fighting overseas. The negotiations dragged on, prolonged by Burgoyne who hoped that Clinton might yet arrive in time to help him; but when it seemed that Clinton would never come and that Gates would agree to the British army being sent home to Europe, Burgoyne agreed to sign the terms, provided they were headed 'Convention' rather than 'Capitulation'. General Gates made this concession; and, to the amazement of several members of his staff, having required a few small alterations in the wording of the 'Convention', not merely accepted it but seemed to be more than satisfied with it. 'If old England is not by this lesson taught humility,' he wrote to his wife, 'then she is an obstinate old slut, bent on her ruin.'

So it was that on the morning of 17 October, with their drums beating, the British and German troops marched out of their lines to pile their arms in front of the American camp, the men in stained and torn uniforms, several of them with pets – foxes, a raccoon, a bear, a deer – most of the officers in full dress so smart that observers were astonished to see that it had been preserved in such perfect condition. In all there were scarcely half the number that had left Quebec in such confidence that summer – less than four thousand British, some twenty-four hundred Germans.

William Digby confessed that, 'unmanly' though it was, there were tears in his eyes as he led his men out to the forlorn tapping of a drum. 'I shall never forget the appearance of their troops on our marching past them,' he wrote, praising, as others did, the courteous forbearance of the rebels who appeared more sympathetic than exultant, who, as Lieutenant Anburey confirmed, showed 'not the least disrespect or even a taunting look but all was mute astonishment and pity'. One of the rebel bands derisively played 'Yankee Doodle Dandy', a British army song of the Seven Years' War, which the soldiers had sung, and continued to sing, in mockery of the bumpkins who had then been their allies; and there were a few angry shouts when Burgoyne appeared, and some threats of tarring and feathering. But these soon died away and then, so Digby continued, 'a dead silence universally reigned through their numerous columns. I must say their decent behaviour . . . meritted the utmost approbation and praise.' Another officer confirmed:

> They stood like soldiers, erect with a military bearing, so still that we were greatly amazed . . . Not one of them was properly uniformed but each man had on the clothes in which he goes to the field, the church or to the tavern . . . The officers wore very few uniforms and those they did wear were of their own invention. All colors of cloth are usable, e.g. brown coats with sea green facings, white lining, and silver sword knots; also gray coats with straw facings and yellow buttons were frequently seen . . . [Some of them had] snow-white wigs with mighty long bushy hair at the sides and thick lambs'-tails behind! There were glistening black abbots' wigs, which especially set off red or copper-coloured faces! There were also white or gray English pastors' wigs whose horse or goat hair was done up in a dangerously huge roll standing up in the air. You think such a man has a whole sheep under his hat and hanging down the back of his neck. The respected wearers of these various wigs are in part between their fiftieth and sixtieth year and have perhaps at this age followed the drum for the first time.

The meeting between Burgoyne in his spotless full-dress uniform and gold epaulettes and Gates in a plain dark blue coat was, in Digby's opinion, 'well worth seeing':

> Gates paid Burgoyne almost as much respect as if he was the conqueror.
> 'The fortunes of war, General,' Burgoyne said, 'have made me your prisoner.'
> 'I shall always be ready,' Gates politely replied, 'to bear testimony that it has not been through any fault of Your Excellency.'

This was, indeed, characteristic of Gates's behaviour throughout the engagement: he seemed almost apologetic in his manner of fighting the battle and punctiliously correct in his conduct after Benedict Arnold had won it for him. When Simon Fraser's funeral, through some mistake, became the object of a fierce bombardment, he sent the enemy a message of deep regret that such an error should have been made and ordered a minute-gun to be fired in honour of the 'gallant dead'; when Major John Dyke Acland's pretty, pregnant wife, Lady Harriet, was rowed downriver to the American camp to tend her wounded husband who was held prisoner there, Gates received her with the utmost politeness, said how sorry he was that her perilous journey had been interrupted by an over-zealous sentry, and had her escorted to her husband's bedside. And when Baroness von Riedesel drove into the American camp with her children she was greeted with the most polite respect, with not a hint of the coarseness she had expected. Indeed she was almost inclined to believe that the Americans were more gentlemanly than the British, between whom and the Germans there had been much bad feeling of late. One German officer had written home to criticize the 'confounded pride and arrogant bearing of the English, who treat everyone that was not born on their ragamuffin Island with contempt'. Baroness von Riedesel herself had had cause to complain of some slighting remarks that Burgoyne had made after one of General Breymann's officers had lost his way while leading a sortie. The British General was, indeed, in her opinion as arrogant as he was incompetent.

The Americans, on the contrary, could not have been kinder to her. When she arrived outside the marquee, where Burgoyne and Gates were having lunch with their respective staffs and other senior officers, and pleaded that she had nowhere to go, General Philip Schuyler immediately rose from the plank which, resting on powder barrels, was serving as a table. He went outside, lifted her children down, kissed them with unaccustomed tears in his eyes, and took the family to his own tent where his cook gave them a meal.

In the Commander-in-Chief's marquee the lunch party continued amicably, General Gates and his principal guest drinking rum and water from the only two available glasses, the other officers using bowls, all evidently enjoying the ham and beef, goose and boiled mutton spread before them, and, much to the disapproval of the Baroness, laughing together. At the end of the meal Burgoyne was asked to propose a toast. He stood and, with his glass in his hand, announced, 'George Washington!' They drank the toast, and waited for General Gates to respond. He rose and said, 'King George III!'

The British troops were then marched 'upwards of two hundred miles to the vicinity of Boston', reported Sergeant Lamb. And in Boston, since Congress refused to honour the Convention of Saratoga which would have permitted them to go home, they were held as prisoners of war in boarded huts on Winter and Prospect Hills.

> It is true [Lamb continued] the court of Massachusetts passed resolutions for procuring suitable accommodation, but from the general unwillingness of the people to administer the least civility, and from the feebleness of the authority which the American rulers had at that time over the property of their fellow citizens, their situation was rendered truly deplorable.
>
> Such were the disagreeable and distressing circumstances, which on every side increased the miseries of confinement, that, at this time the most faithful recital must despair of credence. It was not infrequent for thirty, or forty persons, men, women and children to be indiscriminately crowded together in one small, miserable, open hut; their provisions and fire-wood on short allowance; and a scanty portion of straw their bed, their own blankets their only covering. In the night time, those that could lie down, and the many who sat up from the cold, were obliged frequently to rise and shake from them the snow which the wind drifted in at the openings.

In the summer of 1778 the British prisoners were removed to an open area some fifty miles south of Boston, where they were enclosed within a stockade and provided with boards and nails so that they could build shelters for themselves. The provisions were rice and salt pork delivered – so Sergeant Lamb observed before he himself escaped to New York – with a scanty hand.

Other camps were later established and, according to Lieutenant Anburey, conditions in most were 'very unpleasant'. Anburey himself was not surprised that so many men were induced by their captors to desert and settle in America, as did the whole band of the 62nd Regiment – who could thereafter be heard playing for an American regiment in Boston – as well as numerous Germans, twelve thousand of whom never returned to Europe.

A few days after the surrender at Saratoga, General Gates, 'presuming upon [their] former friendship', wrote to the Marquess of Rockingham:

> Born & Bred an Englishman, I cannot help feeling for the misfortunes brought upon my country by the wickedness of that Administration who begun & have continued this most unjust, unpolitic and unnatural War . . . The United States of America are willing to be the Friends but will never submit to be the Slaves of the Parent Country. They are by Consanguinity, by Commerce, by Language & by the Affection which naturally flow from these more attached to England than any country under the sun. Therefore, spurn not the Blessings which yet remain. Instantly withdraw your Fleets and Armies, cultivate the Friendship and commerce of America. Thus, and thus only can England hope to be Great and Happy. Seek that in commercial alliance; seek it ere it be too late, for there alone you must expect to find it.

15

THE ENGLISH
DEBATE

---

*'Not one of the Ministers knew
what to say, and so said nothing.'*

Horace Walpole

When reports of Burgoyne's surrender at Saratoga reached London, the government, so one of Lord George Germain's secretaries confided to Edmund Burke, were 'in a state of great distraction'. 'He spoke as if they did not know what to do, or which way to turn themselves,' Burke wrote hurriedly 'over his chop', passing the news on to the Marquess of Buckingham. 'I said that *I* knew – to turn themselves out. However all this is between ourselves. As to Burgoyne his *style* is not in the least altered by his misfortunes. It is just as pompous as ever. What is worse, the *matter* is as pompous as ever, for the *style* he cannot help; it is his mother tongue.'

Lord Rockingham himself wrote contentedly, 'My heart is at ease.' The Opposition had been given the ammunition they needed to mount a devastating attack upon the government's conduct of the war. In the Upper House, Lord Chatham harangued his fellow-peers:

No man thinks more highly than I of the virtue and valour of British troops; I know they can achieve anything except impossibilities; and the conquest of English America is an impossibility. You cannot, I venture to say it, *you cannot conquer America* . . . What is your present situation there? We do not know the worst, but we know that in three campaigns we have done nothing, and suffered much . . .

Conquest is impossible: you may swell every expense and every
effort still more extravagantly; pile and accumulate every assistance
you can buy or borrow; traffic and barter with every pitiful German
prince that sells his subjects to the shambles of a foreign power;
your efforts are forever vain and impotent; doubly so from this
mercenary aid on which you rely; for it irritates to an incurable
resentment the minds of your enemies . . . If I were an American,
as I am an Englishman, while a foreign troop was landed in my
country, I never would lay down my arms, never – never – never!

In the Commons, Charles James Fox also made the most of his
opportunity. He stood up to declare that all those who had supported
the war were as criminally responsible as the Ministers; and demanded
that the orders which had been given to Burgoyne should be laid
before the House. This motion was defeated; but the government
awaited with apprehension a debate on the state of the nation which
had been set down for 2 February 1778.

On the afternoon of that day large crowds gathered outside the
House clamouring to be admitted to what promised to be one of the
most exciting debates in years. The porters, who had orders to keep
the doors locked and to let no one in, were besieged by people
claiming to have passes signed by Members, by swearing men and
by women in tears. Fox's beautiful and extravagant friend, the
Duchess of Devonshire, was there; so was that other fashionable
hostess, Mrs Norton. The uproar continued until the doors were
broken down; then there was a stampede into the galleries, and soon
every seat was occupied. But Members objected to their momentous
deliberations being regarded as an amusing show; and after much
heated argument instructions were given for the galleries to be closed.

The House at last fell into silence to listen to Fox. He spoke for
about two hours and forty minutes with that clear yet rapid delivery
which Tories had come to dread and Whigs to relish. During meetings
at Lord Rockingham's house the Opposition had decided that they
must not affront patriotic opinion in the country by appearing to
rejoice over the British defeat, that their policy, while being 'manly
and firm', must be to 'point out how the public had been deceived
and misled'. Consequently, Fox did not lay into Lord George Germain with that pitilessly caustic invective he had employed on previous occasions. He spoke reasonably, carefully and with telling

The BLOODY MASSACRE perpetrated in King—1—Street BOSTON on March 5 1770 by a party of the 29th REG

Above: 'The Bloody Massacre': a propagandist broadside engraved by Paul Revere, misrepresenting the events of 5 March 1770 which are less inaccurately depicted in the black and white illustration between pages 138 and 139. This engraving – described by Josiah Quincy at the soldiers' trial as having given 'wings to fancy' – was widely distributed in Boston together with a tendentious account of the incident printed in the *Boston Gazette*

Left: The master silversmith and engraver, Paul Revere, at the age of about thirty in 1765, showing him holding one of his celebrated teapots. The painter, Revere's fellow-Bostonian, John Singleton Copley, left America in 1774 to work in England where he was elected to the Royal Academy in 1779

Above: Sir William Howe directing the evacuation of Boston in March 1776. The operation was carried out in an 'Astonishing silence', even though he took with his own soldiers over a thousand American Loyalists whose 'Hurry and Confusion was dreadful to behold'

Left: An engraved portrait of Benedict Arnold, the enterprising rebel general, who was to betray the cause for which he had so bravely fought. The portrait was painted soon after Arnold's ill-fated assault on Quebec, which can be seen in the background

Above: John Trumbull's painting of the death of the Irish-born Brigadier-General Richard Montgomery before Quebec. Montgomery is seen dying in the arms of Lieutenant Ogden, who is wearing a fur-trimmed hat; behind them Colonel Donald Campbell holds aloft the flag. The red coats worn by some of the Americans are the British uniforms which had been captured at Montreal. The artist was a brigade major in the rebel army and occasionally employed by Washington as a cartographer. In 1780 he sailed to London where he studied with his fellow-American Benjamin West, who proposed that he painted a series of historical episodes in the war such as this

Below: The Royal Navy bombards Fort Moultrie on Sullivan's Island, which guarded the approaches to the wide harbour of Charleston, South Carolina. On 28 June 1776 the fort's flag was shot away and restored under heavy fire by Sergeant Jasper

Above: John Trumbull's painting of Thomas Jefferson presenting the Declaration of Independence to Congress. John Hancock, as President of Congress, sits in the chair facing Jefferson; Benjamin Franklin is on Jefferson's left, John Adams, in the brown suit, on his right. Most of the other figures were also painted from life. Trumbull began the picture in Paris in 1786 and took it about with him for eight years with the declared intention of preserving the 'resemblance of the men who were the authors of the memorable act'

Left: Charles Willson Peale's portrait of George Washington at the time of the battle of Princeton when the General was forty-six. Peale, who, like Trumbull, had studied in London with Benjamin West, was an ardent revolutionary. He served at Princeton with the Philadelphia militia

Right: On 3 January 1777 the Americans defeated a British brigade at Princeton. The rebel troops were bravely led by Washington himself, whose aide-de-camp pulled his hat over his eyes so that he should not be witness to the General's death

Below: 'The Battle of Germantown' by Xavier della Gatta. Taking advantage of his superiority in numbers, Washington attacked Howe on 4 October 1777. The engagement was savage and confused, and the casualties heavy on both sides

Left: In Trumbull's painting of the British surrender at Saratoga in October 1777, Burgoyne makes a gesture offering his sword to Gates who gracefully declines it. On Gates's left, in white buckskins, is Daniel Morgan then a colonel in the 11th Virginia Regiment, who was later to win a notable victory at Hannah's Cowpens. Although shown here in a smart uniform, Gates was in fact wearing a plain blue frock coat

Above: Christmas Day 1777: General Washington and his wife visit the troops in encampment at Valley Forge, Pennsylvania

Below: After a short siege, Charleston was surrendered on 12 May 1780 to Sir Henry Clinton, who took an immense amount of ammunition and weapons and over four thousand prisoners

Banastre Tarleton, the dashing and brutally ruthless cavalry commander, in a portrait by Sir Joshua Reynolds painted for his mother, widow of a Liverpool merchant

Left: John Singleton Copley's portrait of Lord Cornwallis, commander of British troops in the south, whose relations with nominal superior, Sir Henry Clinton, were so strained

Below: The Surrender at Yorktown from the painting by John Trumbull. Since Lord Cornwa pleaded that he was too ill to appear at the ceremony, his pla was taken by his second-in-command, Brigadier General Charles O'Hara. Washington accordingly appointed his own second-in-command, Major-General Benjamin Lincoln, to accept the formal surrender

effect. 'I would wish gentlemen to forget their animosities,' he said, 'and consider themselves neither friends nor enemies to America, nor that country either with love or hatred, but regard it with calm and dispassionate mind, as a part, and a very considerable part, of the British Empire.'

In a speech which the *London Chronicle* described as 'masterly, forcible, and expressive', containing the 'most striking proofs of judgment, sound reasoning and astonishing memory', Fox went on to survey the course of England's dispute with America and to show how the war had been mismanaged. He suggested that to recognize independence was not necessarily to harm Britain's interests: an independent America could be a powerful friend. To continue to seek blood in America would endanger the hope of that friendship. Now that there were so many reasons to fear that France would enter the war on America's side, it would be unwise to send reinforcements across the Atlantic. He proposed a motion that no more regiments of the Old Corps, that was to say of the existing Army, should be allowed to leave England.

This motion posed a serious problem for the government. It was well known that the establishment of the Old Corps was well under strength, that the King himself had warned against the folly 'of sending in our present Weak State another Old Corps out of Great Britain'. Yet events had already shown that the present strength of the army in America was not enough to defeat the rebels.

At the end of Fox's highly effective speech, Members waited for a government spokesman to reply. Ministers looked at each other and glanced away. The Solicitor General, Alexander Wedderburn, who had a high reputation as a parliamentary debater, had been seen making copious notes during Fox's speech, but he now remained silent like the others. By a performance 'marvellous for method and memory', which, in Horace Walpole's opinion, had tumbled Chatham from his oratorical throne, Fox had reduced the government to silence. 'Not one of the Ministers knew what to say,' Walpole added, 'and so said nothing, and that silence cost them many votes.'

The government could draw little comfort from the defeat of Fox's motion by 259 votes to 165, for the minority was a good deal larger than it had been of late; and, according to the *Gazetteer*, this 'greatly alarmed Administration'. But worse than this was press comment on the 'open degeneracy' of the present times when a speech replete with 'good sense, precision and a detail of woeful information' could be passed over in complete silence by Ministers who 'declined answering a single syllable'.

'We are in a damned bad way,' one supporter of the government lamented; and no one was more bitterly conscious of this than Lord North, who recognized only too well the fateful consequences of a British defeat. 'If America should grow into a separate empire,' he maintained, 'it must cause a revolution in the political system of the world, and if Europe did not support Britain now, it would one day find itself ruled by America imbued with democratic fanaticism.' Yet Europe was far from inclined to support Britain. 'Every nation in Europe,' Benjamin Franklin reported from France, 'wishes to see Britain humbled, having all in their time been offended by her insolence.' And France itself, delighted by Britain's predicament, was prepared to spend large sums of money in support of a democratic revolution which in other circumstances would have been abhorrent. Well aware of his limitations, Lord North wrote to the King once more emphasizing his unsuitability for holding his high office at such a critical time. 'Your Majesty's service requires a man of great abilities, and who is confident of his abilities, who can choose decisively, and carry his determination authoritatively into execution . . . I am certainly not such a man.'

He knew himself to be a highly effective leader of the House of Commons, but he had not the forceful and demanding character necessary to master a government in time of crisis. He suggested that the King should turn for help to Lord Chatham; but this proposal was rejected with horror. Nothing, the King protested, could ever induce him to approach Lord Chatham 'or any other branch of the Opposition'. 'Honestly,' he continued, 'I would rather lose the crown I now wear than bear the ignominy of possessing it under their shackles . . . No consideration in life will make me stoop to Opposition . . . It is impossible that the nation will not stand by me . . . If they will not, they shall have another King.'

North persisted: he would rather be executed than continue in office; his 'former incapacity' was 'so much aggravated by his present distress of mind' that he would 'soon be totally unfit for the performance of any ministerial duty'. In one of those moods of black despair that occasionally overwhelmed him, he confessed that his mind was 'ten times weaker than it was'. 'Let me not go to the grave,' he begged, 'with the guilt of having been the ruin of my King and country.'

The King partially relented: he would agree 'to accept any description of person' who would 'come devotedly' to the support of North's administration, provided it still remained North's. He would even have Chatham and Fox, provided he did not have to negotiate with them personally and it was understood that they were to be colleagues in the existing administration – not leaders of a new one. North knew, however, that Chatham would not be persuaded to agree to this: he would have to be head of any administration in which he served. But then, at the beginning of April, Chatham had a seizure in the House of Lords.

He had arrived in the House from his sick bed, leaning on the arm of his son as he hobbled to his place on crutches, a pale, thin, wasted figure, determined to oppose Rockingham's friend, the Duke of Richmond, who was to propose the withdrawal of British forces from America. Although well known to be a champion of the colonies, Chatham was strongly opposed to acceptance of their Declaration of Independence and to the dismemberment of an empire which he himself had done so much to create. He strongly advocated conciliation, but just as strongly condemned capitulation. He began to make his speech, protesting that it would be preferable to fight the whole of Europe rather than agree to the independence of America under duress from foreign powers. Suddenly he fell back in a fit. He was taken home and died a few weeks later.

By then the King had reluctantly agreed to release North at the end of the parliamentary session; but it appeared that North was not now after all so set upon going. Weary as he was, he said, he would continue beyond the end of the session and until such time as His Majesty was able 'to arrange his servants in the manner most agreeable to himself and the most advantageous to the public', if the King 'really found it necessary to detain him'.

Once the King appeared to be ready to offer him the comforts of retirement, North began to regard with dismay the loss of the pleasures of office. When all was going well, it was very enjoyable to be the King's chief minister. Besides, His Majesty had been extremely generous to him: he had arranged for him to receive £20,000 – worth over £1 million today – from the secret service account to pay his debts; he had appointed him Lord Warden of the

Cinque Ports, worth £4000 a year; and had promised him another sinecure worth a further £10,000 a year. 'I am anxious to give that to your family,' the King had assured him, 'whether or not you remain in your present situation.' On 23 May the King received a profoundly comforting reply: 'Lord North thinks it is his duty to repeat that, though his earnest wish certainly is to retire, yet he is ready to continue in his present office as long as His Majesty deems it for his service that he should continue there.'

The King's anxiety to retain North was not entirely due to his unwillingness to lose so compatible and amenable a prime minister. He knew that no one commanded so much respect among independent Members as North did, and that, however much he protested about the burdens of high office and his incapacity to bear them, he remained a highly popular and reassuring figure in the House. The King also believed that North's policy towards America commanded far more support in the country at large than Fox's opposition to it.

It seemed to the King that the readiness of the country to support North, once the disaster of Saratoga made the intervention of France more likely, was amply demonstrated by the response to calls for volunteers for the Army in the provinces. Manchester undertook to raise a battalion of eleven hundred men at its own expense. Liverpool followed suit; so did Edinburgh and Glasgow. In the Midlands, Coventry, Birmingham and Warwick indicated that they also would raise battalions if permitted to do so. In Scotland several landowners undertook to create their own regiments; and it was consequently at this time that the 71st Highland Light Infantry was formed by Lord Macleod and the 72nd Highlanders by Lord Seaforth. In Wales the 75th or Prince of Wales's Regiment came into existence. In London John Wilkes, still a vigorous opponent of the government's American policy, attacked these regimental creations and brought in a Bill forbidding the raising of money for the Crown without the consent of Parliament; but, although supported by Burke, the motion was not in tune with feeling in the country as a whole and was defeated. Even those City merchants who had strongly opposed the government's policies in the past were softening their attitude; and from now on only a small minority of the members of the governing Court of Common Council persisted in their attacks.

★　　★　　★

The Franco-American alliance which had contributed so much to the surge of patriotic enthusiasm in England had been in the making for a long time, and had been virtually assured by Burgoyne's surrender at Saratoga and Washington's attack at Germantown. As early as 1775, according to a secret report submitted to the government in August and based on the evidence of two French officers who had travelled widely in America, there were 'at least 200 french amongst the Troops of the Rebels [acting] as Artillerists and Engineers'. There were also several French emissaries in America sounding out public opinion for the Comte de Vergennes, the French Foreign Minister, who was eager to recover for France all that she had lost in the Seven Years' War and who was known to be strongly in favour of the colonists being given clandestine financial assistance in their struggle against Britain. 'It is certain, my Lord,' the British Ambassador at Versailles had warned the Secretary of State, Lord Weymouth, 'that the general animosity against us and the wild enthusiasm in favour of the rebels was never greater than it is at present . . . That M. de Vergennes is hostile in his heart and anxious for the success of the rebels I have not a shadow of a doubt . . . notwithstanding all the friendly professions of this court.'

The Comte de Vergennes's principal agent was the *intrigant* and none too honest Pierre-Augustin Caron de Beaumarchais, a watchmaker's son and author of *The Barber of Seville* and *The Marriage of Figaro*. Through a fictitious company he supplied arms to the Americans, for which Vergennes expected them to pay but which the colonists' principal representative, Arthur Lee, assured Congress were a gift.

Arthur Lee, Richard Henry Lee's brother, a Virginian pamphleteer who had been at school in England and had given up the study of medicine for law, was a self-regarding and opinionated man but esteemed for his political essays in the *Virginian Gazette* and for the good work he had done as agent for the colony of Massachusetts in 1770. In 1776, after Thomas Jefferson had declined the appointment because he felt unable to leave a delicate and pregnant wife, Lee, together with Benjamin Franklin, had been chosen to join Silas Deane, a delegate from Connecticut to the Continental Congress who had been sent to France the year before in the guise of a merchant to represent Congress on a Committee of Secret Correspondence, and to buy arms for which he would receive 5 per cent commission.

Franklin had been an ideal choice: his interest in natural science was shared by many members of the Parisian *beau monde* who were likely to sympathize with the opinions he was to disseminate in France, while his openness and charm of manner were calculated to leave a lasting impression upon all who met him. With his heavily accented and ungrammatical French, his plain clothes, cheap-looking spectacles and rough fur hat, his amusing remarks and evident fondness of female company, he became an extremely well-liked as well as respected figure in Parisian society.

The choice of Deane was, however, not so fortunate. An astute lawyer and man of business, he had managed to obtain arms in France valued at over 6 million livres and had had them safely consigned to America, where they had made a significant contribution to Gates's success at Saratoga. But Deane was not a sound judge of men, and the volunteers he accepted for service in America were mostly officers of as little skill as modesty, as often as not with more pressing reasons for wanting to get out of Europe than for serving the American cause. They were, indeed, in many cases, as a chaplain in the Soissonais Regiment conceded,

> men who had lost their reputations and were wholly in debt and who generally presented themselves under false names and titles of nobility to which they had not the least right. Under these false pretences some of them obtained high rank in the American army, also considerable advances of money, and then disappeared. The simplicity of the Americans and their lack of world experience made tricks like this very easy.

As well as being a poor judge of character, Deane was suspected – and accused by the jealous and quarrelsome Arthur Lee – of embezzlement and fraud. The charges were strongly denied and never proved; but when Deane returned to France as a private citizen and wrote letters home condemning the French alliance and urging a *rapprochement* with England, it was widely held that they may well have been justified. Before leaving France, however, he had played an important part in negotiating the treaties with America, reports of which had long since reached London by way of Edward Bancroft, the secretary of the American Embassy in Paris who, on his own later admission, 'regularly informed the British Government of every transaction of the American Commissioners [and] of every step and vessel taken to supply the revolted colonies' in exchange for a pension which would now be worth about £30,000 a year.

The prospect of renewed war with the French, who would certainly try to seize the West Indian sugar islands, and with their ally Spain, made a review of British strategy in America essential. It had already been reluctantly recognized in London that the rebels in America could not be defeated without the British army there being greatly reinforced. Since the raising of the large force which was considered essential would present insuperable difficulties, efforts on land, so it was suggested, would have to be limited to keeping footholds on the coast, and to defending Canada and the West Indies, while the war at sea was intensified. This was the policy advocated by Lord Amherst, the government's principal military adviser, who maintained that 'the object of the war being now changed, and the contest in America being a secondary consideration, our principal object must be distressing France'.

This, too, was the policy recommended by the King, who told North in January that, without the large army essential for victory in America, offensive operations there would have to be abandoned. 'Should a French [war] be our fate,' he had added in February, 'I trust you will concur with me in [believing that] the only means of making it successful, [would be] the withdrawing the greatest part of the [troops] from America and employing them against the French and Spanish settlements. But if we are to be carrying on a land war against the rebels and against those two powers it must be feeble in all parts and consequently unsuccessful.'

Lord North and his colleagues had initially been reluctant to withdraw troops from America for service against the French and Spanish in the West Indies and elsewhere, since this would have seemed tantamount to an admission of defeat in the colonies. They had proposed sending three more battalions to America, one of them composed of soldiers from the Old Corps, an idea still strongly opposed in principle by the King who did not, however, intend to 'object on this occasion'.

As well as threatening the American rebels with British reinforcements, North at the same time proposed to make one more effort at conciliation. He instructed plenipotentiaries to go to America and tell the rebel leaders that the British government was prepared to recognize Congress, to suspend all objectionable Acts of Parliament, to give up the right of taxation, even to consider admitting American representatives to the House of Commons, provided that Loyalists were restored to their property, that debts due to Englishmen were honoured, that military commands were held as from the King, that the British Parliament regulated trade and, above all, that the Declaration of Independence was withdrawn.

The three principal plenipotentiaries chosen were Commodore George Johnstone, the outspoken and ill-tempered former Governor of West Florida who had fought a duel with Lord George Germain; William Eden, later first Baron Auckland, then the young and promising Member for Woodstock; and Eden's intimate friend since their days at Eton together, the Earl of Carlisle, who was accounted one of the two best-dressed men in London – the other being Fox – a heavy gambler who had recently been appointed Treasurer of the Royal Household, and was rudely described by Walpole as 'being very fit to make a treaty that will not be made'. The treaty was not made; and, even had the plenipotentiaries been more carefully chosen, there had never been much likelihood of their mission proving successful, in view of Congress's refusal even to contemplate withdrawal of the Declaration of Independence. The British diplomats, affronted by the unyielding attitude of Congress, sailed for home, leaving the Commander-in-Chief in America with advice to stop treating the rebels as subjects whose loyalty might be regained but as enemies who must be fought with ruthless animosity. The Commander-in-Chief who rejected this advice as quite contrary to the instructions he had received from London was Sir Henry Clinton.

General Clinton had himself repeatedly asked to be recalled. He had lost all patience with Howe, who had failed to keep him informed of his movements in Pennsylvania; and although he had assured Burgoyne that he continued to feel for him as a friend, he had been much annoyed with him, too, when, with the prospect of disaster at Saratoga in view, Burgoyne had asked for orders which he had never sought before and which Clinton, so far from the scene of action, was, of course, unable to give. 'I cannot presume to order,' he had told Burgoyne, 'or even to advise, for reasons obvious.' Clinton had done what he could to help. But then he had been commanded by

Howe to send four thousand men to Pennsylvania at the earliest opportunity; and he had consequently had to abandon all operations on the Hudson River, although, as he commented derisively, he could not imagine what Howe planned to do with the men he was instructed to send him 'after all the victories we have heard of'.

Clinton had deeply regretted having agreed to return to America as Howe's subordinate and had been determined not to remain in this invidious position any longer than necessary. But Howe, complaining that the government had not given him the support he had a right to expect and had ignored his advice, had also demanded to be recalled. In their search for a successor the government had at first turned to Lord Amherst and had turned to him in vain. Just to keep the territories now under British control would require the services of some forty-four thousand men, Amherst protested; in order to crush the rebels seventy-five thousand would be needed. Such numbers being far beyond the government's reckoning, the King and his Ministers would have to look elsewhere for a Commander-in-Chief in America. Lord North had then suggested making such overtures as would have induced Howe to stay on. To be sure, this would mean losing Clinton; but Clinton was a tiresome fellow, always making 'complaints of slights and ill treatment'.

Lord George Germain, however, had not wanted to continue working with Howe, and, since Carleton was anathema to him, since Lord Cornwallis's reputation had suffered such a blow at Trenton, since Burgoyne was a prisoner of war, and since Lord Percy seemed determined to go on sulking in England, there had seemed to him no alternative to Clinton. The name of Duke Ferdinand of Brunswick had been suggested as a possibility. So even had that of the elderly General Philip von Heister, who was senior to all the British generals except Howe. But these two Germans had found little support, and the discussions once more had centred upon Clinton. Admittedly he had not yet proved his ability to conduct a campaign; admittedly, too, he had shown, in his quarrel with Peter Parker, that he was not likely to get on too well with the Navy. Yet there was not really anyone else. So, on 4 February 1778, two days before the Franco-American alliance was signed, the matter had been resolved at last: Germain wrote to Clinton to inform him that he had been appointed Commander-in-Chief.

16

INTRIGUES AT
VALLEY FORGE

'They worry one another like mastiffs.'

John Adams

'It is certain that half the army are naked, and almost the whole army go barefoot,' one of Washington's European officers at Valley Forge, Johann DeKalb, had written to a friend on Christmas Day 1777.

> Our men are also infected with the itch, a matter which attracts very little attention either at the hospitals or in camp. I have seen the poor fellows covered over and over with scab . . . We have hardly been here more than six days, and are already suffering from want of everything. The men have had neither meat nor bread for four days, and our horses are often left without any fodder. What will be done when the roads grow worse, and the season more severe?

Hampered by a lack of hard coin, gold and silver which the British possessed in large supply, Washington had chosen this dreary, unwelcoming and almost deserted valley beneath lines of wooded hills because, as he put it, by retiring to the more pleasant interior parts of Pennsylvania the army would 'leave a vast extent of fertile country to be despoiled and ravaged by the enemy, from which they could draw vast supplies, and where many of our firm friends would be exposed to all the miseries of the most insulting and wanton depredations'. As it was, the British had already scoured Valley Forge the previous September and – sometimes paying for them, sometimes not – had carried off what few provisions and cattle could be found in the poor, scattered settlements by Valley Creek, which wound its way across the low ground between the surrounding hills.

For weeks the American army endured hunger and cold in their tents and roughly built log cabins, the soldiers looking like scarecrows as they appeared on parade in battered uniforms and even in torn blankets, many of them without boots and obliged to stand on their hats when on sentry duty. Living largely on lumps of flour baked on stones and known as 'fire cakes', most of them slept on the ground since straw, like everything else, was in short supply. An American surgeon noted in his journal:

> Poor food – hard lodgings – cold weather – fatigue – nasty clothes – nasty cooking – smoked out of my senses – the Devil's in it – I can't endure it – why are we sent here to starve and freeze – what sweet felicities have I left at home . . . Here, all confusion – smoke and cold – hunger and filthiness – a pox on my bad luck. Here comes a bowl of beef soup – full of burnt leaves and dirt . . . Yesterday upwards of fifty officers resigned their commission, six or seven of our regiment are doing the like today.

Washington's orders of the day made repeated reference to the ill discipline of his army, to officers going off without leave and taking soldiers as servants with them; to men deserting when on guard duty and flagrantly disobeying orders by indulging in the 'vice of gambling'; to 'peaceable inhabitants being plundered and grossly abused'; to soldiers cutting down and burning fences and 'destroying timber by barking of trees'; to commissaries stealing provisions; to sutlers selling 'spirituous liquors contrary to orders, particularly near the pickets and out lines of the camp'; to quartermasters 'embezzling clothing'; to flour being carried off to be sold in Philadelphia; to 'the most pernicious consequences having arisen from suffering persons, particularly women, to pass and repass from Philadelphia to camp, under pretence of coming out to visit their friends in the Army and returning with necessaries to their families, but really with an intent to entice the soldiers to desert'. There were frequent criticisms of such behaviour as that of Colonel George Nagle, who 'was seen on the 15th of May drinking either tea or coffee in Sergeant Howeraft's tent with his whore, her mother, the said Howeraft and his family, to the prejudice of good order and military discipline', and that of 'a soldier of the Virginia line' who was 'executed for attempting mutiny'. 'The fate of this man was confounded hard,' commented the *West Chester Village Record*. 'Released from guard early one morning he returned to his family . . . and found his captain in bed with his wife. Maddened at the sight, he instantly fired at the officer and wounded him, but not mortally. For this he was tried and hung the same evening.'

Offenders were shot as well as hanged, sentenced to receive specified numbers of 'lashes on the bare back', fined or, in the case of senior officers, dismissed from the service. But the offences continued. 'The Commander in Chief is informed that notwithstanding his orders of the 7th of January last,' runs one characteristic order dated 13 March 1778,

> the carcasses of dead horses are lying in and near the camp, and that the offals near many of the commissaries' stalls still lie unburied, that much filth and nastiness is spread amongst the huts, which are, or soon will be, reduced to a state of putrifaction, and occasion a sickly camp. Out of tender regard for the lives and health of the brave soldiers, and with surprise that so little attention has been paid to his orders, he again, in the most positive terms . . . commands . . . that his orders are complied with.

There were those who grumbled that the Commander-in-Chief had to repeat his orders because he was not up to his task, that the idea of camping in this dismal desert must have been put into the head of the commanding general either by one of those all too frequent councils of war called to discuss matters of which most of their members were, so one young colonel said, as entirely ignorant as 'the most honourable body of midwives', or by civilians in Congress who knew as little of military matters as they did of the locality in which their army was supposed to regain its strength for the coming campaign. It was unfortunate that Washington was so easily led, that he was so cautious on occasions, and at other times, as during the siege of Boston, so headstrong that he had to be restrained from foolhardy action. He was the bravest and truest of men, it was conceded; he was well liked and respected by the soldiers of his army, who responded to his kindly manners and sympathetic attitude towards them; he had 'the best intentions and a sound judgement' and could accomplish 'substantial results if he would only act more on his own responsibility'. But he was 'so weak' and had 'the worst of advisers' in the men who enjoyed his confidence. Would not Horatio Gates – who had, after all, forced Burgoyne to surrender at Saratoga – make a better commander? Gates himself thought that he would; so did Samuel and John Adams, who now considered that Washington was becoming too much of a god in America. And so did another more outspoken critic, who advanced the opinion that Washington was proving himself 'not fit to command a Sergeant's Guard'.

This last verdict was expressed by Charles Lee, who had been released in an exchange of prisoners at Washington's specific request and had been welcomed back into camp as though he were a hero returning from exile. An officer on Washington's staff recorded:

> All the principal officers of the Army were drawn up in two lines advanced of the Camp about 2 miles towards the Enemy. Then the troops with their inferior officers formed a line quite to head Quarters. All the music of the Army attended. The General, with a great number of the principal officers, and their suites, rode about four miles on the road towards Philadelphia and waited till Genl. Lee appeared. Genl. Washington dismounted & received Genl. Lee as if he had been his brother. He passed thro' the lines of Officers and the Army, who all paid him the highest military honors to Head quarters, where Mrs Washington was, and there he was entertained with an Elegant Dinner, and the music playing the whole time.
>
> A room was assigned him, Back of Mrs Washington's sitting Room, and all his Baggage was stowed in it. The next morning he lay very late, and Breakfast was detained for him. When he came out he looked as dirty as if he had been in the street all night. Soon after I discovered that he had brought a miserable dirty hussy with him from Philadelphia (a British Sergeant's Wife) and had actually taken her into his Room by a Back Door and she had slept with him that night.

One of those who would have had Washington replaced by Gates was Thomas Conway, an Irishman who made much of the fact that he had served in the French Army and who had been appointed Inspector-General in Washington's. He wrote to Gates to tell him what he thought of the Commander-in-Chief; a copy of the letter was passed to Washington, who reacted sharply to such disloyalty. Gates demanded to know who had been meddling with his correspondence; tempers flared; insults were exchanged; challenges issued; Conway was wounded in the mouth in a duel. Other observers considered that Gates and Conway were equally incompetent; while Dr Benjamin Rush, then serving as a surgeon general at Valley Forge, had little good to say of any of their colleagues. Washington was admittedly the 'idol of America' but under the 'baneful influence' of other generals and certain members of his staff. Nathanael Greene was 'timid, speculative, without enterprise'; Sullivan 'weak, vain, without dignity, fond of scribbling, in the field, a madman'; Stirling, 'a proud, vain, lazy, ignorant drunkard'; Adam Stephen, soon, indeed, to be cashiered for drunkenness, 'a sordid, boasting, cowardly sot'.

John Adams professed himself 'wearied to death with the wrangles between military officers high and low'. 'They quarrel like cats and dogs,' he complained. 'They worry one another like mastiffs . . . I believe there is no one principle which dominates in human nature so much as this passion for superiority . . . But I never saw it to operate with such keenness, ferocity and fury as among military officers. They will go to terrible lengths in their emulation, their envy, and revenge in consequence of it.'

More quarrelsome than most were the French officers who had been recruited by Silas Deane and Arthur Lee and who were constantly demanding promotion, higher pay or more important commands. And as tiresome as any of these was the Polish officer Count Casimir Pulaski, who declined to take orders from the Commander-in-Chief, insisting that he was beholden only to the Continental Congress to whom he sent his voluminous reports direct.

There were, however, several foreign officers whose service to the American cause was invaluable. One of these was a soldier of fortune who called himself Baron Friedrich Wilhelm von Steuben and who, on the strength of his vaunted experiences in the Prussian Army, was appointed Inspector-General at Valley Forge in succession to Thomas Conway. This officer was quite as successful in drilling American troops as he assured Congress he would be, once he had learned that it was no good treating an American like a Prussian soldier. With a Prussian, Steuben told a friend, 'You say, "Do this", and he does it. But [here] I have to say, "This is why you ought to do this." And *then* he does it.' Steuben's English was atrocious, his outbursts of swearing legendary, his fits of temper so explosive that he became in his fury an object of amusement rather than a tyrant to fear and, enjoying the performance as much as anyone, he made himself a caricature for the entertainment of the men, who grew to respect his well-concealed intelligence as well as to like him.

He had them on parade at six o'clock in the morning for two hours of marching and drill in squads of eight. There was an hour's break and at nine o'clock the men were turned out for parade again, this time for practice in arms drill. At noon they had another break while their non-commissioned officers were given special training. There were more parades in the afternoons, and courses in tactics and manoeuvring for the officers, who were repeatedly told that their men must be treated with kindness, that they must get to know the names and characters of every soldier in their companies.

From time to time the whole army was called out for manoeuvres and given lectures on the importance of hygiene, on keeping kitchens well away from latrines, on airing bedding and making sure that cooking utensils were clean, on the need to wash hands at least once a day. Detachments were regularly sent to the sheds where the military equipment was stored to assist in the repair of weapons and the manufacture of gunpowder, or to work on the ramparts and redoubts of the camp under the directions of the French engineer Louis Lebeque Duportail, Brigadier-General of the Corps of Engineers.

No French officer was more generally respected at Valley Forge than the Marquis de Lafayette, General Washington's constant companion, who had arrived in America the year before at the age of nineteen and after whom no fewer than six towns in America were one day to be named. Tall, thin, solemn, rather conceited and extremely rich, he was not at first welcomed by Congress, who had become disillusioned by the quality and pretensions of the foreign officers who had so far arrived in America. But Lafayette's grave demeanour gradually overcame the reluctance of the delegates who interviewed him. 'After the sacrifices I have made, I have the right to exact two favours,' he said to them; 'one is to serve at my own expense, the other to serve at first as a volunteer.' He was promptly appointed major-general.

To one observer, indeed, it seemed that if an officer in Washington's army had claim to any merit at all he was immediately promoted. 'It is safe to accost every man as a colonel who talks to me with familiarity,' said Johann DeKalb who, at fifty-six, was much older than most of his fellow-officers and who, like Lafayette, had been appointed major-general by the Continental Congress. 'In a word the army teems with colonels . . . My blacksmith is a captain! The very numerous assistant-quartermasters are for the most part of no military education whatever, in many cases ordinary pedlars, but always colonels. The same rank is held by the contractors-general and their agents.'

Yet, for all the justified criticism of the army at Valley Forge, Washington's patience and determination, Baron von Steuben's efficient training methods and the patriotic spirit of so many American soldiers combined to transform a collection of discouraged and disintegrating regiments into an efficient fighting force. On 6 May 1778, after hundreds of deserters had returned to camp together with scores of new volunteers who were provided with uniforms captured on a British supply ship, the announcement of the French alliance was celebrated in a manner which reflected the army's new-found confidence. There were parades and open-air services, gun salutes, displays of marksmanship and drill, while shouts of 'Long Live the King of France!', 'Long Live the Friendly European Powers!' and 'The United States!', resounded throughout the camp. Bands played until dark, when fireworks exploded in the sky above the dark surrounding hills. Then 'the whole army returned to its encampment', the *Pennsylvania Gazette* reported,

> and the officers of the several brigades were invited by his Excellency to a collation, which was enlivened by a brilliant company of ladies . . . The spontaneous marks of attachment and respect, which was heaped on our illustrious Commander-in-Chief, when the restraint and formality and etiquette were laid aside, must have given him the most enviable feelings . . . The exact order in which the columns marched to their ground – the celerity and precision with which their lines were formed – the regularity of the fire – the pillars of fleecy smoke ascending in rapid succession – the continued round

of musquetry, not unlike the rolling of distant thunder – the martial appearance of the troops – conspired to exhibit a magnificent scene of joy, worthy of great occasion.

This was now clearly an army which the British would have to treat with caution and respect.

17

FIGHTING AT MONMOUTH COURT HOUSE

*'Sir, these troops are not able to
meet British grenadiers.'*

Charles Lee

As soon as it became known in Philadelphia that their popular commander, Sir William Howe, was to be replaced by Sir Henry Clinton, the young officers of his staff planned an extravagant farewell party, a *'Mischianza'* or 'Medley' as they called it, to speed him on his way. There was to be a mock tournament in which seven Knights of the Blended Rose contended with seven Knights of the Burning Mountain for the favours of Queens of Beauty, both English and American, and all attended by pretty damsels in the draperies of Turkish odalisques. There was to be a grand regatta on the Delaware and a magnificent banquet, at which black slaves in oriental costumes were to serve a meal of twelve hundred dishes, followed by a splendid display of fireworks whose *pièce de résistance* was to be a figure of Fame proclaiming in letters of fire, 'Thy laurels shall never fade.' Elaborate tickets were printed, adorned with military emblems and inscribed in Latin with the words, 'Descending, I shine; I prosper; I shall rise again in splendour.'

These tributes to General Howe seemed to many of his officers and men highly inappropriate. His staff – in the opinion of Colonel Allan Maclean, 'none but very silly fellows' – had certainly contrived to live in comfort in Philadelphia: there were reports of drunken parties and of American girls behaving in a way that deeply shocked the more staid Quaker families of the town and wearing clothes of the most outlandish fashion. 'Their hats, which are of the flat round

kind, are of the size of a large japanned tea-waiter,' wrote one
Philadelphian on his return home to discover that the 'morals of the
inhabitants' had 'suffered vastly in his absence'.

> Their caps exceed any of the fantastic prints you have seen and their
> hair is dressed with the assistance of wool, etc., in such a manner
> as to appear too heavy to be supported by their necks . . . I cannot
> yet learn whether cork rumps have been introduced here, but
> some artificial rumps or other are necessary to counter-balance the
> extraordinary natural weight which some of these ladies carry before
> them . . . Many people do not hesitate in supposing that most of
> the young ladies who were in the city with the enemy, and wear
> the present fashionable dresses, have purchased them at the expense
> of their virtue. It is agreed on all hands that the British played the
> devil with the girls; the privates, I suppose, were satisfied with the
> common prostitutes.

Certainly the women of Philadelphia took part enthusiastically if
not very competently in amateur theatricals with the British officers
stationed there. Lieutenant John Peebles of the 42nd Regiment wrote
in his diary on 2 January 1778:

> The playhouse has open'd and there are plays once or twice a week
> for charity . . . The Performers are Gentl^{mn} of the Army and Navy
> & their mistresses. The Gentl^{mn} do their parts pretty well but the
> Ladies rather deficient . . . The City Tavern is likewise fitted up
> and open'd to receive Company in the style of Public Rooms every
> evening and there is a Ball every Thursday . . . There is also a Pharo
> Bank kept by the Hessians.

To ambitious and dutiful soldiers these weeks of inactivity in
Philadelphia seemed a disgraceful waste of time, offering an unnecessary opportunity for relaxation in discipline. There were complaints,
too, about the poor quality of the food provided for the common
soldiers, the bad water, the unwholesome air, the treatment of the
many sick, the inordinate numbers of rattlesnakes in the countryside
around the outposts. And why, it was often asked, did not Howe
attack Washington, who was encamped no more than twenty miles
away to the east at Valley Forge and whose forces, so spies reported,

were in no fit state to resist a determined assault, despite the rigorous
training instituted by Baron von Steuben? If the British allowed the
training of this army to continue uninterrupted, the consequences of
inaction might be disastrous. To some of Howe's critics there seemed
no reason to look further than the attractive figure of Mrs Loring to
explain Howe's passivity:

> Sir William, he, snug as a flea
> Lay all this time a-snoring
> Nor dreamed of harm, as he lay warm
> In bed with Mrs. ——

Howe's friends protested that there was no need to risk lives in
attacking an enemy whose army was likely to disintegrate in any
case. Nor would victory in a battle at Valley Forge be a foregone
conclusion: Sir Charles Grey, one of the ablest officers in America,
considered the means at Howe's immediate disposal inadequate to
justify an attack. Besides, the Commander-in-Chief could scarcely
be expected to embark on a major enterprise when he had asked to
be recalled and his successor was on the way to relieve him.

Sir Henry Clinton arrived in Philadelphia on 8 May 1778. His orders,
framed in the light of the Americans' new alliance with France, were
to withdraw the troops to New York, and then, if necessary, to
Canada, leaving garrisons at Rhode Island and Halifax. At the same
time he was to embark five thousand men for an attack on St Lucia,
one of the most important French harbours in the West Indies,
another three thousand men for the coast of Florida, and smaller
detachments for Bermuda and the Bahamas.

The most pressing of these duties, the evacuation of Philadelphia,
proved a far more difficult enterprise than Clinton had expected. He
had hoped to withdraw by way of the Delaware, but there were not
enough transports for his men, his horses and his stores, as well as
for the hundreds of American Loyalists who had thrown in their lot
with the British and who claimed their protection. He was obliged,
therefore, to make for New York overland. Setting out on the
morning of 18 June with about ten thousand men fit for duty,
hundreds of wagonloads of baggage, private carriages, bakeries on
wheels, laundries, blacksmiths' shops, boats, pack-horses, hospital

tents and stores, and a twelve-mile-long trail of Loyalists and camp followers, including numerous women who had disobeyed his orders to go to New York by sea, Clinton crossed the Delaware at Gloucester Point and made for Allentown and Amboy.

As soon as he heard of Clinton's departure, Washington was on his tail with a force of similar size but far less heavily encumbered and able to move at a far greater speed. The distance between the two armies narrowed; and after five days' marching, having covered less than thirty miles, Clinton's cumbersome column was in danger of being trapped. The heat in the middle of the day grew ever more intense and the soldiers, in their thick woollen uniforms and weighed down by their heavy packs, ever more exhausted and ill-tempered.

Washington was now advancing quickly on a parallel course on Clinton's left flank, threatening to overtake him, while in front of the British vanguard rebel patrols were demolishing all the bridges he had intended to use. At the same time another enemy force under General Gates was advancing upon Clinton from the north to prevent him getting across the Rariton River to Amboy. Clinton was consequently forced to turn right towards Sandy Hook at the mouth of the Hudson River. He took personal command of the rearguard, sending General Knyphausen ahead with the advance guard.

As they were passing by Monmouth County Court House near the village of Freehold at ten o'clock on the morning of Sunday, 28 June, yet another insufferably hot day with swarms of insects buzzing round their faces, the rearguard came under artillery fire from an American force of six thousand men sent forward by Washington under the command of General Charles Lee. After despatching an urgent message to Knyphausen for reinforcements, Clinton, whose forces outnumbered Lee's by about three to two, immediately gave orders for an attack, hoping that he 'might gain the advantage over [Lee] before Washington came up'. Despite the appalling heat, the British troops responded to their orders with a brave and ready vigour which delighted and amazed their officers. Lee's advance was halted and his men were soon in retreat, falling back through the scrub pine, in some places steadily, in others in confusion, the British grenadiers pressing hard against their front, the light infantry and 16th Light Dragoons racing round their left flank.

Lee had been reluctant to attack until he had learned more of the British dispositions, though urged to do so by Lafayette. 'Sir,' said

Lee, 'You do not know the British soldiers. We cannot stand against them.' As for his own men, they were 'all in confusion'. He repeated as much to Washington when the Commander-in-Chief galloped up on his big white horse demanding to know what was the reason 'for this disorder and confusion'.

'My God, General Lee,' Washington called to him. 'What are you about?'

'Sir,' Lee replied, repeating what he had said to Lafayette, 'these troops are not able to meet British grenadiers.'

After muttering under his breath a few words which a bystander believed to be, 'You never tried them, you damned poltroon', Washington, whom one of his staff described as 'much excited', angrily responded, 'Sir they are able and, by God, they shall do it!'

When it was afterwards reported that these were the very words that Washington had used, doubt was voiced that the General could really have expressed himself so strongly. But Charles Scott, an officer from Virginia, assured a sceptical enquirer that he had indeed done so. 'Yes, sir,' said Scott, who may or may not have been present on this notable occasion. 'Yes, sir, he swore on that day till the leaves shook on the trees – charming, delightful. Never have I enjoyed such swearing before, or since. Sir, on that memorable day he swore like an angel from Heaven.'

Outraged by Washington's criticisms of his conduct, and maintaining that by his evasive and delaying tactics he had saved the Americans from defeat, Charles Lee stormed off the field in a furious temper, calling his black poodle after him. Sent to the rear with the reserves by Washington, he later demanded a general court-martial which, despite his own skilful defence, found him guilty of disobeying orders, of making 'an *unnecessary, disorderly,* and shameful retreat', and of disrespect to the Commander-in-Chief. He was suspended from command for twelve months.

Other witnesses besides Charles Scott testified to Washington's rough words as well as to his bravery and resource at Monmouth Court House. Immediately issuing an order to countermarch Lee's retreating troops, he 'gave a new turn to the action'. 'Always in danger', he 'unfolded surprising abilities which produced uncommon results'.

Clinton, too, displayed remarkable courage, charging on one occasion at the 'head of a few Dragoons', though 'near going raving mad' with the heat which so exhausted his men that one British battalion, after charging up a hill and driving the rebels off it, collapsed helplessly to the ground. 'If the enemy had thrown in fresh troops,' Clinton commented, 'they might have . . . had an easy prey. We had several men die on the spot with thirst and extreme fatigue, and still a greater proportion not able to defend themselves.'

On both sides most officers and men acquitted themselves well throughout the action. Of course there were, as always, those who behaved badly. Joseph Plumb Martin described how he had come upon an American captain who had had his thigh shot off by a cannon ball and appeared to be bleeding to death, neglected by the sergeant who 'pretended to have the care of him'. 'It grieved me to see the poor man in such distress,' Martin wrote, 'and I asked the sergeant why he did not carry his officer to the surgeons, and he said he would directly. Directly! said I, why he will die directly. I then offered to assist in carrying him to a meeting-house, a short distance off, where the rest of the wounded men and the surgeons were. At length he condescended to be persuaded to carry him off.' Martin also related the story of Mary Ludwig Hays, an artillery sergeant's wife, known in the army as Molly Pitcher because of her services as a water-carrier for the gunners both in camp and in battle. At Monmouth Court House, when her husband was wounded, she took his place and worked as hard as he had done; and

> while in the act of reaching for a cartridge and having [one foot] as far from the other as she could step, a cannon shot from the enemy passed directly between her legs without doing any damage than carrying away all the lower part of her petticoat. Looking at it with apparent unconcern, she observed that it was lucky that it did not pass higher, for in that case it might have carried away something else, and then she continued upon her occupation.

As darkness fell, Clinton gave orders for his men to rest and then, soon after midnight, they were roused again and resumed their interrupted march to Sandy Hook, then an island, four miles long, east of Staten Island. Here Clinton embarked his men for the passage across Lower Bay to New York, while Washington marched north, abandoning the pursuit. The British had lost nearly three hundred officers and men in the short engagement at Monmouth Court House;

a further sixty men had died of sunstroke, while another six hundred, mostly Germans, had either fallen behind the straggling column in the insufferable heat to be taken as prisoners of war, or had deserted to return to the girlfriends and families they had met in Philadelphia. The American losses were slightly more than the British; but it was only too clear to General Clinton that Washington's army had been transformed in the six months that had passed since the darkest days of Valley Forge.

18

ENEMIES OF THE FRENCH

'There are not ships enough in readiness to form a squadron fit to meet the Toulon fleet.'

Lord Sandwich

At a Cabinet meeting in early April 1778, Ministers examined intelligence reports about the strength and disposition of the French navy. The number of ships was uncertain, but there was no doubt that most of them were in the two ports of Brest in Brittany and Toulon on the Mediterranean coast. The commander of the fleet at Toulon was the Comte d'Estaing, a charming and well-connected man who had served in India during the Seven Years' War and for three years had been Governor of the Antibes in the West Indies. He was said to be naturally cautious, and his experience of naval warfare was certainly limited; but even so, when he sailed from Toulon with twelve ships of the line and five frigates on 13 April 1778, his departure caused concern in London.

Lord George Germain had already maintained that the Royal Navy should have been used forcefully against France as soon as she entered the war on the rebels' side. He acknowledged that there were risks involved, but these were 'trifling in comparison with what England might suffer by leaving the French at liberty to attack us in North America, the West Indies, or Newfoundland'. Lord Sandwich, the First Lord of the Admiralty, however, had clung to his belief that the security of home waters must not be endangered.

For all his faults and excesses and the favours he bestowed upon incompetent friends, Sandwich was a clever and versatile man, far more responsible than his reputation as a man who invented the sandwich so that he could eat without leaving the gambling table might suggest. He was a Fellow of the Royal Society, and his tastes were intellectual, literary and musical as well as sensual. He was much respected at the Admiralty, where he worked as hard as any eighteenth-century Minister was expected to do. He took long holidays, going off fishing for trout for weeks on end with 'Ladies of Pleasure'; but such, after all, were the habits of his time. Even Lord Howe, who deeply disliked him, conceded that he was 'seldom backward' in answering letters, while Lord George Germain, who did not get on well with him either and who was constantly crossing swords with him, could not complain of his indolence.

During his long tenure of office, the Navy had not been neglected in the way his critics alleged; he had done his best to tend its stores; did all he could to ensure that its strength was maintained; and now warmly urged the impressment of more seamen in British ports and coastal towns, and helped to arrange the loan of both ships and sailors from the East India Company. He was perfectly agreeable to ships being detached from the Home Fleet for service across the Atlantic, but if they were to be detached, they must, he insisted, be replaced by the immediate commissioning of others. 'I lay it down as a maxim,' he wrote, 'that England ought for her own security to have a superior force in readiness at home to anything that France and Spain united have in readiness on their side.'

For the time being, he maintained, there were 'not ships enough in readiness to form a squadron fit to meet the Toulon fleet under Monsieur D'Estaing, unless we were to sacrifice every other intended service to this object'. In this view Sandwich was firmly backed by Admiral Augustus Keppel, commander of the Home Fleet, a supporter of Lord Rockingham and former opponent of the American war, who had been persuaded to accept command only after France's entry changed the war's nature.

Despite the strong objections of Germain, the views of Sandwich and Keppel at first prevailed in the Cabinet. But the American Secretary's vigorous badgering of Lord North and the King gradually induced them to change their minds. 'I have this instant seen dispatches . . . which bring a very particular and interesting account of the sailing of the Toulon squadron, and of the manner of its equipment with stores, clothing, seamen etc., etc.,' Germain told North on 27 April. He was convinced that

> the destination of that fleet must be North America, where it will be joined by all the marine force of the rebellious provinces, and in that case will be able to attack and destroy our fleet in those seas. I must now entreat your Lordship maturely to consider of the very alarming situation of this country, and to lose no time in advising His Majesty immediately to employ such a part of the fleet now at Spithead as may probably prevent the disgrace of this kingdom.

Two days later Germain returned to the attack:

> The fate of the country evidently depends upon the preventing the Toulon Squadron from acting with success against our Fleet and Army and our possessions in North America; and there is every reason to believe it can have no other destination. If we are not able to resist France in this its first offensive operation, what have we not to dread when it shall be joined by the land and sea forces of the revolted provinces? . . .
>
> I must therefore humbly submit my opinion to His Majesty (after lamenting that a fleet was not sent to stop Monsr. d'Estaing passing the straits of Gibraltar) that at least twelve ships of the line should be now immediately detached to [America] . . . If I err in judgement, I hope H.M. will look upon the opinion I offer as proceeding solely from an anxious zeal for maintaining the honour of the Crown by preventing if possible a national disgrace.

Germain's protests at last had their effect: it was decided by the Cabinet, to whom his letter was read out that same day, that thirteen ships of the line, together with reinforcements for the army, should be despatched to America without delay. The command of these ships was to be entrusted to Vice-Admiral the Hon. John Byron, the poet's grandfather, whose extraordinary misfortunes at sea had earned him the nickname 'Foul-Weather Jack'.

Yet, although Sandwich was present at the Cabinet meeting when the decision to send this fleet to America was taken, he was still not convinced that so many ships should be allowed to leave home waters, and he was determined to do what he could to limit their operations off the American coast. At first he tried, unsuccessfully, to prevent Byron's fleet from being given orders to winter abroad; then he refused to spare a frigate to carry the despatches notifying the commander in America of Byron's departure. These vital despatches were eventually sent by a packet, which did not reach the American coast until three months later.

D'Estaing's passage through the Straits of Gibraltar had been watched by a British frigate, the *Proserpine*, sent there for that purpose. On sighting the French fleet sailing westwards out to sea, evidently on course for America, the *Proserpine*'s captain had raced back with the news to England, arriving at Falmouth on 2 June. Until then Byron's departure from Plymouth had been held up, Lord Sandwich arguing, even now, that there should be no detachment from the Home Fleet and that d'Estaing might after all have orders to sail to Cadiz for a junction with the Spanish fleet. In supporting Sandwich, Keppel warned that the loss of Byron's ships to America might well result in a catastrophic defeat in the Channel with the most appalling consequences for the country's safety. Alarmed by these prognostications, the Cabinet had decided that Byron must be kept at Plymouth until d'Estaing's destination was known for certain.

There had been uproar in the Commons when the government's handling of the crisis became known: Burke had eloquently attacked the Cabinet's disgracefully inadequate response to the French threat; Fox had asked how it was possible to estimate the guilt of Ministers who could tamely suffer a hostile squadron to carry destruction to the British army in America; William Pulteney, Member for Shrewsbury, considered that if they could not despatch a fleet at twenty-four hours' notice they ought to lose their heads. Germain did his best to defend a policy of which he strongly disapproved. Lord North, lamenting that he 'never could . . . decide between different opinions', again begged to be allowed to resign before the country was ruined.

Once d'Estaing's destination was at last established and Byron had been given orders to sail, there were yet further delays. Contrary winds held up his departure for a week; and once at sea the weather was as stormy as even he had ever known. Several ships were dismasted; their crews went down with scurvy and – since so many of their number had only recently been released from prison – with gaol fever. Soon the fleet was dispersed and it was not until 8 August, after two months at sea, that Byron came within sight of the enemy squadron sailing off the coast of New York. Of his own ships there was no sign. So he decided to take his flagship to Halifax.

The Comte d'Estaing had arrived off the Delaware a month before. Finding that the British had evacuated Philadelphia and marched to New York, d'Estaing followed them in the hope of falling upon their army as it was being ferried across from Sandy Hook. He was much discouraged to arrive too late and to discover that all Clinton's battalions had been disembarked and that Lord Howe's ships, drawing less water than his own, had sailed across the sand bar that stretched from Sandy Hook to Staten Island.

Behind this bar Howe's ships were well disposed. Having personally taken soundings and studied the set of the currents at different times of the tide, he had had seven of them anchored with springs on their cables in a line across the channel, their broadsides ready to bear on each enemy ship that might attempt to cross the bar into the harbour. The British ships were supported by a battery on the island and by smaller ships commanding the bar and in reserve.

After lying off Shrewsbury Inlet for eleven days and discussing his problem with pilots sent to him by Washington, d'Estaing decided that his larger ships could not be manoeuvred across the bar. So, on 22 July, when tide and winds brought thirty feet of water over the bar and the British captains prepared for an attack, he weighed anchor, came off the entrance to the channel and sailed away. A week later his ships were lying off Rhode Island.

Newport, Rhode Island, a fine harbour taken by Sir Henry Clinton two years before, was now held by some three thousand men under Major-General Sir Robert Pigot, a conscientious and brave if not notably imaginative officer who had served as Howe's second-in-command at Bunker Hill. Washington had decided that, since New York was so securely defended by Lord Howe, the combined French and American forces should be turned instead against Rhode Island. Two of his best brigades were accordingly sent north under the Marquis de Lafayette; these were supported by six thousand militiamen from New England commanded by John Hancock, the rich young Bostonian merchant, while Nathanael Greene was sent to serve under the tactless Irish General, John Sullivan, who was already watching Pigot from Providence, some thirty miles north of Newport on the mainland at the head of Narragansett Bay on Providence River.

There was, however, a long delay before the Americans were ready to attack, since over the past few weeks Pigot had sent raiding parties north to Providence where they had succeeded in destroying a number of Sullivan's boats and large stocks of his provisions and ammunition. At last, however, on 8 August the French fleet sailed from their anchorage in the open sea and closed in upon Newport, providing cover for a landing by American troops on the northern end of Rhode Island. No sooner had these troops disembarked than the sails of Lord Howe's fleet, thirty-five ships in all, were seen approaching in a fair wind.

The two fleets sailed warily around each other for two days, Howe, aboard a fast frigate to which he had transferred from his flagship, seeking to avoid an action which his out-gunned ships had little chance of winning, despite the greater experience of their crews, until they had the full advantage of the wind. These manoeuvres were brought to a halt on the evening of 11 August when a violent gale blew the fleets apart, dispersing and dismasting the larger French men of war which were consequently unable to defend themselves against the guns of Howe's smaller ships. The French admiral's flagship, the ninety-gun *Languedoc*, with her tiller broken, her bowsprit as well as all her lower masts lost, was badly mauled by the fifty-gun *Renown* which might well have taken her as a prize had not other French ships come to her help. Others of his ships fared as badly. The French fleet was so badly damaged, in fact, that d'Estaing decided he would have to sail back to Boston for repairs and refitting. Both Nathanael Greene and the Marquis de Lafayette went aboard the *Languedoc* in an effort to dissuade him; but he insisted that the risk of another encounter with his ships in their present state was out of the question. He sailed away south, taking four thousand French troops with him.

Deprived of his support, the Americans could make little headway against Pigot who withdrew his outpost into Newport and prepared to resist attack within his strong entrenchments, content that Howe's fleet, now free from interference by d'Estaing, could keep his troops well supplied. General Sullivan, accepting the futility of mounting a siege with a force weakened by the seasonal desertion to their farms of many of his volunteers, decided to withdraw. He was pursued by Pigot, who forced several skirmishes upon him as he retreated across the island. Sir Henry Clinton, who had long been preparing a move in support of Pigot, arrived at last on 30 August. But by then he was too late: Sullivan's rearguard, capably commanded by Nathanael Greene, had crossed over to the mainland only a few hours before. Pigot, so Clinton complained, had been too headstrong and energetic in his pursuit. Eager to throw the rebels off the island, he had failed to destroy them; he had made the same kind of mistake that Sir William Howe had made against Washington in New York. This time, however, it was not because a British commander had been too cautious but because he had been too impetuous. 'Knowing I was coming,' Sir Henry wrote, 'he should have been a little less so.'

While Clinton blamed Pigot for letting the rebels escape, the Americans blamed the French for the failure of their assault. They were accused of being worse than useless as allies; their supercilious officers – one of whom described the New England militia as a 'laughable spectacle' of 'tailors and apothecaries' looking like 'a flock of ducks in cross belts' – became more unpopular than ever. Staunch republicans were now satisfied that royalist France should not have been called upon for help in the first place. 'By heavens!' one of these republicans exclaimed, continuing:

> If our rulers had any modesty, they would blush at the idea of calling in foreign aid! 'Tis really abominable that we should send to France for soldiers when we have so many sons of America idle. Such a step ought not . . . to have been taken until the strength of the country had been nearly exhausted, and our freedom tottering on the brink of ruin. Let us be indebted to France, Spain or even the Devil himself, if he could furnish it, for a navy, because we cannot get one reasonably among ourselves. But do let us, unless we are contented to be transmitted to posterity with disgrace, make an exertion of our own strength by land, and not owe our independence entirely to our allies.

There were demonstrations against the French in New York; there was a serious riot in Charleston; and in Boston, when a mob attacked a party of French sailors on shore leave, a French officer who intervened was killed. The Massachusetts Assembly, anxious to placate their allies, immediately raised money for a monument to the dead officer, while several of its delegates invited French officers to dinner. The people of Boston, however, continued to denigrate the French for some time, regarding them less as friends than as interlopers; and were not sorry when d'Estaing sailed away to Martinique for operations in the West Indies.

In the West Indies d'Estaing took the islands of St Vincent and Grenada; but he failed to recapture St Lucia, which had been recently occupied by five thousand British troops sent from New York under Major-General James Grant, and he lost over five hundred men against British casualties of less than two hundred. The French also failed to destroy a much smaller British squadron which was operating in West Indian waters under the skilful command of Rear Admiral the Hon. Samuel Barrington, who had gone to sea as a midshipman at the age of eleven. D'Estaing returned to America with his reputation still further damaged.

In his absence little of importance had occurred before the opposing armies went into winter quarters in 1778. Lord Cornwallis and General von Knyphausen had both left New York and marched up opposite banks of the Hudson River on foraging expeditions; and Washington had sent out parties to do what they could to prevent them, without being drawn into battle. One of these small harassing parties, commanded by Anthony Wayne, included a detachment of the Third Continental Dragoons under Lieutenant-Colonel George Baylor, whose men were known as Mrs Washington's Guards. They had sought shelter for the night in a barn at New Tappan where, in a repetition of the night attack on Wayne's men at Paoli the year before, they were suddenly attacked by Charles 'No Flint' Grey whose 'savage' men, in the words of the surgeon, James Thacher, 'commenced the horrid work of slaughter', totally disregarding the Virginians' 'entreaties and cries for mercy'.

> It has been well ascertained [he went on] that the British soldiers were ordered by their inhuman officers to bayonet every man they could find, and to give no quarter . . . Thomas Hutchinson, sergeant of the third troop, escaped unhurt; but heard the British soldiers cry out 'Sliver him,' repeatedly. Cullency, of the first troop, who

received twelve wounds, says, 'that when the enemy entered the barn where his troops lay, he and the men asked for quarter, and were refused; that the British Captain Bull, after inquiring how many of the rebels were dead, on being told the number, ordered all the rest knocked on the head, and that his orders were executed on five or six of the wounded.'

Sir Henry Clinton maintained that, with the meagre forces at his disposal, he could do little more than despatch such raiding parties as Charles Grey's from New York. More self-distrusting than ever now that he was in supreme command in America, he bombarded London with gloomy letters of complaint, as though convinced he was being singled out for peculiar and personal neglect. 'Shackled' by his lack of men, instead of being reinforced, he was required to weaken his already exiguous forces by sending them elsewhere, to support 'all efforts in America other than his own'.

Ever since the surrender at Saratoga, the government had been gradually coming to the conclusion that the main fight against the rebels should be transferred to the south; here it was believed there was a greater proportion of Loyalists in a sparser population than in the north, and that these loyalist sympathizers included thousands of black slaves for whom the cause of the revolutionaries held no appeal and of whom the white population were always more or less in fear. The government, prompted by the Governor of East Florida, consequently decided that a landing should be made in Georgia; and Clinton was ordered to prepare a force of Germans, Highlanders and Loyalists for this expedition to the south.

THE SOUTHERN CAMPAIGNS

PENNSYLVANIA

Susquehannah R.

Philadelphia

Delaware R.

Head of the Elk

NEW JERSEY

Potomac R.

Baltimore

MARYLAND

DELAWARE

VIRGINIA

Alexandria
Mount Vernon

Annapolis

Delaware Bay

Fredericksburg

Charlottesville

Chesapeake Bay

James R.

Williamsburg

York R.

Gloucester Pt.

Petersburg

Jamestown

Yorktown

Cape Charles

Cape Henry

Portsmouth

Norfolk

Dan R.

Roanoke R.

Guilford

Hillsboro

Neuse R.

King's Mountain

Charlotte

NORTH CAROLINA

Hannah's Cowpens

Cheraw

Cape Fear R.

Peedee R.

Winnsboro

Camden

Ninety-Six

Wilmington

SOUTH CAROLINA

Cape Fear

Augusta

Orangeburg

Santee R.

Georgetown

ATLANTIC OCEAN

N

Savannah R.

W — E

Charleston

Ogeechee R.

GEORGIA

Savannah

Miles 0   50   100   150

PART THREE

19

MARCHING THROUGH
GEORGIA

'Such a scene of confusion as there
appeared is not often equalled.'

Thomas Pinckney

The officer chosen for this operation in Georgia was Archibald Campbell, Member of Parliament for the Stirling burghs of Scotland and son of the Commissioner of the Western Isles. A 'Scotsman through and through', as he put it himself, he had served in Canada in the Seven Years' War with Fraser's Highlanders and had been wounded at the taking of Quebec in 1759. He had later served in India with the 42nd Highlanders and had then come out to America again with Fraser's Highlanders as commanding officer of the second battalion. Having been landed in Boston harbour while the city was in the hands of the rebels, he had been taken prisoner and had not long since been exchanged for Ethan Allen.

After enduring a long sea voyage and a storm which dispersed his transports, Campbell disembarked his 3500 men on Tynbee Island at the mouth of the Savannah River on 29 December 1778. The pretty, orderly town of Savannah, which lay a little way upstream beyond a bend in the river, had been laid out on a plan of linked squares by James Oglethorpe, the English general and philanthropist, who had received a charter for what became Georgia in 1732. Around it were swamps and forests and a landscape of almost tropical luxuriance.

Under Campbell's command were two battalions of Fraser's Highlanders, two of Germans and four of American volunteers, including deserters of Irish descent from Washington's army of whom there were so many that an entire battalion of them, the Volunteers of

Ireland, had been formed in Philadelphia by Lieutenant-Colonel Lord
Rawdon. There being no sign of the enemy, Campbell rounded up
a few local inhabitants from whom he learned that the American
officer in command, Major-General Robert Howe of North Carolina,
had just returned from the south, after conducting a predatory
expedition into East Florida. He had, so Campbell's informants
said, only about fifteen hundred men under his command, though
reinforcements were expected. There were rumours that he had been
recalled and was awaiting his successor, either because of some
disagreements among the politicians of South Carolina or because of
a scandal involving a woman. Anyway, he had not gone home yet
and his reinforcements had not arrived; his camp was about half a
mile east of Savannah on Girardeau's Plantation.

Acting on this information, Campbell decided to march immediately. His orders were to co-operate with Major-General Augustin
Prevost, another of Wolfe's former officers, who was to move up to
Georgia from East Florida with as many men as could be spared from
their garrison duties there. But Campbell, realizing that he would do
well to strike without delay, re-embarked his men in their transports
and sailed upriver to a landing place less than two miles below the
town. From here he advanced over a causeway between rice swamps
for almost half a mile. At the end of the causeway the path led
upwards steadily towards a low hill, from which there suddenly came
a rattling burst of fire from an American outpost.

The Highlanders who were leading the advance immediately
dashed forward, brandishing their claymores in so determined a
manner and making so frightful a din that the Americans fled headlong
from the hill. Coming up on to the ground which they had occupied,
Campbell saw the American main strength drawn up across the road
in front of the town, their left stretching as far as the rice fields that
bordered the river, their right protected by a wooded swamp. On
either side of the road that ran through their position they had dug
a deep trench which was protected by two field-guns. Their front
was also protected by a marshy rivulet running parallel with the
trench. It was a strong position which looked as though it would be
as difficult to turn as it would be to take by frontal assault. But,
informed by a black slave of a private path through a swamp which
led to the enemy's right, Campbell made up his mind to make his
attack in that direction at once, even though nearly half his force was

still aboard the transports and the rest were still feeling the ill effects of their protracted sea voyage. So, while making a pretended attack on their left which they evidently considered their weakest point, he ordered the main force at his disposal to withdraw behind a fold in the ground that conveniently concealed them from view and then to turn the Americans' right.

While these operations were taking place Campbell kept his guns concealed, though the enemy, to use his own phrase, 'continued to amuse themselves with theirs'. As soon as the infantry were in position, however, he ran his guns forward on to the mound which had up till now concealed their movements and ordered a general advance. His well-conducted operation was entirely successful, and that evening he could report with justifiable pride to Lord George Germain:

> Thirty-eight officers of different distinctions, and four hundred and fifteen non-commissioned officers and privates . . . forty-eight pieces of cannon, twenty-three mortars, ninety-four barrels of powder, the fort with all its stores . . . and, in short, the capital of Georgia, the shipping in the harbour, with a large quantity of provisions, fell into our possession before it was dark, without any other loss on our side than that of Captain Peter Campbell, a gallant officer of Skinner's light infantry, and two privates killed, one sergeant and nine privates wounded. By the accounts received from their prisoners, thirty lost their lives in the swamp, endeavouring to make their escape.

After a rest of less than two days during which the American prisoners were put aboard the ships in the harbour, where many of them died in the appalling heat, Campbell continued his advance upriver, even though the ships carrying his horses had still not arrived and his men were compelled to drag the guns and carts across country with the help of the few animals they could lay their hands on. A number of the local inhabitants volunteered to join him and were organized into scouting units or militia, while the few bands of rebels he encountered were soon overpowered. On 10 January 1779 he returned to Savannah where, a week later, he was joined by Prevost.

★   ★   ★

Prevost had had a difficult march from East Florida. He, too, was without horses, and his men had been reduced to living on such oysters as they could scrape together as they marched through the swamps. Nevertheless, on entering Georgia he had sent a detachment under his brother, Mark, to capture a rebel stronghold at Sunbury which yielded plenty of provisions as well as stores of ammunition, forty guns and two hundred more prisoners.

Yet, although Prevost and Campbell had now joined forces in Savannah after their respective successes and had restored British authority in Georgia by establishing a chain of forts between Savannah and Augusta, the campaign in the province was far from over, for Robert Howe's successor had now appeared in the person of Major-General Benjamin Lincoln, a farmer from Hingham in Massachusetts whose tubby frame, ruddy complexion and genial expression belied a mind at once sharp and devious. Soon after his arrival at Purysburg, a company of Loyalists on their way to offer their services to the British at Augusta were waylaid by American militiamen who, having taken them all prisoner, brought seventy of them before a court on charges of treason and hanged five. Already furious with the British for encouraging black slaves to run away from their masters and employing them on fatigue duties in British camps, the militiamen in the south were in no mood to have mercy on their fellow-countrymen who threw in their lot with the redcoats. They were eager to face the enemy in open battle; and, when General Lincoln sent fifteen hundred men under Major-General Ashe up the Savannah River towards Augusta, they marched with a ready determination which induced the British, whose strength was insufficient to hold the riverside forts with confidence, to withdraw from the town and move back to Briar Creek. Here Mark Prevost cleverly contrived to get around behind the American column to attack them in the rear, to inflict four hundred casualties, and to take two hundred prisoners and seven guns. But this was no more than a brief interruption to the march of Benjamin Lincoln who, soon reinforced, continued to threaten Augusta, leaving William Moultrie to guard the upper Savannah.

Prevost, whose promised reinforcements and supplies had not arrived because of the capture of a British convoy at sea, and whose supply lines to the west had been cut, now decided upon a bold stroke: in the hope of drawing Lincoln away from his objective, he took two thousand men across the Savannah and invaded South Carolina. Lincoln, however, was not distracted. He went on towards Augusta, while Prevost, encouraged by the friendly attitude of the people east of the Savannah and learning that Charleston, the capital of the colony, was virtually defenceless, marched quickly down towards the Atlantic, fording rivers whose bridges had been destroyed, and throwing up makeshift pontoons, while his men, mostly American volunteers, ruthlessly plundered the homesteads they passed. On 12 May he reached the outskirts of Charleston and summoned it to surrender. The summons was rejected; Prevost, realizing that the garrison was a good deal stronger than his own forces, thought it prudent not to attack, and so recrossed the Ashley River and occupied James's Island and John's Island where his men could be sure of supplies and, if necessary, could be taken off by the fleet.

Although he had succeeded in alarming Lincoln who, as soon as he understood the British were making a determined effort to seize Charleston, turned on his tracks and came hurrying after him, Prevost was disappointed not to have done more. 'I am in bad health,' he complained to Germain dispiritedly, 'and too infirm for the command. Had I possessed my old activity when pursuing the rebels through Carolina, I should have been at Charleston as soon as they, and taken it without firing a shot.' As it was, when Lincoln came up to Charleston, Prevost felt obliged to go back to Savannah, leaving a rearguard of five hundred men on John's Island where they were severely mauled and lost a quarter of their strength before evacuating the island.

By now the summer days were so hot that further campaigning by land was out of the question; and Prevost could feel fairly secure against attack by Lincoln. Plans were being prepared, however, for an assault on Savannah from the sea.

Already a fast sailing ship had been sent to the West Indies with a request from Congress for the help of the French fleet. D'Estaing had had orders to go home with some of his ships; but he was quite ready to listen to Congress's request, since it offered him the opportunity of striking the successful blow in America which had so far eluded him and, in any case, the approaching hurricane season ruled out any large-scale operations in West Indian waters.

So d'Estaing set sail immediately and by 2 September 1779 the white sails of his large fleet were fluttering in the breeze before the mouth of the Savannah River. There were twenty-two ships of the line and eleven frigates as well as numerous transports packed with troops. Their arrival had been so sudden and unexpected that, after a quick fight with the ill-prepared British ships standing off-shore, a frigate, a fifty-gun ship and two storeships were captured. It was not until the next day that news of the French fleet's appearance reached Prevost, who immediately called in his outposts to Savannah and began urgently strengthening the defences of the town, putting over seven hundred blacks to long hours of work.

A week later d'Estaing started to move slowly up the river, with his transports trailing behind him, forcing the British brigs to tack away before his far superior force. He landed his troops on the western shore just below Savannah and, in excessively high-flown language, without waiting for General Sullivan to join him, summoned Prevost to surrender. Prevost asked for twenty-four hours to consider the summons, hoping that this might give time for him to be reached by Colonel Maitland, who had been left with a garrison at Beaufort on Port Royal Island when the rest of the army had been withdrawn from the islands off Charleston. As soon as he received Prevost's call for help, Maitland paraded his men and marched them at exhausting speed back to Savannah, which they reached just before d'Estaing's ultimatum was due to expire. Maitland brought with him between eight and nine hundred men, thus bringing the total British force to about 3700, mostly Highlanders, light infantry, a battalion of Germans and American Loyalists. Prevost now felt justified in replying to d'Estaing's summons with defiance, even though only a proportion of his men were fit for duty.

He was, at least, in quite a strong position. The north side of the town looked down upon the river; the western side was covered by a swamp; to the south and east strong fortifications had been formed by entrenchments, earthworks and ramparts of felled trees. And, as the enemy's heavy guns had not yet been brought up for lack of horses, Prevost was given time to mount more of his own guns and to send out sorties by night across ground with which his men had opportunities to grow familiar.

When the sixty-seven French guns and mortars did at last open fire on 4 October they made little impression on the defences, though causing widespread damage to the houses in the town. One of these, occupied by an American judge of loyalist sympathies, was hit by a shell:

> We all jumped up, and before I could dress myself, my quarters were so much in flames that I could not venture further than the door, for fear of an explosion from the rum . . . For a moment I expected that the explosion of the rum would blow up the house and kill every-one near it; and as soon as the French observed flames, they kept up a very heavy cannonade and bombardment . . . The appearance of the town afforded a melancholy prospect, for there was hardly a house which had not been shot through, and some of them were almost destroyed . . . Old Mrs Habersham's house, in which Major Prevost lived, was almost destroyed with shot and shells. In the streets and on the common there was a large number of large holes made in the ground by the shells . . . and in the church and Mr Jones's house I observed that the shells came in at the roof and went through to the ground . . . the troops in the lines were much safer than the people in town.

After four days of this shelling, d'Estaing was forced to accept that the bombardment was having little effect upon the British defences. Yet he decided upon an immediate assault. Lincoln was aghast; it seemed to him a suicidal venture. But d'Estaing was adamant: it would not be long before the British fleet sailed over from the West Indies; and, even if the British did not appear, the French fleet was in imminent danger of being driven off the coast by the gales to be expected here at this time of the year. Were they to strike at all, they must strike now. Lincoln gave way with the utmost reluctance, grudgingly consenting to his own troops being used in support of the French in what he continued to insist was a foolhardy venture.

It was agreed that units of militiamen from Georgia and South Carolina should make feints against the southern and eastern flanks of the British position, while the real attack was made by two columns of about two thousand regular troops each, one of these assaulting a redoubt, known as the Springhill redoubt, at the south-west corner of the lines, the other making its way along the edge of the swamp that covered the western defences and then falling upon the enemy from the rear.

The ensuing engagement was almost as confused as the battle in the fog at Germantown. The column which was intended to creep round upon the British rear began its advance as planned before dawn, but soon lost its way in the swamp and when the sun came up found itself exposed to the full fury of the British guns. The men of the other column of the main attack, under the personal direction of the Comte d'Estaing, also came under savage fire from the chief Springhill redoubt. They nevertheless pressed on bravely through this fire up to the very edge of the earthwork, where a furious hand-to-hand struggle took place. Captain Taws of the 60th, the British officer in charge, cut down two men and had his sword in the body of a third when he was killed himself. The Comte d'Estaing, badly wounded in the arm, endeavoured to rally his men when they seemed to be faltering. For a time an American colour flew on the parapet, but was soon shot away. Major Thomas Pinckney of the South Carolina militia wrote:

> Such a scene of confusion as there appeared is not often equalled. The Count ordered that we should move more to the left, and by no means interfere with the troops he was endeavouring to rally. In pursuing this direction we were thrown too much to the left and had to pass through Yamacraw Swamp [which was] wet and boggy [and here] we were annoyed with grapeshot. Count Pulaski, who with the cavalry preceded the right column, proceeded gallantly until stopped by the abbatis, and before he could force it, received his mortal wound . . . When [he] was about to be removed from the field, Colonel D. Horry, to whom the command of the cavalry devolved, asked what were his directions. Pulaski answered 'Follow my lancers to whom I have given orders to attack.' But the lancers were so severely galled by the enemy's fire that they also inclined off to the left, and were followed by all the cavalry breaking through the American column.

A heavy mist had now fallen, exacerbating the muddle and, when the French and Americans gave up the fight, preventing Prevost from pursuing them. He had lost no more than fifty-four men, whereas the French had lost 637 and the Americans 264. Dismayed by this defeat in a battle which, so he contended, should never have been fought, Lincoln withdrew his discouraged and resentful men to

Charleston where they were put to work on the defences that were soon surely now to come under attack. D'Estaing sailed home for France, taking part of his fleet with him and sending the rest back to the West Indies.

20

QUARRELS IN
NEW YORK

*'I am determined to return home;
the Minister has used me so ill that
I can no longer bear with this life.'*

Sir Henry Clinton

Ever since he had had to despatch Colonel Campbell to Georgia
to undertake combined operations in the south with General Prevost,
Sir Henry Clinton had been obliged to remain in New York, constantly complaining of his inability to strike a decisive blow at
Washington for lack of troops. Hard put to it even to man his outposts satisfactorily, not only did he have insufficient men for any
major offensive action, he had very little money and very few
supplies, although when it was a matter of his own comfort he
appears not to have stinted himself, food and liquor, beef, shell-
fish and brandy being ordered for his headquarters in the most
lavish quantities. Germain kept promising to reinforce him, but
the number of troops mentioned decreased as one communication followed another.

Occasionally he could be seen riding out with his staff, 'following
a Hessian jäger who dragged a bone pursued by a dog at full speed
over fences, through fields, etc.'. But most of the time he spent
indoors, worrying and fretting, making plans which were at present
impossible to execute, writing reports and letters full of grievances.
'For God's sake, my Lord,' he wrote to Germain in May 1779 after
the receipt of yet another letter containing advice which he considered
impossible to follow,

if you wish me to do anything, leave me to myself, and let me adapt my efforts to the hourly change of circumstances. If not, tie me down to a certain point and take the risk of my want of success . . . Your Lordship only recommends. But by that recommendation you secure the right of blaming me if I should adopt other measures and fail; and, should I follow that system with success, I appear to have no merit but the bare execution . . . Why, my Lord, without consulting me, you will adopt the ill digested or interested suggestions of people who cannot be competent judges of the subject, and puzzle me by hinting wishes with which I cannot agree but am loath to disregard.

For months Clinton had been demanding either to be sent sufficient reinforcements to carry out a positive and decisive strategy in America or permission to return home, as so many other commanders had done, exasperated by what they took to be the incompetence or wilful perversity of the government. Lord Percy had gone home; so had Lord Cornwallis; so had Pigot and Grey; and so, following the example of his brother, had Lord Howe, who had sailed protesting his anger with the King's Minister, and in the belief, so Clinton believed, that America was already as good as lost.

To press his views and grievances upon the government, Clinton once again sent Duncan Drummond to London. Warned of Drummond's imminent arrival, the Duke of Newcastle fled to the country. 'However, that won't do,' Drummond assured his chief. '*I'll hunt him*, go where he will.'

Before pursuing his quarry, however, Drummond called upon Lord George Germain who pretended astonishment at the Commander-in-Chief's reiterated demands. 'Good God, Mr Drummond!' he exclaimed. 'Is it possible that Sir Henry Clinton can think of desiring to come home at this critical time, when [the country] looks upon him as the only chance we have of saving America?'

Drummond had no more success with either the Duke of Newcastle or with the King, who maintained that Sir Henry was the only officer he could trust to bring matters in America to a satisfactory conclusion. Without the Commander-in-Chief's services, so it was generally held, America was lost; and, so that he should have the resources necessary to hold it, 3600 troops would shortly be despatched to him, followed by others as soon as possible.

'All agree that with your assistance things might still be brought to a happy conclusion,' Drummond assured Sir Henry. But, as though convinced by the Cabinet's arguments, he added, 'Good God, my dear General, could you but know the situation this country is drove to! . . . How can a Minister send supplies when there are so few resources and so many demands? . . . If the force you require is not, cannot, be sent you to effect the service wished for, I think I can assure you no blame will fall to your share.'

Refusing to believe that the government were doing all that they could to help him, Clinton became more and more gloomy and dispirited. Speaking with that uninhibited frankness which occasionally burst forth in the presence of officers much younger than himself, he revealed the extent of his misery to Lieutenant-Colonel Charles Stuart, one of his young confidants. 'With tears in his eyes', Clinton told Stuart that he was 'quite an altered man', that business now 'oppressed him', that he felt 'incapable of his station'.

'Believe me, my dear Colonel Stuart,' he said. 'I envy even that grenadier who is passing the door, and would exchange with joy situations. No, let me advise you never to take command of an army. I know I am hated – nay, detested – in this army. But I am indifferent about it because I know it is without a cause. But I am determined to return home; the Minister has used me so ill that I can no longer bear with this life.'

Clinton's depression had been deepened by his inability to get on with Lord Howe's temporary successor, Rear-Admiral James Gambier. Lord Howe was far from being a friendly or convivial man; indeed, he was even more unclubbable than Clinton. 'We cannot make a rake of Lord Howe,' General Pigot once commented, 'though we got him to a supper party and kept him there till one. Pains were taken to get him to play at *vingt-et-un* but . . . he could not be prevailed upon.' Clinton, however, found Lord Howe's sobriety no bar to the regard in which he held him. In all his service connected with the Navy he had never, so he said, met with an officer in whom he had so much confidence. With the ill-educated Gambier, grandson of a Huguenot immigrant, there was to be no such rapport, for Gambier, a dandified officer who behaved as though he were still a midshipman, was 'in every respect a horrid performer', the most 'impracticable man' Clinton had ever come across. Yet, if Gambier were bad enough, the Admiral who was eventually appointed to succeed Howe in command was far worse. Had the Admiralty racked their brains to find a man less likely to appeal to Sir Henry Clinton, they could scarcely have improved upon the sixty-year-old Marriot Arbuthnot, an unreliable, self-satisfied and unprepossessing officer, by turns absurdly self-confident and fussily hesitant, of whom even his Victorian biographer found far more to say in listing his faults than in describing his talents: 'Ignorant of the discipline of his profession . . . destitute of even a rudimentary knowledge of naval tactics . . . for the rest he appears in contemporary stories as a coarse, blustering, foul-mouthed bully, and in history as a sample of the extremity to which the maladministration of Lord Sandwich had reduced the Navy.'

Relations between Clinton and Arbuthnot grew worse and worse until they were scarcely on speaking terms. Clinton, according to Colonel Stuart, abused the Admiral 'in the grossest terms, called him full of deceit and artifice, and declared that he never could agree with one who meant to mislead him'. Arbuthnot, in turn, 'giving way to his passion', declared that he was 'tired to death' by General Clinton and 'abused him for want of candour and folly'.

By now Clinton was unable to seek solace in the company of the two officers on his staff, Major Drummond and Lord Rawdon, whose support and sympathy in the past had meant so much to him, for he had fallen out with them both. Already annoyed with Drummond for what appeared to be his acceptance of the Cabinet's plea that they were doing all they could to help him, Clinton had subsequently quarrelled with him over the difficult problem of the status of American loyalist officers in the army. In Sir William Howe's day it had been decided that these officers, many of whom had had little military training, should be a rank inferior to their counterparts in a regular regiment, that was to say a captain in a British regiment of the line, for example, was given authority to issue orders to a loyalist major. The government, anxious not to give offence to loyalist officers and to encourage their recruitment, decided to countermand this order and to direct that only if they were of the same rank could a British regular officer give instructions to an American. While he was in London, Major Drummond had been consulted about this; he had said that he was sure Sir Henry would have no objection to the new ruling. But Sir Henry did have objections to it, strong objections; and when Drummond returned to

America he was informed that the Commander-in-Chief had lost all confidence in him and that the time had come for them to part.

Lord Rawdon, the Adjutant-General, also angered Sir Henry not only by interceding on Major Drummond's behalf but also by his attitude to the Volunteers of Ireland, the provincial regiment of Irish immigrants. Clinton had taken a particular interest in them, being convinced that, despite the reasons that had induced them or their forbears to leave Ireland, their 'pride of having sprung in the old country . . . prevented them from entirely assimilating with the Americans'. The Irish made good soldiers; many of their fellow-countrymen were in the British Army; every effort should be made to bring all Irish-Americans over to the British side. Clinton's trusted friend, Lord Rawdon, had been placed in command of the Volunteers of Ireland.

But Rawdon, so Clinton complained, had become absurdly proud of his Irishmen, unwilling to admit their faults, bridling at any criticism of their behaviour. Clinton was 'perhaps a choleric old gentleman', as he admitted; yet Rawdon was without question a 'hot-headed young one'. His attitude was intolerable; and Clinton told him so. Rawdon resigned as Adjutant-General.

This latest quarrel at headquarters could not but increase Clinton's unpopularity. Rawdon was a well-liked and respected officer, whereas Clinton was regarded more widely than ever as unfitted for his command. His reputation, so William Smith, a loyalist New York lawyer, said, was 'going down hill'. There was not now a single, 'sensible, experienced officer' about him. As a replacement for Rawdon as Adjutant-General he appointed the twenty-seven-year-old Major John André, having rejected the claims of Rawdon's assistant, Lieutenant-Colonel Stephen Kemble, who promptly resigned as well.

The son of a merchant from Geneva who had settled in London, André had himself considered a business career before deciding to join the Army. A handsome and attractive young man, he was a highly skilled draughtsman as well as a linguist, and was expected to reach high rank in his chosen profession, though when Clinton asked the government to confirm André in his new appointment Lord Amherst refused to do so, commenting that he had 'never heard of one John André', a dismissive remark which Clinton characteristically – in this case, understandably – took as a personal slight. 'No general,' he remarked, 'had ever been used so.' Admittedly André seemed to spend as much time acting in amateur theatricals in New York as working at headquarters, but he was reckoned by far the best of Clinton's aides-de-camp, the others being dismissed by William Franklin, the Governor of New Jersey, as 'a parcel of blockheads'. Most of the more senior staff were not much more highly regarded: the Quartermaster General, for example, was a young nobleman 'so short-sighted as not to distinguish a man from an ox at twenty yards'.

The quality of the Commander-in-Chief's staff would not have mattered so much had he himself appeared to be in firm control of the army's affairs and future. But he seemed to have no system, said William Tryon, Governor of New York, voicing a general complaint; his apparent unwillingness to act was responsible for 'a mutinous spirit in an inactive army'. A friend of Lady Grimston's wrote to her from New York:

> Nothing, surely, can be more shameful than our perfect inactivity . . . Not a single attempt has been made to annoy the enemy [since] it is unfortunately our fate to be commanded by a person that has no abilities to plan, nor firmness to execute, the most trivial military operation . . . The campaign before Charleston some years since was such a series of misconduct that it was not to be expected that this army would be better conducted by the same commander. For God's sake let us have a man of resolution or abilities! . . . To have an ignorant, capricious, irresolute commander is the excess of madness.

The trouble was that Clinton, as he so often complained, could not act decisively until the reinforcements promised him arrived. He was constantly being asked to send troops elsewhere, to the West Indies or to Canada, and when reinforcements did arrive, on 26 August 1779, there were no more than about 3400 of them, scarcely more than half the number he had been promised; and nearly all of these were either recovering from the fever that had spread throughout the fleet or still suffering from it. Soon no fewer than six thousand soldiers were in hospital or in those large private houses like William Smith's which had been commandeered to serve as such. Even the coastal raids which had been carried out earlier that year had to be suspended.

★   ★   ★

These raids upon ammunition depots, shipping and ports harbouring privateers, sometimes involving the destruction of churches and houses as well as military stores and naval establishments, were carried out with a ruthlessness which Clinton protested was against his orders and which he knew would provide useful ammunition for the Opposition at home – as, indeed, it did: General Henry Conway, Member for Bury St Edmunds, spoke in the Commons of 'rivers of blood, spreading terror, devastation and death over the whole continent of America'. One such raid had been made to the Chesapeake in May, others had been made in July upon Norfolk, New Haven and Fairfield where, according to the *New London Gazette*, the British and German troops 'entered the houses, attacked the persons of Whig and Tory indiscriminately, breaking open desks, trunks, chests, closets, and taking away everything of value; they robbed women of buckles, rings, bonnets, aprons, and handkerchiefs'.

The Americans had retaliated with expeditions of their own: on 16 July, for instance, 'Mad' Anthony Wayne had attacked the British fort at Stony Point on the Hudson River, had captured it, and come away with over five hundred prisoners after a dashing bayonet charge, without committing the brutalities for which the British were condemned. 'No inhumanity was shown to any of the unhappy captives,' one of Clinton's staff, Major-General James Pattison, was forced to admit. 'No one was unnecessarily put to the sword or wantonly wounded.' On 18 August the young, Princeton-educated Major Henry Lee, 'Light Horse Harry', father of Robert E. Lee, took a further 150 prisoners during an assault upon another British fort, Paulus Hook. 'This affair, treading upon the heels of the former contretemps served to inspirit the rebels and gave a degree of venom to the General's enemies,' Charles Stuart commented. 'I pitied and felt for him, and indeed he was tremendously depressed; and I am afraid his temper from these two unlucky blows of fortune became much soured.'

These 'unlucky blows' were compounded by a more serious affair, far to the north at Penobscot, on the coast of what is now south Maine, where it was decided that a fort should be built to protect a settlement of loyalist refugees. Brigadier-General Francis MacLean, commander of British forces in Nova Scotia, was accordingly sent down to Penobscot with two Scottish regiments to construct this fort, which was intended to give protection to his own territory as well as to the refugees. But, as soon as news of the enterprise reached Boston, feelings against Americans who had chosen the British side, as well as the offer of a bounty, encouraged large numbers of men to volunteer to join an expedition which was expected to be short and neither too difficult nor too risky. Three thousand men were enlisted; nineteen ships were commissioned; and the expeditionary force was landed while the fort was still under construction and the settlement itself scarcely begun.

As the Americans poured ashore, the British outposts retreated with the exception of one small picquet of twenty men commanded by the eighteen-year-old John Moore, the future General, then a lieutenant in the 82nd Regiment and a 'really pretty youth', in the opinion of his father. Moore, in action for the first time, obstinately stood his ground until, over a third of his men having been killed or wounded, General MacLean sent a stronger party forward to bring him in. For a fortnight thereafter the two Scottish regiments in Penobscot held out against the besieging force whose guns maintained a persistent cannonade against their incomplete earthworks, while Lieutenant Moore, with fifty men under his command, lay waiting, ready to fulfil his orders to charge the Americans in the flank should an assault be attempted.

Such an attempt was never made. The Americans disappeared as suddenly as they had come; for, on 14 August 1779, a British squadron sailed towards the mouth of Penobscot Bay under Vice-Admiral Sir George Collier whose own ship, the sixty-four-gun *Raisonnable*, was accompanied by four frigates. The American ships seemed at first to be in the process of forming line to offer battle. But then, apart from two which put out to sea, they quickly turned about and sailed back up the river with the British ships in close pursuit. Most were driven on to the banks; some were intercepted and captured; not one escaped either being taken or destroyed by fire. Sailors and volunteers jumped overboard and ran away into the forest where, without shelter or provisions, they quarrelled over the blame for the disaster. Arguments developed into fights, fights into a general affray in which about fifty men were killed. The survivors wandered away in search of sustenance; but most died in the wilderness without encountering the least sign of civilization.

21

BUTCHERS AND PATRIOTS

---

*'The mad, cruel and accursed
American War.'*

Lord George Gordon

When Admiral Collier arrived back in New York with his prizes
from Penobscot he was indignant to discover that the widely disliked
and little respected Marriot Arbuthnot had come out with orders to
assume the command. Arbuthnot had also brought with him news
of Spain's imminent entry into the war and letters from Lord George
Germain. From these letters Clinton learned that Germain now
wanted an attack to be made on New Orleans, though there was
no practicable advice as to how this could be done without the
reinforcements which had often been promised him but which never
arrived in the numbers blithely suggested. As frustrated as his predecessor, Sir William Howe, had ever been, Clinton had again asked a
few weeks before to resign. He now repeated his request, proposing
that Lord Cornwallis, who was shortly due to return to America,
might succeed him.

Cornwallis had been given leave to go home to England, where
his wife was critically ill and where he hoped to remain in retirement
until the troubles in America were over. But after his wife's death he
had no desire to stay in England. 'This country now has no charms
for me,' he told Clinton, 'and I am perfectly indifferent as to what
part of the world I may go to . . . If you should think that you have
any material employment for me, send for me and I will readily come
to you. I shall really come with pleasure.'

He assured him that he had no wish for high command and that, if Clinton were coming home, he did not want to go out to America anyway. Even before he sailed, however, he had changed his mind about this; and had told his brother, 'If he insists on coming away, of course I cannot decline taking the command and must make the best of it.'

Nor did he conceal from the Commander-in-Chief his readiness to succeed him. But, while Clinton professed himself delighted to have so talented an officer to take over his duties, he continued in private to doubt that Cornwallis had the wits and fortitude for the post to which he aspired; and it was soon clear that the two men were no better able to get on well together than Clinton and Howe had been.

Meanwhile, Clinton's difficulties appeared to be increasing on every side: he had felt obliged to send two thousand men from his distressingly small army to General Sir Frederick Haldimand, Carleton's successor as Commander-in-Chief in Canada, who had written to give warning of the worrying change in the attitude of the Canadian people to Britain now that war with France had broken out. Yet the reinforcements which Admiral Arbuthnot had brought out with him barely compensated Clinton for this loss. More than a hundred men had died during the long voyage of 116 days across the Atlantic. Since landing, almost eight hundred had been taken to the military hospitals in New York where, by the beginning of October, most of his force were suffering from various forms of fever and other illnesses. While waiting for news from Georgia, Clinton had felt compelled to evacuate Rhode Island and to concentrate all his available men in and around New York.

There were days and nights that summer and autumn when he was beset with anxiety that the American forces would take advantage of his weakness and throw him out of New York. He could only hope that Washington would continue to find it almost as difficult to increase the strength of his army as he did his own, that the various provinces would continue to put their own individual safety above that of the United States as a whole, and that, when bounties were offered by Congress to men prepared to enlist in the Continental Army, larger bounties would go on being offered by the individual states to those willing to join their own militia.

Clinton's hopes were well founded. Indeed, there were times when Washington was as disillusioned with Congress as the British General was with his own government. 'Speculation, peculation, and an insatiable thirst for riches seem to have got the better of almost every order of men,' Washington wrote. 'Virtue and patriotism are almost extinct. Stock-jobbing, speculating, engrossing seem to be the great business of the multitude.' The value of the paper money issued by Congress had sunk so low that it was now but a fortieth or even a fiftieth of that of hard coin, while counterfeit dollars were circulating everywhere and fortunes were being made by crafty speculators and lost by the unfortunate. 'The great depreciation of Congress money,' wrote Lieutenant Anburey, one of the British officers taken prisoner at Saratoga and now on parole in Virginia,

> means that at the present rate five hundred paper dollars [can be exchanged] for one guinea. The depreciation arises from the vast quantity of counterfeit, which any person who hazards the risk may have gratis at New York to circulate throughout the province . . . There are many persons now in actual possession of plantations which they purchased with the counterfeit money they brought from New York.

While civilians speculated, soldiers continued to desert. 'We hear there is a great Number of Men Deserts Dayly,' wrote one observer. 'Yesterday three men belonging to the Maryland line were found going to the enemy. They were brought to their camp. The one was shot and his head cut off and this morning was brought to the Virginia Camp and put on top of the gallows of a man who was executed and hung. The man who is hung is said to have deserted and repreaved twice before and expected to be repreaved the third time.'

Sir Henry Clinton might have been forgiven for believing that the hanging of certain of its more exasperating members would have wonderfully concentrated the minds of the British government. But Ministers had more problems on their minds than those they faced in America.

In the first place there was trouble in the Royal Navy, which was still in the care of Lord Sandwich. His harrying of Admiral Lord Keppel, a prominent Whig, led to such discontent and ill-feeling in the service that other Whig officers of proven ability refused to accept commands while Sandwich remained in office.

Sandwich's continuing fears of a French assault upon England were widely shared; and when, on 16 June 1779, Spain, as had long been expected, also declared war, the danger of foreign invasion became more real than ever. In July a combined French and Spanish fleet of sixty-six ships entered the English Channel where it remained for several weeks; and, although it succeeded in taking only one British ship of the line, had it not been for the sickness of their crews and an easterly gale that blew them off course the enemy could well have taken the dockyard at Plymouth in a matter of hours, as the General in the command of the port himself readily admitted.

Nor was it only the south coast of England which was threatened. In Scotland there were constant alarms when the sails of American privateers, after having raised crews and refitted in French ports, appeared on the horizon; and the name of John Paul Jones, the Scottish-born seaman who had secured a commission to roam through European waters preying on British ships – and had won a dramatic victory in a celebrated battle with the *Serapis* and the *Countess of Scarborough* – was invoked by nursemaids to terrify children into obedience as that of Bonaparte was a generation later.

To protect themselves against possible invaders, the Scots and Irish formed voluntary associations of armed men in the seaports along their coasts; and, although these were illegal, the authorities turned a blind eye to their establishment. In England, too, volunteer companies came into existence, twenty-four of them in Middlesex and almost as many even in the remote county of Devon. At the same time official encouragement was given to the raising of regular regiments in England, as well as Scotland, by noblemen and landed gentry at their own expense. Regiments of Fencible Infantry, regular troops enlisted for home service only, were also enlisted; while at the end of June 1779 a Bill was brought into Parliament providing for the doubling of the strength of the militia.

Much of this sudden access of patriotic activity exasperated the Opposition, several of whose parliamentary spokesmen had been vying with each other in the display of their knowledge of military and naval affairs ever since the conduct of both Howe and Burgoyne had been examined in the House of Commons. Indeed, in the country as a whole, despite the recent surge of enthusiasm for the government's American policy, there was still support in certain

quarters for the American 'patriots' whom Samuel Johnson so ve-
hemently condemned.

The friends of William Hickey, the diarist and attorney, were characteristic of the kind of people who protested their admiration for the
American rebels and their contempt for all endeavours to suppress
their cry for freedom. One of these friends was Lord George Gordon,
youngest son of the beautiful and eccentric Duchess of Gordon who
had married as her second husband an American from New York,
Staates Long Morris, a dashing and adventurous subaltern in the
British Army seventeen years younger than herself. Her son, Lord
George, was to achieve notoriety as the leader of the Protestant
Association's demonstration which provoked the so-called Gordon
Riots in London, and was to die, a convert to Judaism, in Newgate
Prison. But in the late 1770s Gordon was a 'gay, volatile and elegant
young man of the most engaging manners', Member of Parliament
for the pocket borough of Luggershall in Wiltshire, a seat that was
bought for him when his energetic electioneering in Inverness-shire
threatened to take a seat there away from an old general, a friend of
his family. He had formerly been in the Navy and, as a midshipman,
had served in the West Indies, where he was appalled by the 'bloody
treatment of the Negroes', and in America, where he found a society
he deeply respected and a people whose sincerity and kindness he
never forgot. Once in Parliament he had generally cast his vote for
the Opposition but this seemed more out of loyalty to Edmund
Burke, under whose powerful influence he had fallen, than through
any definite convictions of his own. But as the military operations
against the American colonies had developed, his voice had been
more and more often raised in violent protest at what he called the
'mad, cruel and accursed American War'.

   During one long summer recess he went on holiday with several
friends who shared his views. As well as William Hickey, there were
William Cane, a generous, charming and extravagant young man
upon whose yacht, the *Henrietta*, the holiday was to be spent; George
Dempster, son of an immensely rich Scottish merchant and recently
created Secretary of the Order of the Thistle, whose badge he proudly
wore on a ribbon round his neck; Sir Charles Bingham, afterwards
created Earl of Lucan; and John Stephenson, a brilliant businessman
who had just returned from India with an immense fortune made

while serving in the office of the East India Company at Bombay.

The mood of the party was set when his young friends had been in Cane's house for a few hours. After dinner, as soon as his wife and mother-in-law had retired to the drawing room, Cane stood up and asked each guest to fill a bumper of champagne and drink a toast to 'the American patriots'. The toast was well received and his guests drank it with enthusiasm, not only that first evening but every day they were at sea.

They sailed to Boulogne, 'dashed off to Paris for a couple of days' and returned with an enormous quantity of champagne which, smuggled through the customs, they drank plentifully with their supper. When the conversation turned, as it nearly always did, to the American war, Lord George suggested that 'in compliment to the worthy patriots of our injured colonies', Cane's yacht should be renamed *The Congress*. The others agreed to this with the usual enthusiasm which any reference to American patriotism aroused. Bumper after bumper was drunk to 'the success of the Congress' and a bowl of punch was ordered for the crew.

The next day, as the yacht sailed towards Spithead, a lieutenant on board a warship lying at anchor watched it approach and asked Johnson, its master, to whom it belonged. 'Squire Cane's, sir,' Johnson called back, adding as the yacht glided past, the name *Henrietta* clearly visible on the stern, 'Name of *The Congress*, Sir.'

'Damn your blood, you impudent scoundrel!' shouted the lieutenant, 'I wish I had you here and I'd "congress" you!'

Sympathy for the American rebels was not confined to upper-class Whigs. In April 1779 a draft of sixty men from the 71st Highlanders mutinied when they were told they were to go to America and refused to march aboard the transports. A Fencible Regiment was called up to force them to do so. Fighting broke out; and several men on both sides were killed.

There was no such reluctance in the Army to fight the French or Spaniards. But the Admiralty, American and War Departments were all only too well aware of the difficulties of maintaining successful campaigns against both the French and the Spanish and, at the same time, keeping British commanders in America satisfied. As it was, although Gibraltar was held, Minorca was lost; and in America, Germain's plans for taking the Spanish port of New Orleans had to

be abandoned for lack of a sufficient force to secure success, while
Omoa in the Gulf of Honduras, which was captured in October, had
to be abandoned in December when the small British garrison there
was weakened by disease.

In New York, Sir Henry Clinton was waiting anxiously for a reply
to his request to be recalled. With every month, he complained, his
problems grew more intractable. The continued British presence in
Savannah was having so damaging an effect on the French merchants,
whose prosperity depended upon their trade with the American
South, that Germain was eager to repeat the successes which had
been won in Georgia by further victories in Carolina, and thus reduce
American exports and credit still further. Germain had no doubt that
an attack on Charleston, South Carolina was essential if the benefits
of Prevost's successes in Georgia were to be exploited to the full.

Clinton agreed; but, as so often in the past, his ability to pursue
the course recommended in London was hampered by his lack of
men, by his regiments of regular troops being so much under strength
and by the disinclination of loyalist Americans to come forward to
offer their services in anything like the numbers which had for so
long been – and continued to be – predicted. Clinton had need, he
said, of at least two strong armies instead of a single weak one divided
between New York and the south. He felt obliged to remain in New
York, otherwise the rebels, no longer threatened in New England,
would be certain to attempt another attack on Canada; and so he was
unable to reinforce the troops in Georgia in the way he would have
liked. At the end of 1779 he could, in fact, muster only what he
termed a 'pathetically small army'; and by then he had lost several
more of his best officers, including Francis MacLean who had so
distinguished himself at Penobscot and was on his deathbed in Halifax, Colonel Campbell who had won Savannah and was already
dead, and Sir George Collier who had gone home, leaving the fleet,
without whose support Clinton was doomed, in the incapable hands
of Marriot Arbuthnot. For much of the past year Clinton had had to
content himself with raids upon the coastal towns along the Atlantic
seaboard, destroying stores, harassing rebel camps, burning privateers and making it difficult for the Americans to concentrate their
forces since they never knew where the next lightning attack might
strike.

For these operations he did have good officers as well as enterprising squads of irregulars recruited in America, part cavalry, part infantry, ideally suited for that kind of warfare which was to become known as guerrilla after the Spanish bands which fell upon the French during the Peninsular War of 1808–13. Among these commanders of irregular troops was Major Patrick Ferguson, a small, clever, wilful, amiable man known as 'Bulldog', whom some found a trifle too cocky for their taste. The son of a Scottish lawyer, Ferguson was the inventor of the breech-loading rifle which had been so successfully demonstrated at Woolwich in 1776. A form of this rifle was supplied to an all too small corps of riflemen which had performed valuable service at the Battle of the Brandywine, where Ferguson had received a wound that cost him the use of an arm and where he had refrained from shooting General Washington in the back. Despite his injuries, Ferguson continued in command of his riflemen after they were re-formed – having been disbanded by Sir William Howe, who had taken offence at their being organized without his being consulted – and he was with them in December 1778 when they helped to root out a nest of privateers from Little Egg harbour.

A similar irregular corps was commanded by Lieutenant-Colonel John Graves Simcoe, an old Etonian who had also been severely wounded at the Brandywine. As a captain in the 40th Foot his offer to raise a corps of blacks was not accepted; but he was soon afterwards placed in command of a loyalist corps known as the Queen's Rangers.

Both Simcoe and Ferguson were honourable and chivalrous men, despite the ruthless partisan warfare which they were required to wage and which led to so much anger and bitterness among the American people whose homes and livelihood they put at risk. The more celebrated commander of the irregular corps known as the British Legion enjoyed, however, a less enviable reputation. Since capturing General Charles Lee at Basking Ridge, Banastre Tarleton, the Oxford-educated son of a Liverpool merchant, had been in action in most of the principal operations in which the army had been engaged. He was a captain of twenty-three when chosen by Clinton to command the British Legion, a mixed force of cavalry and light infantry. He was 'almost femininely beautiful', extremely vain, argumentative and none too scrupulous, well deserving many of the unfavourable comments upon his character and activities to be found in the newspapers printed in America in those areas controlled by Congress. He boasted, so Horace Walpole said, 'of having butchered more men and lain with more women than anyone else in the Army', though Sheridan thought 'raped' would have been a more exact description than 'lain'. His method of breaking in an unruly horse was characteristic: wearing huge spurs and wielding a heavy scourge with a piece of iron lashed into its knot, he would kick and lash 'like a fiend', according to one of Cornwallis's messengers, until the animal was possibly ruined but certainly subdued, with 'mingled blood and foam [pouring from its mangled sides] in a thick and clotted stream'.

Yet Tarleton was undeniably one of the most successful cavalry officers of his day, and the raids of the British Legion – though carried out with as little respect for private property and as careless of civilian life as the depredations of militant rebels in the homes of Loyalists – did all that Clinton could expect of them.

As the Christmas of 1779 approached, in a winter so cold that heavy guns were soon able to cross the thick ice on the Hudson River, Clinton decided that the time had come to put a stop to the predatory raids of his irregular corps and to mount the operation in South Carolina which Germain was pressing upon him. On 26 December he accordingly set out for Charleston with some 7600 men aboard ninety transports, leaving Baron von Knyphausen in command in New York. As so often when a British army set sail in American waters, the voyage was a long and stormy one. Off the perilous Outer Banks of North Carolina, the winter winds buffeted the ships whose masts crashed down upon the decks, ripping the sails to shreds. Two frigates foundered; the *Anna* was blown off course; the transport *George* sank beneath the waves, and Captain Johann Hinrichs of the Jäger Corps watched the soldiers 'throwing their belongings and themselves head over heels into the boats'. Many horses were killed and their carcasses tossed overboard, together with some that were sacrificed to lighten cargoes. It was over a month before Clinton reached John's Island and by then nine transports had been lost, seven of them destroyed by ice, and one, dismasted, blown away across the Atlantic as far as Cornwall. His men clambered ashore and advanced to James's Island through a strange countryside of desolate sand, marshland and dense forest, of rice fields and cotton and of fine white houses past which the figures of black slaves could be seen hurrying with bundles on their heads.

Beyond James's Island were the dark, tidal waters of the Ashley River, and parallel with the Ashley ran another river, the Cooper, also named after Charles II's Minister, Ashley Cooper, first Earl of Shaftesbury. Between the two rivers, at the end of a strip of land little more than two miles across at its widest point, was the town of Charleston, the largest city in the southern states, behind whose defences were the seven thousand men of the American Major-General Benjamin Lincoln. The approaches to Charleston harbour were guarded by a fort, Fort Johnston, on the northern shore of James's Island, and, opposite this, on the other side of the harbour, by Fort Moultrie on Sullivan's Island.

On 9 April, a strong easterly breeze filling their sails, the ships of the British flotilla sailed through the harbour under the guns of Fort Moultrie, replying to the rebels' batteries in what the loyalist Lieutenant Anthony Allaire described as a 'spirit becoming Britons'. They were watched by a captain in the Hessian Jäger corps:

This afternoon our men-of-war passed Fort Moultrie. At four o'clock they came out of Five Fathom Hole with a splendid wind and a strong tide, and aided by fog. The Admiral [Arbuthnot] went ahead in a jolly boat and piloted each ship. Sir Andrew Snape Hammond led the vanguard with the *Roebuck*. At half past four he passed the fort which belched fire out of forty pieces, most of them 24 pounders. As soon as this ship in all her glory came under the fort she defiantly replied with a broadside and then sailed by without loss and without delay . . . Then came the *Richmond* . . . She lost her fore-topmast. The *Renown* formed the rear guard, and when she arrived at the fort she lay to, took in her sails, and gave such an unrelenting, murderous fire that the whole ship seemed to flare up. Then she covered the rear of the squadron.

One transport ran aground and was so shot to pieces that the sailors had to set her alight and abandon her. Several cannon balls went through the ships without doing any damage. By half past six our ships lay at anchor on this side, having [twenty-seven] killed and one midshipman and thirteen men wounded . . . What a trifling loss under so enormous a fire.

The next day, 10 April, Clinton, who had marched further up the Ashley, crossed it about twelve miles above Charleston and established his men across the whole tongue of land west of the town. Having delivered a formal summons to Lincoln to surrender and been as formally rebuffed, Clinton next set about cutting the Americans' line of supplies with the north which were kept open by three regiments of cavalry under General Isaac Huger, thirty miles upriver at Biggins Bridge. With this end in view he sent Patrick Ferguson's Queen's Rangers and Tarleton's British Legion with orders to destroy the American camp in a surprise attack by night.

The attack was completely successful. The enemy, taken off guard, were utterly dispersed. General Huger and other officers fled into the swamps, while all those who attempted to defend themselves were cut down. 'Four hundred horses belonging to the officers and dragoons with their arms and appointments fell into the hands of the victors,' Tarleton reported in his notoriously vainglorious manner. 'About one hundred, officers, dragoons and hussars, together with fifty wagons loaded with arms, clothing and ammunition, shared the same fate.' The operation was indeed carried out, as Tarleton added, with 'great promptitude and success'.

It was also marked by great brutality. So ferocious were Tarleton's British Legion, in fact, that Major Ferguson was outraged. He threatened to have some of the worst offenders shot, and would have done so had he not been restrained. For a time he and 'the Butcher', as Tarleton became known, refused to speak to each other.

The operation had, however, enabled Clinton to push on with his siege of Charleston without fear of interference from the north; and by 5 May, when some American ladies came to headquarters to seek permission 'to go into town to take leave of their sons', his third parallel had been opened less than three hundred yards from the rebels' earthworks. He again called upon Lincoln to surrender.

The day before, a party of British marines had landed on Sullivan's Island, and Fort Moultrie had also been summoned to surrender. The fort's commander had replied that his men would resist assault 'to the last extremity'; but on being warned that if he did not hand the fort over in a quarter of an hour every man in it would be put to the sword, he gave way. General Lincoln also refused at first to surrender Charleston when called upon to do so, although the town had been bombarded in so merciless a manner that Clinton upbraided the artillery commander for allowing his men to fire their guns so indiscriminately: it was 'absurd, impolitic, inhuman to burn a town you mean to occupy'. One of Lincoln's officers recalled:

> We remained near an hour silent, all calm and ready, each waiting for the other to begin. At length we fired the first gun, and immediately followed a tremendous number of shells; it was a glorious sight to see them like meteors crossing each other, and bursting in the air; it appeared as if the stars were tumbling down. The fire was incessant almost the whole night, cannon-balls whizzing and shells hissing continually amongst us; ammunition chests and temporary magazines blowing up; great guns bursting, and wounded men groaning along the lines. It was a dreadful night! It was our last great effort, but it availed us nothing.

Three days later on 12 May 1780, after almost ceaseless bombardment, the town surrendered; and an immense amount of ammunition and weapons fell into British hands. Although the Americans' losses in killed and wounded were astonishingly few, over four thousand men, including a thousand sailors, were taken prisoner. The militiamen could not at first 'be prevailed upon to come out', so a British observer said; but the 'poor creatures began to creep out of their Holes the next Day', and were 'allowed to go home and plow the ground', their officers being permitted to keep their swords until their repeated shouts of 'Long Live Congress!' provoked their captors into confiscating them. The losses of the British during the siege were less than three hundred men, though several more were killed when a captured musket was thrown, still loaded, into a shed where gunpowder was stored, the consequent explosion scattering and mutilating bodies so that it was impossible to 'make out a single human figure'.

Clinton, who had behaved with great energy and bravery throughout the siege, was still worried and fretful. He had been warned that a new enemy fleet had set sail from France and that he must lose no time in getting back to New York. Before leaving, he issued proclamations offering pardons to all rebels who returned to their proper allegiance, and who took an oath of loyalty to the royal government, and requiring those who did not actively support the British to be treated as though they were rebels. These proclamations, he hoped, would enable the army to differentiate clearly between friends and enemies; but in fact it achieved no such purpose. Those who had decided to remain neutral in the struggle now found themselves required to take sides, while genuine Loyalists complained that known rebels could gain the privilege of British subjects by taking an oath they would break at the first opportunity. 'I should be very sorry to trust any of them out of my sight,' Captain Bowater told Lord Denbigh. 'They swallow the Oaths of Allegience to the King and Congress Alternately with as much ease as your Lordship does poached Eggs.' Five days after this unfortunate proclamation was issued, on 8 June, Clinton returned to New York, leaving Cornwallis in command in the south with four thousand men.

Lord Cornwallis was thankful to see Clinton go. Throughout the siege, relations between the two men had been slowly deteriorating as they had between Clinton and Admiral Arbuthnot. 'I am sure he is FALSE AS HELL,' Clinton wrote of Arbuthnot. 'He swore he would act with me in [everything] . . . and if he ever did otherwise or deceived me, he hoped he would be damned. The gentleman swears most horribly and I believe will LIE – NAY, I KNOW HE WILL IN A THOUSAND INSTANCES . . . He forgets all he says and does, and talks nonsense.' Clinton made up his mind that the best way to behave towards the man was with the utmost reserve, even hauteur. He did so, and the antagonism deepened. Never again, Clinton concluded, would he serve 'with such an old woman'.

One of the principal troubles was that Arbuthnot could never make up his mind and was constantly consulting his subordinates; and Clinton's opinion of some of these was not much higher than his opinion of Arbuthnot himself. Indeed, he held few naval officers in high esteem, and was perpetually going over past disagreements in an effort to satisfy himself and others that he had been in the right: one day after the siege of Charleston he went out to sound the water off the fort on Sullivan's Island at low tide. He returned confident that the water was quite deep enough for ships of the line and uttered in triumph, 'What say you now, S. P. Parker!'

The weeks of siege at Charleston had seen an end to the wary friendship between Cornwallis and Clinton as well as a worsening in the already tense relationship between the Commander-in-Chief and the Royal Navy. Clinton had long been aware that Cornwallis hoped his offer to resign would be accepted and that he himself would succeed to the command. Clinton was also well aware that the army would welcome the change, and he suspected that his second-in-command was encouraging officers in the belief that Clinton's days were numbered and that Cornwallis should already be regarded as their new chief. 'I can never be cordial with such a man,' Clinton recorded in his journal. 'He will play me false, I fear.' Months before, Cornwallis had inadvertently let slip to Howe a derogatory remark that Clinton had made about his then superior; and Clinton had never forgiven Cornwallis for the betrayal of this confidence.

When it became known in America that the King was reluctant to agree to any change in the command of the Army there, relations between Clinton and Cornwallis became more strained than ever. Cornwallis told Clinton that he did not want to be consulted any longer and asked for a separate command. Clinton was furious, and summoned Cornwallis to a meeting at which old grievances were brought up once more and new ones aired, in particular Cornwallis's friendly relations with that 'hypocrite' Arbuthnot. 'Whenever [Cornwallis] is with me,' Clinton concluded, 'there are symptoms I do not like.'

Clinton was as thankful to get away to New York as Cornwallis was to see him sail. 'I leave Cornwallis here with sufficient force to keep [Charleston] against the world,' Clinton wrote, 'without a superior fleet shows itself, in which case I shall despair of ever seeing peace restored to this miserable country.'

22

SLAUGHTER ON
KING'S MOUNTAIN

*'The violence and passions of these
people are beyond every curb of
religion and humanity.'*

Charles O'Hara

After Clinton's departure, Cornwallis, leaving a garrison in Charleston, divided the rest of his army into three colums for simultaneous expeditions into the interior. One column was to march upon Ninety-Six, a village some 150 miles inland between the Savannah and Saluda Rivers; another was to go up the Savannah to Augusta; while the third, commanded by Cornwallis himself, was to make for Camden by way of the Santee River.

Cornwallis's column had not proceeded far when he was told that a regiment of Virginian infantry under Colonel Abraham Buford, which had been ordered to the relief of Charleston, was now retreating in front of him towards North Carolina. Cornwallis promptly ordered Banastre Tarleton, whose British Legion formed part of his column, to race ahead to catch Buford before he escaped. Tarleton, eager as always to accept such an assignment, galloped off immediately with his own cavalry and a detachment of men from the 17th Light Dragoons, 270 men in all. He took them at such a rate that many horses collapsed under their riders; but, seizing others from settlements by the roadside, he dashed on, through Camden and past Rugeley's Mills until the men who had been able to keep up with him, having been on the road for 54 hours, came upon the American rearguard and overtook it on 29 May 1780 on the borders of the two Carolinas, forcing Colonel Buford to halt and turn round.

Buford drew up his regiment, less than four hundred strong, in a single line in the clearing of a wood. Tarleton decided to press home the attack without delay, despite the exhaustion of his men, and sent them forward in three groups, one on each flank, and one at the centre. As the cavalry of the British Legion charged the centre, Buford's men obeyed his strict orders to hold their fire. Closer and closer the cavalry came towards the steady line of American rifles, the earth flying at their galloping horses' hooves, until no more than ten yards separated them. The order was given at last; the Americans opened fire; but they fired just too late. The impetus of the charge could not be stopped; several horsemen fell, but the rest came on, waving their sabres.

In the ensuing mêlée at Waxhaw Tarleton's horse was killed, several others were wounded, three of his officers and sixteen of his men were shot from their saddles; but the havoc the Legion wreaked with their sabres was such that Buford decided to surrender. One of his ensigns raised a flag but, according to a surgeon who was present, the ensign was 'instantly shot down'. The surgeon, Robert Brownfield, wrote:

> Viewing this as an earnest of what they were to expect, [the Virginians took up their arms again] to sell their lives as dearly as possible; but before this was fully affected, Tarleton with his cruel myrmidons was in the midst of them, when commenced a scene of indiscriminate carnage, never surpassed by the ruthless atrocities of the most barbarous savages.
>
> The demand for quarters, seldom refused to a vanquished foe was at once found to be in vain. Not a man was spared . . . [Tarleton's dragoons] went over the ground plunging their bayonets into everyone that exhibited any signs of life, and in some instances, where several had fallen over the others, these monsters were seen to throw off on the point of the bayonet the uppermost, to come at those underneath.

As though encouraged by this massacre coming so soon after the fall of Charleston, the Loyalists in South Carolina, many of whom had been in hiding for months, now came out to settle old scores with the rebels; and from the sea to the Blue Ridge Mountains, from the Savannah to the Pee Dee River there were riots, fighting and murders as antagonistic factions vindictively attacked each other in a province whose inhabitants were of unusually diverse origins. The first Europeans to have arrived in any number were English, then came Huguenots from France, then Dutch, Swiss, Germans and Scottish; and their descendants, together with other immigrants from the north, had settled in isolated communities whose wariness and jealousy of each other had been exacerbated over the past few restless years, and were now further increased by the proclamation issued by Clinton before his departure offering a pardon to all rebels who took an oath of allegiance to the King.

Had Cornwallis been a less humane man, he might have temporarily put down the unrest in the south by a systematic policy of forceful cruelty, as Banastre Tarleton would have done and as several other officers urged him to do. The rebels, after all, did not hesitate to terrorize the people, even those who wished to remain neutral, behaving on occasion like bands of outlaws and so easily intimidating peaceable farmers that Cornwallis was exasperated. 'When I see a whole settlement running away from 20 or 30 robbers,' he once wrote, 'I think they deserve to be robbed.' But since his duty was to conciliate the people, not to provoke or inflame them, he felt he had to content himself with threats which – although he did not intend to carry them out – became useful propaganda in the hands of rebels, who spread about exaggerated versions of them amongst a people persuaded to believe that the commanding general was personally responsible for all the excesses of the time in South Carolina.

'The violence and passions of these people are beyond every curb of religion and humanity,' wrote an Irish officer. 'They are unbounded and every hour exhibit dreadful wanton mischiefs, murders and violences of every kind, unheard of before. We find the country in great measure abandoned, and the few who venture to remain at home are in hourly expectation of being murdered, or stripped of all their property.' The whole country was in 'an absolute state of rebellion', Cornwallis confirmed to Clinton. 'Every friend of government has been carried off and his plantation destroyed.' Vast amounts of tobacco and other crops and stores were seized; horses and cattle were driven away; houses were broken into and plundered; over two thousand slaves were packed aboard ships and sent off for sale in the West Indies; women robbed of jewellery, wedding rings, shoe buckles and even hat pins by gangs of cruel men, waving swords and, as one victim said, 'bellowing out the most horrid curses imaginable'. Many women considered themselves lucky to escape with the loss of jewellery. Karl Gustav Tornquist, a Swedish officer serving with the French navy in the southern colonies at this time, reported that 'on a beautiful estate a pregnant woman was found murdered in her bed through several bayonet stabs [according to another account, her unborn baby was cut out of her womb and hanged on a tree]. The barbarians had opened both of her breasts and written above the bed canopy: "Thou shalt never give birth to a rebel."' In an adjoining room the floor was covered with the broken pieces of plaster-cast figures; arranged in a cupboard in their place were five decapitated human heads.

Malevolent Whig rebels were often as vindictive as revengeful Tories, while the 'outliers' who attacked and plundered both, with utter indifference to their respective loyalties, were worse than either. After one skirmish between Tories and rebels, a young militiaman was witness of a scene which 'made a lasting impression on his mind':

> I was invited by some of my comrades to go and see some of the Tory prisoners. We went to where six were standing together. Some discussion taking place, I heard some of our men cry out, 'Remember Buford', and the prisoners were immediately hewed to pieces with broadswords. At first I bore the scene without any emotion, but upon a moment's reflection, I felt such horror as I never did before nor have since, and, returning to my quarters and throwing myself upon my blanket, I contemplated the cruelties of war until overcome and unmanned by a distressing gloom from which I was not relieved until commencing our march next morning before day by moonlight. I came to Tarleton's camp, which he had just abandoned leaving lively rail fires. Being on the left of the road as we marched along, I discovered lying upon the ground something with the appearance of a man. Upon approaching him, he proved to be a youth about sixteen who, having come out to view the British through curiosity, for fear he might give information to our troops, they had run him through with a bayonet and left him for dead. Though able to speak, he was mortally wounded. The sight of this unoffending butchered boy . . . relieved me of my distressful feelings for the slaughter of the Tories, and I desired nothing so much as the opportunity of participating in their destruction.

Such brutalities as these were repeated all over the province and, indeed, in other provinces where the struggle had taken on the aspects of a bitterly ferocious civil war. At Bennington, so a loyalist officer related,

> a little before the Royalists gave way, the Rebels pushed with a strong party on the Front of the Loyalists where I commanded. As they were coming up I observed a Man fire at me, and, crying out: 'Peters, you damned Tory, I have got you,' he rushed on me with his Bayonet, which entered just below my left Breast, but was turned by the Bone. By this time I was loaded and I saw that it was a Rebel Captain, and old Schoolfellow & Playmate, and a Couzin of my Wife's. Tho' his Bayonet was in my Body, I felt regret at being obliged to destroy him.

> The whole country was struck with terror [runs another typical account] . . . The outrages were committed mostly by a train of loyal refugees, as they termed themselves, whose business it was to follow the camps and under the protection of the army enrich themselves on the plunder they took from the distressed inhabitants who were not able to defend it.
>
> We were also distressed by another swarm of beings (not better than harpies). These were women who followed the army in the character of soldiers' and officers' wives. They were generally considered by the inhabitants to be more insolent than the soldiers. They were generally mounted on the best horses and side saddles, dressed in the finest and best clothes that could be taken from the inhabitants as the army marched through the country.

It was idle, Cornwallis later added, to expect the militia to help in restoring order and submission to British rule. Such loyalist militia as could be raised in the south were inefficient and unreliable, even worse than the rebel militia, the officers being scarcely more dependable than the men. The provincial regiments were admittedly far superior to the militia; but they were few in number, and recruitment to them proved extremely difficult since their requirement of long-term service, generally in provinces far from those in which enlistment took place, was an obligation which most would-be recruits refused to accept.

Cornwallis's task in keeping order in so large a territory with rather less than four thousand regular troops and an uncertain number of militia and provincials was one of immense difficulty. His garrisons on the coast were far apart at Savannah, Georgetown, Beaufort and Charleston. As well as at Augusta and Ninety-Six, there were also widely separated inland posts at Cheraw Hill, Cross Creek, Rocky Mount and at Camden some fifty miles south of Hanging Rock on the Wateree River. Hard enough as it was to keep a secure hold on South Carolina in the weeks immediately following the capture of Charleston, Cornwallis's difficulties were much increased when, in the middle of June, reports reached him of two thousand men from Washington's army having marched into Hillsboro, and of the activities of Thomas Sumter, a clever leader of irregular troops known as the 'Carolina Gamecock', with years of experience fighting on the Indian frontier, who was gathering strength around the upper reaches of the Pee Dee River. Already an officer who had taken the oath of loyalty to the King had persuaded an entire regiment of militia to join Sumter, and other supposedly loyal troops were expected to follow this example.

It was not long before Sumter felt himself strong enough to make raids on the garrisons at Rocky Mount and Hanging Rock, in both of which the British suffered severe losses; nor was it long before General Gates began to march south from Hillsboro with the main body of the American Army. Gates was warned that provisions would be difficult to come by and the people far from friendly in the country of pine forests through which he intended to pass; but he was bent on going that way, the shortest way, to Camden rather than through less inhospitable terrain which would have prolonged his march. His army accordingly made for Lynch's Creek on 27 July by a path which soon ensured that the 'distresses of the soldiery daily increased', in the words of the Deputy Adjutant-General, Colonel Otho Williams, who had strongly advised against this chosen route:

> They were told that the banks of the Pee Dee River were extremely fertile – and so indeed they were; but the preceding crop of corn (the principal article of produce) was exhausted, and the new grain, although luxuriant and fine, was unfit for use. Many of the soldiery,

urged by necessity, plucked green ears and boiled them with the
lean beef, which was collected in the woods, made for themselves
a repast, not unpalatable to be sure, but which was attended with
painful effects. Green peaches also were substituted for bread, and
had similar consequences . . . It occurred to some that the hair
powder which remained in their bags, would thicken soup, and it
was actually applied . . . As there were no spirits yet arrived in
camp, and as it was unusual for troops to make a forced march, or
prepare to meet an enemy without some extraordinary allowance,
it was unluckily conceived that molasses would, for once, make an
acceptable substitute.

Dispirited by their meagre rations and weakened by a fast and
difficult march and by diarrhoea induced by a recent 'hasty meal of
quick-baked bread and fresh beef, with a dessert of molasses mixed
with mush or dumplings', Gates's men approached Camden, a small,
neat, flourishing town known as Pine Tree Hill until its name was
changed in honour of one of the leading opponents of government
policy in England. Here Cornwallis had established his headquarters
in the house of one of the town's leading citizens, a merchant by the
name of Kershaw, a violent patriot and persecutor of Loyalists
who was shipped off to Bermuda while his wife and children were
relegated to a room in the attic.

On 15 August, Cornwallis left this house for Rugeley's Mills at
the head of a small force of just over two thousand men, of whom
380 were Loyalist militiamen and about 850 provincials. And, at two
o'clock the next morning, he stumbled upon Gates's army, some
3050 strong, at Parker's Old Field, a stretch of open land bordered
by dreary gum swamps and sparsely dotted with tall pines. There
was a sudden outburst of haphazard firing which ceased as suddenly
as it had broken out; then all remained quiet until dawn. Gates
consulted his subordinates, who clearly considered that he would
have been well advised to do so earlier. One of them, Edward
Stevens, offered the opinion that there was now nothing for it but
to fight. The others, who up till then had remained silent, appeared
to agree.

Satisfied by his examination of two or three prisoners that he had
come across the body of Gates's army, Cornwallis called back his
vanguard and made preparations for an attack at sunrise. One brigade,

consisting of Irish volunteers, the infantry of the British Legion and
a corps of North Carolina Loyalists, both militia and provincials, he
placed under Lord Rawdon on the left; a second brigade, under
Lieutenant-Colonel James Webster and comprising three companies
of light infantry, the 23rd Fusiliers and 33rd Foot, was ordered to the
right. In support were two battalions of the 71st Highlanders, with
Tarleton's cavalry drawn up behind them.

Soon after it was light the men of Webster's brigade discerned
parties of American militia advancing unsteadily towards them in the
haze of the hot and windless morning. So uncertain and hesitant was
their approach that Cornwallis ordered Webster to charge them
immediately. At the sight of the redcoats' determined assault and
their intimidating roar, the militia turned and fled for the safety of
the swamps.

'I confess that I was amongst the first that fled,' one of these
militiamen admitted.

> The cause of that I cannot tell, except that everyone I saw was about
> to do the same. It was instantaneous. There was no effort to rally,
> no encouragement to fight. Officers and men joined in the flight. I
> threw away my gun, and, reflecting I might be punished for being
> found without arms, I picked up a drum, which gave forth such
> sounds when touched by the twigs I cast it away. When we had
> gone, we heard the roar of guns still.

Webster, deciding that these militiamen were not worth following,
halted his men, wheeled them to the left and transferred his attack to
the right of Gates's line where the 2nd Maryland Brigade and the
Delaware Regiment, under command of the immense Bavarian volunteer who chose to be known as Baron DeKalb, were already under
heavy fire from Rawdon's brigade. For almost an hour the Americans,
under DeKalb's brave leadership, courageously stood their ground,
meeting bayonet attack with counter-attack; but then the cavalry of
Tarleton's British Legion, which had trotted unnoticed around their
other side, charged headlong upon them from the rear, scattered
them and chased them off the field, slashing at their shoulders as they
tried to escape, catching up with the militia and despatching many
of them too. Soon the road for 'some miles', so an observer wrote,
'was strewed with the wounded and killed, who had been over-

taken by the Legion in their pursuit. The number of dead horses, broken wagons, and baggage, scattered on the road, formed a perfect scene of horror and confusion – arms, knapsacks and accoutrements found were innumerable: such was the terror and dismay of the Americans.'

Almost a thousand of the rebel army were killed in all, including DeKalb; almost as many were taken prisoner, hundreds of them being herded into the grounds of Kershaw's house where the merchant's daughter, looking out of her attic window, saw the British soldiers passing round water to them in tin cups. In addition, Gates had lost all his stores and baggage and all his seven brass cannon. He himself escaped and fled nearly two hundred miles on a panting horse. His reputation, undeservedly high ever since Burgoyne's surrender at Saratoga, was lost for ever; and, though charges were never pressed, an official inquiry into his conduct was ordered.

It now seemed inevitable that Sumter, who had also been advancing on Camden, must retire; and, to hasten him on his way, Cornwallis, having lost three hundred of the men whom he could so ill spare, advanced north, sending Tarleton's Legion ahead up the eastern bank of the Wateree River to intercept him. Tarleton's men galloped off and came upon him at Rocky Mountain Ferry, where his camp fires could be seen burning on the far bank of the river. By the time boats for his men and horses had been found, however, Tarleton's quarry had disappeared. Continuing the chase until less than two hundred men could keep pace with him in the scorching summer heat, Tarleton came at last upon two of Sumter's mounted sentries on 18 August. There was an exchange of shots; one of Tarleton's dragoons fell dead; both sentries were cut down. Thereafter all was quiet again. The shots had been heard in the American camp, but it was supposed that someone had killed an animal for supper.

Tarleton's men crept on until they could distinctly hear the Americans talking and the clatter of their cooking pots. Several of the men lay on the ground, their arms piled. The Legion struck with their customary sudden violence. There was brief resistance from a few militiamen who had taken shelter behind the wagons, but their rifles were soon silenced. Sumter himself, half undressed, managed to escape like Gates had done after the battle outside Camden. Over a hundred and fifty of his eight hundred men were killed or wounded, however, and more than two hundred taken prisoner. The British also captured all Sumter's stores and two of his guns, and released a hundred prisoners. Only one of their own officers was killed and no more than fifteen men wounded.

When news of Gates's defeat and of Sumter's subsequent dispersal reached London, Ministers looked forward eagerly to Cornwallis's invasion of North Carolina. Cornwallis, himself, however, could not view such a move without serious disquiet. Besides, it was all very well for Ministers in London to persist in setting such store by American Loyalists in the south: the reality was that they were always fewer in number than they were said to be and usually unreliable, sometimes all too ready to desert the British, to whose cause they were said to be devoted, for such partisan leaders as Thomas Sumter. Moreover, while Sumter had been surprised by Tarleton, he had not been captured. He was certain to be heard of again; and, even if he were not, there were other partisan leaders, such as William Lee Davidson and Joseph Graham, William R. Davie, Andrew Pickens and the wily and elusive Francis Marion who was known as 'the Swamp Fox', a man experienced in fighting the Cherokee Indians, who were proving themselves quite as troublesome and dangerous. To make matters worse, so alarming a number of Cornwallis's men were on the sick list that any invasion of North Carolina would have to be supported by a strong diversion by Clinton from New York; yet Clinton continued to insist that he could not move until he had stronger support from the sea than the Royal Navy were at present able to supply him.

Yet, despite Clinton's unwillingness to help him, Cornwallis decided that the invasion must be carried out; and so, with just over two thousand men, he began to move up the Wateree River from Camden on 8 September. He had to advance so slowly, because of the ill health of many of his men and the difficulty of gathering supplies in a countryside whose inhabitants were almost all supporters of the rebels, that a fortnight later he had still not reached Charlotte, 'an agreeable village', as one of his officers was to describe it, 'but in a damned rebellious country'. And all the way his outposts and the guards on the baggage wagons had been fired upon and occasionally attacked in force by partisans. On 25 September, as he came within sight of Charlotte, Cornwallis sent Tarleton's British Legion on ahead of his main body to reconnoitre.

Tarleton himself was not in command, since he, like so many

others in the army, was ill with fever; his place had to be taken by Major the Hon. George Hanger, the youngest son of Lord Coleraine, an irresponsible and opinionated young rake who was one of the Prince of Wales's favourite cronies and had joined the Prince on some of his wildest escapades. Once an officer in the Guards, from which he had resigned in a huff when passed over for promotion, Hanger later contrived to obtain a captaincy in the Hessian Jäger corps. After the war, having dissipated all his money on women, drink, clothes and gambling, he was to be imprisoned as a debtor and, upon his release, to set himself up as an extremely unreliable coal merchant.

Possessing all Tarleton's reckless dash and little of his skill as a cavalry leader, Hanger could scarcely have been a worse choice for the task with which Cornwallis entrusted him. He galloped off into Charlotte with the British Legion, leaving his infantry straggled behind; and, disdainful of the orders he had been given for a cautious, exploratory approach, dashed headlong into a heavy fire from the rebel militia in the surrounding houses. He was immediately wounded; his men, disconcerted by the disruption of their charge, fell back upon the infantry; and it was left to Cornwallis, coming up with the main body, to restore order. By now even more of Cornwallis's men had fallen sick; and he felt constrained to halt his advance in Charlotte where he received confirmation of an assault upon the British garrison in Augusta which, although repulsed with severe loss to the Americans, was a reminder of how vulnerable such posts were.

Meanwhile Patrick Ferguson, recently promoted lieutenant-colonel and Inspector of Militia for the Southern Provinces, had left Ninety-Six, also bound for Charlotte. He took a circuitous route to the west to cover the left flank of Cornwallis's march, to scatter such rebel militia as he might come across along the frontier, and in the hope, which nearly all his brother-officers felt convinced would not be realized, of enlisting recruits for the King's cause from the scattered inhabitants of the upper reaches of the Saluda River and the foothills of the South Carolina Blue Ridge. It was, indeed, a forlorn hope. The area was 'composed of the most violent young rebels' one of Ferguson's officers had ever seen, 'particularly the young ladies'. And, instead of the recruits he had been seeking, Ferguson found a force of three thousand rough backwoodsmen, all armed with rifles which they used with uncommon skill, intent upon his destruction. He turned immediately for Charlotte, sending urgent messages by several different routes requesting immediate support from Ninety-Six where the hard-pressed American loyalist commander, Lieutenant-Colonel John Harris Cruger, was in no position to help him. Every one of Ferguson's despatch riders was killed by the backwoodsmen who were now gathering support from settlements from all along the foothills of the Blue Ridge Mountains and were so close upon Ferguson's heels that by 6 October he felt compelled to take up a defensive position on King's Mountain, a spur of the South Carolina Blue Ridge where he turned to face his pursuers, hoping to drive them off.

It was a strong position on the crest of a steep hill littered with thousands of pine needles and immense lichen-encrusted boulders lying between trees that grew to an imposing height. One of his flanks was protected by an escarpment which, for all their renowned agility, the backwoodsmen could not possibly climb. Ferguson evidently felt confident that his men, a thousand or so militia and a hundred provincials, all of them American, would have no difficulty in withstanding attacks from the front and his other side by a force even twice as strong as the two thousand or so men he believed himself to be facing.

Below the plateau, where Ferguson awaited their assault, the frontiersmen, having tied their baggage to their saddles and their horses to nearby trees, began their ascent of the steep, thickly wooded slopes in four separate bands commanded by various chosen leaders, including a miller, an innkeeper, a future member of Congress and a man named Isaac Shelby who was to be the first Governor of the new state of Kentucky. All of them were under the general direction of Colonel William Campbell of the Virginia Militia, Patrick Henry's brother-in-law, who had been elected 'Officer of the Day'. Captain Alexander Chesney, a loyalist officer from South Carolina, reported:

> So rapid was the attack that I was in the act of dismounting to report that all was quiet when we heard their firing about half a mile distant. I immediately paraded the men and posted the officers. During this short interval I received a wound . . . and on going towards my horse I found he had been killed. King's Mountain,

from its height, would have enabled us to oppose a superior force
with advantage had it not been covered with wood which sheltered
the Americans and enabled them to fight in their favourite manner.
In fact, after driving in our pickets, they were enabled to advance
to the crest of the hill in perfect safety, until they took post and
opened an irregular but destructive fire from behind trees and other
cover . . . In this manner the engagement was maintained for near
an hour, the mountaineers flying when there was danger of being
charged with bayonet, and returning again so soon as [Ferguson's
Loyalists] had faced about to repel another of their parties.

Climbing up the slope below Captain Chesney was one of the
frontiersmen, Thomas Young, a boy not yet seventeen, who later
wrote that he could 'well remember' how he behaved that day, how
he fought his way to the summit from tree to tree, standing behind
each trunk 'until the bark was nearly all knocked off' and his eyes
'pretty well filled with it'. 'One fellow shaved me pretty close,'
Young continued, 'for his bullet took a piece out of my gun stock.
Before I was aware of it, I found myself apparently between my own
regiment and the enemy, as I judged, from seeing the paper which
the Whigs wore in their hats, and the pine knots the Tories wore in
theirs, these being the badges of distinction.'

Directing his men by blasts on a shrill silver whistle, Ferguson, a
hunting shirt over his uniform, hurried from one company to the
next as the enemy drew closer, both in the front and flank. Driven
back by the bayonet at one point, the frontiersmen, darting behind
the trees in their dun-coloured buckskins and coats of dark cloth,
would then appear at another, their long rifles in hand, ammunition
in their mouths, creeping around Ferguson's rear. One after the other
his militiamen fell; and the rest began to falter. In a desperate bid to
rally them, Ferguson charged forward on his horse, shouting, 'Hur-
rah, brave boys, the day is ours!', brandishing his sword, knocking
aside two white flags raised in surrender, riding on through the shot,
his hat and hunting shirt shot to pieces, wounded in both arms and
in the chest, until he fell dead from the saddle and his horse tumbled
over down the slope.

It was some time before the firing finally stopped, since some of
the backwoodsmen were unaware of the surrender, while others,
eager to be revenged for the British Legion's brutality, were deter-

mined to kill as many as they could of the accursed Tories. Shouting, 'Tarleton's quarter!' they attacked their fellow-countrymen, shooting them, cutting them down with their own bayonets, killing both the wounded and those trying to surrender. James Collins, a sixteen-year-old boy who had climbed the hill in Isaac Shelby's column, recorded:

> The dead lay in heaps on all sides, while the groans of the wounded were heard in every direction. I could not help turning away from the scene before me, with horror, and though exulting in victory, could not refrain from shedding tears . . .
>
> On examining [Ferguson's body] it appeared that almost fifty rifles must have been leveled at him at the same time. Seven rifle balls had passed through his body, both his arms were broken, and his hat and clothing were literally shot to pieces. Their great elevation above us had proved their ruin; they overshot us altogether, scarce touching a man except those on horseback, while every rifle from below seemed to have the desired effect . . .
>
> We proceeded to bury the dead, but it was badly done. They were thrown into convenient piles and covered with old logs, the bark of old trees and rocks, yet not so as to secure them from becoming a prey to the beasts of the forest, or the vultures of the air; and the wolves became so plenty, that it was dangerous for anyone to be out at night for several miles around. Also the hogs in the neighborhood gathered into the place to devour the flesh of men . . . I saw myself in passing the place, a few weeks after, all parts of the human frame . . . scattered in every direction . . .
>
> In the evening, there was a distribution of the plunder, and we were dismissed. My father and myself drew two fine horses, two guns, and some articles of clothing with a share of powder and lead. Every man repaired to his tent or home.

The injured who escaped slaughter were herded together some way off where they were left, without blankets, under the guard of a single frontiersman who could do nothing to help them in their suffering. Colonel Ferguson's corpse, so it was afterwards said, was mangled cruelly before being buried, wrapped in oxhide, beneath a heap of stones on a slope of the mountain. Nor did all the prisoners who were marched off to Gilbert Town survive when it was learned that there had been executions at Augusta of American militiamen who, though once in the service of the British, had been captured while fighting against them. Despite orders issued by Colonel Campbell against 'the disorderly manner of slaughtering and disturbing the prisoners', several of the Loyalists captured on King's Mountain were tried at Gilbert Town for treason. One of those prisoners reported:

> We were kept and bound under the gallows throughout the day in the rain, spectators of this disagreeable days work. At seven o'clock in the evening, they began to execute them. Coll. Mills, Capt. Wilson, Capt. Chitwood, and six others were hanged for their loyalty to their sovereign. They died like Romans, saying they died for their King and his Laws.
>
> What increased this melancholy scene was the seeing Mrs. Mills, take leave of her husband & two of Capt. Chitwood's daughters take leave of their father. The latter were comforted with being told their father was pardoned. They then went to our fire where we had made a shed to keep out the rain. They had scarce sat down, when news was brought that their father was dead. Here words can scarce describe the melancholy scene, the two ladies swoon'd away and continued in fits all night. – Mrs. Mills with a young child in her arms sat out all night in the rain with her husband's corps & not even a blanket to cover her from the inclemency of the weather.

The next morning the surviving prisoners were marched away, without food, down the mud-covered road towards Bethabara, being halted on the way to listen to a sermon which one of them described as 'a Presbyterian sermon truly adapted to the rebels' principles and the times; or, rather, stuffed as full of Republicanism as their camp is of horse thieves'. Some, exhausted and despairing, fell down and were abandoned or even trodden on and given parting blows; others, a hundred or so in number, contrived to escape. One who was shot and wounded in the attempt was later executed. At Bethabara there were further brutalities: a loyalist officer was kicked out of the bed he had at last found by a drunken captain of rebel militia; a loyalist surgeon, Dr Johnson, was beaten up for presuming to dress the wounds of an injured prisoner. A friend of this surgeon, Lieutenant

Anthony Allaire, contrived to escape with a few companions at Bethabara and eventually made his way to Ninety-Six. The following extracts from his diary reveal the strength of loyalist sympathy in the area at that time:

> Sunday 5th November 1780. Set off from Bethabara in company with Lieutenant Taylor, Lieutenant Stephenson and William Gist, a militiaman, about six o'clock in the evening. We marched fifteen miles to Yadkin River; forded it, found it very disagreeable. We continued on twenty miles farther to Miller's plantation, an exceeding good subject . . . At ten o'clock sent Mr Gist to the house for some victuals. He found Mr Miller at home, who very readily gave us all the assistance that lay in his power. About two o'clock he bought us some victuals . . . He told us he knew a Militia Captain Turner, and one or two more subjects there lying in the bushes [who] would be very happy to join Lord Cornwallis and they were excellent guides . . . Mr Miller then fetched us a blanket and immediately set out to find these people.
>
> Tuesday 7th. Mr Miller returned and told us one of these men would be with us at six o'clock . . . Marched six miles to one Carpenter's. When we arrived there Mr Carpenter advised us to remain there [for the moment] . . .
>
> Wednesday 8th. Lay very snug in the bushes . . .
>
> Thursday 9th. Heard of the rebels following us but they being given false information returned again . . . Marched thirty miles and halted in the woods at daybreak . . .
>
> Friday 10th. Suffered very much with the cold. At six o'clock in the evening set out again . . . Heard several wolves bark. Passed a rebel party consisting of twelve or fourteen who lay about twenty yards from the road by a fire; but, very fortunately for us, they were all asleep. We marched thirty miles and arrived at Colbert Blair's just at daybreak . . . This good man directed us to his fodder house and gave us the best his house afforded.
>
> Sunday 12th. Remained at Mr Blair's; raining; disagreeable day.
>
> Monday 13th. Set out from the good man's fodder house. He conducted us about three miles to a Mr F. Rider's, who guided us seven miles farther over the Brushey Mountains to Catawba River. Mr John Murray, who lived on the banks, put us over in a canoe, and conducted us three miles to Mr Ballon's. This old man was

about sixty years of age, but his love for his King and his subjects induced him to get up, although very late at night and guide us seven miles to a Mr Hilterbrine. On the way the old man informed us he had two sons who lay out in the woods that were anxious to go to our army . . . We arrived at Mr Hilterbrine's at about six o'clock in the morning of the fourteenth. He received us with great caution lest we should be treacherous, but when he found we were [loyalist] officers he was very kind.

Wednesday 15th.   Just as we were drinking a dish of coffee on a rock after dusk [three guides sent to us by Mr Hilterbrine] came to us on horseback . . . We set out immediately and marched twenty miles over the Brushey Mountains where there was nothing but Indian paths. Crossed several rivers. Arrived at one Sheppard's plantation just at daybreak . . . This poor family was so completely stripped of everything they had by the rebels that they could give us nothing but a hoe cake and some dried beef . . . Marched sixteen miles to Camp's Ford, [then to] Townsend's plantation . . . This man was very happy to see us and gave the best his house afforded . . .

Friday 17th.   Marched twelve miles to a Mr Morris's. Here we were told that a party of rebels was directly in our front; that we had better remain a night there.

Saturday 18th.   Lay in the woods; fared pretty well.

Sunday 19th.   . . . We got Mr Murray to guide us . . . Took by paths and got to the main road just at dusk . . . Crossed Pacolet River and . . . marched thirty-seven miles and arrived at James Duncan's plantation half an hour before daybreak . . . About ten o'clock Mrs Duncan rode out to see if she could get any intelligence of our army and rebel army that we might shun the latter. Mrs Duncan returned in less than an hour with the disagreeable news that the rebel army was marching within two miles of us . . . At six o'clock a Mr Jackson came to see us and . . . advised us to go to his house and stay all night as we would be perfectly safe there and the next morning go to Mr Smith's . . . We agreed to what the man said; staid all night at his house where we were treated very kindly . . .

Tuesday 21st.   Mr Duncan conducted us to Mr Smith's . . .

Wednesday 22nd.   Set out from Archey Smith's on horseback, which the subjects in that neighbourhood supplied us with. They

brought us on thirteen miles to one Adair's. Here we dismounted
and those good people returned . . .

Thursday 23rd. Set out from Colonel Kirkland's who was kind
enough to lend us horses as far as Saluda. Left the horses here;
crossed in a scow; walked a mile to Colonel Mason's . . . Got horses
and rode to Ninety-Six.

At Charlotte, Lord Cornwallis read of the sufferings of the defeated
American Loyalists with deep distress. Already dismayed by his
continuing failure to raise militia, by reports of threats to the garrison
at Ninety-Six, of dwindling supplies at Camden, and by the spreading
sickness in his army, he was now forced to accept that his plans for
his future campaign could not be realized. He gave orders for a
withdrawal to Winnsboro in South Carolina; and, falling ill with the
fever which had laid low so many of his men, he delegated his
authority to Lord Rawdon.

It was a retreat of appalling hardship in which men were harnessed
to carts which the army's few horses were too weak to move. The
rain poured down, turning the roads into morasses of thick mud;
provisions were so low that, for days on end, the men had nothing
to eat other than the sweet corn that could be gathered in the fields;
the water was so thick that it had to be filtered through the teeth. At
night there were no tents in which the soldiers might have taken
shelter from the rain; by day the retreating men were under constant
fire from rebel snipers. The wounded in hospital wagons were
agonizingly jolted together on heaps of straw which were soaked by
muddy water as yet another swollen stream was crossed. Nor were
their sufferings over when Winnsboro was reached at last on 29
October.

Here, throughout the coldest days of that bleak winter, the British
troops, occupying the rough log cabins they had constructed and
wearing the most ragged of uniforms, were deprived not only of the
most rudimentary medical supplies but also of the rum to which they
could normally look for comfort; and, despite the efforts of Charles
Stedman, the Pennsylvania Loyalist whom Cornwallis appointed
commissary in charge of collecting provisions, they had to make do
with the most meagre rations of food. Stedman employed well over
a hundred blacks at the mills in the district including those belonging
to the rich rebel merchant Joseph Kershaw, whose wife had cause to

complain that the exacting commissary was so anxious to keep the British army well supplied that he had no concern for her own welfare or, indeed, for that of any of the other inhabitants of South Carolina. Yet, zealous and even ruthless as Stedman was in the exercise of his office, the food he was able to bring in was never enough to satisfy the hunger of the soldiers. Hampered by the shortage of both horses and carts and by General Clinton's having taken so many wagons with him when he left for New York, Stedman was also frustrated in his efforts by the perversity and dishonesty of the officers of the quartermaster-general's department, who bought on their own account as many horses as they could lay their hands on and then asked prohibitive prices for their use. When horses and carts could be found, their drivers were perpetually at risk from rebel raiding parties; and it was not until a reliable and relatively safe river route had been opened up from Charleston that a satisfactory supply of provisions began to come through both to Lord Rawdon, now in command at Camden, and to Lord Cornwallis at Winnsboro.

During these winter months Cornwallis had not been able to fulfil his hopes of improving his intelligence service at Winnsboro. Nor had he managed to secure his tenuous lines of communication which were constantly plagued by partisan bands, by Francis Marion whose men were gathering recruits and supplies from settlements in the wide lands between the Pee Dee and Santee Rivers, and by Thomas Sumter whose militia were as active and troublesome as ever north of Winnsboro and whose presence in the area enabled gangs of marauders to make life miserable for all those Loyalists, or presumed Loyalists, who lived in the shadow of the Blue Ridge Mountains along the upper reaches of the Tiger and Pacolet Rivers.

Nor yet had their recent brushes with the enemy given Cornwallis confidence in the abilities of the officers upon whom he would have to rely in future engagements: a small force of regular infantry and cavalry of the British Legion under Major James Wemyss had been repulsed by Thomas Sumter at Fishdam Ford on 9 November; a fortnight later another British force under Banastre Tarleton, who contentiously claimed a victory, was badly mauled at Blackstock's Plantation where Tarleton, after an impetuous charge, had lost almost a quarter of his men; and in December a blockhouse held by Henry Rugeley, owner of Rugeley's Mills and a colonel of loyalist militia, was surrendered to the dashing rebel cavalry leader, Colonel William

Washington, a kinsman of George Washington, who approached it with a tree trunk carved to look like a cannon.

Disheartened by these setbacks, Cornwallis prepared his plans for the forthcoming campaign of 1781 in grim mood.

23

THE TRAITOR AND
THE SPY

---

*'I never saw a man whom I so
sincerely pitied.'*

Benjamin Tallmadge

It would be miraculous, George Washington had written in August
1780, if American military affairs could 'maintain themselves
much longer in their present train'. Throughout the previous
winter his army had been half starved, and, for much of the time,
shivering in one of the coldest winters that Morristown, New
Jersey had ever known. Desertion became common again; and
Washington endeavoured to maintain discipline by the lash, flogging
the worst offenders over several days so that new wounds were
opened up while the old ones were still unhealed. Between New
York and the fort of Paulus Hook, which had been evacuated immediately after its capture by Henry Lee, the Hudson River was
frozen so solidly that even the most heavily laden carts could be
driven across it, a circumstance never known before. Private Joseph
Plumb recorded:

> At one time it snowed the greatest part of four days successively,
> and there fell nearly as many feet of snow . . . We were absolutely,
> literally starved: I do solemnly declare that I did not put a single
> morsel of Victuals into my mouth for four days and as many nights,
> except a little black birch bark which I gnawed off a stick of wood,
> if that can be called victuals. I saw several of the men roast their old

shoes and eat them, and I was afterwards informed by one of the officers' waiters, that some of the officers killed and ate a favourite little dog that belonged to one of them . . . The fourth day, just at dark, we obtained a half pound of lean beef and a gill of wheat for each man. Whether we had any salt to season so delicious a morsel, I have forgotten, but I am sure we had no bread . . . When the wheat was so swelled by boiling as to be beyond the danger of swelling in the stomach, it was deposited there without ceremony.

By the time warmer weather came, the sufferings of the army were but little alleviated. Two regiments mutinied, and in another the surliness and indiscipline of the soldiers gave officers cause for the deepest concern. 'Instead of having everything in readiness to take the field,' Washington complained, 'we have nothing and instead of having the prospect of a glorious campaign before us we have a bewildered and gloomy defensive one unless we should receive a powerful aid of ships, land troops, and money from our generous allies.' The arrival of Admiral de Ternay with a French fleet of seven ships of the line, three frigates and transports with six thousand troops commanded by the Comte de Rochambeau had brought some comfort to the Americans; but the essential British command of the sea was almost immediately restored when, three days later, Thomas Graves brought a fleet from England into Long Island Sound with reinforcements for Admiral Arbuthnot. Clinton immediately seized the opportunity to embark part of his army for an attack on the French in Rhode Island; but when Washington made a counterstroke by marching on Kingsbridge, Clinton withdrew, leaving Arbuthnot to sail on to blockade Newport alone.

So the stalemate continued; and Admiral de Ternay expressed the opinion that 'the fate of North America' was 'still very uncertain', that the revolution was 'not so far advanced' as was believed in Europe. Rations in the American army were still paltry; recruits joined in scattered groups and then with little enthusiasm; veterans of past campaigns refused to accept the paper money which was still in circulation, though now virtually worthless. One of Washington's most trusted officers, Nathanael Greene, who had 'lost all confidence in the justice and rectitude of the intentions of Congress', resigned as quartermaster-general, protesting that 'honest intentions and faithful services are but a poor shield against the machinations of men without principles, honour or modesty'. Then Washington was further troubled by the Benedict Arnold affair.

Never fully recovered from the injuries sustained at Saratoga, Arnold had been appointed by Washington to command in Philadelphia where he lived far beyond his severely limited means, enjoying to the full the town's social life, riding about in a splendid carriage with liveried attendants, raising money by the manipulation of military finances, employing troops as servants and labourers, and spending immense sums on horses and on parties at Mount Pleasant, his large house on the Schuylkill. Here his guests were often of known loyalist sympathies, and he eventually married one of them, an exceptionally attractive nineteen-year-old girl named Margaret Shippen, as his second wife. Soon after his marriage he announced that he intended to resign his commission and to obtain a grant of land near New York where he would live as a retired country gentleman, expressing his dissatisfaction with the scant notice which Congress had taken of his services to their cause and his disillusionment with that cause now that, for selfish reasons, it was being supported by an autocratic Catholic kingdom against whose soldiers he had once fought.

By then Arnold's peculations in Philadelphia had come to the attention of Pennsylvania's supreme executive council, who referred the charges brought against him to Congress. Although acquitted of some of the charges, Arnold demanded a court-martial to clear himself of the others, at the same time entering into secret correspondence with the British headquarters. Asked not to leave the American service yet, but to endeavour to obtain some more important post than the one he held in Philadelphia, he sought and – on the strength of his past valuable services – was given command of the fortress of West Point on the Hudson River, 'the Rockyest Mountainest Place' that Dr Estes Howe had ever seen. This he undertook to betray to the British for £20,000, asking for £10,000 if he attempted to do so but failed.

Sir Henry Clinton placed high hopes on the capture of West Point. He had done little since his return to New York from Charleston in June, even after the arrival on 14 September of Admiral Sir George Rodney with ten sail of the line. Rodney was a cheerful, elegant and gregarious if rather contentious man, a lucky and resolute naval commander who had become a national hero since his recent victories over the Spanish fleet. Clinton had a higher regard for him than for any other naval officer; but the respect was not reciprocated. Upon his arrival, Rodney had been eager to attack Rhode Island where the French had established themselves as Washington's invaluable allies. But Clinton had opposed the idea: he could spare no more than three thousand men, and the enemy garrison in Newport numbered over three times as many. Rodney was dismayed by the General's lack of enterprise. What the army needed was a leader who hated the Americans from principle, not one who found such ready excuses not to attack them. In a letter to Lord Sandwich he strongly condemned his colleague's weak behaviour:

> Nature has not given him an enterprising and active spirit, capable of pushing the advantages he may have gained . . . his affection for New York (in which island he has four different houses) induces him to retire to that place, where without any settled plan he idles his time and . . . suffers himself to be cooped up by Washington with an inferior army, without making any attempt to dislodge him.
>
> I could not help declaring to him that, if his Majesty's service called me again to America, if affairs were not carried on with more alacrity and a quicker decision it would be impossible for us to agree, for that I came to act and not to amuse myself with the diversions of New York.

Clinton himself believed that the capture of West Point would have far greater consequence than an attack on Rhode Island. He accordingly supervised the negotiations with Benedict Arnold with the utmost care, instructing his young Adjutant-General, John André, to act as go-between.

An opportunity for André to meet Arnold presented itself after Admiral Rodney's arrival in North American waters enabled Clinton to embark troops for what was put out to be an expedition to the Chesapeake. Washington hurried north to Rhode Island to consult the Comte de Rochambeau, while André sailed up the Hudson in the British sloop *Vulture* to discuss with Arnold the attack upon West Point which the British were to make within the next few days.

While he was discussing the assault with Arnold and learning all he could about the defences of the fort, the *Vulture* had to drop downriver when it came under heavy fire from the American batteries. André's boatman refused to row him back, so he was compelled to spend the night in a farmhouse about a mile inland from West Point belonging to one Joshua Smith, a man in Arnold's confidence; and the following morning, having removed the uniform he had been wearing up till now, he set off back to headquarters, disguised as a countryman in one of Smith's coats.

At nine o'clock, just as he was in sight of the British lines, he was stopped by three men, militiamen who had joined a band of 'skinners' preying on Tory families in the area between the opposing armies. Believing them to be in the British service and seeing that one of them was wearing a British Army coat, André decided at first to confess that he was an English officer and not to make use of the pass which Arnold had given him. An American officer to whose care André was later assigned reported:

> One of the men then took his watch from him and ordered him to dismount. The moment this was done, he said he found he was mistaken and he must shift his tone. He says, 'I am happy, gentlemen, to find that I am mistaken. You belong to the Upper Party, and so do I. A man must make use of any shift to get along, and to convince you of it, here is General Arnold's pass,' handing it to them, 'and I am at your service.'
>
> 'Damn Arnold's pass,' says they, 'You said you was a British officer; where is your money?'
>
> 'Gentlemen, I have none about me,' he replied.
>
> 'You a British officer and no money,' says they, 'Let's search him.' They did so, but found none. Says one, 'He has got his money in his boots,' and there they found his papers, but no money. Then they examined his saddle, but found none.
>
> He said he saw they had such a thirst for money, he could put them in a way to get it, if they would be but directed by him. He asked them to name their sum for to deliver him to King's Bridge.
>
> They answered him in this way, 'If we deliver you at King's Bridge, we shall be sent to the Sugar House [a local prison] and you will save your money.'
>
> He says to them, 'If you will not trust my honor, two of you

may stay with me, and one shall go with a letter I shall write. Name your sum.'

The sum was agreed upon, but I cannot recollect whether it was five hundred or a thousand guineas, the latter, I think, was the sum. They held a consultation a considerable time, and finally they told him, if he wrote, a party would be sent out to take them, and then they would all be prisoners. They said they had concluded to take him to the commanding officer on the lines.

Arnold was having breakfast when news of André's capture reached him. He sprang up, kissed his young wife goodbye, rushed down to the river where his official barge was moored, and ordered the crew to row for all they were worth to the *Vulture*. A member of his guard saw him go limping down to the water's edge, wearing a large red shoe on the foot of his wounded leg, drawing his sword as he stepped into the barge, then sitting down as 'the barge started off in great speed'. On board the *Vulture* he told the captain that André had been taken prisoner, that there was no point in waiting longer and that he must sail immediately for New York.

In New York, Arnold at once set about claiming the rewards of his treachery. He did not get as much as he had hoped; but, considering that there could now be no question of an attack upon West Point, which Washington had strengthened as soon as he heard of its commander's precipitate departure, he was eventually, in Clinton's opinion, more than amply rewarded: he was appointed brigadier-general in the British Army, and awarded £6315 and an annuity of £500 for his wife. His three sons by his first marriage were all granted commissions; and the two sons of his second marriage were later given pensions of £100 a year each. Less generous rewards had been offered to other officers in the American service in exchange for secret intelligence and several had accepted them, though Philip Schuyler, Daniel Morgan and Israel Putnam, all of whom were approached, had conspicuously not done so, while Sir George Rodney's belief, expressed to Germain, that Washington could 'certainly be bought – honours will do it', was peculiarly misleading.

Major André was not so fortunate as Arnold. Condemned to death as a spy by a board whose members included Lafayette, Baron von Steuben and Henry Knox, he was sentenced to be hanged. He asked to be allowed to die as a soldier in a less dishonourable way. But this was denied him, though one of Washington's favourite young officers, Alexander Hamilton, entered a strong plea on André's behalf; and General Robertson went under a flag of truce to discuss the matter with Nathanael Greene. There could be no concessions where spies were concerned, Greene insisted. Robertson replied that in Europe not even a military casuist would call André a spy. 'Greene now with a blush told me that the army must be satisfied by seeing spies executed,' Robertson reported. 'But there was one thing would satisfy them – they expected, if André was set free, Arnold should be given up. This I answered with a look only, which threw Greene into confusion. I am persuaded André will not be hurt.' Arrangements for his execution, however, had already been made; and a Tory prisoner, who was to be released when the job was done, was found to act as hangman.

André accepted his fate with the most impressive calm, astonishing those who had dismissed him as a foppish dilettante, one of those largely responsible for Sir William Howe's extravagant 'Mischianza' in Philadelphia. The day before his execution on 2 October 1780 he sketched himself at a writing desk, looking sad after Washington's rejection of his request to be spared hanging, but calm and collected. 'By heavens, Colonel Webb,' one of his visitors, Washington's chief of intelligence, Major Benjamin Tallmadge, exclaimed, 'By heavens I never saw a man whom I so sincerely pitied . . . He seems to be as cheerful as if he was going to an assembly. I am sure he will go to the gallows less fearful of his fate and with less concern than I shall behold the tragedy.' Another observer recorded the scene:

> The Commander-in-Chief and Staff were not present at the execution; and this mark of decorum, I was told, was feelingly appreciated by the sufferer . . .
>
> When the procession was on the main road, the gallows was not visible; but when it wheeled at an angle, the place of execution was seen directly in front. On viewing it, the sufferer made a halt, and exhibited emotion. To an enquiry made by the captain of the guard, Major André gave the answer . . . 'I am reconciled to my death, but detest the mode of it.' The captain rejoined – 'It is unavoidable, sir.' Arrived at the scaffold, André after a short conversation with his servant, (who arrested much attention by the vehemence of his grief and loud lamentation) ascended with gaiety the baggage-wagon.

The General Order of execution was then read . . . The reading was very impressive, and at the conclusion Major André uncovered, bowed to the General and other officers and said with dignity and firmness, *'All I request of you, gentlemen, is that you will bear witness to the world that I die like a brave man.'* He added nothing more aloud, but while the preparations for immediate execution were being made, he said, in an under tone, *'It will be but a momentary pang.'*

Thus died Major John André, Adjutant-General to the British Army. The sympathy of the American Officers was universally expressed, and the Father of our country, in announcing his death to Congress, pronounced that he met his fate like a brave man.

'Both officers and men are so enraged by this business,' a British officer commented in a letter home, 'that they swear they will have revenge whenever they can get an opportunity, and I make no doubt that before this Rebellion is over there will be no quarter given on either side . . . There never was so melancholy a thing. It is not an easy matter to describe how much the whole army is shocked.'

Sir Henry Clinton was almost as distressed as he had been when his wife had died. So concerned were they by his grief that his staff sent for his old friend, William Phillips, who, taken prisoner at Saratoga, had recently been exchanged for General Lincoln. Phillips did his best to comfort Clinton, to persuade him that André's death was 'an event of war'. But it was a long time before the Commander-in-Chief overcame his bitter sorrow.

24

WITH CORNWALLIS IN THE CAROLINAS

'We fight, get beat, rise, and fight again.'

Nathanael Greene

At the end of the first week of January 1781, Lord Cornwallis began to march north from Winnsboro with about thirteen hundred men. Encouraged by a letter from Lord George Germain which seemed to give him a command virtually independent of his superior, Sir Henry Clinton, he appeared to his staff to be in a much more confident mood than he had been of late. Germain had emphasized that 'the prosecution of the war by pushing our conquests from south to north is to be considered as the chief and principal object'. And this was a view which Cornwallis fully shared.

He had made his preparations with great care. Assured by the home government that thousands of men in North Carolina were ready to join him once he entered that province, he had decided to seek out and destroy the American troops across the state border under the command of Gates's successor, the wily Nathanael Greene who had now returned to the army. Although the force which Cornwallis took with him from Winnsboro was a small one, he expected shortly to be joined by almost two thousand men under Major-General Alexander Leslie whom Clinton had sent as reinforcements from the Chesapeake to the mouth of the Cape Fear River. Clinton had also sent Benedict Arnold into Virginia to harass Greene by cutting his lines of communication, destroying his stores and raiding his outposts. To secure his own communications with the Cape Fear River, Cornwallis sent a small detachment to Wilmington under Major James Craig; and to safeguard his position in South Carolina he left garrisons at Charleston, Camden, Ninety-Six, Augusta and Savannah, nearly five thousand men in all under the general command of Lord Rawdon.

At the time of Cornwallis's departure from Winnsboro, Nathanael Greene had fewer than eight hundred men fit for duty in the camps around Charlotte in North Carolina, but more were expected both from other depots in the state and from Virginia. Nor was Greene the only able officer in Charlotte. Also there were the Polish engineer Tadeusz Kościuszko, who had spent the past two years improving the defences of West Point; Henry Green, who had won rather more than his fair share of fame in the storming of Paulus Hook; the cavalry leader William Washington; and Daniel Morgan, the tough yet kindly officer who had recently come out of the retirement which his rheumatism, sciatica and disappointment at not being given a higher command had induced him to seek.

Morgan had once driven a supply wagon in the British Army, and in the Seven Years' War had been wounded in the mouth by a bullet which had carried off most of the teeth in his lower jaw. He had been flogged for striking an English officer, and the 499 strokes he had then received had left permanent scars which he was far from reluctant to show his men, with whom he was on terms that some other officers considered over-familiar. No one, however, doubted his reliability or his bravery in battle; and when Greene decided to divide his army into two, he had no hesitation in appointing Morgan to the command of that part which he sent south-west to threaten the Loyalists under Colonel Cruger at Ninety-Six. This garrison had recently been weakened by the defection of an American militia colonel who had left in fury, taking several of his men with him, when his farm had been over-run by marauders, despite the protection the British had promised him.

Presented with this opportunity of defeating at least a part of Greene's army, Cornwallis also divided his forces. He himself advanced north up the Catawba River to the proposed junction with General Leslie, while sending Banastre Tarleton with a thousand men, both from the British Legion and from British infantry regiments, up the Broad River on his left.

Tarleton caught up with Morgan in the bitter cold morning of 17 January 1781 at a place known as Hannah's Cowpens, an area of land in the process of being cleared of the pine, oak and hickory trees which grew on the banks of the river. The American militiamen had been drawn up to face Tarleton with their backs to the river so that there could be no question of retreat. 'Had I crossed the river,' Morgan said, 'one half of the militia would have immediately abandoned me.' He had put them in the front line, trusting in their skill as marksmen to break Tarleton's first charge, urging them to hold their fire until the enemy were within 'killing distance' and to stand firm until they had fired at least two volleys. After they had fired these shots they could then run away. Behind these militiamen Morgan had posted his regular troops, the Maryland, Delaware and Virginia Continentals commanded by Colonel John Eager Howard, on a long ridge of rising ground; while behind another slightly steeper hill he had hidden his cavalry under Colonel Washington and his mounted infantry under James McCall.

Although Tarleton's men had been on the march for much of the night on bad roads and through deep fords, he decided predictably upon an immediate attack, expecting to be able to drive the militiamen, whom his force slightly outnumbered, back into the river. Leaving two hundred of his cavalry in reserve with the 71st Highlanders, he formed his line with a troop of fifty dragoons on each flank of his infantry and gave the order to advance. One of the American militiamen in the opposing front line recalled:

> We were formed in the order of battle and the men were clapping their hands together to keep warm – an exertion not long necessary . . . The British line advanced at a sort of trot, with a loud halloo. It was the most beautiful line I ever saw. When they shouted, I heard Morgan say, 'They give us the British halloo, boys. Give them the Indian halloo, by God!' and he galloped along the lines, cheering the men and telling them not to fire until we could see the whites of their eyes. Every officer was crying, 'Don't fire!' for it was a hard matter for us to keep from it.

The British infantry came to within about forty yards of the militiamen who, sheltered behind the trees, fired their first volley with telling effect, taking careful aim at the officers and sergeants. They fired another, equally devastating volley before withdrawing.

Tarleton let loose the 17th Light Dragoons at them as they retreated;

but no sooner had he done so than William Washington's cavalry came galloping from behind their hill, outnumbering the dragoons by almost two to one, forcing them back, knocking them out of their saddles. 'The shock was so violent, they could not stand it,' a militiaman noted. 'There was no time to rally and they appeared to be as hard to stop as a drove of wild choctaw steers going to a Pennsylvania market. In a few moments the clashing of swords was out of hearing and quickly out of sight.'

The appearance of Colonel Washington's cavalry had given the militia opportunity to re-form. 'Form! Form! my brave fellows,' Morgan shouted at them, giving them the decoy call which he used to lure wild turkeys and which all his men had learned to recognize. 'Give them one more brisk fire and the day is ours! Old Morgan was never beaten yet!' Responding to his call, the militiamen retreated in good order to the higher ground in the rear, where they faced about and stood ready to fire again.

The British infantry continued to advance, though in noticeably ragged order, with few officers to direct them and those as out of breath as their men. Realizing that he was about to lose the initiative, Tarleton now ordered his dragoons and reserve of cavalry to come down hard on the enemy right. When he saw this movement developing, Morgan rode across from the militia to give orders to his right-hand battalion to pull back to present a new front to the threat; and, as the men of that battalion did so, the remainder of the line followed suit, their officers supposing an order had been given for a general retreat. They withdrew in excellent order, however, while the British advance was becoming more and more disorderly. 'They are coming on like a mob,' a messenger from Colonel Washington told Morgan. 'Give them a fire and I will charge them.'

Morgan immediately halted the withdrawal; and at his command his men turned round and opened fire at the enemy, now less than a hundred feet away. The unexpectedness of this volley brought the ragged line of British troops to a sudden halt. Several more men fell; others ran off; most of Tarleton's dragoons galloped away. A few soldiers of the 71st Highlanders bravely refused to submit for a time; so did ten or twelve artillerymen with Tarleton's two three-pounders. But it was clear to the Americans that the battle was over and that they had won triumphantly. Tarleton, with a few other officers, made a last desperate charge with some forty men of the 17th Light

Dragoons to save the guns, but they were too late. Those who managed to escape trotted off the field disconsolately, while the rest were taken prisoner.

'They laid down their arms and the officers delivered up their swords,' wrote the American Colonel John Eager Howard. 'Captain Duncanson of the 71st Grenadiers gave me his sword and stood by me. Upon getting on my horse, I found him pulling at my saddle and he nearly unhorsed me. I expressed my displeasure and asked him what he was about. The explanation was that they had orders to give no quarter, and they did not expect any, and as my men were coming up, he was afraid they would use him ill. I admitted his excuse and put him in care of a sergeant.'

He was one of nearly eight hundred prisoners taken after the battle, one of the rare tactical defeats inflicted upon the British in the whole course of the war. Over a hundred more of Tarleton's force had been killed or wounded, and ten officers were among the dead. Morgan's losses were no more than seventy-two in all. Among the prizes with which he rode away were thirty-five wagons, the two British cannon, a large number of musical instruments, a hundred horses, sixty black servants and the colours of the 7th Foot. Much of the rest of the baggage was dragged off by American Loyalists who had been serving as spies and guides to the British and who claimed to be saving the loot from falling into the hands of the rebels. When Tarleton's dragoons caught up with them, they were, to use Tarleton's own euphemism, 'dispersed'. Whether or not recognized for what they were, they were all hacked to pieces.

Determined that the main body of the British Army should not cut off his retreat, Morgan lost no time in getting his men across the Broad River and marching fast eastwards for the Catawba. He left the local militia to look after the wounded and bury the dead.

Anxious to head him off, Cornwallis also made for the Catawba, though he realized only too well the dangers of such a move after the catastrophic loss of so many of his light troops at Hannah's Cowpens, a disaster for which he did not expose Tarleton to either public or private censure but which, so he confessed to Lord Rawdon, almost broke his heart and which one of his aides-de-camp described as 'the most serious calamity since Saratoga'. At Ramsour's Mill he reported to Clinton on the steps he had taken to 'remedy his loss by the activity of the whole corps'. 'I employed a halt of two days,' he wrote,

> in collecting some flour and in destroying the superfluous baggage and all my waggons, except those loaded with hospital stores, salt and ammunition, and four reserved empty in readiness for sick and wounded. In this measure, though at the expense of a great deal of officers' baggage, and of all prospect in future of rum and even a regular supply of provisions to the soldiers, I must, in justice to this army, say that there was the most general and cheerful acquiescence.

After allowing them their brief rest, Cornwallis, now joined by Leslie and in command of 2400 men, resumed his march, pushing hard through the cold winter days, as Morgan and Greene retreated before him, drawing him ever deeper into North Carolina. In a thick fog they crossed the fast-flowing Catawba, swollen to over a quarter of a mile in width by the recent rains, struggling to keep their balance and unable, with their cartouche boxes tied round their necks, to return the fire, 'hollerin and a snortin and a drownin', as a Loyalist described them.

Lord Cornwallis, who had been among the first to dash into the river, had his horse shot under him. Several other horses were killed or wounded, and a number of men, floundering in the strong current, stumbled and were swept away between the rocks. The survivors, having got rid of the remaining cumbersome wagons on the way, marched on quickly towards Salisbury. They halted there for two days to collect supplies, then marched on fast again over the rough country roads of the district for the Yadkin River, often catching up with the American rearguard but finding on reaching every creek that the main body of the enemy had already crossed in safety to the far side, where their cavalry were drawn up, obliging the pursuers to deploy. The British passed the Yadkin on 8 February and, a week later, reached the Dan on the border of North Carolina and Virginia, to find as usual that the Americans, whose rearguard had marched forty miles in sixteen hours, were already on the far bank.

Cornwallis now concluded that he had gone quite far enough. In the hope that he might enlist Loyalists in the area he drew back to Hillsboro, but few Loyalists were forthcoming, and one group that did appear, mistaking a party of American cavalry for Tarleton's

British Legion, were surrounded and slaughtered, discouraging other Loyalists from making a similar attempt. Informed that they would feel more secure in coming forward if he moved south, Cornwallis withdrew across the Deep River and there established his camp by the road to Wilmington, down which he could retreat to the coast if forced to do so. From this base, where 350 men were left to guard his baggage, he advanced north-east again to offer battle.

General Greene was now ready to receive him in a position of the Americans' choice. Reinforcements had increased the strength of the rebels to some 4500 men, whereas the British force, tired, ill clothed and hungry, driven to eking out their meagre rations with unripe turnips and Indian corn, were reduced to less than two thousand. The unevenly matched armies met at Guilford, just south of the county court house, on 15 March 1781.

The court house stood in a clearing of the woods through which the high road from Salisbury passed. Greene's troops were hidden from view in these woods on either side of the road, with a reserve immediately in front of the court house. Cornwallis also placed his men on either side of the road; his German troops, the 71st Highlanders and a battalion of Guards on the right, under Major-General Leslie; and on the left, commanded by Brigadier-General O'Hara, the grenadiers, the 23rd Foot and another battalion of Guards. His three guns remained in the road; and in support were a corps of German Jägers, the light infantry and the cavalry of the British Legion, all under the command of Banastre Tarleton, in great pain from a hand badly wounded in a recent skirmish.

The British began their attack at about half past one in the afternoon after a brief artillery duel; and, although met by a heavy and continuous fire from the enemy hidden behind the trees, they came on steadily, their fixed bayonets glinting in the rays of the sun, struggling to keep in line as they trotted over the heavy, red earth, newly ploughed and soggy from the recent rain. Greene's first line of North Carolina militia broke and fled, 'throwing away arms, knapsacks, and even canteens [as] they rushed like a current headlong through the woods'. The sharpshooters on either side of them also withdrew from tree to tree, while the cavalry under William Washington and Henry Lee moved slowly back with them. The Virginian militiamen in Greene's second line held firm for a time, firing their rifles with unhurried accuracy and telling effect, until they too fell back upon the third line of American troops, two brigades of regulars from Maryland and two from Virginia drawn up on a hill in front of Guilford Court House.

Here the British advance faltered. One of the regiments of Greene's third line was the 1st Maryland, whose reputation in the American army stood as high as any; and this regiment stolidly stood their ground as the British light infantry, with the 23rd Foot and the Jägers under Colonel Webster, came towards them, out of breath now but still shouting loudly. The Americans allowed them to get within a few yards then they themselves charged with the bayonet, driving the enemy back in confusion, right out of the clearing and into the woods.

Cornwallis now sent his three guns up to the edge of the woods where, rapidly unlimbered, they opened fire, while General O'Hara brought up the grenadiers and his battalion of Guards to charge the 2nd Maryland Regiment which, giving way before this sudden and unexpected onslaught, might well have been driven far beyond the court house had not Colonel Washington dashed forward with the cavalry to fall on the Guards in the rear, while the 1st Maryland Regiment turned to attack them in flank. The subsequent fighting was exceptionally savage:

> While the Americans and British Troops were intermixed with a charge of Bayonets, Captain John Smith [of the Maryland Regiment] and his men were in the throng, killing the Guards and Grenadiers like so many Furies. [Lieutenant-Colonel Duncan] Stewart, seeing the mischief Smith was doing, made [towards] him through the crowd, Dust and Smoke unperceived and made a violent lunge at him with his Sword. The first that Smith saw was the shining Metal like lightning at his Bosom, he only had time to lean a little to the right, and lift up his left arm so as to let the polished steel pass under it when the Hilt struck his Breast. It would have run through his Body but for the haste of the [Colonel who happened] to set his foot on the Arm of a Man Smith had just cut down . . . The Guards came rushing up very strong. Smith had no alternative but to wheel round and give Stewart a back-handed Blow across the head, on which he fell.
>
> His Orderly Sergeant attacked Smith, but Smith's Sergeant dis-

patched him. A 2d attacked him. Smith hewed him down. A 3d
behind him . . . shot him in the back of the Head. Smith now fell
among the slain . . .

The massacre was halted by Cornwallis's three field guns, but, when
the firing ceased, it was seen that their grapeshot had brought down
as many British guardsmen as American cavalry.

By now General O'Hara and Colonel Webster were both badly
wounded; but, as long as their strength lasted, they helped Cornwallis
re-form the line and rally the men for the second stage of the
battle. This was soon concluded. Tarleton's Legion, having made a
successful charge against the American right, now fell upon their left,
supported by the Hessians under General Bose. The rest of his force
Cornwallis sent forward with orders to make a last, determined effort
against their front. Although they had been fighting since the early
afternoon after a march of twelve miles on empty stomachs, his men
responded with remarkable spirit to his call. They crashed through
the American lines with such desperate courage that Greene decided
to retreat. His losses had already been severe and most of the militia,
who were soon to desert to their homes, had had more than enough.
He rode off the field, leaving his guns and their ammunition behind
him.

The British could, therefore, claim 'a compleat victory over the
rebels'; but it was yet another victory very dearly won. 'The enemy
got the ground the other Day,' Nathanael Greene conceded. 'They
had the splendour but we the advantage.' As the British General
Harvey had forecast, 'Our army will be destroyed by damned drib-
lets.' Already outnumbered by more than two to one at the outset
of the battle, Cornwallis's army could ill afford the heavy losses it
had sustained. Between a third and a quarter of the men who had
fought had been killed or wounded. 'Another such victory,' as
Charles James Fox commented when he heard reports of the battle,
'would destroy the British army.' In the Guards alone, eleven of the
nineteen officers were casualties and over two hundred of the 462
men. Colonel Webster died of his wounds; General O'Hara, who
observed that the spirit of the army had 'evaporated a good deal',
took a long time to recover from his; and O'Hara's son, a promising
lieutenant of artillery, was among the dead. The survivors lay down
in the now steadily falling rain without shelter and without food,

having had nothing to eat since their four ounces of flour and four ounces of dry beef on the afternoon of the previous day. General O'Hara wrote:

> I never did and I never shall experience two such days and nights as those immediately after the battle. We remained on the very ground on which it had been fought, covered with dead, with dying and with hundreds of wounded, rebels as well as our own. A violent and constant rain that lasted over forty hours made it equally impracticable to remove or administer the smallest comfort to many of the wounded. In this situation we expected every moment to be attacked. There could be no doubt that the enemy must be very well informed of our loss, and, whatever their loss might be, their numbers were still so great as to make them very formidable.

Cornwallis had no alternative now but to abandon his chase of Greene into the interior of North Carolina and to withdraw towards the coast. On 18 March, having sent away seventeen wagonloads of wounded with most of the army's women, and having had the American wounded carried into Guilford Court House, he began the long march down towards the Cape Fear River, through a country bereft of provisions for his men and of forage for his horses. Three weeks later his small, exhausted army, many of the soldiers by now barefoot, came down to the coast at Wilmington.

'Now my dear friend, what is our plan?' Lord Cornwallis wrote to William Phillips soon after arriving in Wilmington.

> Without one we cannot succeed, and I assure you that I am quite tired of marching about the country in quest of adventure. If we mean an offensive war in America, we must abandon New York and bring our whole force into Virginia; we then have a stake to fight for, and a successful battle may give us America. If our plan is defensive . . . let us quit the Carolinas . . . and stick to our salt pork and New York, sending now and then a detachment to steal tobacco, etc.

On the same day he wrote to Clinton, also proposing the abandonment of New York and an offensive in Virginia and complaining, as though to an inferior rather than to his Commander-in-Chief, of being 'as yet totally in the dark as to the intended operations of the summer'. A week later Cornwallis wrote to Lord George Germain to make the same proposals and similar complaints.

He had had sufficient experience now of campaigning in the south to know how difficult and dangerous it was with the small force at his command. There were so few committed Loyalists and so many determined rebels; there were also so many rivers to obstruct the passage of an army; above all, it was virtually impossible to find adequate provisions and forage in that inhospitable land.

He had still, of course, to consider young Lord Rawdon who had been left behind at Camden; but, if Rawdon were to be defeated there by Nathanael Greene, there was little Cornwallis could hope to achieve by exposing his diminished force to a similar fate, and if Rawdon were to defeat Greene his own return to South Carolina would be pointless. Much better, he argued, to make a movement inland to the north which might draw Greene away from Camden. So, without consulting Clinton – who had written to ask him to come to the Chesapeake to discuss future operations as soon as the Carolinas were secured and there was no danger to Charleston – Cornwallis left Wilmington for Virginia on the morning of 25 April with no more than 1435 men fit for duty, leaving behind a small garrison under the command of Major James Craig.

On that same morning Lord Rawdon marched out of Camden with eight hundred men, many of them convalescents or non-combatants, to prevent a threatened junction north of Camden of Nathanael Greene's regulars and militia with Francis Marion's partisans. Over the past fortnight Marion had been mounting attacks with Henry Lee on British posts between Camden and Charleston and had forced the surrender of one of the most important of these, Fort Watson, an apparently unassailable stockade on the summit of a hill standing high above the surrounding plain. It was taken after a tall tower, such as those used in siege operations by the centurions of ancient Rome, had been constructed from felled trees and erected in less than a week. Soon after the surrender of Fort Watson, which broke the British line of communications between Camden and Charleston, Marion had moved north up the Wateree to join Greene who had taken post with rather more than twelve hundred men at Hobkirk's Hill.

It was here, two miles north of Camden, that Lord Rawdon seized the initiative by launching an assault before Greene could attack him. Having taken his men, mostly American Loyalists, on a long march through the forest, Rawdon fell upon Greene's left flank. His little army, greatly outnumbered by Greene's, consisted of the 63rd Foot, the New York Volunteers, the Volunteers of Ireland and the King's American Regiment, a corps raised in New York in 1776. The infantry were supported by about sixty dragoons enlisted in America, while other Loyalists were employed as snipers to pick off as many of their fellow-countrymen as they could.

Rawdon's front line approached Greene's four Maryland and Virginia regiments at a slow trot on a narrow front, the men keeping shoulder to shoulder as the distance between the two armies narrowed. When less than a hundred yards separated them, Greene quickly withdrew his front line to right and left revealing three formidable pieces of artillery, all of which immediately opened up with grapeshot. As Rawdon's infantry recoiled under the heavy fire, Greene sent his cavalry against the British rear, two battalions of infantry against their centre and two more against their flanks. Rawdon's response was immediate and admirably conceived. Allowing the American centre to advance, he pushed his reserves to either side of his front line, outflanking the enemy movement and, escaping their trap, catching them in his own. Within this trap the fighting was ferocious for several minutes. For a time Rawdon was surrounded by Colonel Washington's cavalrymen, one of whom demanded his sword. Rawdon appeared to acquiesce but, seeing his own infantry advancing towards him, he pretended to have difficulty in disentangling it and by the time he had done so his would-be captors had been driven off. Both the 1st and 2nd Maryland Regiments had by now lost several officers, brought down by loyalist sharpshooters; and as their men fell back under a sharp fire, Greene struggled to rescue his guns, tugging at the drag ropes himself, until Colonel Washington, who had been occupied in taking prisoners, including several surgeons, galloped up to help him get them away. The guns were saved but a hundred of Greene's men were left on the field to be taken prisoner.

The victory was indisputably Rawdon's, but, like Cornwallis's at

Guilford, it was a victory too expensively bought. Rawdon had lost 270 officers and men killed and wounded; and was now so weak, despite reinforcements of five hundred men of the 64th Regiment, and so uncertain of his communications which were constantly being threatened and cut by Marion and Sumter, that he felt obliged to retreat south to Monk's Corner on the Cooper River thirty miles above Charleston. And as he withdrew, one after the other the British forts in South Carolina fell to American attacks. First Fort Granby surrendered, then Fort Motte, then Orangeburg. Fort Galpin also fell; so did Georgetown. On 5 June a Loyalist, Colonel Browne, who had once had the soles of his bare feet held over a fire in a vain effort to force him to go over to the rebel side, surrendered Augusta after a wooden tower, like that built at Fort Watson, had enabled the besiegers to fire down on his gunners. The village of Ninety-Six, the last remaining British stronghold in South Carolina, would also have fallen had not help arrived to save it just in time.

Ninety-Six was still held by Lieutenant-Colonel John Harris Cruger, whose force included a large proportion of American Loyalists. He had been ordered by Rawdon to evacuate it and march down to Charleston, since it could obviously not be held as an isolated garrison surrounded by enemies. But Rawdon's messengers carrying his order had been intercepted; and the five hundred and fifty men behind the stockade and earthworks which surrounded the village prepared to defend Ninety-Six to the death, fearful of the fate which might attend surrender and which certainly befell two officers taken prisoner at Augusta, one of whom was murdered and another severely wounded. One day, according to a loyalist officer inside the fort, Lieutenant Hatton of the New Jersey Volunteers,

> the garrison had the mortification to see that of Augusta marched by them as prisoners of war . . . Colonel Lee by whom they were taken, enjoyed the gratification of a little mind in exhibiting them before Ninety-Six, with a British Standard reversed, drums beating and pipes playing, to ridicule their situation. This pitiful recourse had an effect quite contrary to that which it was intended to produce. The soldiers were easily convinced that death was preferable to captivity with such an enemy.

The siege was conducted by Nathanael Greene, assisted by the Polish engineer Tadeusz Kościuszko who, to the delight of the Loyalists, was wounded in the bottom while bending down to examine a mine. The operations progressed slowly as the Americans dug parallels in the hot June weather and the besieged garrison, having sunk a well in a vain attempt to obtain water to augment the village's meagre supply, sent out blacks at night to bring in a supply from within pistol shot of the American pickets – their naked bodies not being distinguishable in the darkness from the fallen trees with which the place abounded. On 17 June, however, the defenders had to abandon the stockade and were facing the prospect of annihilation or surrender when Lord Rawdon suddenly appeared with three regiments, the 3rd (the Buffs) and the 19th and 30th Foot, which had arrived as reinforcements at Charleston and which would have gone to New York had not an order directing them there been intercepted by an American privateer. Greene, therefore, abandoned the siege of Ninety-Six and retreated east once more, while Lord Rawdon – who had fallen ill in the dreadful heat of that summer, in which over fifty of his men had died of sunstroke on the march – had to go home on sick leave, leaving the command to Lieutenant-Colonel Stuart who had arrived at Charleston with the Buffs.

Thankful to see the end of Rawdon, Greene hoped to find a less skilful opponent in Colonel Stuart, an older man but not so experienced in American warfare. The two men faced each other for the first time on 8 September when an American deserter walked into the British camp to report that Greene, whose movements had up till then been successfully concealed from Stuart, was actually on the march to attack him. Supposing that the enemy were far away to the north, Stuart had allowed an unarmed party of some hundred men to go forward under a small cavalry escort to collect some sweet potatoes. All the men were captured, while the escort galloped back to camp where their shouts of warning caused the utmost confusion. Hurriedly Stuart took stock of his dangerous position, disposing eighteen hundred men as best he could in the forest clearing where the tents of his camp had been pitched, placing his front line beyond the clearing across the road down which the Americans were reported to be marching, and sending one of his best officers, Major Marjoribanks, with three hundred men slightly forward of his right flank to take up position by the waters of Eutaw Springs. He placed his cavalry on the left and his three guns on the road in the middle of his front line. Behind them at the far end of the clearing was a house which one of his other most trusted officers was ordered to occupy should circumstances require it.

The Americans, some two thousand strong, advanced up the road as the artillery on both sides hurled grapeshot at each other until one of Stuart's guns and two of Greene's were put out of action. The militia of Greene's first line came on bravely through the fire until their guns were silenced; then they faltered and, as they began to give way, the British infantry on the left rushed forward excitedly, only to be stopped almost immediately by a volley from the regular troops in Greene's second line who dashed forward with the bayonet, driving them back in utter disarray. The British right and centre held for a time; but then they too fell back with heavy losses and soon the entire British front was in retreat, the living stumbling over the bodies of the wounded and the dead, the only troops to hold their ground being Major Marjoribanks's detachment and the men who, in obedience to Stuart's orders, had occupied the house at the back of the clearing.

Colonel Washington made a headlong charge against Marjoribanks with his cavalry, many of whom were killed in the assault, Washington himself being wounded. An attack by infantry was also repulsed by Marjoribanks, on whose left the American infantry poured almost unopposed into the British camp where the tents, the piles of stores and stocks of liquor proved too great a temptation for them. Leaving their officers to dash on towards the house and garden beyond, they ran into the tents in search of plunder, filling their pockets with anything that took their fancy, cracking open casks and bottles and drinking so heavily that they were soon uncontrollable. Many of them were shot as they were drinking; several of their officers were also killed in the garden by marksmen shooting from the windows of the house and from behind the railings of the fence. To extricate the survivors, Greene brought up the cavalry to cover their retreat, while Stuart ordered his own cavalry forward to prevent them. Seizing his opportunity, Marjoribanks rushed forward to capture the Americans' guns and to fall upon the infantry still intent upon the plunder of the tents.

The day ended as it had begun in utter confusion, the camp strewn with bodies, both armies devastated, with losses on each side of over six hundred, a large proportion of them officers. Greene withdrew seven miles to the north, Stuart to Charleston Neck. The last battle in Carolina was over. Nathanael Greene had won none of them. Yet, as he wrote to the French Minister, the Chevalier La Luzerne, 'We fight, get beat, rise, and fight again.'

25

THE ROAD TO YORKTOWN

*'I see this in so serious a light that
I dare not look at it.'*

Sir Henry Clinton

The circuitous march of Cornwallis's army north from Wilmington was an extremely unpleasant one. Banastre Tarleton raced ahead with his cavalry, seizing as many stores as he could but finding little food for the hungry army on the road behind him. Occasionally the troops would come across a store of grain, but the level of the water in the rivers had fallen so low in the past few dry weeks that the mills could not be worked to grind the corn. Many men fell ill; and by the time they reached Petersburg on 20 May a large proportion of the 1435 men who had left Wilmington the previous month were scarcely fit for duty. On his arrival Cornwallis learned that the British general there, William Phillips, had died the week before of a fever and that the American, Benedict Arnold, had assumed command – much to the annoyance of his subordinates, most of whom disliked him as much as did the Americans whom he had betrayed.

Both Phillips and Arnold had been sent to Virginia by Sir Henry Clinton with orders not only to send out raiding parties to harass the rebels in the province, so as to create diversions from Cornwallis's operations in South Carolina, but also to fortify a coastal town, preferably Portsmouth, as a base for the Royal Navy. Arnold had arrived first with two thousand men, followed in March by Phillips with another two thousand five hundred. Together with seventeen hundred reinforcements recently landed at the mouth of the James River, there were now over seven thousand men under Cornwallis's command; a far larger force than he considered necessary for carrying out the orders which Clinton had given Arnold and Phillips. Yet Cornwallis was reluctant to use them for the offensive in Virginia which he had long advocated until he had the agreement of the Commander-in-Chief. Already he had exceeded his instructions by coming north, pleading the excuse that the 'delay and difficulty of conveying letters' in America were as inhibiting as 'the impossibility of waiting for answers'. He had accordingly abandoned North Carolina for Virginia, without waiting for instructions from Clinton who had sent the seventeen hundred reinforcements from New York to support Cornwallis's operations in the south. 'I hope Cornwallis may have gone back to Carolina,' Clinton wrote when his subordinate was, in fact – in a move which he was to describe as 'inexcusable' and 'extraordinary' – marching in the opposite direction. 'If he joins Phillips I shall tremble for every post except Charleston, and even for Georgia.'

Now that he was at Petersburg in Virginia, Cornwallis decided that he would not content himself merely with raiding parties and the fortification of a naval base. For the time being he was prepared to hold on to Portsmouth, sending Alexander Leslie there as garrison commander; but he agreed with Arnold – who returned to New York soon after Cornwallis's arrival at Petersburg – that Portsmouth was not really suitable as a naval base. He therefore proposed to Clinton that he should fortify Yorktown instead; this would not only be a healthier place for the troops, but it could also be more easily defended and could offer a more secure harbour for the Navy. At the same time Cornwallis reiterated his conviction that the British should have as few posts as possible in America and that, if offensive war was intended, Virginia was the province where it should be carried on. While awaiting Clinton's concurrence, he planned first to attack the Marquis de Lafayette, who was in camp with a small force at Richmond, then to withdraw to Williamsburg to await the Commander-in-Chief's orders and the reinforcements he would need once agreement to an offensive campaign had been given.

'I shall now proceed to dislodge Lafayette from Richmond,' Cornwallis told Clinton on 26 May, 'and with my light troops to destroy any magazines or stores in the neighbourhood which may have been collected either for his use or for General Greene's army.' He succeeded in dislodging Lafayette, but was unable to catch up with him when he retreated north-west from Richmond. So Cornwallis also withdrew and, destroying stores on the way, marched down to Williamsburg where, towards the end of June, he received the despatches from Clinton which he had been awaiting.

They were a profound disappointment to him. Far from giving his consent to the offensive campaign in Virginia which he and Germain had in mind, the Commander-in-Chief now required Cornwallis to send men from his own army to New York. For Clinton had heard of a meeting at Wethersfield, Connecticut between George Washington and the Comte de Rochambeau whose five thousand French soldiers, in camp around Newport, Rhode Island, were now ready to join the Americans in combined operations. A large French fleet commanded by the tall, grim Comte de Grasse was on its way across the Atlantic with more French troops. As soon as it arrived, if not before, Clinton was likely to come under attack. He had little hope that de Grasse's fleet would be intercepted by that dreadful 'old gentleman', Marriot Arbuthnot. He would, therefore, he contended – distorting figures to support his argument – be faced with an army far stronger than his own; and, since Cornwallis's force was almost four times as strong as that commanded by Lafayette, he felt obliged to ask for most of his subordinate's troops to be sent to New York as soon as possible 'after reserving such Troops as may [be] necessary for an ample defensive, and desultory movements by water for the purpose of annoying the Enemy's communications, destroying Magazines etc.'. These troops, which Cornwallis was to retain in Virginia, were to take a defensive position in any 'healthy situation' Cornwallis chose, 'be it at Williamsburg or Yorktown'.

The almost deferential tone of the letters in which Clinton's instructions were contained reflected the impression which the Commander-in-Chief had been given by Germain that Cornwallis rather than himself was considered in London to be the more gifted and successful as well as the far more active general of the two. Clinton knew that Germain had written direct to Cornwallis and had given him orders as though he held a quite independent command; he also suspected that the government would like to see Cornwallis supersede him and that Cornwallis would still like this well enough himself. Fearful of giving categoric orders that might prove disastrous, he issued instructions in the form of suggestions, repeatedly modifying these instructions in subsequent letters and even contradicting them.

In his reply to Clinton's first letter Cornwallis did not hide his annoyance that the Commander-in-Chief, who had so far been idle in New York, should now ask for the bulk of his own army to be sent there to help withstand a problematical siege, thus destroying all hope of a successful campaign in Virginia. Cornwallis reminded Clinton that his victories further south had been ultimately worthless because the rebels could always rely on Virginia for supplies and support. Of course, he would defer to the opinions of his superior, to whose commands it was his 'duty implicitly to submit'; and, of course, he would send the troops specified to New York when sufficient transports arrived for their embarkation. But he could not forbear advancing his own opinions; and, at the same time, he was bound to report that he had so far been unable to find any 'defensive station' in Virginia which would answer the Commander-in-Chief's purposes. If a naval station in the south was essential to Clinton's plans, it might perhaps be better to return to Charleston, a move which, he contended grumpily, he would now probably be obliged to make in any case, since he could not establish a post in Virginia if he had to send to New York the men that Clinton wanted. In the meantime Lafayette was still at large in Virginia, and it might be necessary to exchange blows with him first.

Indeed, Cornwallis was already anticipating a fight with Lafayette, who was now only twenty miles from Williamsburg and who would certainly follow him as soon as he moved his army towards the coast. On 4 July, at Tyree's Plantation, Lafayette's men celebrated the fifth anniversary of the Declaration of Independence. Bands played; flags were waved; passages from the Declaration were declaimed; guns were fired; soldiers marched and trotted by, Continentals from New England and New Jersey, from Pennsylvania and Virginia, militiamen and artillerymen, dragoons in new uniforms, riflemen in buckskin breeches and coonskin caps.

The next morning Lafayette set off in pursuit of Cornwallis; and on 6 July he sent Anthony Wayne ahead with five hundred men to follow as closely as they could upon the British rearguard. Wayne was approaching the James River that day when a dragoon and a black, claiming to be deserters from the British army, were brought

to his headquarters. They told him that only a small party of infantry
and a detachment of Tarleton's British Legion remained on the north
side of the river, the rest of the British army having crossed to the
other bank.

In fact, the two supposed deserters were spies and Cornwallis's
entire force, apart from a detachment of the Queen's Rangers guarding the baggage, was still on the same side of the river as the
Americans, well concealed by woods and protected from encircle-
ment by ponds and swamps. But, confident that he had only the
British rearguard to deal with, Wayne rode impetuously forward
from a group of buildings known as Green Hill Farm, urging his
men forward as the British pickets fell back enticingly before him.
When, in the late afternoon, he was well within the trap that Cornwallis had set for him, the British guns opened fire in his front, while
Germans and guardsmen suddenly appeared on his left. Undeterred,
he ordered his men to charge with the bayonet. The resultant clash
of arms was a brief one. Wayne soon realized the mistake he had
made, and called his men away. They struggled back through the
swamp towards Green Hill Farm, many of them being shot before
they reached it and others dying of their wounds after getting there.

Tarleton longed to gallop after them; but the marshy ground and
the gathering darkness combined to make pursuit that evening too
hazardous; and the next day Cornwallis reminded him that he had
his orders from Clinton to consider. These did not permit him to
risk a full-scale battle with Lafayette. He had already lost seventy-five
men killed and wounded in this short engagement. To endanger the
lives of more might well be interpreted as insubordination.

Before Cornwallis could execute the directions contained in Clinton's letters of 11 and 15 June, however, further despatches arrived
from New York. Their wording was convoluted and ambiguous and
Cornwallis's exasperation at receiving them was increased by their
not arriving in the order in which they had been written. One was
handed to him on 8 July; three more, all written before it, arrived
four days later; another, countermanding previous instructions but
advising contradictory measures, came on 20 July; this was followed
by several others. In the earliest letters Clinton, while repeating
his disappointment at Cornwallis's march into Virginia from the
Carolinas, emphasized the importance of receiving reinforcements at
New York which the enemy was 'certain' to attack. Subsequent

despatches recommended a raid into Philadelphia, for which Cornwallis was making preparations when he was told to halt the embarkation of troops, to await further despatches and, in the meantime, 'to hold Old Point Comfort which secures Hampton Road'. Cornwallis was told that he must not return to Charleston, and that he could, if necessary, employ the whole force at his disposal for the fortification and defence of Old Point Comfort which commanded the approach to James River. Yet he was also told that, when he had decided how many men he needed for this purpose, he should send the 'remainder' to New York.

On receipt of this final letter Cornwallis sent a responsible engineer to Old Point Comfort to make a survey of it to ensure that it was a suitable place for the purpose the Commander-in-Chief had in mind. The engineer found it to be entirely unsuitable: earth would have to be carried an unacceptably long distance for the erection of fortifications for the protection of ships, and, even if constructed, the fort would be useless since there was no bay where ships could lie at anchor beneath its guns. Cornwallis went to look at the place himself, taking with him the captains of the vessels then lying in Hampton Road. They all agreed that the engineer was right: Old Point Comfort could not be turned into a satisfactory naval base.

But then further letters from Clinton arrived. A naval base in the Chesapeake Bay area was really essential. This, it was emphasized, was not only the Commander-in-Chief's own view; it was the opinion also of the Royal Navy. The base at Old Point Comfort could, if necessary, be protected by fortifications. Fortifications ought also to be constructed at Yorktown, further north by the mouth of the York River. Cornwallis should be able to erect both these forts with three thousand men, but he was 'at full liberty to detain' all the troops if he considered them necessary. This 'very liberal concession,' Clinton added, 'will, I am persuaded, convince your Lordship of the high estimation in which I hold a Naval station in Chesapeake.'

Subsequent letters arrived elaborating and underlining this point; and so, although he still declined to consider the possibility of a base at Old Point Comfort, Cornwallis reluctantly set off for Yorktown with the intention of fortifying both that place and Gloucester, which stood opposite it on the northern bank of the York River. There were strong objections to both places as naval stations: they were on low ground, and in order to make them safe fortifications of excep-

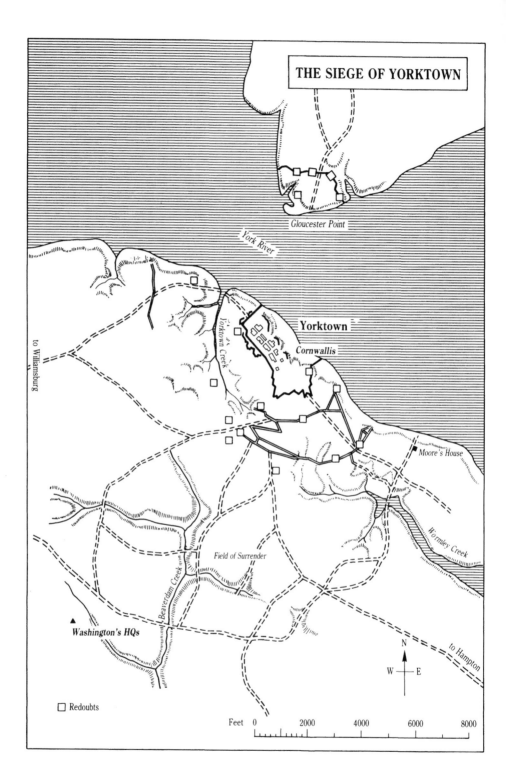

THE SIEGE OF YORKTOWN

Gloucester Point

York River

to Williamsburg

Yorktown Creek

Yorktown

Cornwallis

Moore's House

Wormley Creek

Field of Surrender

Beaverdam Creek

Washington's HQs

N
W — E

to Hampton

☐ Redoubts

Feet   0   2000   4000   6000   8000

tional strength would have to be built at a cost of enormous effort, time and labour by men whom Cornwallis believed could be far better employed in other ways. Even with the help of as many blacks as he could muster he would have to retain the whole army for the purpose, either in labouring on the fortifications with the few entrenching tools with which his army was supplied or in guarding the working parties. But since the Commander-in-Chief and, evidently, the Royal Navy, were so intent upon the project, he would have to carry it out as best he could with the seven thousand or so men at his disposal.

Fortunately the position of Yorktown did offer some natural advantages. Gloucester was less than a mile to the north; and into the anchorage between the two towns a strong British squadron was expected to sail by 5 October. To the east and west were swamps. It was in the south that the Americans could be expected to concentrate their forces; and here Cornwallis constructed an outer line of redoubts and an inner line of stockades and earthen parapets covered by batteries.

The Americans and French, however, were gathering for the siege in far greater numbers than Cornwallis had expected. Soon almost sixteen thousand men were to be assembled at Williamsburg, and it was clear that Cornwallis could not hold Yorktown unless reinforcements arrived without delay. Clinton had promised to come to his help, but Cornwallis had long since abandoned all hope of assistance from that 'unreliable quarter'.

Not so long ago, after his capture of Charleston, Clinton's reputation had stood so high that he was, in William Eden's phrase, 'the most *popular* man in England'. Yet the government did not share the general enthusiasm; and, when undertaking to send him reinforcements far more modest in number than he had requested, Lord George Germain had told him either to 'remain in good humour, in full confidence to be supported as much as the nature of the service will admit of, or avail himself of the leave of coming home, as no good can arise to the service if there is not a full confidence between the General and the Ministers'. By the beginning of 1781 newspapers which reflected the government's views, such as the *Morning Post* and the *Morning Herald*, were openly criticizing Clinton for not doing more to help Cornwallis. It seemed clear to Clinton's family and supporters that

Ministers were ready to abandon him if he did not win another victory soon and were preparing the ground for giving the supreme command to Cornwallis as soon as they could. 'You must look to yourself,' Charles Grey warned him, 'for no person here will. Their only aim seems to be screening themselves by laying the blame if possible elsewhere.'

Sir Henry, it seems, was not above screening himself. When he learned by means of intercepted despatches of Washington's meeting with Rochambeau at Wethersfield and of de Grasse's departure with a strong French fleet from Brest, he later claimed that the despatches also revealed that this was to be France's last effort in America, 'the last campaign in which the Americans were to expect assistance of either troops or ships from that nation'.

Before France's large-scale intervention, the rebels, so Clinton contended, had been losing heart and their army, ill-supplied and largely unpaid, had been on the verge of disintegration. This belief was not unfounded: American troops had mutinied in January 1781 and in April Washington had written despairingly, 'We are at the end of our tether . . . Now or never our deliverance must come.' The French commanders shared Washington's pessimism. 'Send us troops, ships and money,' Rochambeau had written after his first sight of the American army. 'But do not count on these people, nor on their resources. They have neither money nor credit; their forces only exist momentarily, and when they are about to be attacked in their own homes they assemble during the time of personal danger to defend themselves.' After his meeting with Washington at Wethersfield, Rochambeau remained of the same opinion: the Americans were at the end of their resources, he told de Grasse, and only the support of a strong French fleet to wrest command of American waters from the British could save them. The two allied generals had considered the possibility of an attack upon New York; but the strength of the British there, and the presence of the Royal Navy, had dissuaded them from attempting it. They decided to march south against Cornwallis instead; and so, by the middle of August, a powerful French-American army was on the march for the Chesapeake where more French soldiers were to join it, the Americans' reluctance to go so far away from their homes being overcome by the payment of money borrowed from their allies.

★　　★　　★

So far the French alliance had profited the rebels little; but now that de Grasse and the tactful Rochambeau – whose orders were to submit himself and his troops to Washington's command – had crossed the Atlantic, the situation had changed dramatically. Yet, if this were to be France's last campaign in America, as Clinton claimed the intercepted despatches indicated, his policy must be to avoid 'all risks as much as possible', since 'time alone would soon bring about every success we could wish'.

In the months that followed he toyed with the idea of a raid on Philadelphia to disrupt the enemy's supplies; but Arbuthnot was unco-operative and nothing came of the plan. 'For some time back no operations had been concerted between the disagreeing Commanders in Chief,' commented Rear Admiral Thomas Graves who succeeded Arbuthnot, to Clinton's profound relief, in July. Yet Clinton soon found Graves, a highly conventional and unimaginative sailor, scarcely an improvement upon his predecessor. Sir George Rodney, the finest admiral in the Royal Navy, was the man for the American command, Clinton insisted; but Rodney was too ill to take it and was on the point of sailing home to England from the West Indies. Before doing so he was faced with the problem presented by de Grasse's arrival. He dare not send too many ships from the West Indies to meet the challenge in North America for fear of defeat in the Caribbean; but the few which he felt able to spare and which he despatched under command of Samuel Hood were, even when combined with Graves's, no match for the French.

Before Hood arrived, Graves set out with his squadron to intercept a convoy believed to comprise 'one of the most important supplies the French have ever sent the rebels'; and, when Graves returned to New York a month later, three of his ships had been so badly damaged in high seas that he protested he could do nothing until they had been repaired. His subsequent inaction exasperated men like Arnold and Major-General James Robertson, now Governor of New York, who were both urging the need for immediate action and were already dismayed by the supineness of Clinton and his preoccupation with the minutiae of plans that never materialized.

Arnold suggested an expedition to the Chesapeake, but 'nothing takes'; Robertson proposed a sortie to find Washington's army, but Clinton objected that the rebels might burn New York while he was away. In any case, it might well be that Washington still intended to attack New York and that his move south was an elaborate diversion. At last, when it was clear that Cornwallis's plight was desperate, Graves and Hood left New York to save him, believing that their combined forces stood more than a fair chance against the French fleet and sailing straight for the Chesapeake rather than attempting to fall upon the Comte de Barras, whose fleet was known to have left Rhode Island to join the Comte de Grasse.

Already, however, de Grasse's fleet was in Chesapeake Bay at the mouth of the York River, where de Barras was sailing to join him. On 31 August Cornwallis, so he told Clinton in a coded message, could clearly see the sails of about forty enemy vessels between Cape Charles and Cape Henry, 'mostly ships of war and some of them very large'. Clinton replied to the effect that he would do what he could to help, either by sending reinforcements or by mounting a diversion. A diversion was certainly put in hand, Benedict Arnold being sent on a raid to New London, Connecticut. But the reinforcements, Clinton decided, could not be sent until the Royal Navy could undertake to transport them or to protect them were they to make the long march overland.

'Things appear to be coming fast to a crisis,' Clinton reported to Lord George Germain on 7 September. 'We are therefore no longer to compare forces with the enemy, but to endeavour to act in the best manner we can against them . . . With what I have, inadequate as it is, I will exert myself to the utmost to save Lord Cornwallis.'

Soon after writing this letter, Clinton received news from Admiral Graves that gave him pause: on 5 September the French fleet had put out to sea from the Chesapeake, and manoeuvred into line of battle. There had been an ill-conducted and inconclusive engagement in which both fleets were badly damaged, no fewer than four of the British ships being seriously holed. After this battle, de Grasse had withdrawn to his anchorage within the Chesapeake where de Barras, with several heavy cannon and tons of salt beef aboard his ships, had joined him and where their combined fleets were, in Graves's view, inviolate. Indeed, in the English Admiral's words, the enemy now had 'so great a naval force in the Chesapeake that they [were] absolute masters of its navigation'. Graves turned for advice to Hood, his second-in-command, who replied, 'Sir Samuel would be very glad to send an opinion, but he really knows not what to say in the truly lamentable state we have brought ourselves.' So Graves decided that he had no alternative but to bring back his 'shattered fleet' to New York.

On receipt of this letter Clinton called a Council of War at which General Robertson, the Governor, pleaded for immediate and decisive action, making proposals, subsequently amended and put into writing, which Clinton rejected, giving his reasons for doing so in a memorandum as useless as it was verbose. Other members of the Council expressed the view, gratifying to Clinton, that Cornwallis was not in immediate danger, that he should be able to hold out for at least another three weeks, that it would be foolhardy to risk an attempt to save him now when Rear Admiral Robert Digby was reported to be coming out with more ships. Digby, however, had only been spared three ships by the Admiralty, who were still far more concerned with the Mediterranean than with America; and, when he arrived on 24 September, the British fleet still remained greatly outgunned, with twenty-five ships of the line to thirty-six.

Even so, General Robertson continued to press for help to be sent, whatever the risks, to Cornwallis who had written to say, 'If you cannot relieve me very soon, you must be prepared to hear the worst.' 'The man who deliberates is lost,' Robertson insisted in his strong Scottish accent. 'America is at stake and Great Britain, too.' But Robertson was an elderly man, a former sergeant who had shown no great distinction as an officer and who was, in the opinion of Thomas Jones, the loyalist historian, so infirm, paralytic and absurdly libidinous as to be dismissed as a dotard. Other members of the Council of War could not agree with Robertson; nor could Clinton himself. Certainly Cornwallis should be told that help was on the way; but no firm date should be given until the Royal Navy was ready. The Navy was not ready; and Sir Samuel Hood was the only senior naval officer whose views coincided with Robertson's. Admiral Graves, for his part, appeared to have given up all hope and lost all confidence. Fearing that if his fleet were to be destroyed off the Chesapeake the West Indies would be lost also, he appeared to have decided that he dared not risk another battle. Sir Henry Clinton seemed equally dazed by his problems. 'I see this in so serious a light,' he wrote on 30 September, 'that I dare not look [at] it.'

A fortnight later, after yet more dates set for departure had come and gone, Admiral Graves gloomily reported that the ships were ready at last: if the Commander-in-Chief were to go at all, he had better go now. But was it now, Clinton wondered, too late? 'Our generals and admirals,' commented Captain Mackenzie in exasperation, 'don't seem to be in earnest about this business.' They seemed, indeed, to be more concerned with entertaining the King's sixteen-year-old son, Prince William Henry, who had been sent out as a midshipman with Admiral Digby in the hope that his presence in New York would raise the morale of the Loyalists. The Prince was greeted with great ceremony and by large crowds at the quayside. He was entertained at dinners and concerts; he reviewed troops both English and German; he listened to sermons preached in his honour; he was introduced to Benedict Arnold; he was taken on tours of New York which did not impress him, the streets being 'narrow and very ill-paved', so he told his father, and there being only one church, 'all the others converted into magazines or Barracks'.

A rebel colonel proposed that if the Prince were taken prisoner he might be useful as a bargaining counter in future negotiations, and sought permission from Washington to make the attempt in a sea-borne operation. 'The spirit of enterprise so conspicuous in your plan for surprising in their quarters and bringing off the Prince William Henry and Admiral Digby merits applause,' Washington decided, 'and you have my authority to make the attempt . . . I am fully persuaded that it is unnecessary to caution you against offering insult or indignity, to the persons of the Prince or Admiral.' The colonel's plans were betrayed to the British, however; the Prince's guards were doubled; and the expedition was cancelled.

While the Prince was being entertained in New York, Cornwallis, with a large part of his small force ill in hospital, anxiously awaited the arrival of the reinforcements and ships, without which his defence of Yorktown was doomed to failure. He had considered the possibility of breaking out and attacking the approaching enemy. But since relief was promised him, he did not think himself justified 'in putting the fate of the war on so desperate an attempt'.

Washington had been so excited by the news that de Grasse's fleet had arrived in Chesapeake Bay with three thousand French troops, and that Cornwallis was thus trapped in Yorktown, that he amazed his companions by throwing off all his normal restraints, jumping up and down and wildly waving his arms in the air, a handkerchief in one hand, his hat in the other. His army had marched out of Williamsburg at five o'clock on the morning of 28 September, the Americans, not to be outdone by their allies, looking uncommonly smart in their new, French-made uniforms of blue and of brown faced with red, their faces cleanly shaved and even, in one brigade, with their hair powdered.

On arriving before Yorktown, Washington was surprised to discover that three of the British outposts had been abandoned. Supposing that Cornwallis was preparing to evacuate the position altogether, he gave orders for his troops to occupy them; and on the afternoon of 9 October he himself fired the first shot from a heavy gun at a range of about six hundred yards to hasten the British on their way. Philip van Cortlandt of the 2nd New York Regiment 'distinctly heard' the shot pass through the town, striking from house to house. 'And I was afterwards informed,' he continued, 'that it went through the one where many of the officers were at dinner, and over the tables, discomposing the dishes, and either killed or wounded the one at the head of the table.'

This shot was the signal for an intense bombardment: on the first day 3600 shot crashed into the British lines; and on the day after that, having undergone a barrage for hours on end from forty cannon and sixteen mortars, Cornwallis was forced to conclude that 'against so powerful an attack, [he could] not hope to make a very long resistance'. With scarcely more than 3250 men fit for duty, he was facing an allied army almost sixteen thousand strong. By 11 October the American artillery had been advanced to within three hundred yards of the British inner defences; and by the 14th two advance British redoubts had been captured, one by the French, the other by Alexander Hamilton, the illegitimate son of a Scottish merchant and until recently aide-de-camp and secretary to General Washington, with whom he had quarrelled over his request to see more active service. A soldier who took part in Hamilton's attack remembered:

We arrived at the trenches a little before sunset. I saw several officers fixing bayonets on long staves. I then concluded we were about to make a general assault upon the enemy's works, but before dark I was informed of the whole plan . . .

The sappers and miners were furnished with axes and were to proceed in front and cut a passage for the troops through the abatis

. . . At dark the detachment . . . advanced beyond the trenches and lay down on the ground to await the signal for the attack, which was to be three shells from a certain battery . . . All the batteries in our line were silent, and we lay anxiously waiting for the signal . . .

We had not lain here long before the . . . signal was given for us and the French . . . the three shells with their fiery trains mounting the air in quick succession. The word, 'up up' was then reiterated through the detachment. We moved towards the redoubt we were to attack with unloaded muskets.

The next morning Cornwallis wrote to Clinton:

The enemy carried two advanced redoubts by storm . . . My situation now becomes very critical; we dare not show a gun to their old batteries, and I expect that their new ones will open tomorrow morning . . . The safety of the place is therefore so precarious that I cannot recommend that the fleet and army should run great risque in endeavouring to save us.

Food supplies, even of putrid meat and worm-holed biscuits, were running so low that blacks were driven out of the town and several were killed between the two armies; the numbers of sick were rising daily; so were the numbers of dead. A German soldier noted with revulsion the bodies lying unburied in the town, some of them with 'heads, arms and legs shot off'. Farrier sergeants in black coats were performing the 'melancholy duty' of killing horses so weakened by starvation that they could scarcely stand. 'We could find no refuge in or out of the town,' one of the besieged recalled. 'The people fled to the waterside and hid in hastily contrived shelters on the banks, but many of them were killed by bursting bombs . . . Our ships suffered, too, under the heavy fire, for the enemy fired in one day thirty-six hundred shot from their heavy guns and batteries. Soldiers and sailors deserted in great numbers.'

Cornwallis made up his mind that he would have to try to get his army across the York River to Gloucester. So, having sent out 350 men on a desperate sortie to spike the enemy's guns, he gave orders for part of his force to embark. The first wave reached Gloucester in safety. But that night a storm blew up; the boats were scattered; and hope of getting the rest of his men across had to be abandoned.

In the haze of the early morning of 17 October the American artillery opened up as usual, cannon and mortars hurling their shot flying across the lines, and sending showers of red earth and fragments of metal over the British emplacements. There must have been at least a hundred guns at work, the surgeon, James Thacher, thought. 'The whole peninsula,' he wrote, 'trembles under the incessant thunderings of our infernal machines.' From the British batteries there was so little response that an American militiaman pranced about on a parapet, declaring that he would 'damn his soul if he would dodge for the buggers' and brandishing his spade at the occasional shot that flew across towards him until, as an officer recorded, 'a ball came and put an end to his capers'.

While the bombardment continued, on the far left of the British lines, a drummer boy in a shabby bearskin hat followed by an officer waving a white handkerchief appeared from behind a British earthwork and walked down the slope towards the American lines in the drifting gun smoke. One of Washington's staff officers went forward to meet them, sent the drummer back to his own lines, and took the officer, blindfolded, to his headquarters. To Cornwallis's overtures, which this officer delivered, Washington replied, 'An ardent desire to spare the further effusion of blood will readily incline me to listen to such terms for the surrender of your post and garrisons of York and Gloucester as are admissible.'

What was not admissible, as Washington soon made clear, was Cornwallis's request that Tory civilians and American army deserters at Yorktown and Gloucester should not be punished on account of their support of the British cause. Also inadmissible was the permission, which Cornwallis sought, for his troops to return to Europe as General Gates had agreed that Burgoyne's should do at Saratoga. Nor was it to be allowed that they should march out with drums beating and flags flying, since that concession had been denied by Sir Henry Clinton to General Lincoln at Charleston. Cornwallis protested that he had not been responsible for Clinton's harshness at Charleston. 'It is not the individual that is here considered,' one of the American negotiators replied. 'It is the nation.' While the discussions continued, soldiers on both sides lay down in the sun and their bands entertained each other with music, the musicians and drummers of a French regiment replying to the skirling of the Highlanders' bagpipes on the British parapets. In the end Washington agreed that the British could emerge from their lines to the sound of music, provided the music was not one of those parodical versions of American tunes which British bands were so fond of playing.

The ceremony of surrender took place in a field encircled by mounted French troops. The British soldiers marched towards this field down the Hampton Road, wearing new uniforms issued to them that morning so that these would not have to be handed over to the enemy. They passed between the two lines of allied troops, the French in their white uniforms with black gaiters on one side, white standards with gold fleurs-de-lis flying above their heads, the Americans, from whom the British ostentatiously averted their gaze, in their darker, drabber clothes on the other. The British drums were beating and their fifes playing a sad tune, afterwards incorrectly reported to be 'The World Turned Upside Down'. They entered the field, and in the middle of the circle of French hussars they laid down their arms; some of them, until prevented from doing so by General O'Hara, hurled them down angrily, as though they wished to smash them on the ground. As they marched out of the circle, it was noticed that some appeared drunk and many were close to tears, biting their lips or actually weeping.

'To do them justice,' a British officer recorded, 'the Americans behaved with great delicacy and forbearance, while the French, by what motive I will not pretend to say, were profuse in their protestations of sympathy . . . When I visited their lines immediately after our parade had been dismissed, I was overwhelmed by the civilities of my late enemies.'

Lord Cornwallis, pleading illness, had told Brigadier-General Charles O'Hara to represent him. O'Hara tried to hand over his sword to the Comte de Rochambeau but the French officer would not accept it. 'We are subordinates to the Americans,' he said, 'General Washington will give you your orders.'

O'Hara turned away and rode over to offer his sword to the American Commander-in-Chief. But, as Lord Cornwallis was not there, Washington gave up the honour of receiving it to Benjamin Lincoln, who tapped it in silent acceptance of surrender.

'The play, sir,' Lafayette told a friend, 'is over.'

On the day that the surrender was signed, Admiral Graves and Sir Henry Clinton, with seven thousand men aboard their fleet, sailed at last out into the Atlantic past Sandy Hook south of New York. Five days later they reached the mouth of Chesapeake Bay, where they encountered a small boat with a white man and two blacks who brought them the news from Yorktown.

The ships turned round and sailed away north again, back to New York.

EPILOGUE

Within five weeks despatches containing news of Cornwallis's surrender at Yorktown were brought to London and handed to Lord George Germain, who took them immediately to Lord North. Their effect on North, so Germain recounted, was like that of a ball to the breast. He paced up and down the room, exclaiming in mingled horror and relief, 'O God! It is all over!'

The King affected to believe that British arms had suffered merely a setback with the loss of his forces in the province of Virginia; and in the House of Commons government speakers assured Members that the war would go on, that the unfortunate effects at Yorktown had been brought about by the interference of the French, that more encouraging news could soon be expected. Such unwarranted optimism was met by Fox with scorn. He recognized that the mood of the country had changed since the 1770s; then there was widespread support for the war and the government; now that support was waning fast.

In debate after debate, Fox and his supporters had spoken of the folly of attempting to wage a war on the far side of the Atlantic against a people becoming ever more united as the years went by. It was admittedly ridiculous to suppose – as the more romantic English supporters of the rebels liked to think – that the Americans were a nation in arms, having deserted the plough for the sword. Yet the army which Washington had done so much to form and keep intact, combined with that of his allies and supported by the French Navy, was certainly a formidable force, with several highly talented commanders both American and European. 'They have got a great many Foreigners amongst them,' as one of Lord Denbigh's correspondents, Captain John Bowater, told him, 'Runegadoes & partisans from all Countrys which are Very great Rascals but are generall[y] Very

Clever fellows.' It might well prove possible to defeat the rebel forces if they were the only enemy with whom the government had to contend. But there were enemies in Europe too, apart from the French and Spanish: England was at war also with the Dutch, whose powerful fleet was giving its support to the rebels; the Russians, while ostensibly neutral, had combined with Sweden and Denmark to close the Baltic to British warships; and there was trouble as well in India.

The British and German soldiers who had been sent to America had, for the most part, fought bravely; but neither the generals commanding them nor the Ministers directing them had been fully equal to their tasks, while the system of army administration had proved to be inept. Moreover, as Fox emphasized, the terrain over which the army had had to fight was one presenting 'a unique diversity of difficulties' to a regular force, 'obstacles of rivers, of a deep intersected country, of impassable marshes, of a disaffected people, of "timid friends and of inveterate enemies"'.

'Mr Fox,' commented the *London Courant* after one debate, 'daily rises in public estimation. His arguments against the nefarious war were unanswered and unanswerable.' The Earl of Chatham's second son, William Pitt, was also praised for speeches of remarkable fluency in one so young, for the passion with which he deplored 'the accursed, cruel, unnatural, wicked American war, a war of injustice and moral depravity, marked by blood, slaughter, persecution and devastation'. Even Members who were predisposed in Lord North's favour and who, like Edward Gibbon, considered the colonists to be in the wrong, were forced to conclude, as Gibbon himself concluded, that it was 'easier to defend the justice than the policy of [the government's] measures'. 'I shall never give my consent,' Gibbon had said some time before, 'to exhaust still further the finest country in the world in this prosecution of a war from whence no reasonable man entertains any hope of success. It is better to be humbled than ruined.'

Other Members, more vocal in the House, rose to condemn the absurdities of government strategy or to emphasize the appalling problems with which Ministers were beset, the shortage of troops, despite all attempts to raise more, and the shortage of shipping. It was difficult for the layman to comprehend how many vessels were required to prevent rebel importations of such war supplies as gunpowder – almost all of which, up until the end of 1777, was brought into the colonies by sea – and to keep the British army in America stocked with the essential provisions which it proved impossible to obtain locally: every year each soldier in America had to be supplied with a third of a ton of food, excluding the weight of the chests and casks in which were packed the salt beef, pork and flour, the oatmeal, pease and butter, the barley and biscuits and all the other comestibles which could not be obtained on the often dangerous foraging expeditions sent out in search of fodder and hay for the horses. Inevitably a proportion of most shipments was lost either through theft, careless packing or unloading, or through goods being kept too long in the hot holds of ships whose destination was often changed by the exigencies of strategy after the vessels had set sail. Then there were the difficulties of communication: although the crossing of the Atlantic from America could be completed in four or five weeks, even a fast ship carrying urgent despatches seldom took much less than two months to cross over from an English port. Some despatches took three or even four months to reach America; and transatlantic voyages of six or even seven months were not unknown.

Faced by such problems as these, and by the difficulties experienced in organizing and supporting the Loyalists, the government had become involved in a war it was eventually impossible to win. 'No opinion was clearer,' one of the Comte de Rochambeau's aides-de-camp remarked to a friend of Charles James Fox, 'than that, while the American people might well be conquered by well-disciplined European troops, the country of America was unconquerable.'

When Cornwallis surrendered at Yorktown, although there were still thirty thousand British and American troops fit for duty in America, the truth of this observation was felt to be inescapable. 'What we are to do after Lord Cornwallis's catastrophe, God knows,' one of his old school friends wrote to Lord Carlisle. 'How anybody can think there is the least glimmering of hope for this nation surpasses my comprehension.'

Yet when the House of Commons debated the motion that 'all further attempts to reduce the revolted colonies to obedience are contrary to the true interests of this Kingdom', government supporters were able to gain a majority after a lively speech by Lord North. Subsequent anti-government motions were also defeated, though with such slender majorities that Lord North was persuaded to drop Lord George Germain from his administration. But neither this nor the replacement of Sir Henry Clinton by Sir Guy Carleton could save the government now. On 22 February 1782 Horace Walpole's friend, General Henry Conway, rose in the House and, in a memorable speech, proposed that the American war be abandoned. The government survived by a single vote. Five days later, however, when the motion was brought forward again, it was carried by nineteen votes; at two o'clock the next morning, Lord North wrote to the King to propose that a new administration should be formed.

The King was reluctant to agree, protesting again that he would rather lose his crown than call in a set of men who would make him a slave, that no consideration would ever make him 'in the smallest degree an instrument in a measure that would annihilate the rank in which the British Empire stood among the European States'. So the government tottered along for a month; and when Lord North again tendered his resignation, His Majesty crossly replied, 'If you resign before I have decided what I will do, you will certainly for ever forfeit my regard.'

It was, therefore, not known for certain whether or not Lord North was to remain as First Lord of the Treasury when the House of Commons met on 20 March to debate a proposal that the King's Ministers should be removed from office. Sir Nathaniel Wraxall, Member of Parliament for the Wiltshire borough of Hindon, as well as various parliamentary correspondents for the London newspapers, described the scene as Wraxall's fellow-Members entered the chamber that Wednesday afternoon in their bag wigs and flowered waistcoats, swords at their sides, taking their seats on the benches, looking up as each new arrival came through the door, anxious not to miss the appearance of Lord North. Four hundred Members had arrived in the chamber before the clock struck four. The hum of their talk could be heard in the street outside. At last Lord North appeared, uncommonly well dressed in what appeared to be a new suit, a ribbon over his coat.

The House fell into silence at the behest of the Speaker. Lord Surrey rose to make the proposal which had already been advertised. But before he could speak, Lord North also stood up and declared, 'I rise to speak to that motion.' There followed a noisy wrangle about parliamentary procedure. Surrey eventually gave way, and North was allowed his say: he opposed the motion, he said, for the good reasons that he had already handed in his resignation and that his administration was, in any case, dissolved. A man of greater abilities, he conceded, might well succeed to his office but 'a successor more zealous for the interests of his country, more anxious to promote those interests, more loyal to his sovereign, and more desirous of preserving the constitution whole and entire', would not so easily be found. As so often in the past, Lord North had contrived to have the last word.

He left the chamber to go home. It was an exceptionally cold afternoon and the snow was falling outside in Old Palace Yard. Members stamped their feet as they waited for their carriages to come to the door. Lord North's was among the first to arrive. 'I have my carriage,' he announced with cheerful complacency to the Members of the Opposition still waiting for theirs. 'You see, gentlemen, the advantages of being in the secret.'

Some eighteen months later, on 3 September 1783, the King's new Ministers concluded the negotiations which resulted in the Treaty of Paris. The independence of the United States was recognized; and the boundaries of the new country were drawn on lines whose generosity owed much to the skill of the American negotiators, Benjamin Franklin, John Adams and John Jay, the New York lawyer who had stated the claims of the colonists in his *Address to the People of Great Britain*.

A few weeks later General Washington prepared to enter New York as the British left it. There had been a recent threat of mutiny in his army over pay. He had appealed to the officers of the disaffected regiments and, before reading a paper in his hands, had said to them, 'Gentlemen, you must pardon me. I have grown grey in your service and now find myself going blind.' A few weeks later, the mutiny suppressed, he said goodbye to his officers in New York, shaking each of them by the hand. He then set out for Virginia for what he vainly hoped would be a peaceful retirement at Mount Vernon. The history of the United States of America as an independent republic had begun.

While America had won her freedom, and France by spending so many millions of livres in helping her to do so had done much to precipitate her own revolution, England had gained a new awareness of her place in the world, a new conception of empire which was now seen not merely as a means to riches through trade, but as a political organization of peoples involving responsibilities as well as rights. The Crown, the old aristocratic society, and the Army which they controlled between them, had suffered a defeat from which they never fully recovered and a loss of confidence which was never fully restored. Power was already passing to the middle classes, the merchants of the Midlands and the industrialists of the North, to men like Sir John Gladstone, corn and sugar merchant of Liverpool, and Sir Robert Peel, calico printer of Blackburn, both fathers of future Prime Ministers and representatives of a growing class whose protests against the continuance of the war had found expression in the parliamentary speeches of the opponents of its prosecution, the statesmen and politicians who came into office with its ending.

As Horace Walpole told his friend Horace Mann, a new chapter had been opened in the history of their country. What America might now become it was impossible yet to say; but sure it was that a new nation had been born, and that the old world, by its creation, had been changed for ever.

The Fate of Characters Whose End Is Not Recorded in the Text

John Adams: While serving as American Minister in London in 1787 he published his *Defence of the Constitution of the United States.* Two years later he became Vice-President under Washington; and in 1796 second President of the United States. Defeated on seeking re-election in 1800, he returned home to Quincy, Massachusetts where he died a few hours after Thomas Jefferson, on 4 July 1826, the fiftieth anniversary of the Declaration of Independence.

Samuel Adams: Became Lieutenant Governor of Massachusetts in 1789 and Governor in 1797. He died in Boston in 1803.

Ethan Allen: Released from imprisonment in May 1778, he did not return to the Army but settled in Vermont where, having failed to obtain independence for that state, he tried to arrange for its annexation to Canada. His *Vindication of the Opposition of the Inhabitants of Vermont to the Government of New York* was published in 1779. He died in Burlington, Vermont ten years later.

Marriot Arbuthnot: After his replacement by Admiral Graves, he returned home and had no further employment at sea. He was promoted Admiral of the Blue by seniority in 1793 and died in London the following year.

Benedict Arnold: Sailed in 1782 to England where he tried to obtain employment in the Army, in which he had been given the rank of brigadier-general. Disappointed in this endeavour and in his efforts to gain promotion, he went into business in Canada, then in the West Indies; but was not successful and would have been ruined had not his wife saved him by her acute commercial sense. He died, a broken man, in London in 1810.

William Eden, Baron Auckland: Became successively Minister-Plenipotentiary to France, Ambassador to Spain, Ambassador to Holland, Postmaster-General and President of the Board of Trade, dying at Beckenham, Kent in 1814.

Alexander Lindsay, Earl of Balcarres: Captured at Saratoga, he was released in 1779. Gazetted major-general in 1793, he was appointed Governor of Jamaica, returning to England in 1801. When George III introduced him to Benedict Arnold, he is said to have protested 'What, the traitor Arnold?' This remark led to a duel. Arnold fired, but Balcarres then walked away. 'Why don't you fire, my Lord?' Arnold called. Balcarres called back over his shoulder, 'I leave you to the executioner.' He died at Haigh Hall, his wife's family home, in 1825.

John Burgoyne: Given permission by Washington to return home after his surrender at Saratoga, he was subjected to harsh attacks in both Parliament and the press. These attacks continued after publication of his defensive *State of the Expedition from Canada* (1779). Deprived by the King of his command of the 16th Light Dragoons, he lent his support to the Opposition and was appointed Commander-in-Chief in Ireland when the Whigs came into office under the Marquess of Rockingham. He held this appointment for a short time only, however; and after Charles James Fox's resignation in 1783 he devoted himself to the theatre, enjoying great success with *The Heiress*, of which Horace Walpole wrote: 'Burgoyne's battles and speeches will be forgotten; but his delicious comedy of "The Heiress" still continues the delight of the stage.' Burgoyne died at his home in Mayfair in 1792.

John Byron: Suffering from a 'nervous fever', he returned home in 1779 and saw no further service. He died in 1786.

Archibald Campbell: Returned to England in 1779 and was promoted major-general in 1782, having been appointed Governor of Jamaica. He later became Governor of Madras. His health broken, he went home in 1789 and died in London two years later.

Guy Carleton: Evacuated New York in November 1783; and, after spending some time in London, was again appointed Governor of Quebec and created 1st Lord Dorchester. Leaving Canada in 1796, he lived in retirement in England until his death near Maidenhead in 1808.

Frederick Howard, Earl of Carlisle: Appointed President of the Board of Trade on his return from America, he was successively Lord Lieutenant of Ireland and Lord Privy Seal. He died at Castle Howard, Yorkshire in 1825.

Henry Clinton: Published his contentious *Narrative* in 1783 and consequently quarrelled with Cornwallis and, later, with his cousin, the Duke of Newcastle. He was, however, promoted general in 1793 and in 1794 Governor of Gibraltar, where he died in 1795.

George Collier: Dismayed by Admiral Arbuthnot having succeeded to the command, he returned home in 1779. He commanded the *Canada* at the relief of Gibraltar but resigned the command shortly afterwards, following further disagreements with the Admiralty. Appointed to be Commander-in-Chief at the Nore in January 1795, he gave up this post because of ill health a few weeks later and died in April.

Henry Seymour Conway: Appointed Commander-in-Chief when the war, which he had consistently opposed, was over. He resigned in 1784 and died at Park Place, Henley-on-Thames in 1795.

Thomas Conway: Left the American Army under a cloud in 1778, and afterwards joined the French Army in which he did not distinguish himself. He died in *c.*1800.

Charles Cornwallis: Appointed Governor General and Commander-in-Chief in India in 1786, returning to England to be created a marquess in 1793. He distinguished himself also as Lord Lieutenant of Ireland and in 1802 as Plenipotentiary to France, where he helped to negotiate the Peace of Amiens that year. He died in India in 1805.

Silas Deane: Denounced as a traitor, lived in exile in Ghent and afterwards in London where his *Address to the Free and Independent Citizens of the United States* was published in 1784. In 1789 he decided to return to America, but died off the coast of Kent in the Boston packet.

Comte d'Estaing: Elected to the Assembly of Notables after his return to France. He was commander of the National Guard at Versailles when the Revolution broke out in 1789 and was guillotined in Paris during the Terror of 1794, three weeks after the execution of Danton.

John Murray, Earl of Dunmore: Having disbanded his troops in Virginia, returned to England in July 1776. Appointed Governor of the Bahama Islands in 1787, he remained in the West Indies until 1796 and died in Kent in 1809.

Benjamin Franklin: Remained in France for two years after the signing of the peace treaty of 1783. On his return to America he became a member of the Constitutional Convention of 1787. The last years of his life were spent in intermittent pain from a stone in his bladder, until in 1790, at the age of eighty-four, he died in Philadelphia.

Thomas Gage: Although promoted to the rank of general in 1782, his career was effectively over on his return from Boston in 1775. He died in 1787.

James Gambier: Appointed Commander-in-Chief at Jamaica in 1783; but ill health obliged him to return to England where he died at Bath in 1789.

Horatio Gates: Although he served for a time in the state legislature of New York after the war, he played no further significant part in American affairs after his defeat at Camden. He died in New York City in 1806.

George Germain: Upon the resignation of Lord North, created 1st Viscount Sackville. Thereafter he lived largely in retirement, dying at his country house, Stoneland Lodge, Sussex, in 1785.

James Grant: Retired from active service after his return from America. Promoted general in 1796, he was for several years Member of Parliament for Sutherlandshire. When he died, aged eighty-five, at Ballindalloch in 1806, he was said to be the fattest man of his age in Scotland.

Thomas Graves: Sailed to Jamaica after the surrender at Yorktown, thence for England in the *Ramillies* which was wrecked on the way. He arrived aboard a merchant ship in England where he was appointed Commander-in-Chief at Plymouth. On the outbreak of war with France, he was placed in command of the Channel Fleet and was badly wounded on the 'Glorious First of June', 1794. Raised to the peerage as Baron Graves, he died in 1802.

Nathanael Greene: Having declined the post of Secretary of War, retired in 1785 to an estate in Georgia where he had been granted both land and money. He died in Georgia, at Mulberry Grove near Savannah, in 1786.

Charles Grey: The end of the war prevented his taking up his appointment as Commander-in-Chief in America. After distinguished service in the West Indies, he was promoted general and made a Privy Councillor. In 1801 he was created first Earl Grey and died at Howick, Northumberland, his family home and birthplace.

Alexander Hamilton: As a distinguished lawyer and writer, he pleaded for justice to Loyalists. He was elected to the New York legislature in 1787; and in 1789 was appointed First Secretary of the Treasury. Having helped to restore the country's finances, he resigned from office in 1795 but remained highly influential in the government. He helped to found the *New York Evening Post* which voiced his Federalist ideas. He was mortally wounded in 1804 in a duel with Aaron Burr which was fought on the heights of Weehawken, New

Jersey, where the eldest of his seven children, the nineteen-year-old Philip, had been killed not long before.

John Hancock: Became Governor of Massachusetts in 1780 and died still in that office at Quincy in 1793.

George Hanger: Became increasingly eccentric with the passing years until his friend, the Prince Regent, found his manners 'too free and coarse for the royal taste'. On the death of his brother he became the fourth Lord Coleraine but he refused to adopt the title and died unmarried in 1824.

Patrick Henry: Having served as Governor of Virginia during the war, he was reappointed to that office in 1784 and remained Governor until 1786. He was offered various high offices in the federal government but declined them on the grounds of his poor health. He died at Red Hill, near Brookneal, Virginia in 1799.

Richard, Viscount Howe: Became First Lord of the Admiralty in 1783 and was created Earl Howe in 1788. He was given command of the Channel Fleet upon the outbreak of war with France in 1793, and defeated the French fleet west of Ushant in his greatest victory on the 'Glorious First of June', 1794. After an attempt had been made to cure his gout by 'electricity', he died in 1799.

William Howe: Demanded a parliamentary committee to enquire into his conduct in America after his return to England in 1778. The findings of this committee were inconclusive, and its members adjourned in 1779. On the outbreak of war with France, he was placed first in command of the northern, then of the eastern, district of England. In 1814 he died at Plymouth where he had been Governor for several years.

Thomas Hutchinson: Having been replaced as Governor of Massachusetts by General Gage, sailed to London where he became an adviser to the government on American affairs. Although counselling moderation, he was proscribed in America where his estate was put up for sale. Offered a baronetcy, he declined it on the grounds of poverty. He was, however, created DCL at Oxford in 1776. He died in London in 1780.

Thomas Jefferson: Succeeded Franklin as Minister in Paris, and was appointed Secretary of State by Washington in 1789. He became Vice-President of the United States in 1797 and in 1801 the third President. He retired in 1809 and died at Monticello, the house in Virginia which he designed himself, on 4 July 1826, the same day as John Adams.

George Johnstone: On his return to England after the failure of the peace commission he became a vociferous, cantankerous, and far from knowledgeable supporter of the government. He was appointed commodore in 1779, but his subsequent career in the Navy was notably unfortunate. He died in 1787 with the reputation of being a 'noted duellist'.

Augustus Keppel, First Viscount Keppel: Dismissed from his command in 1779, he was nevertheless appointed First Lord of the Admiralty on the fall of Lord North's ministry. Already in poor health, however, he died in 1786 after an unsuccessful attempt to recuperate at Naples.

Henry Knox: Succeeded Washington as Commander-in-Chief of the American Army in 1783, and became Secretary of War in 1785. He retired in 1795 to his estate in Maine, where he died in 1806.

Wilhelm, Baron von Knyphausen: Returned in 1782 to Germany where he was appointed Military Governor of Kassel. He died there in 1800.

Tadeusz Kościuszko: Returning to Poland after the war, he became one of the heroes of the nationalist movement. He established a provisional government after defeating the Russians at Raclawice, but was himself defeated at Maciejowice in 1794. Having lived for a time in England, then in America, he settled in France, where he became a farmer, and afterwards in Switzerland. He died at Solothurn in 1817 after the horse he was riding fell over a precipice.

Marquis de Lafayette: Returned to France in 1782, taking with him some American earth in which to be buried, and was promoted *maréchal de camp*. He was appointed Commander of the National Guard of Paris in 1789, resigning in 1791. After the overthrow of the monarchy, he defected to the Austrians. Returning again to France in 1802, he spent a period of rustic retirement on his Lagrange estate during the First Empire before being elected deputy for the Sarthe, which he represented until 1824. In the 1830 revolution he was once more appointed Commander of the National Guard and died in 1834.

Arthur Lee: Elected to the Virginia House of Delegates in 1781 and was a delegate to the Continental Congress from 1782 to 1784. Retiring to Lansdowne, his Virginian estate, in 1789, he died three years later.

Charles Lee: Retired in 1779 to his estate in the Shenandoah valley where he lived as a recluse, breeding horses and dogs. He died alone in a tavern in Philadelphia at the age of fifty-one in 1782. 'I desire most earnestly,' he wrote in his will, 'that I may not be buried in any church, or church-yard, or within a mile of any Presbyterian or Anabaptist meeting-house; for since I have resided in this country, I have had so much bad company while living, that I do not chuse to continue it when dead.'

Henry ('Light Horse Harry') Lee: Became Governor of Virginia in 1791, and from 1799 to 1801 served in the United States House of Representatives. He was imprisoned for debt after speculating unsuccessfully in landed property, and was badly hurt in a riot in Baltimore where he had come to the defence of an unpopular newspaper editor. His health seriously impaired, he died in 1818 on his way back from a visit to the West Indies.

Richard Henry Lee: Remained a leading member of Congress until his retirement in 1792. He died at Chantilly, Virginia two years later.

Benjamin Lincoln: Became Secretary of War in 1781 and Lieutenant-Governor of Massachusetts in 1788. From 1789 to 1809 he was Collector for the port of Boston, where he died in 1810.

Francis Marion: From 1782 to 1790 served in the Senate of South Carolina, and died in that state in Berkeley County in 1795.

Daniel Morgan: Commanded the federal troops sent into Western Pennsylvania in 1794 to suppress the Whiskey Rebellion, an uprising of farmers against the liquor tax. A Federalist representative in Congress during 1797–9, he died at Winchester, Virginia in 1802.

William Moultrie: Appointed Governor of Georgia in 1785 and served in that office until 1787 and from 1792 to 1794. He died at Charleston in 1805.

Charles O'Hara: A prisoner in America until his exchange in 1782, he served first in Gibraltar and then at Toulon, where he was again captured. Exchanged for the Comte de Rochambeau, he was promoted general in 1798 and appointed Governor of Gibraltar where he died, an extremely rich man, in 1802, leaving his fortune to his two mistresses and their respective children.

Thomas Paine: Received a grant of money and a farm from Congress in 1785, but in 1787 returned home to England where he published *The Rights of Man*. Elected to the French National Convention, he annoyed Robespierre by proposing that Louis XVI should be offered asylum in America. He was imprisoned during the Terror of 1794 but escaped the guillotine; and in 1802, still blaming Washington for not having come to his rescue while imprisoned in Paris, he returned to America where, as the author of *The Age of Reason*, his advocacy of deism, he was not well received. He died in New York City in 1809.

Peter Parker: Became Commander-in-Chief at Jamaica in 1777 and returned to England in 1782, taking with him the Comte de Grasse and other French officers as prisoners. Promoted admiral in 1787 and admiral of the fleet in 1799, he was Commander-in-Chief at Portsmouth from 1793 to 1799. He died in London in 1811.

Hugh, Lord Percy: His return home to England, 'disgusted with Howe', as Horace Walpole put it, marked the end of his active military career, though he was promoted general in 1793. He succeeded his father as second Duke of Northumberland of the third creation in 1786, and died in 1817.

Robert Pigot: Promoted lieutenant-general in 1782, he died at his family's home in Staffordshire in 1796 without having further distinguished himself.

Casimir (Kazimierz) Pulaski: Wounded at Savannah in 1779, he died on his way to Charleston aboard the *Wasp*.

Francis, Lord Rawdon: In compliance with the terms of an uncle's will, took the surname of Hastings in addition to his own, and in 1793 succeeded his father as second Earl of Moira. He became Governor General of India in 1813 and Marquess of Hastings in 1817. Resigning from this post in 1821, he was Governor of Malta from 1824. He died off Naples in 1826 on board HMS *Revenge*, having requested that his right hand be cut off after his death and preserved until it could be placed in his widow's coffin.

Paul Revere: Appointed to command Castle William in Boston harbour in 1776; after the war, not having further distinguished himself, he returned to his business enterprises. His rolling mill at Canton, Massachusetts provided the sheet copper for several ships of the United States Navy. He died at Boston in 1818.

James Robertson: Appointed Commander-in-Chief in Virginia in May 1781, but returned to New York on learning that Cornwallis's commission superseded his own. He returned to England in 1782 and died in London six years later.

Comte de Rochambeau: Sailed home to France in 1783; and in 1791 was appointed to the command of the Army of the North. Imprisoned during the Terror, he escaped the guillotine and was created a Marshal of France in 1803. He died in Vendôme in 1807.

George Rodney: Defeated a Spanish fleet off Cape St Vincent in January 1780 and captured seven ships of the French fleet, as well as the Comte de Grasse, in an action off Dominica in

April 1782. Raised to the peerage on his return home, he died in London in 1792.

John Montagu, Earl of Sandwich: Upon the fall of Lord North's administration, retired into a private life which was rendered particularly unhappy by the murder of his beloved mistress by a clergyman whose offer of marriage she had declined. He died in London in 1792 three weeks before Lord Rodney.

John Simcoe: Appointed the first Lieutenant-Governor of Upper Canada in 1791. On his return to England, he was appointed to the command at Plymouth; then, in 1806, Commander-in-Chief in India, but died at Exeter before he could take up the appointment.

John Stark: Promoted major-general in 1783, he died at Manchester, New Hampshire, in 1822.

Frederick William, Baron von Steuben: After the war, settled in New York where his extravagant way of life led to his incurring heavy debts, even though he had been granted large sums of money as well as 16,000 acres of land. In 1790 he was given an annuity for life of $2500. He died near Remsen, New York in 1794.

John Sullivan: Fought against the Six Nations in 1779 and defeated the Iroquois and their allies under the Mohawk chief Joseph Brant (Thayendanegea) at Newtown, New York. He became Governor of New Hampshire in 1786 and was United States district judge from 1789 to 1795, the year of his death in Durham, New Hampshire.

Thomas Sumter: Served in the House of Representatives from 1789 to 1793 and 1797 to 1801, and in the Senate from 1801 to 1810. The last surviving general officer of the war, he died in South Carolina at the age of ninety-seven in 1832.

Banastre Tarleton: Returned to England on parole in 1782, the year in which Reynolds' celebrated portrait of him was painted for his mother, and became Member of Parliament for Liverpool in 1790. He lived for several years with the notoriously exhibitionistic actress Mary Robinson, formerly mistress of his friend, the Prince of Wales. His ungenerous and vainglorious *History of the Campaigns of 1780 and 1781 in the Southern Provinces of North America* was published in 1787. He died in Shropshire in 1833, having been promoted general in 1812.

George Washington: Became first President of the United States in 1789 and died at Mount Vernon in 1799.

Anthony Wayne: Appointed Commander-in-Chief of the American Army in 1791 and in 1794 defeated the Northwest Indian Confederation at the Battle of Fallen Timbers in Ohio. He subsequently (1795) negotiated the Treaty of Greenville, by which the Indians surrendered to the United States most of Ohio and large parts of Illinois, Michigan and Indiana. He died in Pennsylvania in 1796.

BIBLIOGRAPHY

Manuscript Sources

Diary of Lieutenant Anthony Allaire, State Historical Society of Wisconsin, Madison

Amherst Manuscripts, Kent Archives Office

David Avery Papers, Connecticut Historical Society, Hartford

Barcroft Letters, Lancashire Record Office

John Barr's Journal, Library of Congress, Washington

William Barton Collection, New Jersey Historical Society, Newark

Boucher Papers, East Sussex Record Office

Buckinghamshire Letters, Norfolk Record Office

Buckle Manuscripts, West Sussex Record Office

Burgon MSS, Devon Record Office

Camden Manuscripts, Kent Archives Office

Letters of Guy Carleton, first Baron Dorchester, Huntington Library, San Marino

Clerke Letters, Bedfordshire Record Office

Congreve Papers, Staffordshire Record Office

Crosier Papers, Essex Record Office

Diaries of Captain John Davis, Schenectady, NY

Denbigh Archives, Warwickshire Record Office

Lyman Copeland Draper Collection, State Historical Society of Wisconsin, Madison

Extracts from the journal of a corporal serving with Captain Hendrick's riflemen from Pennsylvania, Sandwich Papers

Feilding Papers, Warwickshire Record Office

FitzWilliam (Burke) Papers, Northamptonshire Record Office

Peter Force Papers, Library of Congress, Washington

Thomas Gage Papers, William L. Clements Library, Ann Arbor

Gage Papers, East Sussex Record Office

Gardner Letters, Hertfordshire Record Office

Horatio Gates Papers, New York Public Library

Grafton Manuscripts, Suffolk Record Office

Great Britain Army Collection, 1770–1782, William L. Clements Library, Ann Arbor

Simon Griffin Papers, Yale University Library, New Haven

Grimston Papers, Humberside Record Office

Hamilton-Dalrymple of North Berwick Muniments, Scottish Record Office

Herrick Manuscripts, Leicestershire Record Office

Diary of Dr West Hill, New England Historic and Genealogical Society, Boston

Journal of Dr Estes Howe, New York Public Library

Diary of William Jenison, Historical Society of Pennsylvania, Philadelphia

Legge Papers, Staffordshire Record Office

Records of the Leicestershire Regiment, Leicestershire Record Office

The Lexington and Concord Collection, William L. Clements Library, Ann Arbor

Lonsdale Manuscripts, Cumbria Record Office

Manchester Papers, Cambridgeshire Record Office

Diary of Joseph Merriam, Boston Public Library

Murray of Murraythwaite Muniments, Scottish Record Office

Journal of John Peebles, 42nd Regiment, in the Cunningham of Thorntoun Muniments, Scottish Record Office

Percy Papers, Northumberland Record Office

Phelps Collection, Somerset Record Office

Polhill-Drabble Collections, Kent Archives Office

Military journal and commonplace book

of Richard Pope, 47th Regiment, Huntington Library, San Marino

Reeve Letters in the manuscripts of Sir George Howard, Buckinghamshire Record Office

Robertson of Kindeace Muniments, Scottish Record Office

Rockingham Letters in the Ramsden Archive, West Yorkshire Archive Service, Leeds

Records of the Royal Sussex Regiment, West Sussex Record Office

Hartley Russell Papers, Berkshire Record Office

Schoff Revolutionary War Collection, William L. Clements Library, Ann Arbor

Seafield Muniments, Scottish Record Office

John Graves Simcoe Collection, William L. Clements Library, Ann Arbor

Stanhope of Chevening Manuscripts, Kent Archives Office

Ezra Stiles's Diary, Library of Congress, Washington

Diary of Thomas Sullivan, Historical Society of Pennsylvania, Philadelphia

Ephraim Squire's Journal, Library of Congress, Washington

J. M. Toner Papers, Library of Congress, Washington

Trumbull Manuscripts, Berkshire Record Office

Earl of Verulam MSS, Bedfordshire Record Office

Published Sources

ABBALT, William (ed.), *Memoirs of Major-General William Heath* (New York, 1901)

ALDEN, John R., *General Gage in America: His Role in the American Revolution* (Baton Rouge, 1948)

—— *General Charles Lee, Traitor or Patriot* (Baton Rouge, 1951)

—— *The South in the Revolution 1763–89* (Baton Rouge, 1957)

—— *The American Revolution, 1775–1783* (New York, 1963)

ALDRIDGE, Alfred Owen, *Benjamin Franklin* (Philadelphia and New York, 1965)

ALLAN, Herbert S., *John Hancock* (New York, 1948)

ALLEN, Robert S., *The Loyal Americans* (Ottawa, 1983)

ANDERSON, Troyer S., *The Command of the Howe Brothers during the American Revolution* (New York and London, 1936)

ANDRÉ, John, *Journal* (ed. Henry Cabot Lodge, 2 vols, Boston, 1903)

ANDREWS, Stuart, 'Classicism and the American Revolution', (*History Today*, vol. 37, January 1987)

ARNOLD, Isaac N., *The Life of Benedict Arnold* (London, 1980)

ATKINSON, C. T., 'British Forces in North America' (*Journal of the Society for Army Historical Research*, vols 16 and 19)

AUGER, Helen, *The Secret War of Independence* (New York, 1955)

AYER, A. J., *Thomas Paine* (London, 1988)

BAILYN, Bernard, *The Ideological Origins of the American Revolution* (Cambridge, Mass., 1967)

—— *The Ordeal of Thomas Hutchinson* (Cambridge, Mass., 1975)

BAKELESS, John, *Turncoats, Traitors and Heroes* (New York, 1959)

BAKER, Norman, *Government and Contractors: The British Treasury and War Supplies, 1775–1783* (London, 1971)

BALDERSTON, Marion and David Syrett (eds), *The Lost War: Letters from British Officers during the American Revolution* (New York, 1975)

BANCROFT, George, *History of the United States of America* (6 vols, Boston, 1876)

BANGOR, Thomas Williams (ed.), *The Revolutionary Journal of Colonel Jedutha Baldwin* (Bangor, 1906)

BANGS, Edward (ed.), *Journal of Lt. Isaac Bangs* (Cambridge, Mass., 1890)

BARNES, G. R., and J. H. Owen (eds), *The Private Papers of John, Earl of Sandwich, 1771–82* (4 vols, London, 1932–8)

BARRINGTON, Shute, *Political Life of Viscount Barrington* (London, 1814)

BARROW, Sir John, *Life of Richard, Earl Howe* (London, 1835)

BASS, Robert D., *The Green Dragoon* (New York, 1957)

BAXTER, James Phinney, *The British Invasion of the North . . . with the Journal of Lt. William Digby* (Albany, NY, 1887)

BEMIS, Samuel Flagg, *The Diplomacy of the American Revolution* (Bloomington, Indiana, 1957)

BERNIER, Olivier, *Lafayette* (New York, 1983)

BILL, Alfred Hoyt, *The Campaign of Princeton, 1776–1777* (Princeton, 1948)

BILLIAS, George Athan (ed.), *George Washington's Generals* (New York, 1964)

—— *George Washington's Opponents* (New York, 1969)

BINNEY, J. E. D., *British Public Finance and Administration, 1774–1792* (Oxford, 1959)

BIRD, Harrison, *The March to Saratoga* (London, 1963)

BIRNBAUM, Louis, *Red Dawn at Lexington* (Boston, 1986)

BLANCHARD, Claude, *Journal of 1780–83* (Albany, 1867)

BOATNER, Mark M., *Encyclopaedia of the American Revolution* (New York, 1976)

BOLTON, Charles K., *The Private Soldier under Washington* (New York, 1902)

—— (ed.) *Letters of Hugh, Earl Percy, from*

Boston and New York, 1774–76 (Boston, 1902)

BONWICK, Colin, *English Radicals and the American Revolution* (Chapel Hill, 1977)

BOOTH, Christopher C., 'Taxation no Tyranny' (*Johnson Society Transactions*, 1988)

BOWEN, Catherine Drinker, *John Adams and the American Revolution* (Boston, 1950)

BOWLER, R. Arthur, *Logistics and the Failure of the British Army in America 1775–1783* (Princeton, New Jersey, 1975)

BOYLAN, Brian Richard, *Benedict Arnold* (New York, 1973)

BRADLEY, J. E., *Popular Politics and the American Revolution in England* (Macon, 1986)

BREWER, John, *Party Ideology and Popular Politics at the Accession of George III* (New York, 1976)

BRIDENBAUGH, Carl, *The Spirit of '76: The Growth of American Patriotism Before Independence* (New York, 1975)

The British in Boston: Being the Diary of Lt. John Barker of the King's Own Regiment (Cambridge, Mass., 1924)

BRODIE, Fawn M., *Thomas Jefferson* (New York, 1985)

BROGAN, Hugh, *Longman History of the United States of America* (London, 1985)

BROOKE, John, *King George III* (London, 1972)

BROWN, Gerald Saxon, *The American Secretary: The Colonial Policy of Lord George Germain, 1775–1778* (Ann Arbor, 1963)

BROWN, Lloyd A. and Howard H. Peckham, *Revolutionary War Journals of Henry Dearborn, 1775–83* (new edition, Freeport, 1969)

BROWN, Wallace, *The Good Americans* (Boston, 1965)

BULLION, John L., *A Great and Necessary Measure: George Grenville and the Genesis of the Stamp Act, 1763–65* (Columbia, 1983)

BURT, A. L., *Guy Carleton, Lord Dorchester, 1724–1808* (London, 1955)

BUTTERFIELD, Herbert, *George III, Lord North and the People* (London, 1949)

CALHOON, Robert McCluer, *The Loyalists in Revolutionary America, 1760–1781* (New York, 1973)

CARP, E. Wayne, *To Starve the Army at Pleasure: Continental Army Administration and American Political Culture, 1775–1783* (Chapel Hill, 1984)

CARRINGTON, Henry B., *Battles of the American Revolution, 1775–83* (New York, 1876)

DE CHASTELLUX, Marquis de, *Travels in North America in the Years 1780, 1781 and 1782* (2 vols, New York, 1968)

CHRISTIE, Ian R., *The End of North's Ministry, 1780–82* (London, 1958)

—— *Wilkes, Wyvill and Reform, The Parliamentary Reform Movement in British Politics, 1760–1785* (London, 1962)

—— *Crisis of Empire: Great Britain and the American Colonies, 1754–1783* (London, 1966)

—— *Wars and Revolutions: Britain 1760–1815* (London, 1982)

CHRISTIE, Ian R. and Benjamin W. Labaree, *Empire or Independence, 1760–1776: A British-American Dialogue* (New York, 1976)

CLARK, Jonathan, 'The American Revolution: A War of Religion' (*History Today*, vol. 39, December 1989)

CLARK, Ronald W., *Benjamin Franklin* (New York, 1983)

CLARK, William Bell (ed.), *Naval Documents of the American Revolution* (Washington, 1976)

CLOSEN, Baron Ludwig von, *The Revolutionary Journal of 1780–83* (Chapel Hill, 1958)

COUNTRYMAN, Edward, *The American Revolution* (New York, 1985)

CRARY, Catherine, *The Price of Loyalty* (New York, 1973)

CRÈVECOEUR, J. Hector St John, *Letters from an American Farmer* (new edition, London, 1912)

CUMBERLAND, Richard, *The Character of the Late Lord Sackville* (London, 1785)

—— *Memoirs* (London, 1807)

CUMMING, William P. and Hugh F. Rankin, *The Fate of a Nation: The American Revolution through Contemporary Eyes* (London, 1975)

CUNLIFFE, Marcus, *George Washington* (London, 1958)

CURTIS, Edward E., *The Organisation of the British Army in the American Revolution* (New Haven, 1926)

DALLAS, C. Donald, *The Spirit of Paul Revere* (Princeton, NJ, 1944)

DANN, John C. (ed.), *The Revolution Remembered: Eyewitness Accounts of the War of Independence* (Chicago, 1980)

DAVIS, Burke, *The Cowpens-Guilford Courthouse Campaign* (Philadelphia, 1962)

—— *The Campaign That Won America* (New York, 1970)

—— *George Washington and the American Revolution* (New York, 1975)

DE PUY, Henry W., *Ethan Allen and the Green-Mountain Heroes of '76* (New York, 1970)

DEFONBLANQUE, Edward Barrington, *Political and Military Episodes . . . of the Eighteenth Century, Derived from the Life and Correspondence of the Rt. Hon. John Burgoyne* (London, 1876)

DERRY, John, *English Politics and the American Revolution* (New York, 1976)

DEUX-PONTS, Count William de, *My Campaigns in America* (Boston, 1868)

DONOGHUE, Bernard, *British Politics and the American Revolution, The Path to War, 1773–1789* (Chicago, 1956)

DRAPER, Lyman C., *King's Mountain and its Heroes* (Cincinnati, 1881)

DULL, Jonathan R., *A Diplomatic History of the American Revolution* (New Haven, 1985)

DUPUY, R. Ernest and Trevor N. Dupuy, *The Compact History of the Revolutionary War* (New York, 1963)

DWYER, William M., *The Day is Ours!* (New York, 1983)

EAST, Robert A. and Jacob Judd (eds), *The Loyalist Americans: A Focus on Greater New York* (Tarrytown, NY, 1975)

EELKING, Max von, *The German Allied Troops in the North American War of Independence* (trans. J. G. Rosengarten, London, 1893)

EVANS, G. N. D., *Allegiance in America: The Case of the Loyalists* (Reading, Mass., 1969)

FLEMMING, Thomas, *Beat the Last Drum* (New York, 1963)

—— *1776: The Year of Illusion* (New York, 1975)

FLEXNER, James Thomas, *The Traitor and the Spy: Benedict Arnold and John André* (New York, 1953)

—— *Washington: The Indispensable Man* (Boston, 1974)

FONER, Eric, *Tom Paine and Revolutionary America* (London and New York, 1976)

FORBES, Esther, *Paul Revere and the World He Lived In* (Boston, 1942)

FORMAN, James D., 'King's Mountain' (*Men at Arms*, vol.3, no.3, May/June, 1981)

FORTESCUE, The Hon. J. W., *A History of the British Army* (vol. VII, London, 1911)

—— *The Correspondence of King George III from 1760 to December 1783* (6 vols, London, 1927–8)

FRASER, Henry S. (ed.), *The Memoranda of William Green, Secretary to Vice-Admiral Marriot Arbuthnot* (Providence, 1924)

FREEMAN, Douglas S., *George Washington: A Biography* (completed by J. A. Carroll and Mary W. Ashworth, 7 vols, New York, 1948–57)

FRENCH, Allen, *The First Year of the American Revolution* (Boston and New York, 1937)

FREY, Sylvia R., *The British Soldier in America: A Social History of Military Life in the Revolutionary Period* (Austin, Texas, 1981)

GALLATIN, Gaspard, *Journal of the Siege of Yorktown* (Washington, 1931)

GERSON, Noel B., *Light Horse Harry* (New York, 1966)

GIPSON, Lawrence Henry, *The Coming of the Revolution, 1763–1775* (New York, 1962)

GLOVER, Michael, *General Burgoyne in Canada and America* (London, 1976)

GOTTSCHALK, Louis, *Lafayette and the Close of the American Revolution* (Chicago, 1942)

GOTTSCHALK, Louis and Donald Lach, *Toward the French Revolution: Europe and America in the 18th-Century World* (New York, 1973)

GREENE, George W., *The Life of Nathanael Greene* (3 vols, New York, 1871)

GREENE, Jack P., *The Reinterpretation of the American Revolution, 1763–1789* (New York, 1968)

—— (ed.), *The American Revolution: Its Characters and Limits* (New York, 1987)

GREENE, Jack P. and J. R. Poole (eds), *Colonial British America: Essays in the New History of the Early Modern Era* (Baltimore, 1984)

GRIFFITH, Samuel B., *In Defense of the Public Liberty* (New York, 1976)

GROSS, Robert A., *The Minutemen and Their World* (New York, 1976)

GRUBER, Ira D., *The Howe Brothers and the American Revolution* (Chapel Hill, 1974)

GUEDALLA, Philip, *Fathers of the Revolution* (New York, 1926)

Guide to British Historical Manuscripts in the Huntington Library (San Marino, Calif., 1982)

HADDEN, James M. A., *Journal Kept in Canada and upon Burgoyne's Campaign in 1776 and 1777* (new edition, Freeport, 1970)

HANNAY, David, *Rodney* (London, 1891)

HARGREAVES, Reginald, *The Bloody Backs: The British Serviceman in North America and the Caribbean, 1655–1783* (London, 1968)

—— 'Washington's Drill Master' (*Army Quarterly*, vol. LXXXXI)

HAYTER, Tony (ed.), *An Eighteenth-Century Secretary at War: The Papers of William, Viscount Barrington* (London, 1988)

HEALE, M. J., *The American Revolution* (London, 1986)

HENRY, J. J., *Account of Arnold's Cam-*

paign against Quebec (New York, 1968)

HIGGINGBOTHAM, Don, *Daniel Morgan, Revolutionary Rifleman* (Chapel Hill, 1961)

—— *The War of American Independence* (New York, 1971)

HIGGINS, W. Robert (ed.), *The Revolutionary War in the South: Power, Conflict and Leadership: Essays in Honor of John Richard Alden* (Durham, North Carolina, 1979)

HOERDER, Dirk, *Crowd Action in Revolutionary Massachusetts, 1765–1780* (New York, 1977)

HOFSTADTER, Richard, *America in 1750; A Social Portrait* (London, 1972)

HOOD, Dorothy, *The Admirals Hood* (London, 1942)

HOULDING, J. A., *Fit For Service: The Training of the British Army, 1715–1795* (Oxford, 1981)

HOWSON, Gerald, *Burgoyne of Saratoga* (New York, 1979)

HUTCHINSON, P. E. (ed.), *Diary and Letters of Thomas Hutchinson* (London, 1886)

JAFFE, Irma B., *John Trumbull: Patriot Artist of the American Revolution* (Boston, 1975)

JAMES, Coy H., *Silas Deane* (East Lansing, Mich., 1975)

JAMES, William M., *The British Navy in Adversity: A Study of the War of Independence* (New York, 1926)

JELLISON, Charles A., *Ethan Allen* (Syracuse, NY, 1969)

JENSEN, Merrill Monroe, *The Founding of a Nation: A History of the American Revolution, 1763–1776* (London and New York, 1968)

—— *The American Revolution within America* (New York, 1974)

JOHANSEN, Bruce E., 'Mohawks, Axes and Taxes: Images of the Amer-

ican Revolution' (*History Today*, vol. 35, April 1985)

JOHNSTON, Henry P., *The Yorktown Campaign and the Surrender of Cornwallis, 1781* (New York, 1881)

JONES, Thomas, *History of New York during the Revolutionary War* (London, 1879)

'Journal of a Physician on the Expedition against Canada in 1776' (*The Pennsylvania Magazine of History and Biography*, vol. LIX, no. 4, October 1935)

KATCHER, Philip, *Rebels and Loyalists: The Revolutionary Soldier in Philadelphia* (Philadelphia, 1976)

—— 'Loyalist Militia in the War of American Independence' (*Journal of the Society for Army Historical Research*, vol. LIV, no. 219, 1976)

KENNEDY, Paul M., *The Rise and Fall of British Naval Mastery* (New York, 1976)

KEPPEL, Thomas, *Life of Augustus, Viscount Keppel* (London, 1842)

KETCHUM, Richard M., *The Winter Soldiers* (Garden City, NY, 1973)

—— *Decisive Day: The Battle for Bunker Hill* (Garden City, NY, 1974)

LABAREE, Benjamin, *The Boston Tea Party* (New York, 1964)

LAMB, Roger, *An Original and Authentic Journal of Occurrences During the Late American War* (Dublin, 1803)

—— *A Memoir of His Own Life* (Dublin, 1811)

LANDERS, H. L., *The Battle of Camden* (Washington, 1929)

LANGGUTH, A. J., *Patriots: The Men Who Started the American Revolution* (New York, 1988)

Letters from America, 1776–1779: Being Letters of Brunswick, Hessian and Waldeck Officers with the British Armies during the

Revolution (trans. Ray W. Pettergill, Boston and New York, 1924)

LEWIS, Charles Lee, *Admiral de Grasse and American Independence* (Annapolis, 1945)

LEWIS, Michael, *History of the British Navy* (London, 1957)

LINCOLN, James Minor (ed.), *The Papers of Captain Rufus Lincoln of Wareham, Mass.* (new edition, New York, 1971)

LOSSING, Benson J., *Pictorial Field Book of the Revolution* (new edition, Rutland, Vermont, 1972)

LOWELL, Edward J., *The Hessians and Other German Auxiliaries of Great Britain in the Revolutionary War* (New York, 1884)

LUARD, John, *History of the Dress of the British Soldier* (London, 1852)

LUNT, James, *John Burgoyne of Saratoga* (London, 1976)

LUTNICK, Solomon, *The American Revolution and the British Press, 1775–83* (Columbia, 1967)

LYDENBERG, Harry M. (ed.), *Archibald Robertson . . . His Diaries and Sketches in America, 1762–80* (New York, 1930)

MACINTYRE, Captain Donald, *Admiral Rodney* (London, 1963)

MACKENZIE, Frederick, *Diary of Frederick Mackenzie, Giving a Daily Narrative of his Military Service . . . 1775–1781* (2 vols, Cambridge, 1930)

MACKESY, Piers, *The War for America, 1775–1783* (London, 1964)

MAHAN, A. T., *The Influence of Sea Power upon History* (Boston, 1890)

—— *Major Operations of the Navies in the American War of Independence* (London, 1913)

MAHON, R. J., *Life of General the Hon. James Murray* (London, 1921)

MAIER, Pauline, *The Old Revolutionaries: Political Lives in the Age of Samuel Adams* (New York, 1980)

Manuscript Sources in the Library of Congress for Research on the American Revolution (Washington, DC, 1975)

MARSHALL, Christopher, *Extracts from the Diary of Christopher Marshall* (New York, 1969)

MARSHALL, Peter and Glynn Williams (eds), *The British Empire Before the American Revolution* (London, 1980)

MARSTON, J. F., *King and Congress: The Transfer of Political Legitimacy* (Princeton, 1987)

MARTELLI, George, *Jeremy Twitcher: A Life of the Fourth Earl of Sandwich* (London, 1962)

MATTHEWS, William, *American Diaries in Manuscript: A Descriptive Bibliography* (University of Georgia Press, Athens, 1974)

Memoirs of the Life of the Late Charles Lee, Esq. . . . . Second in Command in the Service of the United States of America during the Revolution (London, 1792)

MERLANT, Joachim, *Soldiers and Sailors of France in the American War of Independence* (New York, 1920)

MIDDLEKAUFF, Robert, *The Glorious Cause: The American Revolution, 1763–1789* (New York, 1982)

MILLER, John C., *Triumph of Freedom, 1775–1783* (Boston, 1948)

MOORE, George H., *The Treason of Charles Lee* (Port Washington, NY, 1976)

MORGAN, Edmund S. (ed.), *The American Revolution: Two Centuries of Interpretation* (Englewood Cliffs, NJ, 1965)

MORGAN, Edmund S. and Helen M. Morgan, *The Stamp Act Crisis: Prelude to Revolution* (Chapel Hill, 1953)

MORISON, S. E. (ed.), *The American*

Revolution: Sources and Documents (London, 1923)

MORRIS, Richard B. (ed.), *The Era of the American Revolution* (New York, 1939)

MOULTRIE, William, *Memoirs of the American Revolution* (New York, 1802)

MUMBY, Frank Arthur, *George III and the American Revolution* (London, 1924)

MUNDY, Major General G. B., *Life and Correspondence of Lord Rodney* (London, 1830)

MYERS, Albert Cook (ed.), *Sally Wister's Journal* (Philadelphia, 1902)

MYERS, William S. (ed.), *The Battle of Monmouth by the Late William S. Stryker* (Princeton, 1927)

NAMIER, L. B. [Sir Lewis], *England in the Age of the American Revolution* (London, 1930)

NAMIER, Sir Lewis and John Brooke, *Charles Townshend* (London, 1964)

Narrative of John Blatchford detailing his sufferings in the Revolutionary War (New York, 1865)

NEDELHAFT, Jerome J., *The Disorders of War: The Revolution in South Carolina* (Orono, Maine, 1981)

NELSON, Paul David, *General Horatio Gates* (Baton Rouge, 1976)

NELSON, W. H., *The American Tory* (London, 1961)

NICKERSON, Hoffman, *The Turning Point of the Revolution, or Burgoyne in America* (Boston and New York, 1928)

NORTON, Mary Beth, *The British Americans: The Loyalist Exiles in England, 1774–1789* (Boston, 1972)

O'BRIEN, Harriet E. (ed.), *Paul Revere's Own Story* (Boston, 1929)

OLSON, Alison Gilbert, *Anglo-American Politics, 1660–1775: The Relationship between Parties in England and Colonial America* (New York, 1973)

OLSON, Alison Gilbert and Richard Maxwell Brown (eds.), *Anglo-American Political Relations, 1765–1775* (New Brunswick, 1970)

PARES, Richard, *George III and the Politicians* (London, 1953)

PATTERSON, Samuel White, *Horatio Gates: Defender of American Liberties* (New York, 1941)

PEARSON, Michael, *Those Damned Rebels: Britain's American Empire in Revolt* (London, 1972)

PECKHAM, Howard H. (ed.), *The War for Independence: A Military History* (Chicago, 1958)

—— *Memoirs of the Life of John Adlum in the Revolutionary War* (Chicago, 1968)

—— *The Toll of Independence* (Chicago, 1974)

Personal Recollections of Captain Enoch Anderson (Wilmington, 1896)

PETERSON, Merrill D., *Thomas Jefferson and the New Nation* (London and New York, 1970)

PETTENGILL, R. W. (ed.), *Letters from America 1776–79* (New York, 1924)

POTTER, Janie, *The Liberty We Seek: Loyalist Ideology in Colonial New York and Massachusetts* (Cambridge, 1983)

PRESTON, J. H., *A Gentleman Rebel: The Exploits of Anthony Wayne* (London, 1928)

Proceedings of a Board of General Officers . . . Respecting Major John André (Philadelphia, 1780)

RANKIN, Hugh F. (*see also* CUMMING, William P. *and* SCHEER, George F.)

—— *The American Revolution* (London, 1964)

—— *The North Carolina Continentals* (Chapel Hill, 1971)

READ, R. B., *The Life and Times of General John Graves Simcoe* (Toronto, 1901)

REID, Loren, *Charles James Fox: A Man for the People* (London, 1969)

RIEDESEL, Madame de, *Letters and Journals Relating to the American Revolution* (ed. Max von Eelking, trans. W. L. Stone, New York, 1867)

RIEDESEL, Major-General Friedrich von, *Memoirs, Letters and Journals* (ed. Max von Eelking, trans. W. L. Stone, New York, 1868)

RITCHESON, C. R., *British Politics and the American Revolution* (London, 1954)

ROBSON, Eric (ed.), *Letters from America, 1773–80: Being the Letters of a Scots Officer, Sir James Murray* (Manchester, 1951)

—— *The American Revolution in its Political and Military Aspects* (London, 1955)

ROCHAMBEAU, Comte de, *Memoirs . . . Relative to the War of Independence* (New York, 1971)

ROGERS, Horatio (ed.), *A Journal Kept in Canada upon Burgoyne's Campaign in 1776 and 1777* (London, 1884)

ROSS, Charles (ed.), *The Correspondence of Charles, 1st Marquess Cornwallis* (London, 1859)

ROSSIE, Jonathan G., *The Politics of Command in the American Revolution* (Syracuse, NY, 1975)

ROYSTER, Charles, *A Revolutionary People at War: The Continental Army and American Character, 1775–1783* (Chapel Hill, 1979)

RUDÉ, George, *Hanoverian London, 1714–1808* (London, 1971)

SABINE, William H. W. (ed.), *The New York Diary of Lt. Jabez Fitch* (New York, 1954)

—— *Historical Memoirs . . . of William Smith, Historian of the Province of New York* (2 vols, New York, 1958)

SAINSBURY, John, *Disaffected Patriots: London Supporters of Revolutionary America, 1769–82* (Ontario, 1987)

SCHEER, George F. and Hugh F. Rankin, *Rebels and Redcoats* (New York, 1957)

SCHWARTZ, Barry, *George Washington: The Making of an American Symbol* (London, 1988)

SCOTT, Duncan C., *John Graves Simcoe* (London, 1905)

SERLE, Ambrose, *see* TATUM, Edward H.

SHY, Arlene Phillips (assisted by Barbara A. Mitchell), *Guide to the Manuscript Collections of the William L. Clements Library* (3rd edition, Boston, Mass., 1978)

SHY, John, *Toward Lexington* (Princeton, New Jersey, 1965)

—— *A People Numerous and Armed: Reflections on the Military Struggle for American Independence* (New York, 1976)

SIMMONS, R. C., *The American Colonies from Settlement to Independence* (New York, 1976)

SMELSER, Marshal, *The Winning of Independence* (Chicago, 1973)

SMITH, Page, *A New Age Now Begins: A People's History of the American Revolution* (2 vols, New York, 1976)

SMITH, Paul H., *Loyalists and Redcoats: A Study in British Revolutionary Policy* (Chapel Hill, 1964)

—— *English Defenders of American Freedoms, 1774–78* (Washington, 1972)

SOSIN, Jack M., *The Revolutionary Frontier, 1765–1783* (New York, 1967)

SPINNEY, David, *Rodney* (Annapolis, 1969)

STANLEY, F. G. (ed.), *For Want of a Horse: Journal of an Officer Who Served* with Carleton and Burgoyne (Sackville, New Brunswick, 1961)

STEDMAN, Charles, The History of the Origin, Progress and Termination of the American War (2 vols, Dublin, 1794)

STONE, William L., Letters of Brunswick and Hessian Officers during the American Revolution (Albany, 1891)

STRACHAN, Hew, British Military Uniforms, 1768–96 (London, 1975)

STRYKER, William Scudder, The Battles of Trenton and Princeton (Boston, 1898)

SYRETT, David, Shipping and the American War, 1775–1783 (London, 1970); see also BALDERSTON, Marion

TARLETON, Banastre, A History of the Campaigns of 1780 and 1781 in the Southern Provinces of North America (Dublin, 1787)

TATUM, Edward H. (ed.), The American Journal of Ambrose Serle, Secretary to Lord Howe (San Marino, Calif., 1940)

THACHER, James, Military Journal of the American Revolution (New York, 1823)

THAYER, Theodore G., Nathanael Greene, Strategist of the American Revolution (New York, 1960)

THOMAS, P. D. G., British Politics and the Stamp Act Crisis: The First Phase of the American Revolution, 1763–1767 (Oxford, 1975)

TORNQUIST, Karl Gustav, The Naval Campaigns of Count de Grasse (Philadelphia, 1942)

TOWNSHEND, Charles Harvey, The British Invasion of New Haven (New Haven, 1879)

Travels through the Interior Parts of America in a Series of Letters by an Officer [Thomas Anburey] (2 vols, London, 1791)

TREACY, M. F., Prelude to Yorktown, the Southern Campaigns of Nathanael Greene (Chapel Hill, 1963)

TREVELYAN, Sir George O., The American Revolution (4 vols, London and New York, 1905–12)

TRUMBULL, John, Autobiography (ed. T. Sizer, New Haven, 1953)

TUCHMAN, Barbara W., The First Salute (New York, 1988)

TUCKER, Robert W. and David C. Hendrickson, The Fall of the First British Empire: Origin of the War of Independence (Baltimore, 1982)

UHLENDORF, Bernard A. (ed.), The Siege of Charleston with an Account of the Province of South Carolina (Ann Arbor, 1938)

—— Revolution in America: Confidential Letters and Journals, 1776–1784, of Adjutant-General Major Baurmeister (New Brunswick, NJ, 1957)

VALENTINE, Alan, Lord George Germain (Oxford, 1962)

—— Lord North (2 vols, Oxford, 1967)

—— The British Establishment, 1760–1784: An Eighteenth-Century Biographical Dictionary (Oxford, 1970)

VAN DOREN, Carl, Benjamin Franklin (New York, 1938)

—— Secret History of the American Revolution (New York, 1941)

VAN TYNE, Claude H., The Loyalists in the American Revolution (New York, 1902)

WALLACE, Willard M., Appeal to Arms: A Military History of the American Revolution (New York, 1951)

—— Traitorous Hero: The Life and Fortunes of Benedict Arnold (New York, 1954)

WALPOLE, Horace, Letters (ed. W. S. Lewis, 39 vols, London, 1937–79)

WARD, Christopher, *War of the Revolution* (ed. J. R. Alden, 2 vols, New York, 1952)

WHITE, R. J., *The Age of George III* (London, 1968)

WHITRIDGE, Arnold, 'Baron von Steuben: Washington's Drillmaster' (*History Today*, vol. 26, 1976)

WICKWIRE, Franklin and Mary, *Cornwallis and the War of Independence* (London, 1970)

WILDES, Harry Emerson, *Anthony Wayne, Trouble Shooter of the American Revolution* (New York, 1941)

WILLCOX, William B., *Portrait of a General: Sir Henry Clinton in the War of Independence* (New York, 1964)

—— (ed.), *The American Rebellion: Sir Henry Clinton's Narrative of His Campaigns* (New Haven, 1954)

WILLS, Garry, *Inventing America* (Garden City, New York, 1978)

WRAXALL, Sir Nathaniel, *Historical and Posthumous Memoirs* (5 vols, London, 1884)

WRIGHT, Esmond, *Washington and the American Revolution* (London, 1957)

—— *A Tug of Loyalties: Anglo-American Relations, 1765–85* (London, 1975)

—— *The Fire of Liberty* (London, 1984)

—— 'Benedict Arnold and the Loyalists' (*History Today*, vol. 36, Oct. 1986)

—— (ed.), *Causes and Consequences of the American Revolution* (Chicago, 1966)

WRIGHT, Louis B., *Everyday Life in Colonial America* (London, 1965)

WROTTESLEY, Hon. George, *The Life and Correspondence of Field Marshal Sir John Burgoyne Bt.* (2 vols, London, 1873)

ZOBEL, Hiller B., *The Boston Massacre* (New York, 1971)

ILLUSTRATION CREDITS

Black and White Section

Boston Massacre *The Mansell Collection*

Rebels hurling tea into harbour *The Mansell Collection*

Frederick, Lord North *The National Portrait Gallery*

John Burgoyne *The National Portrait Gallery*

Major-General Sir Henry Clinton *Courtesy of the R. W. North Art Gallery, Shreveport, Louisiana*

Lord George Germain *Mary Evans Picture Library*

'Bunker's Hill' *Fotomas Index*

'Six-Pence a Day' *Fotomas Index*

The destruction of the statue of King George III *Fotomas Index*

Fire in New York *Fotomas Index*

General Burgoyne's camp *Fotomas Index*

'The Conference between the Brothers How . . .' *British Museum*

Self-portrait of Major John André *Mary Evans Picture Library*

'The Count de Rochambeau . . .' *British Museum*

The battle of Guilford *Anne S. K. Brown Military Collection, Brown University Library*

'The Savages let loose . . .' *Fotomas Index*

Caricature of May 1782 *Fotomas Index*

British, German and American soldiers *Anne S. K. Brown Collection*

Colour Section

'The Bloody Massacre' *The Metropolitan Museum of Art, Gift of Mrs Russell Sage, 1909*

Paul Revere *The Museum of Fine Arts, Boston, Gift of Joseph W., William B. and Edward H. R. Revere*

Sir William Howe directing the evacuation of Boston *Anne S. K. Brown Military Collection*

Benedict Arnold *Anne S. K. Brown Military Collection*

The death of Brigadier-General Richard Montgomery *Copyright Yale University Art Gallery*

The Royal Navy bombards Fort Moultrie *Anne S. K. Brown Military Collection*

Thomas Jefferson presenting the

Declaration of Independence *Copyright Yale University Art Gallery*

George Washington *The Metropolitan Museum of Art, Gift of Collis P. Huntington, 1896*

The Americans defeating a British brigade at Princeton *Anne S. K. Brown Military Collection*

'The Battle of Germantown' *Courtesy of the Valley Forge Historical Society*

The British surrender at Saratoga *Copyright Yale University Art Gallery*

Christmas Day 1777 *Anne S. K. Brown Military Collection*

The siege of Charleston *Anne S. K. Brown Military Collection*

Banastre Tarleton *The National Gallery*

INDEX

Acland, Lady Harriet, 198

Acland, John Dyke, 193, 198

Adams, Abigail, 64

Adams, John: defends redcoats after Boston Massacre, 14, 15; history, 14–15, 339; personality, 15; and Washington, 66–7; and Tom Paine, 114; and American independence, 115; and Jefferson, 115; Declaration of Independence, 116; and Gates, 215; wrangles among military officers, 216; United States boundaries, 337

Adams, Samuel: personality, 12, 19; denounces Townshend Acts, 12; Harvard, 14; Boston Massacre, 15; and British policy in America, 19; Boston Tea Party, 20; and Boston's predicament, 25; Gage and, 27; receives warnings, 29; in Lexington, 31; opinion of Lee, 70; and American independence, 115; and Gates, 215; later history, 339

Alexander, William, 123

Allaire, Anthony, 265, 284–5

Allen, Ethan, 40–41, 56, 239, 339

Amherst, Jeffrey Amherst, Baron, 209, 211, 252

Anburey, Thomas: on scalping, 167; engagement at Hubbardtown, 170; Battle of Bemis Heights, 185–6; and Saratoga surrender, 196; prisoner of war camps, 199; taken prisoner, 258

André, John: personality and ability, 252–3; Clinton's go-between with Arnold, 293; capture, 294–5; execution, 296–7

Arbuthnot, Marriot: personality, 251, 268; and Clinton, 251, 268, 269, 316; to assume command, 256; brings reinforcements, 257; reinforcements for, 291; and

proposed raid on Philadelphia, 323; later history, 339

arms: artillery at Ticonderoga, 41, 71, 169; of New Hampshire Regiment, 51–2; of rebels at Bunker Hill, 52, 53; Washington enlarges stocks of ammunition, 71; flintlocks, 81–2, 182; in use by British Army, 81–3; breech-loading rifle, 82, 263; captured at Kipp's Bay, 126; bayonets, 150, 187, 271, 305; at Paoli massacre, 158–9; Battle of Bennington, 177; French supply Americans with, 207; French at Savannah, 244; sabres, 271; cannon and mortars at Yorktown, 327, 329

Arnold, Benedict: history, 39, 339; appearance and personality, 40; raid on Ticonderoga fort, 40–41; and Quebec, 89, 92, 93; builds fleet on Lake Champlain, 97; his agents spread rumours, 180; Battle of Bemis Heights, 183, 184–5, 186; Saratoga engagement, 192, 193, 198; extravagant life in Philadelphia, 292; turns traitor, 292; and André, 293, 294; his rewards, 295; Clinton sends into Virginia, 298–9; in command at Petersburg, 314; unpopularity, 314; and Clinton, 323; on diversionary raid, 324; and Prince William Henry, 326

Arnold, Margaret, née Shippen, 292

Ashe, Major-General, 242

Augusta, Georgia, 242, 275, 280, 284, 299, 310

Baddeley, Mary, 59–60, 155

Balcarres, Alexander Lindsay, 6th Earl of, 193, 339–40

Baltimore, Cecil Calvert, 2nd Baron of,

Bancroft, Edward, 208–9
Barber, Francis, 22
Barcroft, Ambrose, 9
Barras, Jacques-Melchior St-Laurent, Comte de, 324
Barré, Isaac, 9, 10, 77
Barrington, Hon. Samuel, 234
Barrington, William Barrington, 2nd Viscount, 48, 78
Basking Ridge, New Jersey, 145–6
Baum, Frederick, 175–7
Bayer, George, 234
Beaumarchais, Pierre-Augustin Caron de, 207
Bemis Heights, New York, Battle of, 182–7
Bennington, New York, Battle of, 175–8
Bernard, Francis, 4
Bill of Rights (1869), xx
Bingham, Sir Charles, later 1st Earl of Lucan, 260
Bingley, Robert Benson, Baron, 46
blacks: American descendants of African, 5; lack of rights, 7; slavery, 8, 242, 265; drummer at Boston Massacre, 12–13; Skene's servants, 166; and Loyalists, 235; informer at Savannah, 240; at work in Savannah, 244; Lord George Gordon and, 260; sent for sale in West Indies, 272–3; at siege of Ninety-Six, 311; and fortification of Yorktown and Gloucester, 321
Bose, General, 306
Boston, Massachusetts: violence against taxation, 3–5, 12–14; East India Company's tea despatched to, 19–20; tarring and feathering, 21; Acts to control, 25; sympathy for, 25–6; British, 33, 48, 55, 59, 60–62, 73; rebels, 37, 67, 70–71, 73–4; burial of officers, 55; condition of countryside around, 70; British evacuate, 74; British prisoners of war in, 199; mob attacks French sailors, 233–4
Boston Massacre, 12–15
Boston Tea Party, 19–21; Revere, 28
Boswell, James, 23
Bowater, John, 61, 75, 77–8, 123, 268, 333
Braddock, Edward, 65
Brandywine, Pennsylvania, Battle of, 156–8, 263

Breed's Hill, Massachusetts, 50, 51, 52, 74
Breymann, Lieutenant-Colonel von, later General von, 177, 183, 193
British armies in America: detachment leaves Boston, 29; Lexington skirmish, 31–3; Concord skirmish, 33, 37; march back to Boston, 33; conduct of troops, 34–5; and rebel raid on Ticonderoga fort, 40–41; deficient in supplies, 48; early days in Boston, 48; attack on Charlestown, 51; Battle of Bunker Hill, 52–5; period of idleness and frustration, 72; rebel reports of behaviour, 76; Hanoverian mercenaries for, 85; men for Canada, 94; raiding party at Long Bridge, 102–3; losses at Sullivan's Island, 109; troops under Howe's command, 119, 121; battle for New York, 122–3, 125–31 passim; losses at Princeton, 150; Philadelphia, 155, 159; Battle of Brandywine, 156, 158; Battle of Germantown, 160–61; Burgoyne's, 163, 167, 170; Battle of Bemis Heights, 183–7; Saratoga engagement, 192–4; prisoners of war after surrender at Saratoga, 199; volunteers from English and Scottish provinces, 206; Battle of Monmouth Court House, 223–5, 226; Volunteers of Ireland, 240, 252; status of loyalist officers, 251; ruthless raids, 254; losses at siege of Charleston, 267; inept administration, 334
British Army: loyalist regiments in, 79; in poor shape, 80–81; regiments distinguished by class, 81; weapons, 81–3; sale of commissions, 83; musicians, surgeons, chaplains, 83; uniform, 84; punishment, 84; recruitment, 84–5; regular regiments raised, 259
British Legion: Tarleton to command, 263; raids by, 264; at Charleston, 266; at Waxhaw, 271; Battle of Camden, 277, 278; disperses Sumter's force, 278–9; reconnoitring expedition under Hanger, 280; Fishdam Ford, 288; Blackstock's Plantation, 288; Battle of Hannah's Cowpens, 299; Battle of Guilford Court House, 304, 306
Brown, Joseph, 157–8
Brunswick, Ferdinand, Duke of, 86, 211
Buford, Abraham, 270, 271

Bunker Hill, Massachusetts: British troops spend night on, 37; militiamen prepare positions, 51; Battle of, 52–5; Rawdon at, 60; Pigot at, 232

Burgoyne, Lady Charlotte, 46, 48

Burgoyne, John: history, 46–7; proposes negotiations with rebels, 48; to America, 49; Charlestown, 50, 51, 52; on Battle of Bunker Hill, 53–4; and Gage, 53; favours New York as offensive position, 56; advice on strategy, 55–6, 57; leaves for England, 57, 100; self-confidence, 63, 163; *The Blockade of Boston*, 72; baggage allowance, 94; cannot postpone departure for Canada, 94; and Indians, 97, 166, 172; and Carleton, 97–8, 136–7, 162–3; appointed to Canadian command, 138; plan for Canadian campaign, 138–41 *passim*; General Orders to his army, 163–4; Germain and, 180–81; question of Howe's co-operation with, 164–5; temperament, 166; confidence in his army, 166; takes Ticonderoga, 167, 169; pursues Americans, 170; march hampered by felled trees, 171; and Loyalists, 171; on anti-British feeling by rebels, 171–2; death of Jane McCrea, 174; his forces weakened, 174; needs baggage animals, 175; losses at Bennington, 178; recreations, 178; transport of his possessions, 178; Battle of Bemis Heights, 183–4, 186; and use of bayonet, 187; and Clinton, 189, 191–2, 210; attacks Hudson River forts, 190; Saratoga engagement, 192–3, 195–7; toasts Washington, 199; later history, 340

Burgoyne, John senior, 46

Burke, Edmund: and Stamp Act, 10; and Burgoyne's warning to Indians, 172–3; and news of Burgoyne's surrender, 201; supports Wilkes, 206; and French threat, 230; Lord George Gordon and, 260

Buttrick, Major, 33

Byrd, William, 66

Byron, Hon. John, 229, 230, 231, 340

Camden, Charles Pratt, 1st Earl, 8, 10

Camden, South Carolina: Cornwallis's headquarters in, 276; Battle of, 276–8; Rawdon at, 288, 308; garrison left at, 299

Campbell, Sir Archibald, 239, 240–41, 262, 340

Campbell, William, 281, 284

Canada: Quebec Act, 26–7, 88; weakness of garrisons, 89; bateaux and gunboats for, 93–4; army raised for, 94; government's handling of Canadian command, 136; Burgoyne's plan of campaign, 138–9; Saratoga engagement, 193; Britain and defence of, 209; change in attitude to Britain, 257

Canadians: few in Burgoyne's army, 163; Battle of Bennington, 175; Battle of Bemis Heights, 185

Cane, William, 260, 261

Carleton, Sir Guy, *later* 1st Baron Dorchester: history, 88, 340; and American attack on Canada, 89; Quebec, 89–90, 92; reinforcements, 93, 95; and Burgoyne, 97–8, 136–7, 162–3; fleet assembled on Lake Champlain, 97, 98; withdraws into Canada, 100; antipathy for Germain, 136, 162; government's lack of confidence in, 137; personality, 138; demand to be recalled, 138; Howe writes to, 164–5; Ticonderoga garrison, 174; North and, 211; replaces Clinton, 336

Carleton, Thomas, 136

Carlisle, Frederick Howard, 5th Earl of, 210, 240

Catawba River, 299, 303

Catherine the Great, Empress of Russia, 85

Chambly, Quebec, 89, 97

Champlain, Lake, New York/Vermont, 93, 97, 98–9, 163

Charles II, King, 5

Charles Edward Stuart, Prince, 103

Charleston, South Carolina: tea agents, 20; commerce, 56; defences and fort, 105; British attack on Sullivan's Island, 106–9; celebrations, 109; riot against French, 233; Prevost calls for surrender, 243; Germain proposes attack on, 262, 264; Lincoln's strength at, 265; British fleet passes Fort Moultrie, 265; destruction of American camp at Biggins Bridge, 266; bombardment and surrender, 266–7; garrison at, 299

Charlestown, Massachusetts, 28, 29, 37, 49, 52

Charlotte, North Carolina, 279, 280, 299
Chatham, 1st Earl of, see Pitt, William
Chesapeake Bay, Maryland, 155, 165, 319,
  324, 326
Chesapeake River, 159–60, 254
Chesney, Alexander, 281–2
Christie, Gabriel, 136
Clerke, Sir Francis Carr, 184, 193
Clinton, Admiral the Hon. George, 43–4
Clinton, George (American Governor of
  New York), 190
Clinton, Sir Henry: aristocratic family, 43;
  history, 44, 45–6, 340; personality, 45, 46,
  138, 142, 235, 323; and attack on
  Charlestown, 50, 51; Battle of Bunker
  Hill, 54, 55, 57; and Duke of Newcastle,
  57–8; worried about condition of the
  army, 58; life in Boston, 59; and Mary
  Baddeley, 59–60; and General Howe, 60,
  62–3, 133, 141–2, 165, 188, 210–11; to
  command expedition to North Carolina,
  62–3; realistic view of Loyalists, 104;
  interest in natural history, 105; invasion of
  South Carolina, 105; and attack on
  Sullivan's Island, 106, 107; blames Parker,
  109; battle for New York, 119, 122–3;
  occupies Rhode Island, 131; leaves for
  England, 134; and Canadian command,
  135, 137, 138; and Charleston, 137–8, 140,
  262, 264, 266–8, 329; knighthood, 140;
  1777 campaigns, 140, 141; and
  Cornwallis, 142, 256–7, 268–9, 279, 308,
  315–19 passim, 324–6 passim, 340; expense
  on guests, 155; and Burgoyne, 165, 189,
  190, 210; British diplomat's advice to, 210;
  asks to be relieved of command, 210, 249,
  256, 262; Commander-in-Chief, 211;
  evacuation of Philadelphia, 222–3; Battle
  of Monmouth Court House, 223, 225;
  embarks army for New York, 226; blames
  Pigot, 233; and Georgia campaign, 235;
  letters of complaint to London, 235,
  248–9; in comfortable circumstances, 248;
  gloomy and dispirited, 248, 250; need for
  reinforcements, 249, 253, 262; personal
  relationships, 250–52; and Arbuthnot,
  251, 268, 269, 316; protests against
  ruthless raiding, 254; sends force to
  Haldimand, 257; increasing difficulties,
  257, 262; guerrilla raids, 262–4;

proclamation to differentiate between
  Loyalists and rebels, 267–8, 272; and
  Washington, 291; and capture of West
  Point, 292, 293; Rodney and, 293, 323;
  and death of André, 297; orders to Arnold
  and Phillips, 314; government attitude to,
  321–2; and Graves, 323; sails to
  Chesapeake Bay, 330–31; Carleton
  replaces, 336
Colden, Cadwallader, 9
Collier, Sir George, 125, 255, 256, 262, 340
Collins, James, 283
colonies: administration, 5; in frequent
  dispute, 8; Stamp Act Congress, 9;
  taxation after repeal of Stamp Act, 10–11
colonists: day to day life, 6–7; Stamp Act, 7,
  8; Gage on, 55
Concord, Massachusetts, 28, 33
Congress: Washington delegate to, 66;
  American Navy, 67; execution of
  deserters, 68; and American independence,
  115; Philadelphia headquarters, 135; agrees
  to Washington's requests, 145; flees from
  Philadelphia, 159; British government
  and, 210; Washington disillusioned with,
  257–8; Congress money, 258; Greene and,
  291
Congreve, William, 127
Connecticut, 5
Continental Congress, see Congress
Conway, Henry Seymour, 254, 336, 340
Conway, Thomas, 215–16, 341
Copley, John Singleton, 16, 28
Cornwallis, Charles Cornwallis, 2nd Earl
  later 1st Marquess: arrives in North
  Carolina, 105; battle for New York, 122,
  131; supports Howe, 142; marches to
  Trenton, 148–9; personality, 149; Battle of
  Brandywine, 156, 157–8; reputation, 211;
  foraging expeditions, 234; returns to
  England, 249; death of his wife, 256; and
  Clinton, 256–7, 268–9, 315, 340; left in
  command at Charleston, 268; and
  Arbuthnot, 269; orders to Tarleton, 270;
  problem of keeping order in South
  Carolina, 274–5; Battle of Camden,
  276–7; sends Tarleton after Sumter, 278;
  invasion of North Carolina, 279, 280; ill,
  287, 288, 330; withdrawal to Winnsboro,
  287; Battle of Hannah's Cowpens, 302–3;

campaign in Carolinas, 298–9, 303–4; Battle of Guilford Court House, 304–6; leaves North Carolina for Virginia, 315; and Lafayette, 315–16, 317; military proposals to Clinton, 315; plans for offensive campaign in Virginia, 315, 316, 317; despatches from Clinton, summer 1781, 316, 318–19; replies to Clinton, 317; defeats Wayne at James River, 317–18; Old Point Comfort, 319; fortification of Yorktown, 319, 321; in urgent need of reinforcements at Yorktown, 321, 324, 325, 326; and attack on Yorktown, 327, 328; surrender, 329, 330; later history, 341

Cortlandt, Philip van, 327

Craig, James, *later* Sir James, 299, 308

Crown Point, New York, 97, 99, 136, 137

Cruger, John Harris, 281, 299, 310

Dartmouth, William Legge, 2nd Earl of, 25, 87

Davidson, William Lee, 279

Davie, William R., 279

Dawes, William, 29

Deane, Silas, 207–8, 216, 341

Declaration of Independence, 115–17, 210, 317

DeKalb, Johann, 212, 218, 277, 278

Delancy, James, 153

Delaware River: Washington's troops cross, 148; frozen, 149; to be opened to British shipping, 159, 161; farewell regatta for Howe, 220; d'Estaing's fleet off, 231

Dempster, George, 260

Derby, Sir Edward Stanley, 11th Earl of, 46

deserters: pardon offered to, 57; Washington seeks execution of, 68; Indians, 180; scalping of, 191; German, 191, 199, 226; prisoners of war, 199; from rebel army, 131, 213, 240, 258; rebel deserters return, 218; seasonal desertion to farms, 233; Irish, 240; punishment of, 290; militiamen, 306

Devonshire, Georgiana Cavendish, Duchess of, 202

Dickinson, John, 11

Digby, Robert, 325, 326

Digby, William, 166–7, 185, 186, 196, 197

disease: diarrhoea, 276; dysentery, 62; fever, 253, 257, 314; gaol fever, 231; itch, 212; malaria, 97; scurvy, 62, 230; smallpox, 93, 97, 151; sunstroke, 311

Douglas, Captain, 95

Drummond, Duncan, 137–8, 249, 250, 251–2

Dulany, Daniel, 8

Dulany, Walter, 79

Dunmore, John Murray, 4th Earl of, 101–2, 341

Eden, William, *later* 1st Baron Auckland, 210, 339

Emerson, William, 70, 71

Erskine, Sir William, 122, 142

Estaing, Charles-Hector, Comte d': history, 227, 341; British frigate watches his movements, 230; ships leave New York for Rhode Island, 231; his fleet dispersed off Rhode Island, 232; operations in the West Indies, 234; engages British at mouth of Savannah, 244; summons Prevost to surrender, 244; assault on Savannah, 245–6; sails home, 247

Eutaw Springs, South Carolina, Battle of, 312

Fairfax, Thomas Fairfax, 6th Baron, 65, 66

Fairfax, William, 65

Fairfield, Connecticut, 254

Farquier, Francis, 26

Feilding, William, 72, 77

Ferguson, Patrick: personality, 263; breech-loading rifle, 263; and Tarleton, 266; Battle of King's Mountain, 280–81, 282; corpse, 283

Fitzgerald, John, 150

Florida, 6

Fordyce, Charles, 102

Fort Edward, New York, 175

Fort Stanwix, New York, 179, 180

Fort Watson, South Carolina, 308

Fox, Charles James: and American War, 86, 202–3, 334; reduces government to silence, 203–4; George III and, 205; dress, 210; and French threat, 230; on Battle of Guilford Court House, 306; scornful of government optimism, 333

France (*see also* French with rebel army *and* navy, French): Seven Years' War, xviii; supports American revolution, 204; Franco-American alliance, 207; clandestine assistance to America, 208–9; Britain and, 209; trade with American south, 262; impending revolution, 337

Franklin, Benjamin: London agent for colonies, 22; and Johnson, 23; and Tom Paine, 113, 114; and American independence, 115; and Committee of Secret Correspondence, 207; in Paris, 208; United States boundaries, 337; later history, 341

Franklin, William, 79, 253

Fraser, Simon: commands regiments for Canada, 94; engagement at Hubbardtown, 170; Battle of Bemis Heights, 183, 184–5, 186; Saratoga engagement, 192; funeral, 198

French with rebel army: sent against Rhode Island, 231; unpopularity, 233–4; at Savannah, 244; losses after Savannah, 246; and siege of Yorktown, 321; Franco-American army on march for the Chesapeake, 322; musicians at Yorktown, 329; British surrender, 330

Gage, Hon. Thomas: and American affairs, 24; Governor of Massachusetts, 25; alarmed by growing unrest, 27; precautionary measures, 27–8; in Boston, 37; government loses faith in, 42; inactivity, 48; and Prescott, 49; assault on Charlestown, 50–51; on colonists, 55; opinion of Boston as British base, 55; and rebel deserters, 57; and Graves, 59; sails home, 60; later history, 341

Galloway, Joseph, 27

Gambier, James, 250, 341

Garrick, David, 47

Gates, Horatio: history, 69, 341; personality, 69, 183; joins Washington, 148; letter of protest to Burgoyne, 173; Battle of Bemis Heights, 183–6 *passim*; British deserters warn, 194; Burgoyne's surrender, 195–6, 329; courteous conduct, 197–9; toasts George III, 197; writes to Rockingham, 200; office of Commander-in-Chief, 215, 216; advances on Clinton's army, 223; the

march to Camden, 275–6; Battle of Camden, 276, 278; reputation, 278

George I, King, 43

George II, King, 88

George III, King: and Grenville, xvii–xviii, 10; frugality, xviii; and Stamp Act, 10; and North, 18, 204–6, 336; and American affairs, 24, 25; and Howe brothers, 43; Queen's Light Dragoons, 47; and American War, 80, 203, 209; army recruitment, 85; and Catherine the Great, 86; Paine's attack on, 114; American grievances against, 116; statue destroyed in New York, 121; and Percy, 135; and Howe's plan for move against Philadelphia, 135; and Carleton, 136, 137; and Clinton, 138, 140, 249

Georgia, campaign in, 235, 239–47

Germain, Lord George, *later* 1st Viscount Sackville: history, 86, 341; appearance and personality, 87; American Secretary, 87; and American War, 93; orders bateaux and gunboats, 93–4; and proposed and actual assaults on Charleston, 106, 262, 264; and General Howe, 131, 135, 139, 164, 165; and Carleton, 136, 137, 162; and Clinton, 137, 140, 211, 248–9, 321; and optimistic view of 1777 campaign, 141; duel, 210; and Sandwich, 228; and French threat, 229, 230; proposed attack on New Orleans, 256, 261–2; and Cornwallis, 298, 316; news of surrender, 333; dropped from North's administration, 335

Germans: Hanoverian mercenaries, 85; for Canada, 94, 97; lose equipment, 94; among Howe's troops, 119, 121; behaviour on Staten Island, 121–2; battle for New York, 122, 124–6 *passim*, 129–31 *passim*; in Burgoyne's army, 140, 163; immigrant regiment in rebel army, 148; at Trenton, 148, 150; Battle of Brandywine, 156; Battle of Bennington, 175–6, 177; equipment and clothing, 176; Battle of Bemis Heights, 185, 186; deserters, 191, 199; Saratoga engagement, 192, 193; and British, 198; under Campbell's command, 239; at Savannah, 244; ruthless raids by, 254; Battle of Guilford Court House, 304, 305, 306

Germantown, Pennsylvania, Battle of, 160–61

Gibbon, Edward, 22, 334

Gladstone, Sir John, 338

Gloucester, New Jersey, 319, 321, 328

Gloucester, William Henry, Duke of, 45

Gordon, Lord George, 260, 261

Graham, Joseph, 279

Grant, James, 122, 234, 341

Grasse, François-Joseph-Paul, Marquis de Grasse-Tilly, Comte de, 316, 323, 324, 326, 345

Graves, Samuel, 59

Graves, Thomas, *later* Baron Graves: brings reinforcements for Arbuthnot, 291; succeeds Arbuthnot, 323; and French fleet, 324; back to New York, 325; and aid for Cornwallis, 325–6; sails to Chesapeake Bay, 330–31; later history, 341–2

Green, Henry, 299

Greene, Nathanael: battle for New York, 125–6, 130; Battle of Brandywine, 156, 158; criticism of, 216; serves under Sullivan, 231–2, 233; and d'Estaing, 232; resigns as quartermaster-general, 291; and André's execution, 296; in command in North Carolina, 298; Arnold sent to harass, 298–9; men fit for duty, 299; in retreat before Cornwallis, 303; Battle of Guilford Court House, 304–5, 306; Battle of Hobkirk's Hill, 309; siege of Ninety-Six, 311; Battle of Eutaw Springs, 311, 312; on his defeats, 313; later history, 342

Green Mountain Boys, 40, 41, 56

Grenville, George, xvii, xviii, xix, 10

Grey, Charles: Paoli Massacre, 159; discourages attack by Howe on Washington, 222; attack on Baylor's harassing party, 234–5; returned to England, 249; and Clinton, 322; later history, 342

Gridley, Richard, 39

Guilford Court House, North Carolina, Battle of, 304–7

Haldimand, Sir Frederick, 257

Hamilton, Alexander, 296, 327, 342

Hamond, Sir Andrew Snape, 265

Hancock, John: background, 12; Boston Tea Party, 20; receives warnings, 29; in Lexington, 31; his Boston house, 59; personality, 66; post of military commander, Boston, 66; commands militiamen against Rhode Island, 231; later history, 342

Hanger, Hon. George, *later* 4th Baron Coleraine, 280, 342

Hannah's Cowpens, South Carolina, Battle of, 299–302

Harcourt, Hon. William, *later* 3rd Earl Harcourt, 146

Harvey, Edward, 58, 78, 140, 306

Hays, Mary Ludwig, 225

Heister, Philip von, 122, 211

Henry VIII, King, 64

Henry, Patrick, 8, 115, 281, 342

Herkimer, Nicholas, 179

Hickey, William, 260

Hillsboro, North Carolina, 275, 303–4

Hinrichs, Johann, 264

Hobkirk's Hill, South Carolina, Battle of, 309

Hood, Sir Samuel, *later* Viscount Hood, 323, 324, 325

Hotham, Como, 190

Howard, John Eager, 300, 302

Howe, George Augustus Howe, 3rd Viscount, 43

Howe, Richard Howe, 4th Viscount, *later* Earl: inarticulateness, 42; and American trade, 42–3; to treat with rebels, 119; entertains Adams and members of Congress, 125; congratulated, 131, 132; and Sandwich, 228; his ships disposed off New York, 231; engages French off Rhode Island, 232; returns to England, 249; Clinton and, 250; sobriety, 250; later history, 342

Howe, Robert, 240

Howe, William, *later* 5th Viscount Howe: sent to America, 42; sympathetic feelings for Americans, 42, 43; soldier, 43; Clinton and, 46, 60, 62–3, 133, 135, 140, 141, 142, 188, 210–11; negotiations with rebel leaders, 48, 119; plan for attack on Charlestown, 50; Battle of Bunker Hill, 53, 55; and Baddeley, 59; Commander-in-Chief, 60; and evacuation

Howe, William – *cont.*
  of Boston, 72, 74; contemplates attacking
  rebels, 73; in Halifax, 74–5; request for
  more troops, 93, 135; troops under, 119,
  121; battle for New York, 122–3, 126,
  128–31 *passim*; American opinion of, 124;
  inaction, 124, 125, 128, 222; and New
  York fire, 127, 128; congratulated, 131,
  132; criticizes Rhode Island operation, 134;
  and Mrs Loring, 135, 155, 222; and 1777
  campaign, 135, 141; and Burgoyne's
  Canadian campaign, 139; invasion of
  Pennsylvania, 139, 141; capture of Lee,
  147; sea-route to Philadelphia, 155, 165;
  Battle of Brandywine, 156; army enters
  Philadelphia, 159; Paoli Massacre, 158;
  problem of supplies, 159–60; Battle of
  Germantown, 160–61; suggests resigning
  command, 161; Germain ignorant of his
  movements, 164; question of co-operation
  with Burgoyne, 164–5, 181; demands to
  be recalled, 211; farewell party for, 220;
  and Ferguson's corps of riflemen, 263;
  later history, 342–3
Hudson River: strategic importance to
  British, 121; Washington's forts on, 121;
  British ships in, 125; Fort Lee, 127, 129,
  131; Fort Washington, 127–30 *passim*;
  Dobb's Ferry, 130; battle for New York,
  130; Clinton suggests Howe uses, 165;
  Clinton attacks forts on, 190; foraging
  expeditions up, 234; frozen over, 264,
  290
Huger, Isaac, 266
Hutchinson, Thomas, 4–5, 20, 24, 343

independence, American (*see also* Declaration
  of Independence), 114–15, 205, 337
Indians: Proclamation Line, 6; British and,
  57; Burgoyne and, 78, 166, 172; carry
  messages between American commanders,
  92; Dunmore and, 102; and Burgoyne's
  Canadian campaign, 138, 139; in
  Burgoyne's army, 163, 167; dancing,
  166–7; scalping, 167, 191; depredations
  by, 172–4, 175; create terror, 175; Battle
  of Bennington, 175, 176, 177; join St
  Leger, 179; losses at Fort Stanwix,
  179–80; alarmed by rumours, 180; Battle
  of Bemis Heights, 185; in American

  employment, 191; Saratoga engagement,
  192; Treaty of Granville, 346
Irish: Volunteers of Ireland, 239–40, 252,
  309; form associations of armed men, 259;
  Battle of Camden, 277

Jay, John, 337
Jasper, Sergeant, 108, 109
Jefferson, Thomas, 26, 115–17, 207, 343
Johnson, Samuel: attitude to slave owners,
  22; *Taxation no Tyranny*, 22–3; dislike of
  Americans, 23–4; life guardsmen and
  felons, 84; and American independence,
  117, 118; and American 'patriots', 260
Johnstone, George, 210, 343
Jones, John Paul, 259

Kemble, Stephen, 252
Keppel, Augustus, *later* Viscount Keppel,
  228, 230, 258, 343
Kershaw, Joseph, 276, 278, 287–8
King's Mountain, South Carolina, Battle of,
  281–3
Knox, Henry, 41, 71, 295, 343
Knox, William, 139
Knyphausen, Baron Wilhelm von: Battle of
  Brandywine, 156–8; Battle of Monmouth
  Court House, 223; foraging expeditions,
  234; in command in New York, 264; later
  history, 343
Kościuszko, Tadeusz, 182, 299, 311, 343

Lafayette, Marie-Joseph du Motier, Marquis
  de: general respect for, 217;
  major-general, 218; Battle of Monmouth
  Court House, 223–4; sent against Rhode
  Island, 231; and d'Estaing, 232; and
  André's execution, 295; Cornwallis
  dislodges, 315–16; in pursuit of
  Cornwallis, 317; later history, 343–4
Lamb, Sergeant, 199
Lee, Arthur, 207, 208, 216, 344
Lee, Charles: history, 69, 344; appearance
  and personality, 69–70; and Washington,
  70, 145, 215; at Sullivan's Island, 107–8;
  surrenders at Basking Ridge, 145–6;
  dismay over loss of, 147; released in
  exchange of prisoners, 215; Battle of
  Monmouth Court House, 223–4;
  court-martial, 224

Lee, Henry, 254, 304, 308, 344
Lee, Richard Henry, 115, 344
Leslie, Alexander, 298, 299, 303, 304, 315
Lewis, Andrew, 66
Lexington, Kentucky: Revere warns rebel leaders at, 28–9; skirmish at, 31–2
Liberty Tree, 3
Ligonier, Sir John, later Earl Ligonier, 44–5
Lincoln, Benjamin: Battle of Bemis Heights, 182; attacks Ticonderoga, 191; appearance and personality, 242; marches towards Augusta, 242–3; assault on Savannah, 245; withdraws to Charleston, 246–7; his force at Charleston, 265; Clinton's summons to surrender, 266; exchanged for Phillips, 297; and British surrender, 330; later history, 344
Locke, John, 116
London: support for rebels in, 77; news of Declaration of Independence, 117; news of Burgoyne's surrender, 201 et seq., changing policy on American War, 209
Long Bridge, Virginia, engagement at, 102–3
Loring, Elizabeth, 135, 155, 222
Loring, Joshua, 135
Louis XIV, King of France, 115
Loyalists (see also British Legion): Hutchinson, 4–5; British support for, 56; optimistic estimate of numbers of, 63, 80, 101, 179, 235, 279; Fairfax, 66; leave Boston with Howe, 74; numbers, 78; from all classes of society, 79; regiments formed, 79; threat of rebel reprisals, 79; at Long Bridge engagement, 102; Allan MacDonald, 103; defeated at Widow Moore's Creek, 104; Clinton's realistic view of, 104; in attack on Charleston, 106; with Clinton, 141, 155; Germain's optimism over, 141; in Burgoyne's army, 163, 167, 171; on Howe's line of march, 165; Burgoyne and, 166, 171, 175; revolutionary committees intimidate, 171; treachery at Bennington, 176; join St Leger, 179; Battle of Bemis Heights, 186; Saratoga engagement, 192; British demand on behalf of, 210; in British evacuation of Philadelphia, 222–3; black slaves as, 235; at Savannah, 244; annoyed by Clinton's proclamation, 268; and rebels in South Carolina, 271–2; in North Carolina, 277; sufferings of defeated, 284–7, 288; Rugeley, 288; Battle of Hannah's Cowpens, 302; Cornwallis hopes to enlist, 303–4; Battle of Hobkirk's Hill, 309; at siege of Ninety-Six, 310; difficulties in organizing and supporting, 335

McCall, James, 300
McCrea, Jane, 173–4
MacDonald, Allan, 103
MacDonald, Flora, 103
MacIntosh, Ebenezer, 4
McKenzie, Frederick, 34
MacLean, Allan, 92
MacLean, Francis, 254, 255, 262
Magaw, Robert, 130
Maitland, Colonel, 244
Malcolm, John, 21
Marion, Francis, 279, 288, 308, 310, 344
Marjoribanks, Major, 311, 312
Marshall, Christopher, 25
Martin, Joseph Plumb, 225
Martin, Josiah, 103
Maryland, 5, 71
Massachusetts, 8, 25, 27, 43
Mawhood, Charles, 149
Mercer, Hugh, 150
militia, American: expert marksmen, 102; Connecticut, 144; New England, 231, 233; assault on Savannah, 245; bounties for enlistment, 257; after siege of Charleston, 267; Battle of Camden, 277; Battle of Hannah's Cowpens, 300, 301; North Carolina, 304; Virginia, 305
minutemen, 28
Mitchell, Edward, 30–31
money, 258
Monmouth Court House, New Jersey, Battle of, 223–5
Montagu, John, 21
Montgomery, Richard, 89, 92, 93
Montreal, Quebec, 89
Moore, John, later Sir John, 255
Morgan, Daniel: his riflemen at Battle of Bemis Heights, 182, 183; Saratoga engagement, 192; does not sell secret intelligence, 295; history, 299, 344; to threaten British at Ninety-Six, 299; Battle

Morgan, Daniel – *cont.*
  of Hannah's Cowpens, 300, 301, 302; in
  retreat before Cornwallis, 303
Morris, Staates Long, 260
Moultrie, William, 107–8, 109, 344
Murray, James, 55

Narragansett Bay, Rhode Island, 18
navy, American: created 67; flag, 71;
  dispersed at Penobscot Bay, 255
navy, British, *see* Royal Navy
navy, French: British fear effect of Toulon
  squadron in America, 229, 230; leaves
  Toulon, 227; en route for America, 230,
  316; ships leave New York for Rhode
  Island, 231; closes in on Newport, 232;
  dispersed off Rhode Island, 232;
  engagement at mouth of Savannah, 243–4;
  French and Spanish fleet in English
  Channel, 259; fleet under de Tournay in
  America, 291; engagement with British,
  324; in Chesapeake Bay, 324, 326
navy, Spanish, 259
Newcastle, Henry Fiennes Clinton, 2nd
  Duke of, 43, 44, 45, 57–8, 249
New Haven, Connecticut, 254
New Orleans, Louisiana, 256, 261–2
Newport, Rhode Island, 56, 131, 231
New York, New York (*see also* New York,
  Battle for): violence against taxation, 9,
  11; tea agents resign, 20; demonstration
  against tea imports, 21; strategic
  importance, 56; suitability as British base,
  56; Howe requests reinforcements for
  defence of, 93; statue of George III
  destroyed, 121; news of Declaration of
  Independence, 121; Clinton's garrison on
  Manhattan Island, 141; summer of 1777,
  153–5; securely defended by British fleet,
  231; Clinton, 257, 262, 293, 316, 323–4;
  Cornwallis required to send men to, 316,
  317, 319; Prince William Henry in, 326
New York, Battle for: Howe ready for
  assault on, 119, 121; Washington prepares
  defences, 121; British and German soldiers
  landed on Long Island, 121, 122; British
  casualties at Flatbush, 122; Clinton's
  successful plan of attack, 122–3; British
  popularity on Long Island, 123; Howe's
  inaction, 124, 125, 128; Washington

evacuates Brooklyn, 124; fog covers
  Washington's withdrawal, 125; rebel
  decision to abandon New York, 126;
  Washington withdraws forces to Harlem
  Heights, 126–7; British enter New York,
  127; fire devastates New York, 127–8;
  armies face each other on Manhattan
  Island, 128; Howe advances to New
  Rochelle, 128; Washington alters
  dispositions, 128–9; Battle of White
  Plains, 129; rebels surrender at Fort
  Washington, 130; British attack Fort Lee,
  131
Ninety-Six, South Carolina: Cornwallis
  sends column to march on, 270; garrison
  at, 275, 299; Ferguson seeks support from,
  281; Morgan sent to threaten, 299; siege
  of, 310–11
Norfolk, Virginia, 56, 254
North, Frederick, 2nd Earl of Guilford,
  better known as Lord North: history and
  personality, 17; appearance, 18; and
  American affairs, 24; negotiations with
  rebel leaders, 48; American Secretary, 80,
  86, 209, 335; begs to be allowed to resign,
  204–5, 230; agrees to remain in office,
  205–6; popularity, 206; conciliation with
  rebels, 209–10; and Howe, 211; and
  command of army in America, 269; news
  of surrender, 333; George III and, 336;
  announces his resignation to the House,
  336–7
Norton, Caroline, 202

Oglethorpe, James, 239
O'Hara, Charles: Battle of Guilford Court
  House, 304, 305, 306, 307; and surrender at
  Yorktown, 330; later history, 344
Oliver, Andrew, 3–4
Oliver, Peter, 15
Otis, James, 11

Paine, Thomas, 113–14, 344–5
Palmer, Richard, 13
Paoli Massacre, 158–9
Paris, Treaty of, 337
Parker, John, 31, 32
Parker, Sir Peter: history, 104, 345; keen
  for action, 105; attacks Sullivan's Island,
  106, 107; writes letter of apology, 109;

and Clinton, 131, 134, 211; Howe and, 134

Pattinson, James, 254

Peebles, John, 221

Peel, Sir Robert, 338

Pelham, Henry, 16

Penn, Sir William, 5

Penn, William, 5

Pennsylvania, 5, 8, 71

Penobscot, Maine, 254–5

Percy, Hugh, Earl, *later* 2nd Duke of Northumberland of the 3rd creation: covers withdrawal to Boston, 33; and American toughness of spirit, 35; Battle for New York, 122, 125, 130; in command on Rhode Island, 134; returns to England, 134–5, 249; later history, 345

Peters, John, 166

Petersburg, Virginia, 314, 315

Philadelphia, Pennsylvania: tea agents, 20; sympathy with Boston, 25–6; Congress, 26, 27, 66; important commercial centre, 56; Tom Paine settles in, 114; Jefferson, 115; in Burgoyne's Canadian campaign, 139; Howe, 159, 161; extravagant life under British occupation, 220–21; British evacuate, 222; Arnold's way of life in, 292

Phillips, William: and Clinton, 45, 62, 297; and American War, 80; and Burgoyne's Canadian campaign, 139; at Ticonderoga, 169; Battle of Bemis Heights, 183, 186; Saratoga engagement, 192, 193; death, 314

Pickens, Andrew, 279

Pigot, Sir Robert: at Bunker Hill, 53; in Newport, 231, 232; raiding parties to Providence, 232; pursues Sullivan, 233; returned to England, 249; and Lord Howe, 250; later history, 345

Pinckney, Thomas, 246

Pitcairn, John, 29, 32, 33, 54

Pitt, William, *later* 1st Earl of Chatham: and Grenville, xviii; and Stamp Act, 10; and American affairs, 24; on impossibility of conquering America, 201–2; George III and, 204, 205; death of, 205

Pitt, William, the younger, 76, 334

Plumb, Joseph, 290–91

Pontiac, Ottawa Indian chief, 6

Prescott, Samuel, 30

Prescott, William: military service, 39; under fire on Boston earthwork, 49; and Warren, 52; Battle of Bunker Hill, 54–5, 68

Preston, Thomas, 13, 14

Prevost, Augustin, 240–44 *passim*

Prevost, Mark, 242

Princeton, New Jersey: British brigade at, 148; Battle of, 150–51

Proclamation Line, 6, 65

Protestants, 27

Providence, Rhode Island, 18, 134, 232

provisions: local produce in Boston, 59; shortages, 61, 62, 153, 175, 191, 213, 287–8; prices, 74, 155; diet of Clinton's troops, 104, 109; for British prisoners of war, 199; Gates's army, 275, 277; Cornwallis's army, 287–8; Washington's army, 290–91; in Carolinas campaign, 304, 307, 308; at siege of Yorktown, 328; exported to British army in America, 335

Pulaski, Casimir, 216, 246, 345

Pulteney, William, 230

punishment: in British army, 63, 72, 84; in rebel army, 68, 71, 214; for desertion, 258, 290; for treason, 284

Putman, Israel: military service, 39; at Charlestown, 49–50; Battle of Bunker Hill, 54–5; on Howe, 124; stores, 190; does not sell secret intelligence, 295

Quakers, 134, 220

Quebec: white settlement encouraged, 6; Governor of, 89; Arnold commissioned to take, 89; Arnold's army's march to, 90–91; assault on, 92–3; British garrison relieved, 95; Carleton, 136; Burgoyne, 162

Quebec Act, 26, 88

Quincy, Josiah, 14, 15

Rall, Johann Gottlieb, 148

Rawdon, Francis Rawdon, Baron, *later* 1st Marquess of Hastings: at Bunker Hill, 60; and Clinton, 60, 251, 252; his supper, 62; cases of rape, 122; on reconnaissance with Cornwallis, 122; Battle for New York, 126; Volunteers of Ireland, 240, 252; Battle of Camden, 277; commands garrisons in South Carolina, 299; left behind at Camden, 308; Battle of

Rawdon – *cont.*
   Hobkirk's Hill, 308–10; at siege of
   Ninety-Six, 311; ill, 311; later history,
   345
Reeve, Richard, 16, 109
refugees, 175
Regiments: 2nd Foot Guards, 44; 3rd Foot
   (the Buffs), 311; 7th Foot, 302; 9th Foot,
   186; 10th Foot, 29; 16th Light Dragoons,
   47, 146, 223; 17th Light Dragoons, 270,
   300–1, 302; 19th Foot, 311; 20th Foot,
   185, 186; 21st Foot, 185; 23rd Fusiliers
   (Royal Welch Fusiliers), 34, 277, 304, 305;
   29th Foot, 12–16; 30th Foot, 311; 33rd
   Foot, 277; 40th Foot, 263; 42nd
   Highlanders, 131, 221; 43rd Foot, 53; 47th
   Foot, 60; 52nd Foot, 53; 53rd Foot, 188;
   60th Foot (King's American Regiment),
   246, 309; 62nd Foot, 185, 186, 199; 63rd
   Foot, 309; 64th Foot, 310; 71st Highland
   Light Infantry, 206, 261, 277, 300, 301,
   304; 72nd Highlanders, 206; 75th Foot,
   206; 82nd Foot, 255; Fraser's Highlanders,
   239
Revere, Paul, 16, 28–31 *passim*, 37, 345
Rhode Island: chartered colony, 5; Stamp
   Act, 8; Islanders' camp equipment, 70;
   Clinton, 131, 134, 257; d'Estaing's ships
   off, 231; French and Americans sent
   against, 231; French fleet dispersed off,
   232; Pigot retreats across, 233; French
   established on, 293
Richmond, Charles Lennox, 3rd Duke of,
   77, 205
Richmond, Virginia, 315–16
Riedesel, Adolf Friedrich, Baron von, 99;
   commands German regiments in Canada,
   97; engagement at Hubbardtown, 170;
   advice to Burgoyne, 175; Battle of Bemis
   Heights, 183, 185, 186; Saratoga
   engagement, 192, 193
Riedesel, Baroness von, 178, 194–5, 198
Rivoire, Apollos, 28
Robbins, John, 31
Robertson, James: and Loyalists and rebels,
   80; quoted, 123–4; and execution of
   André, 296; and Clinton, 323; advice to
   Council of War, 325; later history, 345
Robinson, Beverley, 60
Robinson, Mary, 346

Rochambeau, Jean Baptiste de Vimeur,
   Comte de: brings troops to America, 291;
   Washington consults, 293; meeting with
   Washington, 316, 322; on situation in
   America, 322; his orders, 323; and British
   surrender, 330; exchanged for O'Hara,
   344; later history, 345
Rockingham, Charles Watson-Wentworth,
   2nd Marquess of, 10, 201, 202
Rockingham, Marchioness of, 7
Rodney, Sir George Brydges, *later* 1st Baron
   Rodney: arrives in New York waters, 292;
   and Clinton, 293; opinion of Washington,
   295; despatches ships to America, 323;
   later history, 345–6
Roman Catholics, 5, 27
Royal Navy: evacuation of Boston, 74; and
   American War, 78; in state of decline,
   80–81; Germain orders bateaux and
   gunboats, 93–4; damage suffered at
   Sullivan's Island, 108–9; and Battle for
   New York, 121, 124, 125, 126, British
   flotilla captured on Lake George, 188;
   under Sandwich, 228; ships under Byron
   for America, 229; Howe's ships disposed
   off New York, 231; French capture frigate
   and storeships, 244; Sandwich and Keppel,
   258; stormy voyage to Charleston, 264;
   Graves brings fleet from England, 291;
   Rodney arrives in New York waters, 282;
   and naval base in Chesapeake Bay, 319,
   321; engagement with French fleet, 324;
   outnumbered and outgunned, 325; aid for
   Cornwallis at Yorktown, 324, 325
Rugeley, Henry, 288
Rush, Benjamin, 216
Rutledge, John, 109

Sackville, Lord, *see* Germain, Lord George
St Clair, Arthur, 169
St Leger, Barry, 139, 178–9, 180
St Lucia, West Indies, 234
Sandwich, John Montagu, 4th Earl of:
   personality, 86, 228; importance of *Isis*
   reaching Quebec, 94–5; congratulates
   Lord Howe, 131; and security of home
   waters, 227; ability, 228; Royal Navy
   under, 228; against despatch of fleet to
   America, 229–30; and Keppel, 258; fears
   assault on England, 259; later history, 346

Sandy Hook, New York, 223, 225–6, 231
Sansevoort, Peter, 179
Saratoga, New York: engagement at, 192–5;
  Burgoyne surrenders, 195–7
Savannah, Georgia: geographical position,
  239; Campbell takes, 240–41; British
  withdraw from, 242; Prevost back to, 243;
  Prevost strengthens defences, 244; under
  French bombardment, 244–5;
  Franco-American assault fails, 245–6;
  effect of British presence in, 262; garrison
  left at, 299
Savannah River, 239, 241, 242, 243, 244
scalping, 33, 167, 191
Schuyler, Philip, 183, 198, 295
Scots: immigrant colony in North Carolina,
  103; Scottish landowners create own
  regiments, 206; Highlanders at Savannah,
  240, 244; Scottish regiments at Penobscot,
  255; John Paul Jones, 259; form voluntary
  associations of armed men, 259; pipers at
  Yorktown, 329
Scott, Charles, 224
Serle, Ambrose, 127
Shaftesbury, Ashley Cooper, 1st Earl of,
  265
Shelby, Isaac, 281
Shippen, Margaret, 292
ships (see also Royal Navy): Actaeon, 108;
  Anna, 264; Apollo, 162; Bristol, 104, 107,
  108; Cerberus, 42, 43; Countess of
  Scarborough, 259; Dartmouth, 19–20; Eagle,
  119; Experiment, 107, 108; Fowey, 101;
  Gaspee, 18; George, 264; Isis, 94–5; Lively,
  49; Magdalen, 101; Maria, 167; Nancy, 21;
  Nautilus, 28; Nonsuch, 155; Pearl, 130;
  Proserpine, 230; Raisonnable, 255; Renown,
  232, 265; Richmond, 265; Roebuck, 265;
  Serapis, 259; Surprise, 95; Vulture, 293–4,
  295
Simcoe, John Graves, 263, 346
Skene, Philip, 166, 170, 176, 177
Skenesborough, New York, 169, 170, 171
slaves: black, 7; South Carolina, 8; Francis
  Barber, 22; Johnson recommends arming,
  22; Wesley, 23; arms for, 57; of
  Washington family, 65, 66; Burgoyne
  proposes enlistment of, 78; Dunmore
  proclaims freedom for, 102; Jefferson, 116;
  blacks as Loyalists, 235; black informer at

Savannah, 240; militiamen angry with
  British over, 242; at Charleston, 265
Smith, Francis, 29, 32–3
Smith, Joshua, 294
smuggling, xviii, xix, 18, 19, 113
Sons of Liberty, 9, 79
Sorel, Quebec, 97
South Carolina: Stamp Act, 8; slaves, 8;
  Prevost invades, 242–3; Loyalists and
  rebels, 271–2; nationalities of immigrants,
  272; in 'absolute state of rebellion', 272–4;
  British garrisons widespread in, 275;
  garrisons under Rawdon, 299; British
  forts fall, 310
Spain, declares war, 259
spies, rebel, 29, 49; British, 318
Stamp Act: Grenville imposes, xix–xx;
  colonial attitude to, xx, 3–4, 7, 8; violence
  in New York, 9; opposition in Britain, 10;
  repealed, 10
Stamp Act Congress (1765), 9
Stanley, Hans, 131–2
Stark, John, 51, 52, 53, 194, 346
Stedman, Charles, 287–8
Stephenson, John, 260–61
Stevens, Edward, 276
Stony Point, New York, 254
Stuart, Charles, later Sir Charles, 250, 254,
  311–12, 313
Sullivan, John: given command at Quebec,
  93; forces at Sorel and Chambly, 97;
  Battle for New York, 122; Battle of
  Brandywine, 156, 157, 158; criticism of,
  216; on Rhode Island, 232–3; later history,
  346
Sullivan, Thomas, 73, 155–6, 187
Sullivan's Island, South Carolina, 106–9
Sumter, Thomas, 275, 278–9, 288, 310,
  346
Surrey, Charles Howard, Earl of, later 11th
  Duke of Norfolk, 336

Tallmadge, Benjamin, 296
Tarleton, Banastre, later Sir Banastre:
  captures Lee, 146; personality, 263–4;
  British Legion raids, 264; at Charleston,
  266; massacre at Waxhaw, 270–71; Battle
  of Camden, 277, 278; disperses Sumter's
  force, 278–9; ill, 280; Blackstock's
  Plantation, 288; Battle of Hannah's

Tarleton – *cont.*
Cowpens, 299–302; Battle of Guilford
Court House, 304; marches north from
Wilmington, 314; and Wayne at James
River, 318; later history, 346
Taws, Captain, 246
taxation (*see also* Stamp Act): of colonies,
xviii, xix, 10–11; and Parliamentary
representation, 7; colonial resistance to
British, 8–9, 11–12; Townshend proposes
customs duties, 11; on tea, 18, 19; British
attempt at conciliation, 210
Taylor, Daniel, 190
tea, 18, 19, 20–21
Ternay, Admiral de, 291
Thomas, John, 39, 93
Thompson, William, 97
Ticonderoga, New York: surrender of fort,
40–41; artillery captured from, 41, 71;
Arnold withdraws to, 99; Burgoyne takes,
167, 169; British garrison at, 174; attack
by Lincoln, 191
Tornquist, Karl Gustav, 273
Townshend, Hon. Charles, 11, 16
trade (*see also* tea): transatlantic, xviii–xix;
Sugar Act, xix; Proclamation Line to
encourage, 6; American embargo, 10, 26,
27; Franco-American, 262
Trenton, New Jersey, 148
Trois Rivières, Quebec, 97, 136, 137
Tryon, William, 253

United States, independence recognized, 337

Valley Forge, Pennsylvania: deprivation
endured by Washington's army, 212, 213;
British scour, 213; transformation of rebel
army, 216–19
Van, Charles, 24
Vergennes, Charles Gravier, Comte de, 207
Virginia: House of Burgesses and Stamp
Act, 8; Washington family settles in, 65;
Washington elected to House of
Burgesses, 65; reinforcements from, 71;
reports to British government on, 101;
Dunmore, 101–2; raiding party at Long
Bridge, 102–3

Wales, George, Prince of, 280, 346
Walker, Patrick, 12

Walpole, Horace, 4th Earl of Orford, 48,
86
Ward, Artemas, 39, 70
Warren, Joseph, 37–8, 52, 54
Washington, Augustine, 65
Washington, George: appearance, 64, 148;
personality, 64, 66; background and
history, 64–6, 346; and post of military
commander, 66–7; Commander-in-Chief,
67; and his army, 67–9 *passim*, 71, 151–2,
213–14, 290–91, 333, 337; raises new flag,
71; and conquest of Canada, 89; declines
to see Lord Howe, 119; New York
defences, 121; Battle for New York,
124–6, 128, 129–30; angry with his
troops, 128; his army retreats to
Pennsylvania, 131; begs soldiers to stay
with army, 143–4; Congress agrees to his
requests, 145; and Charles Lee, 147, 215;
leaves Trenton by stealth, 149–50; Battle
of Princeton, 150; Battle of Brandywine,
156–7, 158; Battle of Germantown, 160,
161; derives encouragement from
Burgoyne's methods, 174; Battle of Bemis
Heights, 182; compatriots criticize,
214–15, 216; and Lafayette, 217; pursues
Clinton's army, 223; Battle of Monmouth
Court House, 224–5; and d'Estaing, 231;
sends brigades against Rhode Island, 231;
disillusioned with Congress, 257–8; and
Rochambeau, 293, 316, 322; pessimism,
322; and Prince William Henry, 326; news
of arrival of French fleet, 326–7; before
Yorktown, 327; and Hamilton, 327;
Cornwallis's surrender, 329–30
Washington, Lawrence, 79
Washington, Martha ('Patsy'), 65–6
Washington, William: Rugeley's Mills
surrenders to, 288–9; at Charlotte, 299;
Battle of Hannah's Cowpens, 300, 301;
Battle of Guilford Court House, 304, 305;
Battle of Hobkirk's Hill, 309; Battle of
Eutaw Springs, 312
Wayne, Anthony: Battle of Brandywine,
156; Paoli Massacre, 159; his harassing
party attacked, 234; captures Stony Point,
254; engagement at Green Hill Farm,
317–18; later history, 346
Webster, James: Battle of Camden, 277;
Battle of Guilford Court House, 305, 306

Wedderburn, Alexander, *later* 1st Earl of Rosslyn, 203
Wemyss, James, 288
Wentworth, Frances, 35–7, 61
Wentworth, John, 35
Wesley, John, 23
West Indies, 209, 234, 243
West Point, New York, 292, 293, 295, 299
White Plains, New York, Battle of, 129
Widow Moore's Creek, North Carolina, 104
Wilkes, John, 76–7, 206
Willard, Abijah, 49
Willett, Marinus, 179
William Henry, Prince *later* King William IV, 326
Williams, Otho, 275
Williamsburg, Virginia, 26, 101–2, 321
Wilmington, North Carolina, 56, 299, 307

women: lack of rights, 7; of Boston, 59; to go with regiments to Canada, 94; rape, 122, 154; join Washington with recruits, 151; Burgoyne's army hampered by, 163; Battle of Bemis Heights, 183; in evacuation of Philadelphia, 223; Battle of Monmouth Court House, 225; robbery and murder in South Carolina, 273
Woodford, William, 102
Wooster, David, 93
Wraxall, Sir Nathaniel, 336
Wynkoop, Jacobus, 98

Yorktown, Virginia: Cornwallis and fortification of, 315, 319, 321; Old Point Comfort, 319; Cornwallis awaits reinforcements, 326; American and French bombardment, 327–8, 329; British surrender, 329–30
Young, Thomas, 282